Reality Television and Arab Politics

Contention in Public Life

What does it mean to be modern outside the West? Based on a wealth of primary data collected during five years, *Reality Television and Arab Politics* analyzes how reality television stirred an explosive mix of religion, politics, and sexuality, fueling heated polemics over cultural authenticity, gender relations, and political participation in the Arab world. The controversies, Marwan M. Kraidy argues, are best understood as a social laboratory in which actors experiment with various forms of modernity, continuing a long-standing Arab preoccupation with specifying terms of engagement with Western modernity. Women and youth take center stage in this process. Against the backdrop of dramatic upheaval in the Middle East, this book challenges the notion of a monolithic "Arab Street" and offers an original perspective on Arab media, shifting attention away from a narrow focus on al-Jazeera and toward a vibrant media sphere that compels broad popular engagement and contentious political performance.

Marwan M. Kraidy is Associate Professor of Communication at the Annenberg School for Communication at the University of Pennsylvania. Previously a Fellow at the Woodrow Wilson International Center for Scholars and Director of the Arab Media and Public Life (AMPLE) project, Kraidy has authored *Hybridity, or the Cultural Logic of Globalization* (2005), and coedited *Global Media Studies: Ethnographic Perspectives* (2003). He has written widely and contributed frequently to media discussions of Arab media and global communication, mostly on National Public Radio.

Politics and relations among individuals in societies across the world are being transformed by new technologies for targeting individuals and sophisticated methods for shaping personalized messages. The new technologies challenge boundaries of many kinds – between news, information, entertainment, and advertising; between media, with the arrival of the World Wide Web; and even between nations. Communication, Society and Politics probes the political and social impacts of these new communication systems in national, comparative, and global perspective.

A list of books in the series follows the index.

Reality Television and Arab Politics

CONTENTION IN PUBLIC LIFE

Marwan M. Kraidy
University of Pennsylvania

CAMBRIDGE
UNIVERSITY PRESS

CAMBRIDGE UNIVERSITY PRESS
Cambridge, New York, Melbourne, Madrid, Cape Town, Singapore,
São Paulo, Delhi, Dubai, Tokyo

Cambridge University Press
32 Avenue of the Americas, New York, NY 10013-2473, USA

www.cambridge.org
Information on this title: www.cambridge.org/9780521749046

First published 2010

Printed in the United States of America

A catalog record for this publication is available from the British Library.

Library of Congress Cataloging in Publication Data

Kraidy, Marwan, 1972–
Reality television and Arab politics : contention in public life / Marwan M. Kraidy.
p. cm. – (Communication, society and politics)
Includes bibliographical references and index.
ISBN 978-0-521-76919-8 (hardback) – ISBN 978-0-521-74904-6 (pbk.)
1. Reality television programs – Arab countries – History and criticism. 2. Reality television
programs – Political aspects – Arab countries. 3. Television viewers – Arab countries – Attitudes.
4. Public opinion – Arab countries. I. Title. II. Series.

PN1992.8.R43K73 2009
791.45′6–dc22   2009010065

ISBN 978-0-521-76919-8 Hardback
ISBN 978-0-521-74904-6 Paperback

For Ute

Reality and the representation of reality are always far apart. But the gap between the two reaches a breaking point when a society experiences a deep crisis in which individuals don't have enough time to formulate discourses to explain to themselves what they are doing.

Fatima Mernissi (1987, x)

If we, in late modernity, have an idea of reality, it cannot be understood as the objectives given lying beneath, or beyond, the images we receive of it from our media. How and where could we arrive at such a reality "in itself"? For us, reality is rather the result of the intersection . . . of a multiplicity of images, interpretations and reconstructions circulated by the media in competition with one another and without any "central" coordination.

Giannni Vattimo (1992, 7)

Even if any terminology is a reflection of reality, by its very nature as a terminology it must be a selection of reality, and to this extent it must function also as a deflection of reality.

Kenneth Burke (1970, 45)

Contents

Acknowledgments

I was fortunate to witness as a teenager in the 1980s the explosion of privately owned media in wartime Lebanon, and to come of age in the 1990s with what has become known as the "Arab media revolution." It is thanks to those firsthand experiences that I began exploring Arab television as a social and political force, and an accounting of everyone who has contributed in some way to my understanding of this puzzling world is simply impossible. This book bears the imprint of numerous friends, colleagues, family members, students, teachers, intellectuals, journalists, directors, producers, and critics who inhabit the various communities and institutions through which I have been fortunate to pass. Without the many media workers throughout the Arab world who have shared their experiences, frustrations, and aspirations, some of whom must remain anonymous, this book would simply not exist. I am grateful to all.

At American University, Louis Goodman and Hamid Mowlana supported preliminary fieldwork. A large research grant from the U.S. Institute of Peace funded extensive field research in Dubai, Kuwait, Beirut, London, and Paris, and a yearlong fellowship at the Woodrow Wilson International Center for Scholars enabled me to analyze my massive data and start writing. At the center I enjoyed edifying conversations about politics and scholarship with Lee Hamilton, Michael Van Dusen, Haleh Esfandiari, and Robert Littwak, and about publishing with Joseph Brinley. Other Fellows, especially Larry Rosen and Michael Suleiman, gave generous feedback. At a crucial stage in the writing process, Barbie Zelizer invited me to spend a semester in residence at the Scholars Program in Culture and Communication at the Annenberg School for Communication at the University of Pennsylvania. During that semester vigorous intellectual stimulation came by way of doctoral students in my Culture and Modernity in the Arab World seminar, my fellow scholar Robin Wagner-Pacifici, the Annenberg faculty, and various visitors. Several times during the writing process, the Stanley Foundation of Muscatine, Iowa, invited me to speak and write about Arab media to the policy world and the public at large. As I was finalizing the manuscript, I benefited from a visit to Amman, Jordan, under the auspices of the Center for Global Communication Studies at Annenberg (thanks to Monroe Price and Susan Abbott).

Since the Annenberg School became my academic home, Michael Delli Carpini, dean of the school, has provided an ideal working environment; Joe Turow has been an irreplaceable mentor and Barbie Zelizer an invaluable supporter; and Bob Hornik, John Jackson, Carolyn Marvin, and Monroe Price have been engaging interlocutors. Fortuitous conversations with Kathleen Hall Jamieson and Klaus Krippendorf helped me crystallize theretofore nebulous ideas. Stimulating colleagues, inquisitive students, dedicated staff, and the activities of the Scholars Program in Culture and Communication and the Center for Global Communication Studies have made this a special place to teach, think, learn, and write.

By inviting me to speak at the University of Texas at Austin half a dozen times during the last five years, Karin Wilkins and Joe Straubhaar contributed more than they imagine to the evolution of this book.

I am grateful to Lewis Bateman, Emily Spangler, and Mark Fox at Cambridge University Press for a smooth editorial and production process, and to Christine Dunn for her copyediting.

Marc Andrejevic, Marlena Badway, Douglas Boyd, Peter Dahlgren, Fabienne Darling-Wolfe, Lauhona Ganguly, Larry Grossberg, Ute Kraidy, Libby Morgan, Patrick Murphy, Monroe Price, Courtney Radsch, Larry Rosen, Mary Anne Tétreault, Graeme Turner, Joe Turow, Bob Vitalis, Robin Wagner-Pacifici, Olesya Wenger, and Barbie Zelizer read and commented on portions of the manuscript. Briar Smith read several renditions of every chapter and caught many infelicities. Michel Kraidy's keen eye helped me get my dates and facts straight. Joe Khalil read the entire manuscript thoroughly and gave generous recommendations. Heidi Khaled marked the index under a tight deadline. The technical support staff at the Annenberg School has been top notch, and Chris Holland deserves special thanks for helping resolve formatting and indexing crises. Heartfelt gratitude to Deb Porter, who keeps the machine running smoothly.

At the risk of forgetting someone, the following colleagues contributed in ways big and small: Ibrahim al-Marashi, Jon Alterman, Hussein Amin,

Jon Anderson, Marc Andrejevic, Walter Armbrust, Pat Aufderheide, Lemi Baruh, Elizabeth Bird, Douglas Boyd, Sandra Braman, Nasser Chour, Edward Comor, Nick Couldry, Michael Curtin, Dima Dabbous-Sensenig, Peter Dahlgren, Nabil Dajani, Susan Douglas, John Downing, Waddick Doyle, Michelle Dunne, Nabil Echchaibi, Tariq Elseewi, Riad Ferghani, Layal Ftouni, Néstor García-Canclini, Yves Gonzalez-Quijano, Larry Gross, Larry Grossberg, Tourya Guaybess, Kai Hafez, Sune Haugbølle, Stewart Hoover, Michael Hudson, Adel Iskandar, Sean Jacobs, François Jost, Joe Khalil, Lina Khatib, Gholam Khiabany, Rami Khouri, Patricia Kubala, Shanti Kumar, Amanda Lotz, Ian Lustick, Dima Matar, Melani McAllister, Toby Miller, Nancy Morris, Patrick Murphy, Silvia Naguy-Zekmi, Assem Nasr, Christine Ogan, Radikha Parameswaran, Trevor Parry-Giles, Andrea Press, Aswin Punathambekar, Yeidy Rivero, Bill Rugh, Tarik Sabry, Naomi Sakr, Christa Salamandra, Paddy Scannell, Mehdi Semati, Jacob Skovgaard-Petersen, Catherine Squires, Annabelle Sreberny, Jonathan Sterne, Helga Tawil-Souri, Zala Volcic, Bruce Williams, Ferruh Yilmaz, and Mohammed Zayani.

Comments and criticism came from audiences at the following universities and institutions: American University, American University of Beirut, American University of Paris, Copenhagen, Georgetown, Hong Kong-Baptist, Indiana-Bloomington, Iowa, Kadir Has (Istanbul), Kuwait, Lyon, Maryland, Michigan, Minnesota, National Defense, North Dakota, North Dakota State, Pittsburgh, Temple, Texas-Austin, Wisconsin-Madison and Wisconsin-Milwaukee, Villanova, Virginia, Westminster, Carnegie Endowment for International Peace, Center for International and Strategic Studies, Palestine Center, Social Science Research Council, State Department, U.S. Institute of Peace, Woodrow Wilson International Center for Scholars, Jordan Media Institute (Amman), and the Stanley Foundation (Dubai, Iowa City, Milwaukee, and Pittsburgh).

From Washington, D.C., Emile el-Hokayem introduced me to Pierre el-Daher in Lebanon, who in turn arranged for me to speak with key people at LBC and generously gave me several boxes of videotapes of *Star Academy* and other LBC programs. My American University colleague 'Abdulaziz Sa'id connected me with 'Abdelrahman al-Rashed, General Manager of al-Arabiya in Dubai, who generously opened the door to the MBC Group. Also in Dubai, Jihad Fakhreddine and Shadi Qandil introduced me to key industry people. Jon Alterman, Director of the Middle East Program at the Center for Strategic and International Studies, provided a key contact in Kuwait, where Nadia and Hadi

Chemaly provided further contacts and Fady Sbeih explained the intricacies of the publishing business. Also in Kuwait, Entesar Alazmi helped me schedule many interviews with journalists, media managers, and activists, and Aisha al-Rshaid pleasantly surprised me with a thick envelope of clippings about the Kuwaiti reality television episodes. Mamoun Fandy connected me to the staff of *Asharq al-Awsat* in London.

I pilfered ideas and segments from my own work previously published in *Arab Media and Society, First Monday, International Journal of Communication, International Journal of Middle Eastern Studies* (Cambridge University Press), *Journal of Communication* (Blackwell), *Middle East Journal of Culture and Communication* (Brill), and *Television and New Media* (Sage), the publishers of which are gratefully acknowledged. The Arab Documentation Center in Beirut sold me world nonexclusive rights for Figure 7.1.

Two friends and collaborators deserve special mention: Patrick Murphy for his advice and support during the years and Joe Khalil, for his insights and introductions into the Arab media industry, welcoming me in his home in Dubai in 2004 and 2005, and having survived being my housemate and coauthor (of another book)!

A supportive extended family was instrumental to the completion of this book. I wrote this book's conclusion while enjoying the hospitality of Julian Flores and Maren Sartorius Flores in Amecameca, Mexico. My parents, Aida and Michel Kraidy, provided a home away from home during many months of field research. They tirelessly recorded and stored dozens of episodes of Arab reality television, collected clippings, and provided unwavering support. My brothers Ziad and Ghassan sent me dozens of valuable articles and were enthusiastically supportive.

Bruno and Maya bravely handled my frequent and long absences, sometimes by learning names and locations on a world map of places "papa" visited. Their love and energy sustained me in magical ways; I hope one day they find this book worth it. Ute, my soul mate, lifepartner, critic extraordinaire, and gifted graphic designer, read various chapters, endured anxious conversations, and created the perfect cover for this book. Without her this book would be a ghost; thanks to her it has blossomed. She selflessly cared for children and home during my physical and mental leaves, all the while tending to her own work. She put up graciously with my recurrent travels, unforgiving writing schedule, and the tensions that inevitably come with it. To her I dedicate this book.

Preface

On a warm summer evening, making our way up a narrow street, we left behind the fishermen's harbor of the ancient city of Byblos, Lebanon. I had been in the country for about two months, since early April 2004, doing research on what I initially conceived as a study of the overlaps between popular culture and politics in the Arab world, guided as much by a long-standing conceptual interest in the issue as by my mounting frustration with the obsession with al-Jazeera as a stand-in for Arab media. We were in Byblos to see my brother giving a piano concert in the old Saint Jean Marc church up the street. Suddenly, my two-year-old son leapt onto the street.

"Bruno!" I called, panicked by the sight of my toddler jumping onto a street that had a fair amount of car traffic. As I hauled my son back to safety, we were quickly surrounded by a group of teenagers, mostly girls, some smiling, others giggling, and several excitedly repeating "Esmo Bruno? Esmo Bruno!" (His name is Bruno? His name is Bruno!) Among them were several school girls wearing the veil, on a school trip from the Northern city of Tripoli to visit Byblos's ancient ruins; some teenage tourists in jeans, t-shirts, and tank tops; and a few local boys and girls stepping out from the souvenir stores and eateries dotting the area. The name Bruno is uncommon though not unheard of in Lebanon. What was it about that name that piqued the interest of these youngsters?

Bruno, they explained to me, was a Lebanese contestant on *Star Academy,* a bilingual (Arabic and French), pelvis-rotating heartthrob, whose popularity turned out to be short lived when viewers voted him out of the show early on. I had watched a few episodes of *Star Academy,* taking detailed notes for what I thought would become one chapter in my book about entertainment media and Arab politics. The encounter on the street of Byblos triggered a chain of ideas and field observations that led me to scrutinize the reality TV fever as it gripped one Arab society after another, and to investigate the social and political implications of the phenomenon.

The timing of the Byblos incident was propitious, as I was about to embark on a two-week trip to Dubai for fieldwork in Dubai Media City and interviews with managers, producers, directors, journalists, and corporate analysts. After several years doing extensive research in several countries, viewing a dizzying amount of Arab reality TV shows, analyzing hundreds of newspaper columns, and poring over institutional histories, I realized that I was on to something more far-reaching than I had imagined: by stirring a volatile mix of politics, religion, business, and gender, the Arab polemics over *al-Ra'is* (Big Brother), *Superstar*, and *Star Academy* crystallized epochal debates about what it meant to be modern in the Arab world. This led me to recast *Reality Television and Arab Politics* as an attempt, however limited, to contribute to what the philosopher Charles Taylor called "perhaps the most important task of social sciences in our day: understanding the full gamut of alternative modernities which are in the making in different parts of the world."[1]

---

[1] Taylor, C. (1999). "Two Theories of Modernity," *Public Culture* 11 (9): 165.

Introduction: Beyond al-Jazeera

On March 3, 2004, the journalist Ahmad Mansour introduced an episode of *Bila Hudud* (*No Boundaries*), a widely followed talk show on al-Jazeera:

> Though the West has made great strides in many fields and human rights . . . Arabs have specialized in mimicking the worst the West has to offer. As soon as there is a strange or deviant fad in food, drink, fashion, triviality and folly, Arabs rush madly upon it, imitating it blindly and ignorantly. The most prominent symptom [of this imitation] is the proliferation of . . . television programs copied from European television and based on degeneration, nudity, gyrating, triviality, void, voyeurism, the end of privacy and the dissemination of Western social ills under the heading of reality TV. This kind of program has infested Arab television as channels compete to acquire reality TV formats, copy them for Arab youth, and mobilize millions of viewers to follow who does what and who says what, thus toppling and destroying the values, culture, civilization and identity of Arab society.[1]

The episode, entitled "Mimicking Western Programs and Imposing Them on Arabs," aired three days after the Saudi-owned Middle East Broadcasting Center (MBC) shut down *al-Ra'is*, the Arabic version of *Big Brother*, and less than three months after the Lebanese Broadcasting Corporation (LBC) aired the first episode of *Star Academy*. Reaching two dozen Arab countries by satellite, these reality shows instigated a firestorm of contention over politics, commerce, religion, and sexuality.

---

[1] Mimicking Western Programs and Imposing Them on Arabs, Episode 1. (March 3, 2004). *Bila Hudud* (Ahmad Mansour, Host). Doha, Qatar: al-Jazeera. Mansour is known for sympathizing with the Muslim Brotherhood.

After years of watching pugilistic talk shows on al-Jazeera, Arab viewers were turning in droves to new and exciting reality TV (Arabic: *telfizion al-waqiʿ*) programs served up by entertainment channels, stirring wide-ranging controversies – some of which Mansour captured in his stinging indictment – and confirming Jon Alterman's quip that "If al-Jazeera indicates that news can be entertainment, LBC indicates that entertainment can be news."[2]

Reality Television and Arab Politics: Contention in Public Life tells the fascinating story of the Arab reality TV controversies, a political earthquake whose shockwaves rumbled from epicenters in Beirut and Dubai all the way to Algeria, Bahrain, Kuwait, Saudi Arabia, and Syria, and whose aftershocks can be felt to this day. What these pan-Arab polemics call for is nothing short of a shift in how we understand the social and political impact of Arab media, a pressing issue since the attacks of September 11, 2001. Looking at the many books published heretofore about Arab television, one is struck by an obsessive focus on al-Jazeera, the Qatari network critical of U.S. policies in the Middle East.[3] Broadcasting videotaped messages by Osama Bin Laden made al-Jazeera infamous, but assuming that a single telecaster shapes Arab "hearts and minds" discounts the vibrancy of Arab media and the complexity of their effects. For a time, this book will demonstrate, popularity and controversy made reality TV as consequential as explicitly political programs: In 2004 *Star Academy* captured the largest audience in pan-Arab television history, reaching up to 80 percent of viewers in some countries. Unlike the predominantly adult male audience of news and current affairs, Arab entertainment television attracts a large and diverse audience that includes women and youth. Reality TV has sparked intense debates about the role of Islam in public life, Western cultural influence, gender relations, and political participation, all hot-button issues that Arabs discuss passionately in private, and increasingly in public. Though Latin American *telenovelas*, Egyptian melodramas, and

---

[2] Alterman, J. (1998). *New Media, New Politics?* Washington, DC: Washington Institute for Near East Policy, 24.

[3] See, e.g., El-Nawawy, M. and Iskandar, A. (2003). *Al-Jazeera: Inside the Arab News Network that Rattles Governments and Redefines Modern Journalism.* Boulder, CO: Westview; Lynch, M. (2005). *Voices of the New Arab Public.* New York: Columbia University Press; Miles, H. (2005). *Al-Jazeera: How Arab TV News Challenges America.* New York: Grove; Zayani, M. and Sahraoui, S. (2007). *The Culture of Al-Jazeera.* Jefferson, NC: McFarland and Company; Lamloum, O. (2004). *Al-Jazira: Miroir rebelle et ambigu du monde arabe.* Paris: La Découverte; al-Zaidi, M. (2003). *The Al-Jazeera Channel: Breaking Taboos in the Arabic Media Space.* Beirut: Dar-al-Taliʿa [Arabic].

televised Hindu epics have generated national debates, Arab reality TV is so controversial that it has triggered street riots, contributed to high-level political resignations, compelled clerics to issue hostile *fatwas*, and fanned transnational media wars. To elucidate these compelling events, this book draws on a rich combination of hitherto unexamined visual, textual, and ethnographic sources collected during extensive fieldwork in Beirut, Dubai, and Kuwait, and also in London, Paris, and Washington, D.C., where many Arab journalists and intellectuals live. Overall, I spent more than fifteen months in the field researching this book, consisting of three major stays in the Arab world, each lasting between three and five months in 2004, 2005, and 2006, in addition to several shorter visits between 2004 and 2009, concluding with a visit to Amman, Jordan in April 2009. However, background sections of the book are also informed by research notes and interviews from the period from 1994 to 2004. In the process of researching and writing, I combed through extensive Arabic print primary sources, watched hundreds of hours of Arab television, conducted more than 120 interviews with journalists, politicians and television professionals (see List of Interviews), and drew on a broad literature from multiple disciplines and in several languages, spanning politics and popular culture, citizenship, reality TV, modernity and authenticity, gender and Islam, and Arab media and politics.

Since 2003 the reality TV controversies have captured the transformation of a protracted Arab malaise into an acute existential crisis precipitated by 9/11, the invasion of Iraq, bloodshed throughout the region, and historic Arab realignments along the U.S.-Iran contest for hegemony over the Middle East. That has been a period of collective soul-searching during which Arabs have debated norms governing their public life and grappled with shifting identities and changing values. This process is public and contentious: it arises in homes, coffeehouses, and intellectual *fora*, and unfolds on television screens, newspaper pages, the Internet, and even mobile phones. By stirring up a volatile mix of politics, religion, business, and sexuality, reality TV has compelled more Arabs to join heated deliberations over long-standing and ponderous issues: Why are Arab states impotent to check Western power? Should Arabs and Muslims identify with their brethren across the region, with their coreligionists across the world, or rather, should they be loyal to modern nation-states? What is the role of religion in matters of state? To what extent should clerics influence politics and public life? How best to ward off Western cultural influence? Is commercial television promoting women's emancipation, or is it turning them into erotic commodities? What is the proper scope of relations between men and women? Where should we draw the boundary between private life and the public sphere? Should we purge the media from foreign values, or should we rather provide indigenous alternatives to Western popular culture? Do Arab media reflect Arab reality, or do they represent foreign attempts to define a new reality? Is there one unified "Arab reality"?

ELABORATING ARAB MODERNITY

Though reality TV did not singlehandedly trigger these polemics, it extended their scale, widened their scope, and broadened their reach. Analyzing these debates allows us to understand the tensions stirring the Arab world and to grasp corresponding changes in social and political relations. At the heart of the controversy, this book will show, is a radical transformation of the ways in which individuals, institutions, and nations compete to define reality. This occurs in the context of a historical struggle to specify the terms of engagement with Western modernity, a litigious and abiding Arab preoccupation since the second part of the nineteenth century.[4] By altering the dynamic between private selves and public life, the reality TV quarrels ushered in new ways of using public space; by compelling Arabs to contemplate the implications of adapting Western programs carrying "foreign" values and images, the debate opened to scrutiny the ways in which Western modernity is selectively adapted in Arab societies. States, political movements, clergies, media institutions, journalists, and individuals contributed to this wide-ranging discussion.

The polemic over how to adapt Western modernity turns public space into a battlefield of beliefs and values. The creation of European modernity, wrote the political theorist Timothy Mitchell, is based on

---

[4] For English-language sources, see al-Azmeh, A. (1993). *Islams and Modernities*. London: Verso; and Hourani, A. (1983). *Arabic Thought in the Liberal Age: 1789–1939*. Cambridge: Cambridge University Press. Arabic-language sources include 'Abdullatif, K. (1999). *Modernity and History: A Critical Dialogue with Some Questions in Arab Thought*. Casablanca: Afriqia al-Sharq; al-Ghaddhami, M. (2005). *The Tale of Modernity in Saudi Arabia*. Beirut and Casablanca: Arab Cultural Centre; Belqziz, A. (2007) *The Arabs and Modernity: A Study in the Writings of the Modernists*. Beirut: Center for Arab Unity Studies; and Bennis, M. (2004). *Fractured Modernity*. Casablanca: Toubqal Press.

"the way in which the modern is staged as representation."[5] Producing acute conflict over representation, the reality TV controversies highlight contrary views of the Arab experience with *al-hadatha* – modernity. What it means to "be modern" in the Arab context has been vigorously contested since the 1850s, but the debate took on a renewed poignancy in the 1990s with the rise of pan-Arab commercial television and its growing linkages to the global media industries. Despite countless debates over its definition, it is generally agreed that modernity entails self-criticism through which societies constantly renew themselves. As the sociologist Anthony Giddens put it, modernity "effectively involves the institutionalization of doubt."[6] On the surface, modernity presents the Arab world with a challenge. Can Arab societies, where Islam permeates social, cultural, and political life, follow the modern path of decreasing the role of religion in public life? The answer may be "no," if we follow Giddens who writes that modernity is "manifestly incompatible with religion as a pervasive influence upon day-to-day life."[7] But the answer could be "yes" according to scholars who have argued that modernity has theological origins, religious speech enabled early European modernity, there are different kinds of modernity, and more specifically, media usage helped Arab and Muslim communities to accommodate modernity without forsaking their heritage.[8] The commotion over reality TV played up tensions associated with modernity – the relation between religion and the state, development of representative forms of governance, rise of nationalism, and conflict over gender roles.[9]

The media have historically played a crucial role in Arab experiences with modernity. A recurrent story in Albert Hourani's classic *Arabic Thought in the Liberal Age: 1798–1939* is the importance of newspapers as platforms for nineteenth-century Arab and Muslim reformers advocating

---

[5] Mitchell, T. (2000). *Questions of Modernity.* Minneapolis: University of Minnesota Press, 16.

[6] Giddens, A. (1990). *The Consequences of Modernity.* Palo Alto, CA: Stanford University Press, 176.

[7] Ibid., 109.

[8] See, e.g., Cole, J. (1999). *Modernity at the Millenium.* New York: Columbia University Press; Gillespie, M. A. (2008). *The Theological Origins of Modernity.* Chicago: University of Chicago Press; Adelkhah, F. (2000). *Being Modern in Iran.* New York: Columbia University Press; Eickelman, D. (1998). "Inside the Islamic Reformation," *Wilson Quarterly* 22 (1): 80–9; al-Azmeh, A. (1993). *Islams and Modernities,* London: Verso; Mitchell, 2000; Deeb, L. (2006). *An Enchanted Modern,* Princeton, NJ: Princeton University Press; Blanks, J. (2001). *Mullahs on the Mainframe,* Chicago: University of Chicago Press.

[9] See Cole, 1999.

selective adoptions from Western modernity and focusing on the question, "how to become part of the modern world while remaining Muslim?"[10] This trend carried over into the early twentieth century, when newspapers in Ottoman cities like Aleppo featured intense debates about what it meant to be modern.[11] In his book *Fractured Modernity*, the Moroccan poet Muhammad Bennis considers the Arab press to be the midwife of modernity, spreading the "alphabet of light" to the Arab population.[12] Arab modernizers found in the press an effective platform for their ideas, especially with the development of the newspaper column. Writing about his country, the Saudi literary and social critic 'Abdallah al-Ghaddhami argues that the appearance of the newspaper column in the 1950s constituted

> a modal change in the individual's position towards himself and in his relation to the world. The individual used to be a cell in a relationship deferring speech to the lord of the people who did not require evidence to back what he said. But in the column the individual came to change the ways of expression and topple the boundaries of the permissible. . . . The column [is] a foundation for the constitution of an independent, individual opinion.[13]

The Saudi modernity wars that lasted from 1985 to 1995, like the polemic over *Star Academy* dissected in Chapter 4, were waged primarily in op-ed columns in the Saudi press.[14] Likewise, in Egypt, Lebanon, and Morocco, media institutions played a crucial role in elaborating local versions of modernity.[15] In Egypt, as the anthropologist Walter Armbrust has shown, television drama since the 1970s has presented "modern" characters that are "educated, sophisticated, worldly, and at

---

[10] Hourani, 1983, 95.

[11] Watenpaugh, K. D. (2006). *Being Modern in the Middle East: Revolution, Nationalism, Colonialism, and the Arab Middle Class.* Princeton, NJ: Princeton University Press.

[12] Bennis, 2004, 121.

[13] al-Ghaddhami, 2005, 126.

[14] Ibid.

[15] Abu-Lughod, L. (2005). *Dramas of Nationhood.* Chicago: University of Chicago Press; Armbrust, W. (1996). *Mass Culture and Modernism in Egypt*, Cambridge University Press; Hirschkind, C. (2006). *The Ethical Soundscape: Cassette Sermons and Islamic Counterpublics.* New York: Columbia University Press; Kraidy, M. M. (1999). "The Global, the Local, and the Hybrid: A Native Ethnography of Glocalization," *Critical Studies in Mass Communication* 16 (4): 458–78; Sabry, T. (2005). "The Day Moroccans Gave Up Couscous for Satellites: Global TV, Structures of Feeling, and Mental Emigration," *Transnational Broadcasting Studies* 14, http://www.tbsjournal.com/Archives/Spring05/sabry.html (accessed December 30, 2005).

the same time clearly tied with *asala* (authenticity)," underscoring an Egyptian modernity that seeks national renewal and at the same time emphasizes continuity with the past.[16] In a similar vein, the anthropologist Lila Abu-Lughod showed that since the beginning of Egypt's *infitah* (open-door economic policies), television has promoted consumption while simultaneously warning against the dangers of consumerism. Following Peter Brook's assertion in *The Melodramatic Imagination* that melodrama was "the central fact of the modern sensibility,"[17] Abu-Lughod argues that television drama is one of several "technologies of modern self-making" in Egypt because it foments a distinct kind of individual emotionality.[18] By carrying conversations about the nation's relation to the world and heightening viewers' subjectivity, television hosts a national debate about modernity and authenticity.

Current reality TV polemics, therefore, continue historical trends; they also constitute a qualitative leap: Though, as we shall see, Arab newspaper columnists played a crucial role in connecting the reality TV battles to wider themes of political participation, social justice, and individual emancipation, Arab media today are not merely a carrier of debate. By virtue of the disputable entertainment it broadcasts, television is an important catalyst for broad-ranging, increasingly public, and often-heated discussions of modernity. This book focuses on how reality TV has sparked debates on vital social and political issues, and how it has been appropriated by various actors as a language of contestation. Further, unlike Saudi modernity wars or Egyptian concerns about authenticity, both national debates, the subject of this book is transnational, involving the traffic of ideas and controversies within and among twenty-two Arabic-speaking countries in addition to the global Arab diaspora.

Though reality TV generated controversy in many countries including Australia, Germany, Malawi, Turkey, and France (see Chapter 1),[19]

---

[16] Armbrust, 1996, 22.

[17] Brooks, P. (1976). *The Melodramatic Imagination: Balzac, Henry James, Melodrama, and the Mode of Excess.* New Haven, CT: Yale University Press.

[18] Abu-Lughod, 2005, 113. The author argues that Egyptian television serials contribute to a modernist project by shaping national political and social debates and by promoting a "distinctive configuration of narrative and emotionality" (113).

[19] See the collection Mathjis, E. and Jones, J., eds. (2004). *Big Brother International: Formats, Critics and Publics.* London: Wallflower Press. For the intellectual debates reality TV fomented in France, see Schneidermann, D. (2004). *Le cauchemar médiatique.* Paris: Denel/Folio documents; Le Guay, D. (2005). *L'empire de la télé-réalité, ou comment accroître le "temps de cerveau humain disponible."* Paris: Presses de la Renaissance.

the upheaval in the Arab world has been all-encompassing and enduring, touching on a broad spectrum of issues and linking to momentous geopolitical crises. However, the distinct form the controversy took in each Arab country suggests that modernity comes in multiple and sometimes contradictory forms. Debates over the meaning of modernity are heated in the non-West because "modernity" conjures up social progress, economic growth, individual emancipation, or cultural modernism, or, alternatively, cultural decline, loss of authenticity, and economic dependency. Complicating these discussions is the widespread belief that modernity is incapable of shedding its Western ethos. Nonetheless, if modernity involves what the philosopher Charles Taylor called "the coming to be of new kinds of public space"[20] then impassioned debates about reality TV constitute crucial episodes of Arab engagement with modernity. It would be too easy to conceive of the Arab reality TV debate as a clash between tradition and modernity. Rather, under the irresistible pull of Western modernity, societies search for what Taylor dubbed "creative adaptation"[21] to adopt constituents of modernity. Though broadly sympathetic to the multiple modernities literature,[22] like Mitchell, I am aware of modernity's insistent claim to universality and its unavoidable linkages to the West. Through a critical engagement with theories of modernity, this book aims to explicate anew how the struggle between rival versions of modernity – what the philosopher Leszek Kolakowski called modernity's "endless trial"[23] – unfolds.

TELEVISION'S NEW ECONOMIC MODEL

Arab reality TV presents a fascinating case of creative adaptation. Widespread format adaptation reflects a growing integration of Arab television in the global media industry, visible in multimedia convergence, intense competition among four hundred and seventy Arabic-language

[20] Taylor, C. (1999). "Two Theories of Modernity," *Public Culture* 11 (9): 153–74.
[21] Ibid., 163.
[22] Gaonkar, D. P. (1999). "On Alternative Modernities," *Public Culture* 11 (1): 1–18; Hervieu-Léger, D. (2003). "Pour une sociologie des 'modernités religieuses multiples': une autre approche de la 'religion invisible' des sociétés européennes," *Social Compass* 50 (3): 287–95; Kaya, I. (2004). "Modernity, Openness, Interpretation: A Perspective on Multiple Modernities," *Social Science Information* 43 (1): 35–47; Mitchell, 2000; Taylor, 1999.
[23] Kolakowski, L. (1990). *Modernity on Endless Trial*. S. Czerniawski, W. Freis, and A. Kolakowska, trans. Chicago: University of Chicago Press.

satcasters, and a trend toward specialization and niche markets.[24] The designation "reality TV" refers to various talent and game shows that are unscripted, feature primarily amateurs, and involve viewer participation through voting for contestants. Two European companies, Endemol in Holland and Fremantle Media in Britain, dominate global "formats," program recipes stipulating creative, technical, and dramatic components, sold worldwide and culturally adapted to local audiences. LBC's *Star Academy* is a knockoff of the identically named French show, and *Superstar*, aired by Beirut-based Future TV, is the Arabic version of *Pop Idol*. Because adapting a format is less risky than creating a brand-new program, Arab producers and directors repeatedly told me that reality TV had changed the way they worked.[25] "It used to be that we aimed to create the next great program; now we compete to adapt the next great format," a director told me in Dubai, succinctly describing the shift from original creation to inventive adaptation.[26]

In theory, Arabic speakers constitute one of the largest language-based audiences in the world, roughly the size of the U.S. audience. In reality, various Arabic accents, uneven socioeconomic levels with wealth concentrated in the Gulf states, and widespread signal piracy undercut the commercial viability of Arab television.[27] The state of corporate audience research compounds the challenges mentioned in the preceding text. Some companies, such as the Pan-Arab Research Center (PARC) in Dubai and IPSOS-STAT in Beirut and Dubai, have achieved a measure of respectability within the media industry, but doubts linger about their reliability, especially when it comes to their major clients. Focusing extensively on oil-rich Gulf Cooperation Council countries

---

[24] Kraidy, M. M. and Khalil, J. (2007). "The Middle East: Transnational Arab Television," in *The Media Globe: Trends in International Mass Media*, ed. L. Artz and Y. Kamalipour. Lanham, MD: Rowman and Littlefield, 79–98. For more details, see Kraidy, M. M. and Khalil, J. (2009, in press). *Arab Television Industries*. London: Palgrave Macmillan/British Film Institute. The number 470 was determined in April 2009 by Arab Advisors Group, author interview with Jawad Abbasi, General Manager, Arab Advisors Group, April 26, 2009, Amman, Jordan.

[25] Less risky does not necessarily mean less costly. See Khalil, J. (2005). "Inside Arab Reality Television: Development, Definitions and Demystification," *Transnational Broadcasting Journal* 15, http://www.tbsjournal.com/Archives/Fall05/khalil.html (accessed December 30, 2005).

[26] See Khalil, J. (2004). "Blending In: Arab Television and the Search for Programming Ideas," *Transnational Broadcasting Journal*, 13, http://www.tbsjournal.com/Archives/Fall04/khalil.html (accessed November 30, 2004).

[27] For a detailed discussion of these issues, see Kraidy, M. M. (2008). "The Arab Audience: From Activity to Interactivity," in *Arab Media: Power and Weakness*, ed. K. Hafez. New York: Continuum, 77–88.

(e.g., Bahrain, Kuwait, Oman, Qatar, Saudi Arabia, and the United Arab Emirates), audience researchers are confronted with resistance grounded in privacy issues.[28] To be sustainable, advertising-supported media require reliable audience research, the lack of which is a major reason for low advertising spending in the Middle East and North Africa, the second lowest in the world after Sub-Saharan Africa. Total "ad spend" in 2005 was near U.S.$5 billion, though this reflects undiscounted "rate cards" figures. The real figure according to Arab advertising mogul Antoine Choueiri was U.S.$2 billion. Newspapers still get the lion's share and television accounts for only 20 percent of the rate card amount.[29] Low advertising receipts have also compelled Arab media companies to aggressively develop new revenue streams from subsidiary rights and "value-added services" like ring tones, CDs, and DVDs, and from Short Messaging System (SMS), Multimedia Messaging System (MMS), and Interactive Video Network (IVN) applications. Pay-as-you-click interactivity is a new source of profit. In the absence of reliable knowledge of the audience, the advent of interactivity has tempered a raging debate over people meters (devices installed in private homes to monitor television use) and other audience-measurement techniques. At a time when controversy continues over whether to introduce people meters to socially conservative Gulf countries, some in the industry began to question the necessity of such a move. An executive at Omnicom Media Group (OMD) Middle East argued that:

> Everyone will tell you that people meters are crucial, and that's all good, but the issue in my opinion is that TV meters are passé, an old story. . . . We should go beyond TV meters and I think in this region we have the opportunity to go to the next stage. *It's about doing engagement studies, how programmes are engaging with viewers – not just how long they're spending watching them.*[30]

The desired shift from quantitatively measuring the time spent watching television to qualitatively assessing viewers' engagement with particular

---

[28] Author interviews with Jihad Fakhreddine, Research Manager, Pan Arab Research Center (PARC), June 1, 2004 and June 25, 2005, Dubai, UAE; Kandil, Shadi, Media Manager, IPSOS-STAT Dubai, June 2, 2004 and Director of Research and Insights, OMD, June 22, 2005, both in Dubai, UAE.

[29] "Choueiri: It's Time to Raise Ad Spending" (December 3, 2006). *Campaign Middle East.*

[30] "We Must Go Past TV Meters, Says OMG Boss" (September 24, 2006). *Campaign Middle East*, 6, emphasis added.

programs springs out of the recognition that interactive programs create new kinds of audience involvement.[31]

Reality TV has been a laboratory for the Arab television industry, allowing it to test new business models based on convergence and inter-activity. It is an attractive genre because it enables the integration of television with the Internet and mobile phones, creating what I call *hypermedia space*.[32] Based on media convergence, hypermedia space has become an important source of profit. Nominating or voting for contestants using text-messaging or Web sites, requesting and voting for a favorite music video, or calling a live music or game show are now established features of the industry. Though it is impossible to obtain completely reliable financial figures from media corporations and market research companies, it is a public secret that few Arab satellite television channels are financially sustainable.[33] The advertising-supported model does not quite work in the Arab world because of fragmented audiences, uneven socioeconomic levels, and unreliable ratings research. A combination of technological developments and commercial imperatives has turned the Arab media industry into an incubator of what is essentially a new economic model for media institutions that rests on a new conception of the audience, which, we should recall, is class-based because it requires economic, social, and educational capital. It is therefore no wonder that in one of several interviews I conducted with him, LBC's General Manager Pierre el-Daher said that "The future of Arab media is interactive television."[34]

LBC has championed the new economic model in various programs, most notably *Star Academy*, its flagship reality TV show. Though in 2008 LBC had only four reality shows (MBC had seven, so did Future TV, the al-Hariri-owned Lebanese channel), all four LBC reality shows had a viewer "online forum" and three had interactive voting, compared to MBC (one show with voting, three with online fora) and Future TV

---

[31] See Badi, I. (February 14, 2006). Where is new television technology taking us? . . . Viewers are now able to retrieve broadcasts they miss. *Al-Hayat* [Arabic]; and Ghosn, Z. (March 18, 2005). Free-to-air channels pull the rug from under encrypted channels. *Assafir* [Arabic].

[32] Kraidy, M. M. (2006). "Governance and Hypermedia in Saudi Arabia," *First Monday* 11 (9), http://firstmonday.org/issues/special11_9/kraidy/index.html (accessed December 30, 2006).

[33] Judging from the many interviews I conducted, industry insiders perceive LBC and MBC to be the most – if not only – profitable channels.

[34] Author interview with Pierre al-Daher, General Manager, LBC, June 30, 2004, Adma, Lebanon.

(two shows with voting, none with online fora).[35] During the 2007–8 season, sixteen out of twenty-six (61.5%) Arab reality shows offered viewer interactivity.[36] Reliance on interactive practices gives media institutions a wealth of demographic information that can in turn be used to target consumers with extreme precision.[37] Without viewers' participation, reality TV shows literally cannot proceed, as their narrative and commercial logics are as dependent on people nominating and voting using the Internet and mobile phones as they are on people watching the television set. Participating, voting, and nominating in reality TV shows is a reversal of economic relations because viewers perform much of the labor customarily executed by professionals.[38] Furthermore, LBC makes additional profits from music contracts and dramatic productions. *Star Academy* spawned two sitcoms in 2007 and 2008, with amateur contestants recycled as professional actors based on their newly acquired fame.

FROM CULTURAL AUTHENTICITY TO CONTENTIOUS POLITICS

Now that we understand the institutional reasons behind the proliferation of reality formats in the Arab world, it is time to ask: Why has reality TV been so controversial in this region? After all, unlike *Baywatch*, previously the *bête noire* of many a cleric, *Star Academy* cannot be rejected as "foreign" – code for sexually bold and culturally inappropriate. Many Arab reality shows are produced in Beirut or Dubai and feature Arab performers who pay homage to the Arab musical canon. In this sense they are celebrations of cultural heritage. So why have they provoked a firestorm of controversy? One answer lies in the cultural mixture featured in these shows. As local adaptations of global formats, Arab reality TV programs are "hybrid texts" that mix foreign and local

---

[35] Snobar, A. (May 2008). *Arab Reality TV Shows.* Amman, Jordan: Arab Advisors Group.

[36] Ibid.; the study covered eight channels and a total of twenty-six shows.

[37] In *Reality TV: The Work of Being Watched* (2004), Lanham, MD: Rowman and Littlefield, Marc Andrejevic writes that reality TV "highlights the increasing importance not just of surveillance but of interactive technologies that rearrange the conventional distinctions between work and play and between consumption and production" (17). In the Arab world, this model is reinforced by the fact that the wealthiest Arab countries in the Gulf have high-speed Internet.

[38] The labor implications of the reality genre are a major concern for reality television studies in the United States, the United Kingdom, and Australia. Andrejevic (2004) offers the most probing and comprehensive treatment.

cultural sensibilities.[39] Reflecting the lifestyle of the socially liberal Lebanese creative class who directs and produces them, Arab reality TV shows clash with the conservative Gulf societies, whose businessmen paradoxically invest in Arab reality TV productions and whose wealthy audiences are prime targets of the companies who advertise on reality TV shows. Writing about Latin America, Néstor García-Canclini pithily remarked that "the uncertainty about the meaning and value of modernity derives not only from what separates nations, ethnic groups and classes, but also from the socio-cultural hybrids in which the traditional and the modern are mixed."[40] Arab literature, cuisine, and poetry are replete with cultural mixtures, but reality TV has given Arabs a highly visible cultural hybrid. Arab reality TV is so intensely controversial, then, because it violates boundaries of identity and authenticity at a time when these boundaries have been hardened by widespread violence in the Middle East and various global controversies over Islam. For some opponents, *al-Ra'is* and *Star Academy* were links in a chain of horrors – Abu Ghrayb, Guantanamo, the infamous Danish cartoons, and others befalling Arabs and Muslims.

Many critics of Arab reality TV were incensed by the gender dynamics staged by shows like *al-Ra'is, Star Academy,* and even *Superstar.*[41] "Woman," the feminist critic Rita Felski wrote in *The Gender of Modernity,* is a "powerful symbol of both the dangers and the promises of the modern age."[42] In the Arab world, the status of women is a touchy issue because of colonial attempts to change personal status laws. This compounded the resonance of the figure of woman as a symbol of group and national identities, turning it into an icon of resistance to foreign domination.[43] At the same time, the rise of women's literacy, education, and employment levels throughout the postcolonial Arab world has created tensions in relations between men and women. By showcasing women's bodies as commodities in advertising, music videos, and game shows, while at the same time increasing the visibility of women as

---

[39] See Kraidy, M. M. (2005). *Hybridity, or the Cultural Logic of Globalization.* Philadelphia, PA: Temple University Press.

[40] García-Canclini, N. (1998). *Consumers and Citizens: Multicultural Conflicts in Globalization.* Minneapolis: University of Minnesota Press, 2.

[41] An earlier, moderately controversial, show called *'al-Hawa Sawa* [*On the Air Together*], aired on ART from December 2003, consisted of eight women living together while competing for an arranged marriage.

[42] Felski, R. (1995). *The Gender of Modernity.* Cambridge, MA: Harvard University Press, 3.

[43] See, e.g., Mernissi, F. (1987). *Beyond the Veil: Male-Female Dynamics in Modern Muslim Society.* Bloomington: Indiana University Press.

actors, directors, and producers, the pan-Arab media explosion of the
1990s compounded already fraught relations between men and women.
It is no wonder, then, that gender was central to the reality TV wars. As
the book unfolds, we will see that critical *fatwas* focused on fears that
reality TV would teach women to "display their charms" and "lose their
modesty" while leading men to succumb to their impulses and lose their
status as guardians of familial honor. In other instances, we will see
women caught in patriotic battles, their bodies claimed by feuding
nations as markers of identity. Modernity establishes a binary between
the notions of "man" and "woman" that puts women in a double bind:
whereas men are allowed latitude to adopt new ways of being and behav-
ing, women are required to be modern while remaining the repository
of tradition.[44] Spotlighting dramatic episodes of contention over the
role of women in society, this work elucidates the role of reality TV in
promoting "new" gender identities and relations in Arab societies.

To its critics, what otherwise elevated reality TV to the status of
imminent threat to Muslim faith and Arab dignity – unlike other television genres, including provocative Arab music videos – was reality
TV's claims to represent reality. Reality TV shows feature amateurs
and, in the case of *Star Academy*, are beamed in live and continuous
satcast or webcast flows, 24/7. This makes their content unpredictable
to their audience and justifies their claim to the real. In the West, some
surveys have shown that most viewers are skeptical of reality TV's
claim to be real,[45] so the genre's claim to "the real" can be dismissed.
In the Arab world, representational claims are contentious not only
because viewers mistrust reality TV's pretense to be real but also
because of long-standing grievances about Western misrepresenta-
tions of Arabs and Muslims, leading to an acute sensitivity toward
representations of Arab and Muslim issues.[46] In the Arab cultural
trenches, as it were, television is rarely dismissed as "just TV." Shortly

---

[44] See Kandiyoti, D. (1994). "Identity and Its Discontents: Women and the Nation,"
in *Colonial Discourse and Post-Colonial Theory: A Reader*, ed. P. Williams and
L. Christman. New York: Columbia University Press. For a discussion of the connection between gender, modernity, patriotism, and the media in the late Ottoman
Empire, see Frierson, E. (2004). "Gender, Consumption and Patriotism: The Emergence of an Ottoman Public Sphere," in *Public Islam and the Common Good*, ed.
A. Salvatore and D. F. Eickelman. Leiden, the Netherlands: Brill, 99–125.

[45] Hill, A. (2005). *Reality TV: Audiences and Popular Factual Television*. London: Routledge.

[46] This has interesting parallels with feelings about race by African Americans, which
my colleague John Jackson Jr. (2008) explicated in *Racial Paranoia: The Unintended
Consequences of Political Correctness*. New York: Basic Books.

we will see that Muslim clerics vigorously contested reality TV's claim to represent reality because the lifestyle, behavior, and values manifest on *al-Ra'is* and *Star Academy* are anathema to these clerics' vision of the virtuous society. From their perspective, they were resisting the imposition of a foreign reality on their world.[47] Reality TV's declarations about reality are antithetical to prevailing forms of social authority and cultural representation.

The discord over the right to represent reality (to be fully discussed in the next chapter) can be understood as a contest between contrary versions of modernity, each casting itself as "real" while labeling others as fake, that is, a mere "image." The dualism between representation and reality, which in Mitchell's view is central to modernity's self-presentation, is a fundamental dimension of the Arab reality TV polemics. In Algeria, Bahrain, Kuwait, Lebanon, Saudi Arabia, and Syria, disputes over reality TV were proxy battles to draw boundaries between reality and image, the masculine and the feminine, the pure and the hybrid, the authentic and the foreign. Marking these boundaries rouses battles in public life over what it means to be Arab and modern.

These struggles are driven by a complicated process of cultural translation. Modernity's Arab advocates and adversaries are forced to grapple with Western sway over their world. Mitchell argued that modernity is born out of the distinction between the West and the non-West;[48] each time the distinction is made, the modern risks contamination by the nonmodern. This book will show how the reality TV upheaval was an opportunity for actors to stage the reverse – a presumptive modern polluting the nonmodern, a volatile issue touching on "authenticity," most acutely in the ways in which reality TV subverted Saudi Wahhabiyya's insistence on cultural and religious purity.[49] Even in less-conservative Arab societies, the reality TV polemics signaled that popular culture was taken hostage by contentious politics.

Since 2004, reality TV's embroilment in Arab politics – elections, diplomatic relations, parliamentary debates, and ministerial performance –

---

[47] Detailed explanations of deep concerns about the impact of reality TV on Arabs and Muslims can be found in Hammoud, A. (2008). *Reality Television: Humans in the Cage of the Image*. Beirut: Dar al-Hadi [Arabic], and in *Satan Academy*, the recorded sermon by Shaykh Muhammad Saleh al-Munajjid discussed in Chapter 4.

[48] Mitchell, 2000, 26.

[49] Kraidy, M. M. (2008). "Critical Transculturalism and Arab Satellite Television: Theoretical Explorations," in *Global Communications: Toward a Transcultural Political Economy*, ed. P. Chakravartty and Y. Zhao. Lanham, MD: Rowman and Littlefield, 189–200.

fueled the upheaval. In Bahrain, the outcry over *al-Ra'is* (the local version of *Big Brother*) led to a parliamentary debate that generated two competing definitions of national reputation, whose prevalent meaning as conformity to Islamic tenets was now challenged by an emerging definition of national reputation as fitness for foreign investment (Chapter 2). After it attracted record audiences in Saudi Arabia, radicals, conservatives, and liberals enlisted *Star Academy* in their rhetorical wars, prompting the highest juridical council to issue a *fatwa* dedicated to the show (see Chapter 4). In Kuwait, Islamist legislators forced a minister of information to resign for allowing *Superstar* contestants to hold a concert, as they fended off women's demands for political rights (Chapter 6). This echoes the existence of contending visions of the common good based on rival fields of authentication, a recurrent debate in Arab/Muslim history.[50] Modernity is open to multiple interpretations because it is unable to unify discrepant worldviews.

In addition to the "chamber politics" of official government described in the preceding text, reality TV entered the fray of "street politics" when activists in Egypt, Kuwait, and Lebanon appropriated its alluring style and operational routines as an *idiom of contention* – a set of media-savvy tricks employed in political battles. Mobilization tactics, campaign slogans, and voting rituals honed during several reality TV shows were transferred to "real" politics because popular culture can hone messages useful in political action. Political agendas were captured in one-word slogans reminiscent of *Star Academy* broadcasts: "Now!" said Kuwaiti women agitating for political rights; "The Truth!"[51] chanted the Lebanese demonstrating against the murder of a former prime minister, as they "nominated" reviled politicians to be "voted off the island"; "Enough!" clamored Egyptian activists protesting Husni Mubarak's one-party rule. By getting mixed up in political spectacle, reality TV augured new uses of public space.[52] Unlike officially staged media events, these demonstrations were orchestrated by media institutions and political groups, managing publics who, like reality TV

---

[50] In addition to Hourani, 1983, see al-Azmeh (1993) and A. Salvatore and D. F. Eickelman, eds. (2004). *Public Islam and the Commmon Good*. Leiden, the Netherlands and Boston: Brill, 75–97.

[51] "Al-Haqiqa," Arabic for "The Truth," *is* one word.

[52] This is seen by some as a harbinger of modernity. See Taylor (1999) and Eickelman, D. (1998). "Inside the Islamic Reformation," *Wilson Quarterly* 22 (1): 80–9. A combination of media was used effectively during the Iranian revolution, but the combination of media convergence and transnational scope make the pan-Arab situation more complex.

fans, use a combination of mobile phones and television to fulfill a strategic goal – the victory of their candidate or the ousting of scorned politicians.

Reality TV increased popular awareness of media convergence. To vote for their favorite contestants in *Superstar* or *Star Academy*, viewers conjoin mobile phones, e-mail, and television in interactive processes, creating a hypermedia space that eludes censorship and facilitates distinct kinds of social and political communication. At the same time, in a vibrant media scene hungry for content, reality TV created a drama with colorful characters: the contest counterposed ultraconservatives and neoliberals, autocrats and democrats, clerics and feminists, who stirred up the controversies on talk shows and opinion pages. In columns titled "*Star Academy*'s Democracy," "The *Star Academy* of Arab Leaders," or "If I Were a Clergyman," journalists excoriated Arab politicians and clerics, mixing irony with desire for alternative politics as they drew "lessons in democracy,"[53] fables of political hypocrisy,[54] and conclusions about clerical abuse of power.[55]

Another feature of modernity is the integration of ethnically diverse and geographically scattered populations into nation-states,[56] a process in which communication has played a crucial role.[57] Reality TV competitions promoted a "new" Arab nationalism centered on reaffirming individual nation-states at the expense of pan-Arab identity, a phenomenon visible throughout this book. Even in war-torn Iraq, *Star Academy* awakened national consciousness at a time of heightened sectarian identification. When a young Iraqi woman, Shadha Hassoun, rose to the finals in 2007, more than seven million Iraqis voted for her; both Sunnis and Shi'a claimed her as one of them, while insurgents posted online diatribes against *Star Academy* for allegedly showcasing a corrupt model for Iraqi women.[58] After the show Shadha starred in public-service announcements on the national channel al-Iraqiyya, promoting unity in Iraq.[59] At a time when facile clichés like "Sunni Triangle" and "Shi'i

---

[53] al-Bishr, B. (April 19, 2005). Star Academy's democracy. *Asharq al-Awsat* [Arabic].

[54] al-Baba, H. (April 6, 2005). The camera rules the world: Star Academy for Arab leaders. *Al-Quds al-Arabi* [Arabic].

[55] al-Jasem, W. J. (April 6, 2004). If I were a clergyman. *Al-Watan* [Arabic].

[56] See Anderson, B. (1993). *Imagined Communities: Reflections on the Origins and Spread of Nationalism.* London: Verso; Cole, 1998.

[57] Gelvin, J. (1999). "Modernity and its Discontents: On the Durability of Nationalism in the Arab Middle East," *Nations and Nationalisms* 5 (1): 71–89.

[58] See First young woman to win the title . . . Shadha Hassoun triumphs for Iraq in Star Academy 4 (April 2, 2007). *Al-Hayat* [Arabic].

[59] Author field notes (January 9, 2008), Beirut, Lebanon.

Crescent" reflect a slide into sectarian discourse in the Arab world and the West alike, reality TV's plebiscitary features appear to promote national unity within Arab states even as it foments discord between them.

The rise of nationalism in the context of the Arab reality TV wars should not be mistaken for enduring expressions of a preexisting and well-defined national identity. Rather, as this book will show, they are better understood as episodic utterances of national identities constantly in the making. It is therefore a "constitutive rhetoric" that works on strengthening national personhood by reminding Arab viewers that they belong to nation-states.[60] The reality TV controversies expose rivalries between incomplete national projects and tensions within each national enterprise, underscoring the contingent and arbitrary character of Arab nation-states as political leaders seek to rekindle national sentiment and reaffirm national loyalties in the face of transnational ethnic, religious, or consumerist affiliations. Watching, nominating, voting, and participating in reality TV shows, in addition to contesting and defending them, all along national lines, showed how, as the scholar of nationalism Roger Brubaker put it, "the nation becomes momentarily yet powerfully realized in practice."[61]

THESIS AND ORGANIZATION

The combined cultural, social and political impact of reality TV – the ultimate reason for the controversies – is best understood as follows: reality TV is a social laboratory where various versions of modernity are elaborated and contested, a courtroom of sorts that hosts modernity's endless trial. During the trial, various ways of being modern emerge, all involving a combination of media and other institutions playing a central role in mediating modernity, a refashioning of individual identities and their relationship to society, and a search for historically resonant and culturally meaningful forms of modernity. Filtering out undesirable aspects of Western modernity and nurturing its locally attractive facets is a driving force of the Arab reality TV polemics. By explaining how reality mixes an explosive cocktail of religion, politics, gender, and

---

[60] See Charland, M. (1987). "Constitutive Rhetoric: The Case of the Peuple Québécois," *Quarterly Journal of Speech* 73 (2): 133–50.

[61] Brubaker, R. (1996). *Nationalism Reframed: Nationhood and the National Question in the New Europe.* Cambridge: Cambridge University Press, 16. For a similar approach in the Arab context, see Wedeen, L. (2008). *Peripheral Visions: Publics, Power, and Performance in Yemen.* Chicago: University of Chicago Press.

commerce; how the ensuing controversies give voice to various themes and polemics associated with modernity; and how this echoes historical debates in Arab public discourse, *Reality Television and Arab Politics* aims to explain the complexity and vibrancy of Arab media, an important story that is too often eclipsed by the excessive focus on al-Jazeera. This book also counters the prosaic idea that reality TV is naturally democratic while demonstrating its unequivocal political salience in non-Western contexts.

Chapters can be read as discrete national cases of contentious politics or as episodes of a transnational controversy beginning with various conflicts over reality TV shows in several countries and building up to a crescendo during the 2005 massive demonstrations in Beirut. Chapter 1, "Screens of Contention: The Battle for Arab Viewers," relies on television transcripts, newspaper columns, and historical research to examine how multiple actors vie to shape social reality. As state media addressing national viewers cede ground to semicommercial satellite channels with transnational audiences, reality TV contributes to changing the dynamics of the battle for Arab viewers because its peculiar commercial applications and political resonance portend a new relationship between individuals and social reality.

The first contentious episode followed the shutdown of *al-Ra'is*, the Arabic version of *Big Brother* in Bahrain in 2004. This touched off heated parliamentary debates between economic liberals and religious conservatives, giving rise to conflicting definitions of national reputation. Based on personal interviews with *al-Ra'is* staff and an analysis of Arab and Bahraini newspapers, Chapter 2, "Voting Islam Off the Island? *Big Brother* in Bahrain," dissects this dispute whose significance resides in its showcasing of the emergence of alternatives to religion as bases for governance, a development symptomatic of modernity.

At the heart of the *al-Ra'is* snafu is an intriguing alliance of Saudi capital and Lebanese talent that drives the battle for Arab viewers. Chapter 3, "The Saudi-Lebanese Connection," explains the paradox at the heart of the Arab media trade: Saudi Arabia, the most socially conservative Arab country, provides capital to companies from Lebanon, ostensibly the most liberal Arab society, to produce television programs focused primarily on the high-income, advertiser-coveted Saudi market. Business and political interests have helped controversial shows survive while pulling others off the air. Elucidating this fascinating connection that underlies the political economy of Arab reality TV, Chapter 3 leads us to *l'affaire Star Academy* in Saudi Arabia, the most contentious episode of the reality television wars explored in Chapter 4, "Contesting Reality: *Star Academy* and Islamic Authenticity in Saudi Arabia." There, incensed critics called the show "Satan Academy" and "moral terrorism," and the Higher Council of 'Ulamas issued a critical *fatwa*. Through an inquisitive analysis of episodes of *Star Academy*, a dissection of the *fatwa*, personal interviews, and analysis of the Saudi press, Chapter 4 argues that the scandal can be understood as a reemergence of the Saudi modernity wars of the 1980s and 1990s, intensified by reality TV's claim to represent reality and by the fear that its participatory rituals subvert Wahhabiyya's view of Islamic authenticity and threaten the core of the Saudi social order.

An equivalent though not similar quarrel stormed Kuwait, where the parliament debated legislation to ban "Lebanese reality shows," "grilled" and fired the minister of information, and forced the creation of a high-level committee to "monitor" controversial television content. Intense deliberations linked the uproar over reality TV to the fraught issue of women's political rights, echoed in op-eds. Chapter 5, "Gendering Reality: Kuwait in the Eye of the Storm," tells this story based on field observations and interviews with Kuwaiti policy makers, media workers, and activists for women's issues, underscoring the unique role of media and political institutions in Kuwait.

Though the reality TV polemics took various forms in different Arab countries, they also echoed larger geopolitical clashes. The remaining chapters examine why and how reality TV entered the fray of the Beirut demonstrations called "Independence Intifada"[62] and the Lebanese-Syrian media war, on the backdrop of an international showdown between the United States and Iran and the Israel-Hizbollah war in the summer of 2006. A primary theater for proxy wars, political spectacles, and reality TV production, Lebanon emerges as a crossroads of political, military, and media confrontations reshaping the Middle East. Chapter 6, "A Battle of Nations: *Superstar* and the Lebanon-Syrian Media War," focuses on the compelling story of *Superstar*'s embroilment in the war of the airwaves between Lebanon and Syria and a stunning reversal between 2003, when Syria controlled Lebanon, and 2006, after Syrian troops withdrew from Lebanon. Broadcast from Beirut by the al-Hariri-owned channel Future TV, *Superstar* was usurped as a patriotic stage, with a Syrian finalist's father bursting on stage to wrap his daughter in a body-sized Syrian flag before she was voted off the show. Chapter 6

---

[62] The prevalent name in Lebanon had been *Intifadat Al-Istiqlal* [Independence Intifada].

anchors primary visual and print sources in the literature on nationalism and political spectacles.

Superstar's stumble into the strained Syrian-Lebanese relation foreshadows momentous events in 2005, coupling inter-Lebanese struggles to regional and global turbulence involving the United States, France, Syria, Israel, Saudi Arabia, and Iran. Chapter 7, "'The New Middle East?' Reality Television and the 'Independence Intifada,'" examines how reality TV was mixed up in political spectacles. Unlike officially staged media events, these demonstrations are hypermedia events orchestrated by media institutions and political groups, managing publics who, like reality TV fans, use a combination of mobile phones and television to fulfill a strategic goal – the victory of their candidate or the ousting of scorned politicians.[63] By inspiring mobilization tactics, protest signs, and indelible images of popular contention, reality TV functions as an idiom of contentious politics.

In addition to spawning new kinds of televised spectacles, nationalistic battles, or institutional differentiations, the reality TV controversies suggest various ways of being modern through the remaking of individual and social identities in a context of cultural translation focused on localizing Western modernity. The conclusion, "Performing Politics, Taming Modernity," explores how reality TV's underlying premises – the exacerbation of desire and emotional conflict, exaltation of individualism, and promotion of self-revealing behavior[64] – are absorbed by socially resonant and culturally meaningful shows. A majority of the most recent Arab reality shows are original creations, not adapted from Western formats, and some of the most successful do not feature singing and dancing. Rather, they stage contests in poetry and Qur'anic recitation, revealing the extent to which reality TV, a controversial genre created in the West, has been localized in the Arab world. In addition to capturing the texture of contemporary cultural practices in the Arab world, the Arab reality television polemics give us a view into the dynamics through which the taming of modernity occurs.

[63] Updating the framework proposed in Dayan, D. and Katz, E. (1992). *Media Events: The Live Broadcasting of History*. Cambridge, MA: Harvard University Press.
[64] Le Guay, D. (2005).

CHAPTER ONE

Screens of Contention: The Battle
for Arab Viewers

When the English philosopher George Edward Moore wrote that "[w]henever a philosopher says something is 'really real,' you can be really sure that what he says is 'really real' isn't real, really,"[1] he could have been describing how Arab viewers related to their state-owned television channels until the 1990s. For decades Arab television had a warped relation to reality. Under the stifling control of the Ministries of Information, media institutions presented a reality that most listeners and viewers knew to be unreal. Every once in a while, Libyan viewers were reportedly treated to what can only be described as surreal: regular programming would be interrupted by a still picture of a pensive Mu'ammar al-Qaddhafi with a caption informing viewers that "the leader" was "contemplating the future of the nation." Even less meditative regimes expediently manufactured their own "reality" through controlled media that rarely gave listeners and viewers access to alternative views. Predictably, Arabs turned *en masse* to foreign broadcasters. In wartime Lebanon, we used to "triangulate" in search of reliable information. Huddled around a battery-operated transistor radio during long, electricity-deprived evenings, we would listen to a couple of local radio news bulletins from opposing camps and then move on to the French Radio Monte-Carlo Middle East, BBC Radio, and, less frequently, Voice of America or Radio Moscow.

The explosive growth of pan-Arab satellite channels since 1990 has demoted broadcasts from Paris, London, Washington, and Moscow. Today the average Arab viewer can "triangulate" by using exclusively Arabic-language media. Even relatively uninformed viewers sense that al-Jazeera and al-Arabiya regularly tell two versions of the same story,

---

[1] Quoted in Geertz, C. (1983), *Local Knowledge: Further Essays in Interpretive Anthropology.* New York: Basic Books, 84.

whose numerous shades of grey are reflected by myriad other channels. Government backing makes for predictable editorial lines: al-Jazeera is a reliable, albeit feisty, tool of Qatari foreign policy, al-Arabiya reflects the priorities of Saudi royals, and Abu Dhabi TV and Dubai TV defer to the ruling princes of the United Arab Emirates. But al-Jazeera spares Qatar from its biting criticism of Arab governments, and al-Arabiya eschews negative coverage of Saudi rulers. The range of voices has retracted as governments develop new levers of control: the restrictive satellite television charter passed by Arab information ministers on February 12, 2008 reflects a Saudi-Egyptian push for a new pan-Arab regulatory regime to reassert state control over transnational media.[2] Even al-Jazeera has moderated its coverage of Saudi affairs in 2007 after a détente in Saudi-Qatari relations. Nonetheless, shifting alliances and inconsistent policies have kept the battle for Arab viewers in flux, with new Arab networks popping up every day – there were four hundred and seventy pan-Arab satellite channels in April 2009. On top of this, the U.S., Iranian, and Russian governments have launched Arabic-language satellite channels, respectively al-Hurra (The Free One), al-Aam (The World), and Rusya al-Yawm (Russia Today); the French and German government expanded Arabic-language broadcasts; and the BBC launched an Arabic television service in March 2008. The capacity to reach Arab "hearts and minds" has become a trapping of great power status.

THE NEW VISIBILITY OF POWER

In this dynamic media environment, state-owned channels are struggling to retain a modicum of relevance. Numerous and contradictory regulatory amendments, policy shifts, and management shuffles in state-owned Arab television channels reflect a scattershot approach motivated by an increasingly desperate search for legitimacy. Jordan's press laws are constantly amended and its media policy chronically unstable.[3] Jordan's first privately owned satellite channel, ATV, was shut down at the eleventh hour after it had been permitted to set up studios, hire staff, and announce its imminent launch, reportedly because the channel's

---

[2] Kraidy, M. M. (March 2008). "Arab States: Emerging Consensus to Muzzle Media?" *Arab Reform Bulletin* 6 (2), http://www.carnegieendowment.org/publications/index .cfm?fa=view&id=19968&prog=zgp&proj=zdrl,zme#kraidy (accessed June 1, 2008).

[3] The situation described in Najjar, O. A. (1998). "The Ebb and Flow of Press Freedom in Jordan, 1985–1997," *Journalism and Mass Communication Quarterly* 75 (1): 127–42, continues to this day with press and broadcast legislation.

owners were less pliant than expected to the concerns of Jordanian military intelligence.[4] More recently, Libyan authorities nationalized al-Libiyya, a new privately owned satellite channel, after a talk show host criticized the Egyptian regime. The Syrian Ba'th party elite has for years been locked in a debate about the need to "modernize the media sector," which was felt most acutely during the spring 2005 Lebanese media onslaught on Asad's regime.[5] Egypt, Jordan, and Libya have struggled for years to establish privately owned channels that would be regime-friendly and popular with viewers. The inability of state-owned media to reach beyond a small segment of the national audience is a source of anxiety for regimes whose version of "reality" has become impossible to sustain. As Egyptian media critic Amina Khairy wrote in a column entitled "'Reality' in official eyes," in the Saudi-owned, Beirut- and London-based pan-Arab daily al-Hayat (Life):

> Most Arab viewers are cognizant that what they watch on "official" television channels is not necessarily what is really happening, but what the state wants them to watch. . . . It is no exaggeration to say that "unofficial" Arab satellite channels have excited . . . Arab viewers, who are no longer content with following the news of the "commander" or the "leader" . . . whose goal is to keep leaders in . . . power for as long as possible. . . . Arab viewers are no longer capable of pretending to accept the "maneuvering" of official television channels around facts . . . [and] . . . sensitive political, social and economic topics. . . . Now television channels discuss all the issues that are on viewers' minds, even when extremely bold . . . viewers have a choice between those and other programs where news, information and even entertainment are presented in a way that is closer to the reality that for decades was lacking for Arab viewers.[6]

This media proliferation goes hand in hand with a fragmented political reality. The channel-surfing Arab viewer sees the same military action described as a "terrorist attack," a "suicide bombing," a "resistance operation," or a "martyrdom operation." In between, our viewer

---

[4] Personal interviews with Jordanian and non-Jordanian sources who requested anonymity.

[5] Kraidy, M. M. (May 2006). "Syria: Media Reform and Its Limitations," *Arab Reform Bulletin* 4 (3). Carnegie Endowment for International Peace, Washington, DC, http://www.carnegieendowment.org/publications/index.cfm?fa=view&id=18341-media (accessed June 1, 2008).

[6] Khairy, A. (May 23, 2006). 'Reality' in official eyes. *Al-Hayat* [Arabic].

can watch financial news and talk shows extolling the virtues of free trade and personal investing on the business network CNBC Arabiya, and then watch talk show guests on the Lebanese leftist channel New TV discussing the dark side of globalization. Someone with more radical political or religious views may enjoy watching newscasts and talk shows on Hizbollah's al-Manar or Hamas's al-Aqsa. If the mood strikes for lighter fare, that viewer can choose from the sexually charged Arab music videos on Melody Hits, a Wahhabi-sanctioned talk show on Iqra' and a softer, hipper Islamist show on the Saudi-owned al-Risala TV. MBC and LBC always have game, variety, or reality TV shows. The menu is topped off by Egyptian bio-dramas and Syrian series with themes ranging from community life to terrorism.

Though Arab prime time is dominated by programs produced for the most part in Beirut, Cairo, Damascus, or Dubai, Western programs are widely available. In the age of multiplatform television groups, affluent Arabs can purchase satellite packages featuring American sitcoms and action movies, police series, news and public affairs, and game and variety shows around the clock. Whether advertising-supported like MBC 4 or fee-charging "pay-TV" like the Saudi-owned Orbit and the partially Kuwaiti-owned Showtime, these channels contribute to segmenting the Arab audience by targeting a small, upscale and cosmopolitan elite: The Saudi executive who acquired a lasting taste for NBA basketball while getting an MBA in Boston, the Tunisian dentist who followed the Franco-German high culture channel Arte while pursuing specialization in Paris, young professionals who have never left Cairo or Kuwait but like to watch U.S. sitcoms, or society ladies who avidly follow Fashion TV. These channels' largely noncontroversial existence indicates that the "Western" provenance of programs does not in itself trigger controversy. Rather, watching them is a sign of distinction – owning a satellite dish ostensibly indicates openness to foreign cultures and involvement in consumption. It signals membership in a modern, cosmopolitan, elite.[7] Whereas government broadcasting in newly independent Arab states focused on consolidating national identity and fostering socioeconomic development, satellite channels now target viewers with political and religious messages in addition to luring tourists regionwide with advertisements for the Egyptian Red Sea resort of Sharm al-Shaykh, Lebanon's ski slopes, Dubai's shopping festival, and Morocco's *medinas*.

---

[7] See Moores, S. (1993). "Satellite TV as Cultural Sign: Consumption, Embedding, and Articulation," *Media, Culture and Society* 15: 621–39.

This is not the first time that the media help to expand consumer society and participation in public life. The contemporary Arab world bears some resemblance to the late Ottoman Empire in the wake of wide-ranging administrative reforms known as the *tanzimat*. As described by historian James Gelvin, during that period

> the domain of formal politics expanded . . . an increasing number of inhabitants of the empire, mobilized by the state or its opponents, began to contend over a growing number of public issues . . . [enabled by] the proliferation of new media outlets – from newspapers to coffeehouses – the efficacy of which was ensured by enlarged urban concentrations, the restructuring of urban space and the introduction of modern technologies for transportation and communication.[8]

Enabled by growing economic integration and administrative reform within the empire, new communication practices contributed to the restructuring of power relations between rulers and masses. Twin processes of cultural standardization and differentiation spawned disparate social groups with divergent responses to change.[9] Soon thereafter, the media had become instrumental to people's experience of modernity. To middle classes in Ottoman Mediterranean cities in the early twentieth century, according to historian Keith Watenpaugh, "being modern had to be observable and reproducible, something that bisected the public and the private, often requiring the use of venues . . . [like] newspapers [and] Western consumer goods . . . in which or with which to perform one's modernity."[10] One century later, Arab satellite television forged new bonds between individuals and society by exposing a large number of viewers to consumer lifestyles. Media consumption and the polemics it generates, this book shows, increasingly shape how Arabs experience modernity in the early twenty-first century.

Comparisons between the early twentieth and early twenty-first centuries encompass media proliferation, public contestation, changing social relations, and the emergence of new, self-conscious middle classes with consumptive links to the Western metropolis. They also include

---

[8] Gelvin, J. (1999). "Modernity *and* Its Discontents: On the Durability of Nationalism in the Arab Middle East," *Nations and Nationalisms* 5 (1): 71–89.

[9] Ibid., 76.

[10] Watenpaugh, K. D. (2006). *Being Modern in the Middle East: Revolution, Nationalism, Colonialism, and the Arab Middle Class.* Princeton, NJ: Princeton University Press, 16.

fluid relations between transnational and national spheres, similar in nature but dissimilar in direction. In the late Ottoman period, local elites adopted Western values and ideologies, including various forms of nationalism that aimed to reshape societies, as Gelvin put it, in "a manner compatible with the dictates of progress and modernity."[11] Whereas the Ottoman *tanzimat* enabled the growth of national groups, the economic, political, and technological changes of the late twentieth century have fostered the development of transnational links: Nowadays, rival discourses of progress, modernity, and identity have a regional (pan-Arab) resonance, even when they take on specific national forms. Due to what the anthropologist Dale Eickelman called a combination of "mass education and mass communication,"[12] the new pan-Arab scale of public discourse overshadows the relatively limited reach of contestation through newspapers, civic associations, or coffeehouses in late Ottoman culture.[13]

The growth of a dynamic transnational Arab media landscape has ushered a new private-public relationship attributable to what the British sociologist John Thompson called the "transformation of visibility."[14] Historically, publicness was concerned with the exaltation rather than the exercise of power. According to the old doctrine of *arcana imperi*, power was invisible because important decisions were made in secret. This resonates with Arab authoritarian politics today: Until his death in 2000, Hafez al-Asad's iron rule of Syria for three decades was predicated on the exaltation of the leader and his conflation with the nation. State media, first radio and later television, played a crucial role in creating the leader's cult. A deft use of the private-public dynamic is central to dictatorial power. In the case of Syria, Asad's cult, through the ubiquity of his image and state-orchestrated political spectacles with massive popular participation, according to political scientist Lisa Wedeen, operated to "personify the state . . . identify the mortal body of the leader with the immortal body of the realm" while at the same time narrowing "the gap between ruler and ruled" because "Asad

---

[11] Gelvin, 1999, 76.

[12] Eickelman, D. (1998). "Inside the Islamic Reformation," *Wilson Quarterly* 22 (1): 80–9.

[13] See Kirli, C. (2004). "Coffeehouses: Public Opinion in the Nineteenth-Century Ottoman Empire," in *Public Islam and the Common Good*, ed. A. Salvatore and D. F. Eickelman. Leiden, the Netherlands and Boston: Brill, 75–97.

[14] Thompson, J. (1994). *The Media and Modernity: A Social Theory of the Media*. Palo Alto, CA: Stanford University Press.

represents ... [both] the extraordinary individual ... [and] the average Syrian."[15] A media-savvier version of his late father, Bashar al-Asad has maintained the core of the personality cult while softening its style. The situation is equivalent in Saudi Arabia, where the clerico-political regime uses Wahhabiyya, a puritanical version of Sunni Islam, to sanctify the regency – what Saudi journalist Badreiah al-Bishr calls "worldly power through religious power."[16] State television plays a crucial role in Saudi governance: the system reproduces itself through constantly repeated rituals of worship broadcast on television: the pilgrimage to Mecca, Friday sermons, religious guidance shows, widely publicized *fatwas* proscribing or allowing specific activities and behaviors.[17] In Syria and Saudi Arabia, citizens and subjects regularly pledge allegiance to the rulers by participating in officially sanctioned rituals that reaffirm prevailing social and political relations.[18] They reflect the importance of rhetoric, symbols, and ritual in Arab politics.[19] New modes of social and political communication that connect various media and mix popular culture with politics subvert regime mastery of symbolic space and threaten prevalent power structures in many Arab countries (Saudi Arabia, Chapter 4; Kuwait, Chapter 5; and Syria, Chapter 6).

Among news channels, al-Jazeera pioneered practices that blurred the private and public.[20] The channel's most enduring legacy resides in "open microphone" programs like *Minbar al-Jazeera* (*al-Jazeera's Pulpit*) that invite viewers to call and express their views live on the air. Al-Jazeera thrives on live or recorded programs in which viewers can express dissenting or controversial opinions. In relinquishing full control over the "script" of some of its programs and inviting viewers to weigh in by phone, fax, and e-mail, the channel made an institutional decision to stoke controversy and foreshadowed reality TV's expansive use of interactive devices and reliance on viewer participation. This public, two-way communication is not unique to the Arab world.

---

[15] Wedeen, L. (1999). *Ambiguities of Domination: Politics, Rhetoric and Symbols in Contemporary Syria.* Chicago: University of Chicago Press, 17.

[16] al-Bishr, B. (2007). *The "Tash Ma Tash" Battles: A Reading of the Prohibition Mentality in Saudi Society.* Casablanca, Morocco, and Beirut, Lebanon: Arab Cultural Centre, 13 [Arabic]. See also al-Rasheed, M. (2007). *Contesting the Saudi State.* Cambridge: Cambridge University Press.

[17] al-Rasheed, 2007.

[18] Ibid.

[19] Barnett, M. (1998). *Dialogues in Arab Politics.* New York: Columbia University Press; Wedeen, 1999.

[20] So much has been written about al-Jazeera that there is no need to rehearse the story. See note 3 in this book's introduction.

In late-twentieth-century Latin America, as the Argentinian intellectual Beatriz Sarlo wrote,

> Disillusioned with state, party and union bureaucracies, the publics turn to radio and television to receive what citizen institutions could not deliver: services, justice, reparation, or just attention. Of course, one cannot claim that the mass media, with their call-in programs or live public forums, are any more successful than public institutions, but they fascinate because they listen and people feel that they do not have to [put up with obstacles and delays].[21]

Rather than bringing actual solutions to people's problems, García-Canclini argues, these programs rearticulate the relation between the private and the public. This blurring of boundaries attracts attention and incites debate. Arab news and entertainment shows that break taboos and involve viewer participation are popular and controversial: popularity makes them potentially controversial and controversy makes them more popular. If al-Jazeera ushered the era of "The opinion, and the other opinion," as its motto proclaims, then the reality TV controversies demonstrate that there are multiple (not merely two) rival voices contesting important issues on the airwaves.

This broad range of voices did not please leaders of the Arab status quo. In early 2003, a group of Saudi, Kuwaiti, and Lebanese businessmen and politicians launched al-Arabiya as a counterweight to al-Jazeera. Based in Dubai Media City in order to benefit from the city's concentration of media talent, the new channel purported to be everything al-Jazeera was not. In contrast to al-Jazeera's trademark live call-in programs, al-Arabiya carried prerecorded shows. (This befits the channel's Saudi owners: In January 2008, Saudi authorities banned live call-in shows on Saudi television after several angry calls during a heated discussion of a salary raise for civil servants, which many callers considered insufficient.) Its airy and futuristic newsroom was meant to reflect transparency in news reporting.[22] Whereas al-Jazeera's logo is a pear-shaped calligraphy of the name of the channel – a classical Islamic art form – in a golden color on dark background, al-Arabiya's logo renders the channel's name in white and in a specially commissioned modernized,

---

[21] García-Canclini, N. (2001). *Consumers and Citizens: Globalization and Multicultural Conflicts.* Minneapolis: University of Minnesota Press, 23.
[22] Author interview with Michel Costandi, Business Development Director, MBC Group, June 3, 2004, Dubai, UAE.

that is, less curvilinear, Arabic font.[23] As a marketing representative for the MBC Group (al-Arabiya's mother company) told me, white was meant to convey transparency, echoing the newsroom's design.[24] In keeping with the theme of transparency, al-Arabiya launched in 2005 a promotional campaign with the theme "Closer to the Truth." Sitting in his corner office in the MBC building in Dubai Media City, I asked 'Abdelrahman al-Rashed, the channel's general manager, if "Closer to the Truth" reflected recognition that the truth always eluded media institutions – whose aim therefore should be to come as close as possible to the truth – or whether the slogan meant that al-Arabiya was closer to the truth than al-Jazeera. He smiled, seemingly acknowledging that it was a bit of both.[25] Two years later, in late summer 2007, when the channel switched its slogan to "So You Know More," al-Arabiya's director of marketing and public relations, Mazen Hayek, explained that "this campaign caters to the viewer's mind, not to his instincts,"[26] a clear attempt to distinguish his channel from al-Jazeera.[27]

Al-Arabiya's agenda was to change the Arab sociopolitical reality construed by al-Jazeera. "We are trying to redefine the news," said al-Arabiya's executive editor, by which he meant downplaying "big" pan-Arab causes like Iraq and Palestine and focusing on practical issues like "health, education, livelihoods" in addition to more human interest stories.[28] In that spirit, the documentary *Eye on Palestine* combined a

---

[23] For a historical explanation of the pear-shaped calligraphic form, see Khan, G. M. (2001). *L'écriture arabe: alphabet, style et calligraphie.* Paris: Flammarion. This form can be found in the work of the Ottoman master Mehmet Shefik Bey in the mid-to-late nineteenth century and more recently in the work of the Lebanese calligraphist Nassib Makarim. For a technical discussion of Al-Arabiya's brand identity, see Shaheen, B. "A Loser Look at Alarabiya's New Identity," *Tasmim: The Arab Design and Creativity Magazine* (Gitex 2003 issue): 3–6.

[24] Author interview with Costandi, Michel, Director of Business Development, MBC Group, June 3, 2004, Dubai, UAE.

[25] Author interview with al-Rashed, 'Abdelrahman, General Manager, al-Arabiya, June 27, 2005, Dubai, UAE.

[26] Habib, V. (August 7, 2006). From "Closer to the Truth" to "So You Know More" . . . Al-Arabiya changes its slogan but says professional essence does not change. *Al-Hayat* [Arabic].

[27] In a column he published during Al-Arabiya's fifth anniversary celebration, Walid al-Ibrahim, owner of MBC Group (Al-Arabiya mother company) confirmed Al-Arabiya's founders aimed to counter al-Jazeera; see al-Ibrahim, W. (March 7, 2008). Al-Ruba'i . . . names "Al-Arabiya" and departed. *Asharq al-Awsat.* See also Mansour, M. (March 7, 2008). Al-Arabiya five years after its launch: A necessity imposed by Al-Jazeera and continuity shaped its identity. *Al-Quds al-Arabi* [Arabic].

[28] Shadid, A. (May 1, 2006). "A Newsman Breaks the Mold in Arab World." *Washington Post*, A01.

concern for Palestine with a focus on daily life. A brainchild of Palestinian-Jordanian journalist Daoud Kuttab, *Eye on Palestine* was produced by O3 Productions, an MBC group company, and aired on al-Arabiya in March and April 2005. In a press interview, Kuttab argued that Palestinians were associated with two stereotypes: evil "terrorists" in the eyes of the West and sacrificial "supermen" in the eyes of the Arabs. *Eye on Palestine* was meant to give a more complex and balanced idea of Palestinians.[29] *Eye on Palestine* was produced reality TV–style, which meant less editing, longer shots, and a naturalistic approach to real, daily Palestinian life.[30] Like reality shows, it followed the lives of six ordinary people including a male Bir Zeit university professor, divorcée from Gaza, pregnant woman, and young man. Like reality TV, it purported to represent Palestinian ordinariness in contrast to the prevailing negative and positive stereotypes of Palestinians.[31] The program was an explicit intervention in the ongoing debate about the relation between television and sociopolitical reality, and producers thought that a reality TV production style was best suited for that purpose.

Entertainment, like news, joined the struggle to describe social reality as Arab satellite channels began acquiring European television formats. Foreign program "plagiarism" began in the early 1990s when Lebanese channels aired copycats of *Wheel of Fortune* (*Dulab al-Huzz*, on Télé-Liban, then half-owned by the state) and *Win, Lose or Draw* (*Min Qaddak*, LBC).[32] As the satellite era dawned, three channels, MBC, LBC, and Future TV, became pan-Arab leaders in format-based entertainment. MBC was initially launched in 1991 in London as a (mostly) news broadcaster, a "CNN in Arabic," by Walid al-Ibrahim, brother-in-law of then Saudi King Fahd. MBC's strategy worked well until expenses ballooned to more than 100 million dollars and royal support was no longer secure because of King Fahd's deteriorating health. At the same time, LBC and Future TV initiated satellite operations in 1996. With their slick production values, depiction of flashy upper-middle-class Lebanese lifestyle, and reliance on attractive and suggestively dressed

---

29 Salih al-Nou'amy (April 23, 2005). "Eye on Palestine" ... a look on people's life. *Asharq al-Awsat* [Arabic].

30 Author interview with Nabil Khatib, Executive Editor, *Al-Arabiya*, Dubai, UAE, June 29, 2005.

31 Salih al-Nou'amy (April 23, 2005).

32 Khalil, J. (2004). "Blending in: Arab Television and the Search for Programming Ideas," *Transnational Broadcasting Journal* 13, http://www.tbsjournal.com/Archives/Fall04/khalil.html.

female anchors and program hosts, LBC and Future TV quickly became popular with Arab audiences. These factors (among others) compelled MBC to recruit a new management team and shift its focus to entertainment in the late 1990s. As it relocated from London to Dubai, MBC launched *Man Sa-Yarbah al Malyoun*, the Arabic version of the Celador format *Who Wants to Be a Millionaire*. First broadcast in November 2000,[33] the "Arab millionaire show" was produced in multiple locations including London and later Cairo. Program structure, set design, and music were identical to the American version of the show. The questions, however, focused on Arab culture, poetry, politics, and history in addition to global issues – the show was not controversial. MBC also purchased the *Big Brother* format from Endemol and customized it as *al-Ra'is* to conservative Arabian Gulf social norms: separate quarters for males and females, in addition to a prayer room. Nonetheless, as will be explained fully in Chapter 2, *al-Ra'is* went on to become the shortest-lived pan-Arab reality TV show when it was shut down within a week of its launch. Future TV, the Lebanese channel owned by the al-Hariri family, purchased the *Pop Idol* format from Fremantle Media and adapted it as *Superstar*. The show was similar to *American Idol*, but its ethos was markedly different, focusing on apprenticeship and mentoring rather than public humiliation (this is a trend: the Arabic version of Reveille LLC's format *The Biggest Loser* was titled *al-Rabeh al-Akbar*, Arabic for "The Biggest *Winner*," emphasis added). *Al-Ra'is*, *Star Academy*, and *Superstar* were pivotal events in the history of Arab satellite television: they were major commercial successes (except *al-Ra'is*), generated controversy, and impacted industry practices.

Of all the programs in the format-based reality TV wave, *Star Academy* was the most controversial.[34] LBC, a private company with a terrestrial channel registered in Lebanon and a satellite channel registered in the Cayman Islands, began a pan-Arab, multiple media casting drive in July 2003. This netted three thousand applicants who were culled down to sixteen finalists from various Arab countries including Egypt, Kuwait,

---

[33] *Man Sa Yarbah Al-Malyun*, as it was called in Arabic, was initially produced in London; production moved to Paris in June 2001 and then to Cairo in February 2002. The 2005 installment was produced in Beirut. Even news and talk shows can be said to be an indirect format adaptation, albeit indirectly, such as al-Jazeera's flagship program *al-Ittijah al-Mu'akess* [*The Opposite Direction*], clearly modeled on CNN's *Crossfire*, or MBC's all-female hosted *Kalam Nawa'em*, clearly inspired by ABC's *The View*.

[34] *Star Academy* was on in France, Belgium, and Canada, in addition to the United Kingdom's *Fame Academy*, when it was first broadcast to the Arab world from Lebanon in December 2003.

Lebanon, Morocco, Saudi Arabia, and Tunisia,[35] the "academy's" *tullab* (students). Starting in December 2003, Arab viewers could watch the contestants twenty-four hours a day for four months on LBC Reality, a dedicated satellite channel that transmitted live footage captured by sixty cameras positioned inside of the four-story building of the academy, in addition to a nightly "access" (in English) show and a weekly Friday evening "prime" (also in English). Each Monday a jury of experts nominated two contestants for expulsion, and each Friday viewers voted one of them out of the "academy" using text messaging, until the winner was crowned in April 2004. As this book unfolds, we shall see how *Star Academy* prompted clerics to issue *fatwas*, pushed legislators to launch inquiries, mobilized fans and detractors on the Internet, and inspired myriad newspapers columns and letters-to-the-editor. The *Star Academy* polemic contributed to redefining the relation between media and politics in the Arab world and is best understood – as I elaborate in Chapter 7 – as a hypermedia event.

THE ENTERTAINMENT-POLITICS NEXUS

With its simplistic slogans, slick packaging, promises of fast gratification, and grounding in consumerist imperatives, entertainment is often described as having a corruptive impact on democratic life. This perception is belied by a long line of entertainers who crossed over into politics in Italy, India, Latin America, and, especially, in the United States,[36] which the nonfiction writer Neil Gabler called the "Republic of Mass Entertainment."[37] The media scholar Liesbet van Zoonen sees three similarities between communities formed around politics and those

---

[35] Author interview with Roula Sa'd, Director of Promotion and Marketing, LBC, Adma, Lebanon, July 5, 2005. Sa'd also played the on-screen role of "Director of the Academy" and is LBC's point person for the program.

[36] In Italy, the porn star Cicciolina was elected to parliament. In India, the televised versions of the Hindu epics, Ramayana and Mahabharata, had active links with the changing political landscape; see Rajagopal, A., *Politics after Television: Hindu Nationalism and the Reshaping of the Public in India*, New York: Cambridge University Press, 2001. In Latin America, sensitive socioeconomic themes are often politicized in the context of telenovelas and other forms of public culture; see García-Canclini, N., *Consumers and Citizens: Globalization and Multicultural Conflicts*, Minneapolis: University of Minnesota Press, 2001, and Martín-Barbero, J., *Communication, Culture and Hegemony: From the Media to Mediations*, Newbury Park, CA: Sage, 1993.

[37] Gabler, N. (1998). *Life the Movie: How Entertainment Conquered Reality*. New York: Knopf, 11.

created around entertainment television.[38] Both kinds of community are created by emotionally invested members through performance, participation, discussion, and mobilization. Van Zoonen rightfully argues that activities like "discussion, participation . . . intervention, judging and voting" among *Pop Idol* and *Big Brother* fans "would qualify as civic competences if they were performed in the domain of politics."[39] The political scientist Stephen Coleman argues that *Big Brother* enables the playing out of ideas and behaviors excluded from democratic politics.[40] Like reality TV contestants, he wrote, politicians must be "extraordinary enough to represent others, but ordinary enough to be representative of others."[41]

The growing visibility of ordinary persons on television does not mean that reality TV is "democratic."[42] Rather, the cultural studies scholar Graeme Turner describes the widening gamut of popular representation and the broadening access as "demotic," a term that refers to the use of average people as raw material for media content and not to increased civic participation. Turner's argument that the democratic aspect of "democratainment" is episodic and unreliable[43] underscores one of this book's key questions: To what extent does the broadening of public space fostered by the reality TV controversies impede or enable sustainable civic engagement? Turner sees a new kind of cultural power in a global media system that is able to breed new collective identities *ex nihilo*.[44] This "demotic turn," as Turner characterizes it, has implications beyond the question of popular culture and political participation. This book's conclusion elaborates the ways in which Arab reality TV contributed to a new relation between individuals and society.

Entertainment-politics overlaps are frequent in Arab history. Decades ago, the singer 'Abdulhalim Hafez was a spokesperson for Gamal Abdulnasser's Egyptian revolution and the diva Umm Kulthum raised

---

[38] Van Zoonen, L. (2004). "Imagining the Fan Democracy," *European Journal of Communication* 19 (1): 39–52.

[39] Ibid., 42.

[40] Coleman, S. (2006) "How the Other Half Votes: Big Brother Viewers and the 2005 British General Election Campaign," *International Journal of Cultural Studies* 9 (4): 457–79.

[41] Ibid., 468.

[42] Andrejevic, M. (2006). Reality TV is Undemocratic. *Flow,* http://flowtv.org/?p=11 (accessed October 1, 2006); Turner, G. (2006). "The Mass Production of Celebrity: 'Celetoids,' Reality TV and the 'Demotic Turn,'" *International Journal of Cultural Studies* 9 (2): 153–65.

[43] Turner, 2006, 157.

[44] Ibid., 162.

funds for Arab war efforts against Israel. But the politics-popular culture nexus has become more dynamic with the growth of commercial electronic media since the 1990s. The Egyptan singer Sha'ban 'Abdulrahim is known for his polemical songs, the most famous of which is "I Hate Israel." More recently, events in Lebanon have spawned a new genre of patriotic songs, ranging from multicast elegies to Rafiq al-Hariri to *Ahibba'i* (*My Loved Ones*), in which Christian-Lebanese singer Julia Boutros sang lyrics cobbled together from speeches by Hezbollah Secretary-General Hassan Nasrallah during his party's war with Israel in 2006. In the socially conservative Gulf monarchies, popular culture is at the forefront of culture wars over Westernization, gender relations, and social change. Though indigenous academic studies focusing on these overlaps are nearly nonexistent, the Arab press reflects a growing awareness of the phenomenon. Under the headline "Stars Return to Politics . . . a Job or a Search for the Audience?"[45] an article in *Asharq al-Awsat* (*The Middle East*) posed a series of questions:

> What is the relation between entertainment and politics? And is it necessary for the entertainer to have a well-defined political stand or to belong to a political party? And do entertainers accept roles with political themes that are not compatible with their tendencies and desires and political orientation?[46]

Several Arab entertainers then declared that political engagement comes "naturally" to public figures, suggesting that patriotism was good for show business. Other headlines like "Fifi Abdo Confronts Corruption and Smuggling of Antiquities"[47] or "Because of their Political Activities, Israel Considers [pop stars] Nancy and Maria and Haifa to Pose a Danger,"[48] reflect active links between entertainment and Arab politics.[49]

Though Arab popular culture has long been politicized, the reality TV polemics placed the entertainment-politics nexus at the center of Arab public life. Taking the Arab world by storm at a time of war, terrorism, and the Bush administration's attempt to remake the Middle East,

---

[45] Stars return to politics . . . a job or a search for the audience? (August 14, 2005). *Asharq al-Awsat* [Arabic].

[46] Ibid.

[47] Yassin, S. Fifi Abdo confronts corruption and smuggling of antiquities (September 16, 2005). *Al-Hayat* [Arabic].

[48] Because of their political activities, Israel considers Nancy and Maria and Haifa to pose a danger (September 14, 2005). Al-Arabiya.net [Arabic].

[49] Street, 2004.

al-Ra'is, *Star Academy*, and *Superstar* became political arenas *par excellence* because they echoed the big questions that Arabs were debating at the time: Is there a Western conspiracy to control the Arab world? Are imported reality TV formats a Trojan horse in that conspiracy, serving to weaken putative Arab values to facilitate Western hegemony? Or do reality TV programs depict a model of meritocracy, equality, and participation that may be Western in inspiration but from which Arab societies can glean social and political lessons? The ensuing controversies articulated an explosive combination of forces that continue to rock the Middle East: radical Islamism, oil geopolitics, U.S.-Iran tensions, political and military conflict in Lebanon, and occupation and violence in Iraq and Palestine. It is against that dreadful backdrop that the reality TV polemics constitute an utmost convergence of entertainment and politics.

Elsewhere in the world, some reality shows were political in the narrow sense of "politics." In 2002, *El Candidato de la Gente*, broadcast in Buenos Aires, invited viewers to select their candidate for legislative elections in Argentina, and in the United States, FOX promoted *The American Candidate*, brainchild of the documentary maker who made *The War Room*, the documentary about Bill Clinton's winning media strategy during the 1992 U.S. presidential election.[50] In Malawi, condemnations of *Big Brother Africa* by social and religious leaders pushed a parliamentary vote to ban the program.[51] In France, *Loft Story* (the French *Big Brother*) triggered heated exchanges between journalists, politicians, and clergymen in the pages of *Le Monde* and other elite newspapers and generated several books.[52] Reality TV was broadly seen as a threat to aesthetic and social Republican values, as expressed by Jean-Jacques Aillagon, then sitting Minister of Culture, in an interview published by the Catholic newspaper *La Croix* (June 6, 2003), in which he said that reality TV programs "pose a threat to the equilibrium

---

[50] See Van Zoonen, 2004. Preparations for *The American Candidate* ceased because of spiraling costs.

[51] See Biltereyst, D. (2004). "*Big Brother* and Its Moral Guardians: Reappraising the Role of Intellectuals in the *Big Brother* Panic," in *Big Brother International: Formats, Critics and Publics*, ed. Mathjis, E. and Jones, J. London: Wallflower Press, 9–15.

[52] See Le Guay, D. (2005). *L'empire de la télé-réalité: ou comment accroître le "temps de cerveau humain disponible."* Paris: Presses de la Renaissance; Schneidermann, D. (2004). *Le Cauchemar médiatique.* Paris: Denoel/Folio documents; Jost, F. (2007). *Le culte du banal. De Duchamp à la télé-réalité.* Paris: CNRS; Jost, F. (2007). *L'empire du Loft.* Paris: La Dispute; Jost, F. and Muzet, D. (2008). *Le Téléprésident: Essai sur un pouvoir médiatique.* Paris: L'Aube.

of our society."[53] Voicing concerns about the genre's social totalitarian tendencies, Arte president Jérôme Clément called reality TV "rampant fascism."[54] The philosopher Damien Le Guay explained French reactions to reality TV trenchantly: "*Loft Story* deflowered television, leading it into an era where nothing is scandalous."[55] Nonetheless, by the end of this book the reader will realize that these national polemics pale in comparison to the transnational Arab political storm kicked up by *Star Academy*.

Reality TV touched a constellation of raw nerves in Arab societies. Whether articulating inter-Arab rivalries, nurturing nationalism, provoking socioeconomic discussions, igniting hostile media campaigns, questioning what constituted reality, or ushering new ways for self-fashioning, reality TV was intensely politicized, invested with rival arguments that competed for the public's attention.[56] As ratings sensations that received heavy and sustained news coverage, reality TV shows became a public preoccupation from workplaces to ruling palaces. They attracted widespread participation in public disputes over a wide range of political, economic, social, and religious issues. Proponents of Wahhabiyya in Saudi Arabia, advocates of commercial media autonomy in Lebanon, women's rights activists in Kuwait, business communities in Bahrain, Egypt, Jordan, and Syria, and ruling parties and families throughout the region were drawn into these controversies. Some entered the fray eagerly, others grudgingly: Arab regimes were compelled to join the debate when their opponents used the issue to score political points. When Algeria's president 'Abdulaziz Boutelfiqa faced active legislative opposition to a bill, he ordered the state television service to cease *Star Academy* broadcasts relayed from LBC, softening Islamist opposition to his policies in parliament.[57] The highest judicial-religious body in Saudi Arabia was compelled to issue a *fatwa* about *Star Academy* because the show became a popular obsession in the kingdom. The Islamist bloc in Kuwait's legislature used the upheaval *Superstar* caused in the small Gulf emirate to force the resignation of an Information Minister

---

[53] Le Guay, 2005, 12.

[54] Ibid., 42.

[55] Ibid., 41.

[56] See Kraidy, M. M. (2006). "Reality TV and Politics in the Arab World (Preliminary Observations)," *Transnational Broadcasting Studies* 2: 7–28.

[57] Algerian television forced to shut down *Star Academy* after widespread criticism in mosques (February 4, 2006). *Al-Quds al-Arabi* [Arabic]; Senoussi, 'Ayyash (April 14, 2006). Algerian television director to al-Hayat: *Star Academy* violated the contract and threats are our daily bread. *Al-Hayat* [Arabic].

it deemed overly liberal. In Arab politics, reality TV is at once lightning rod, political bludgeon, and bargaining chip.

Storming the Arab world during a time of crisis, reality TV expanded the notion of the political, as the Belgian political scientists Fabrizio Cantelli and Olivier Paye put it, because it "circulates in all social spaces and not only in a social area that presents itself as specially or essentially political."[58] The debates analyzed in this book move across realms (political, economic, cultural, and religious) and scales (local, national, regional, and global) of public life, illuminating complicated and indirect struggles – what García-Canclini calls "oblique power."[59] By compelling social and political actors to intervene in public debate, the reality TV controversies brought to the surface latent tensions and hidden interests whose openness to multiple interpretations opened up new spaces of expression – Taylor's signature indicia of the modern.

REALITY TELEVISION AND SOCIAL AUTHORITY

Consider how Arab journalists seized *Star Academy* and *Superstar* as political platforms. For Hakam al-Baba, a Syrian columnist, *Star Academy* reflects Arab political dependence on the United States. In a column titled "The Camera Rules the World: Star Academy for Arab Leaders,"[60] the author skewers Arab autocrats:

> The Arab viewer only needs to zap between official Arab television channels to discover that his leaders' actions, speeches . . . reforms . . . cater to television's lights and cameras and not to their peoples' interests and aspirations. The leaders' highest interest is to improve their image with America (first, second and third) in reality, and with their peoples (finally!) only on the screen.
>
> Since ours is a tailor-made-for-television situation of the reality TV type like *Star Academy*, the Arab viewer follows [Arab politics] with the interest of those reality TV viewers, rather than with the interest warranted by existential . . . reality. And since Arab leaders' view of their televised performance is similar to the viewers' vision

---

[58] Cantellli, F. and Paye, O. (2004), "*Star Academy*: un objet pour la science politique?" in *Star Academy: Un objet pour les sciences sociales?*, ed. Y. Cartuyvels. Bruxelles, Belgique: Publications des Facultés universitaires Saint-Louis, 65–89.

[59] García-Canclini, N. (1994). *Hybrid Cultures: Strategies for Entering and Leaving Modernity.* Minneapolis: University of Minnesota Press.

[60] al-Baba, H. (April 6, 2005). The camera rules the world: A Star Academy for Arab leaders. *Al-Quds al-Arabi* [Arabic].

of it (notice here the exceptional confluence of Arab peoples and leaders), these leaders present their positions, statements and actions as artistic performances, not as political stances. As a result, each one of them (his majesty, his excellence, or his highness) chooses a role through which he will present himself to America . . . the enthusiastic rebel role . . . the clownish comedic role . . . the wise elder role . . . the silent sidekick role.

In addition to mocking the lack of authenticity in official Arab politics, al-Baba's mordant wit underscores Arab political feebleness. Just like *Star Academy* contestants are manipulated by executive producers, Arab leaders are dependent on the United States. He continues,

[T]heir common objective is to please the American producer of this political *Star Academy*, so that they can go on playing acts for their peoples – of course they do not mind some popular applause. The television camera today is the most important and effective Arab parliament, and the image today is the most transparent political analyst.

As the column was published in the staunchly Arabist London-based newspaper *al-Quds al-Arabi* (*Arab Jerusalem*), the thinly veiled jabs at Arab monarchs and autocrats in Egypt, Jordan, and Saudi Arabia, seen as mere peons of the United States, are not surprising. But al-Baba does not spare even those who play the role of "rebel" against the United States – including Bashar al-Asad, the columnist's country's leader. Al-Baba also demonstrates intimate familiarity with the logistics of *Star Academy*, and, through the prism of reality TV, he expresses a somber view of Arab politics and its artificiality. For him, reality TV is a window onto the changing dynamic between the private and the public, between backstage and front stage:

[Arab leaders] try to hide the backstage from the camera and from Arab viewers, so that on the *Star Academy* of Arab leaders only the "prime" evening can be seen. . . . But Arab viewers know by now that their leaders are being rebuked backstage for their *Star Academy* performance, and they know who is doing the rebuking.

Arab viewers of reality TV are attuned to the workings of power in Arab politics, because in the new media environment the camera brings a new level of transparency to public life:

The camera used to be dedicated to the leader's great achieve-ments, unforgettable speeches, and blessed projects; now it has turned against the leader to show his mistakes and record his errors, changing the world and awakening people. The decision about who stays and who exits [the Arab leaders' *Star Academy*] is in the hands of globalized satellite channels, not the canned terrestrial stations. The leader's slogan no longer rules because now the picture opposes it and nullifies it.[61]

Al-Baba is at his most poignant when he suggests that, unlike *Star Academy* contestants, whose daily life is managed by television producers but whose fate ultimately depends on the viewers, Arab autocrats' dependence on the West spurs them to ignore their peoples. Arab kings and presidents strive to present a positive image to the United States because their actual image with their people is not only unimportant to these leaders but also is beyond restoration. In doing so, Arab leaders perform a desultory "modernity" by political association with the West (which enjoys less popularity than reality TV). Nonetheless, satellite television subverts authoritarian power and brings a new level of visibility to Arab politics. At the same time, like reality TV performers who are suspended between their former private selves and their future as public figures, Arab leaders, al-Baba seems to be saying, jockey – without guarantees – for U.S. support instead of an irremediably lost popular legitimacy. The fraught connection between "reality" and "image" central to the elaboration of modernity is a focal point of al-Baba's criticism.

Other commentators broached the same issue earnestly rather than ironically. For example, after a dispute between proponents of tourism and advocates of nature preservation in the southern Lebanese city of Saida was shown live on television, Dalal al-Bizri wrote in *al-Hayat*:

This is the real "reality TV," more deserving of being aired than other "reality TV" programs. It is the real reality, where there is a . . . struggle . . . over . . . the image of that group or that leader. . . . The calculations of the producers of sterile "reality TV" programs, from *Star Academy* to *Journey in the Jungle* [Survivor], to beauty pageants, with their narrow rules, contrived and predictable nature, pale in comparison. What is hidden from viewers – the "disputes" and arguments concealed to preserve a clean image of groups and leaders – is what deserves to be aired. . . . Otherwise

---

[61] Ibid.

television "reality" would be . . . "cleansed," a clean television . . . without reality's warts, twists and turns. . . . If television would reserve some space for the unvarnished reality . . . if it would only do that . . . it would perform its most serious function: the production of reality based on truthful depiction.[62]

Here again, the binary separation of image and reality is front and center, increasingly connecting reality TV with disputes over representations of society. Journalists of various ideological persuasions considered *Star Academy* to be either unambiguously positive or unequivocally negative. Some hailed the spring 2005 Beirut demonstrations as a new kind of Arab politics, peaceful but effective, and making crucial use of the media, which an *Asharq al-Awsat* columnist called "Academy Politics,"[63] while others glimpsed in the Beirut rallies a "coup against the resistance by the public of *Superstar*"[64] (see Chapter 7 for details). Some argued that *Star Academy* was a "channel for dialogue"[65] while others called the show "moral terrorism"[66] (this story is told in Chapter 4). Even an Islamist like the Egyptian Fahmy Howeidy, known for his ties to the Muslim Brotherhood, published a column in *Asharq al-Awsat* asking political and religious leaders to stop complaining about reality TV – repeatedly stating that he had not watched such shows, only read and heard about them, of course! – and prodding them to give youth alternatives to *Star Academy* and *Superstar*.[67]

Why was reality TV so dramatically politicized in the Arab world? Chapters that follow indicate that the embedding of interactive procedure, the plebiscitary nature of reality shows, the affective bonds they forge with viewers, their transnational pan-Arab scope, and, most importantly, the self-made claim that reality TV represents reality, created a volatile combination that made it impossible for *Star Academy*, *al-Ra'is*, and *Superstar* to avert politicization. And politicized they were,

[62] al-Bizri, D. (January 23, 2005). The truthful "reality" which is concealed from television screens . . . ." *Al-Hayat* [Arabic].
[63] Shobokshi, H. (May 6, 2006). Academy politics. *Asharq al-Awsat* [Arabic].
[64] Mazhloum, H. D. (April 11, 2005). A coup against the resistance with the public of Superstar! *Al-Quds al-Arabi* [Arabic].
[65] al-Jabban, M. (February 20, 2004). Star Academy channel . . . ideas for dialogue. *Asharq al-Awsat* [Arabic].
[66] al-'Enezi, H. A. (March 19, 2005). Star Academy . . . the other terrorism. *Al-Riyadh* [Arabic].
[67] Howeidy, F. (May 4, 2005). Do not accuse Arab youth but provide them with an alternative. *Asharq al-Awsat* [Arabic].

instrumentalized by media institutions for business and political reasons, used as an analytical prism by journalists and as bogeyman by clergy, appropriated as a new political language by street demonstrators. A provocative rhetorical act in the Arab world, reality TV's claim to represent the real catalyzed discussions not only about gloomy social and political reality, but often about how social reality is constructed and the role of television in that process. In the prebroadcast marketing campaigns for reality TV shows, LBC, Future TV, and MBC promoted the concept of "reality" in reality TV aggressively, touting the spontaneity of the contestants, the liveness of the primes, and, most importantly, the power of viewers to evict contestants weekly and ultimately to select the winner. In the early months of the Arab reality TV wave, media coverage adroitly managed by the channels' public relations machines echoed the representational claim uncritically.[68] "In its Arab connotation," an article in *Asharq al-Awsat* noted matter-of-factly, "'reality TV' means 'representation of reality.'"[69] But reality TV's claim to represent reality resonated widely and deeply in Arab intellectual, media, and religious circles. Consider *Bila Hudud*, al-Jazeera's talk show that in March 2004 dedicated two episodes to reality TV under the heading "Mimicking Western Programs and Imposing Them on Arabs." The exchange reflected the controversy surrounding reality TV's claim to be real. On March 3 the guest was Ramsay Najjar, Head of the Lebanese Syndicate of Advertising Agencies, who represented the "liberal" view. The host Ahmad Mansour's introduction listed a motley crew of social, political, moral, and religious objections to reality TV. Rather than refuting Mansour's harsh allegations (quoted at the onset of the book's introduction), Ramsay Najjar, a veteran Lebanese ad man known for his penchant for big cigars and CEO of S2C (Strategic Communication Consultancy), immediately put the connection between reality TV and "reality" at the debate's forefront:

> **Ramsay Najjar:** Please allow me to object to the translation of "reality TV" as *telefizion al-waqi'* (television of reality) to help us correct a widespread characterization that is mistaken and imprecise.

---

[68] See, e.g., al-Jacques, S. (January 23, 2004). Star Academy on LBC "represents reality" with amateurs but with outstanding professionalism. *Asharq al-Awsat* [Arabic]; Haddad, V. (April 23, 2005). A new wave of Arab reality TV shows poised to be launched. *Asharq al-Awsat* [Arabic].

[69] Star Academy brings "reality TV fever" to LBCI (December 9, 2003). *Asharq al-Awsat* [Arabic].

Ahmad Mansour: What would a more precise (translation) be?

Ramsay Najjar: It would be the television of realistic representation [*telefizion al-tasweer*[70] *al-waqi'i*].

Ahmad Mansour: (*sounding incredulous*) Television of realistic representation?

Ramsay Najjar: Yes, because "telefizion al-waqi'" is a distortion; if we go back to the English language, it is "reality TV" [in English] and not "television of reality/realistic television" . . .

Ahmad Mansour: Unfortunately *Telefizion al-Waqi'* is the common usage in Arab media.

Ramsay Najjar: Yes, but this poses a danger to Najib Mahfouzh.

Ahmad Mansour: There is a big difference between the two. . . . What exactly do you mean?

Ramsay Najjar: I mean all the writers who have chosen realism in the novel . . . or the short story . . . [belong to] a very noble [literary tradition]. . . .

Ahmad Mansour: Please go on.

Ramsay Najjar: What I want to get at is that *telefizion al-waqi'* is a mistranslation because at the end what does *telefizion al-waqi'* mean? Is it the opposite of *telefizion al-khayal* [television of the imagination]?[71]

Najjar's argument is not new. As the French philosopher Damien Le Guay argued,

> Reality TV is not the television of reality. Its pretension to be the television of reality is exorbitant; false and exorbitant. Its raw matter is constructed, organized, mise-en-scène. Contestants are selected. Narratives are arranged. The morale of the story mostly predictable . . . from show to show appears, recurrently, a way of seeing things, people and situations.[72]

Nonetheless, Najjar's rhetoric was strategic. Cognizant of reality TV's advertising windfall, Najjar invoked Mahfouzh, the Egyptian novelist and Nobel Prize laureate, as an icon of realism, to establish a contrast with reality TV. This was not merely a distinction between high and popular culture. Rather, Najjar adroitly maneuvered to disconnect reality

---

[70] The Arabic word *tasweer* means representation, depiction, portrayal, picturing.

[71] Mimicking Western Programs and Imposing Them on Arabs, Episode 1 (March 3, 2004). *Bila Hudud* (Ahmad Mansour, Host). Doha, Qatar: al-Jazeera [Arabic].

[72] Le Guay, 2005, 30.

TV from "reality" because that connection attracted vociferous attacks against reality TV from clerics whose vision of Islamic social order faces a grave threat in the behavior, values, and lifestyles propagated on *al-Ra'is* or *Star Academy*.

In the second episode, Mansour hosted Muhammad al-'Awadhi, a member of the founding committee of the World Islamic Media Committee affiliated with the League of the Islamic World based in Mecca, Saudi Arabia. Like Najjar, this representative of Wahhabiyya objected to reality TV's claim to represent reality. But in contrast to Najjar, al-Awadhi's objection was not semantic, but rather religious, as reflected in this exchange:

> **Ahmad Mansour:** ... supporters ... claim that reality TV is an expression of human reality, of feelings, a spontaneous expression devoid of artifice, imitation, acting, and fake emotions that most people have?
> **Muhammad al-'Awadhi:** Which reality are they talking about? You chose a certain reality, you create an ambience, you put it under the spotlight, and you tell people this is reality. It is an artificial reality but it is (promoted as) an ideal reality. But what does this reality put under the spotlight? Moments of weakness, instinct, prohibited relations, illegitimate and immoral situations, all that in a society already afflicted (by many problems).[73]

It is tempting to see in Najjar and al-'Awadhi's questioning of the "reality" of reality TV a continuation of previous panics about the impact of "foreign" television on Arab societies. In this view, the new genre exacerbates already existing anxieties about television's representational power, in line with the argument by media scholar Justin Lewis that reality TV brought to the surface inconsistencies that were for a long time implicit in television viewing.[74] Although this applies somewhat to the Arab context, reality TV struck raw nerves in Arab countries for other reasons. Al-'Awadhi reflected visceral reactions in the Saudi clerical establishment, betraying deep anxieties about reality TV's potential for subverting the ritual bases of the Saudi clerico-political order. Also, this book will show, the contests between image and reality driving the

---

[73] Mimicking Western Programs and Imposing Them on Arabs, Episode 2 (March 10, 2004). *Bila Hudud* (Ahmad Mansour, Host). Doha, Qatar: al-Jazeera [Arabic].

[74] Lewis, J. (2004). "The Meaning of Real Life," in *Reality TV: Remaking Television Culture*, ed. S. Murray and L. Ouellette. New York: New York University Press, 288–302.

reality TV polemics created a space for the elaboration of varied representations of modernity.

Though the controversies took distinct national shapes in various Arab countries, reality TV contributed to an overall atmosphere of contentious politics in which Arabs of various nationalities and outlooks contested reality. Clerics, politicians, journalists, artists, and average Arabs found themselves compelled to engage the controversy because reality TV claimed to represent reality and because the "reality" it presented to Arab viewers was contentious. *Star Academy, Superstar,* and *al-Ra'is* thus became code words for various aspects of the Arab malaise, a rhetorical appropriation that made reality TV an idiom of contention. As this compelling account will show, that idiom entered a heavily politicized public space with multiple actors promoting rival agendas, making public claims, staking out ideological territory, and redrawing social and political boundaries between indigenous and foreign, virtuous and immoral, authentic and contaminated.

The al-Jazeera talk show host Ahmad Mansour concluded the two episodes of *Bila Hudud* devoted to the Arab reality TV phenomenon in a manner that left no doubt about his view of reality TV's pretense to represent reality: "we are here in the television of reality and nowhere else," he said, sanctifying al-Jazeera against usurpers of the power to represent the real.[75] Mansour's attempt to foreclose the debate was dissonant with the contentious, multivoiced, and ultimately unresolved debate he had chaperoned on the air. What the many participants in his show, journalists, and viewers throughout the Arab world had begun to realize, was that reality and the struggle over the privilege to define it would go on to animate the battle for Arab viewers for years to come. This became clear in one of the early contentious episodes of the Arab reality TV wars: the shutdown of *al-Ra'is*, the Arabic version of *Big Brother*, in Bahrain, whose story is told in the next chapter.

[75] Mimicking, Episode 1, 2004.

CHAPTER TWO

Voting Islam Off the Island? *Big Brother* in Bahrain

On March 1, 2004, one week after MBC launched *al-Ra'is*, the Arabic version of *Big Brother*, shot in the minuscule Persian Gulf island nation of Bahrain, a company spokesperson leaked to Agence France-Presse that "a decision to suspend the program was taken today."[1] The show appeared to have been doomed when a scarf covering the shoulder of a female Egyptian-Iraqi contestant fell and when, shortly thereafter, Hakim, a male Saudi contestant, kissed Kawthar, a female Tunisian participant, on the cheeks.[2] On February 27, 2004, a few hundred people demonstrated against *al-Ra'is* in Manama, Bahrain's capital. This sequence of events led Arab and Western media to report that MBC canceled *al-Ra'is* after demonstrators objected to the show's foreign values, which they deemed offensive to Islam. As told by the press, the story fits a well-rehearsed archetype: Muslim clerics oppose popular culture that reflects Western values; in turn, "traditional" society bows to religious edicts. In such narratives, Islam is trumpeted, in Olivier Roy's words, as "a discrete entity, a coherent and closed set of beliefs, values and anthropological patterns"[3] – an all-encompassing determinant of social relations.

This chapter advances a different perspective, avoiding ready-made formulae and relying instead on empirical research and careful examination of complicated institutional, national, and regional forces. It shows that religious determinism – analyzing events exclusively through

---

[1] "Arab Network Suspends Big Brother Show" (March 2, 2004). Manama, Bahrain: MASNET and News Agencies.

[2] Bouhaji, S. (February 28, 2004). Islamists demonstrate in Bahrain against al-Ra'is and request its shutdown. *Asharq al-Awsat* [Arabic].

[3] Roy, O. (2004). *Globalized Islam: The Search for a New Umma*. New York: Columbia University Press, 9.

the prism of "Islam" – obscures political agendas and economic interests. The vivid stories told throughout the book demonstrate that Islam
comes in various forms, speaks in different ways, and connects to rival
political agendas. Rather than seeing the shutdown of the Arabic version of *Big Brother* as a clear-cut episode of censorship in the name of
religious conservatism, the scandal that erupted because of *al-Ra'is* is
rather approached as an initial tremor, limited in scope and intensity
but revealing in its dynamics, auguring the major pan-Arab earthquake
that was to come in the form of *Star Academy*. As the remainder of this
chapter will show, the *al-Ra'is* episode was an early indication (alongside early *Superstar* skirmishes in Kuwait and Lebanon discussed in
Chapters 5 and 6) of reality TV's propensity to stir the volatile mix of
gender, religion, business, and politics that animates Arab public life.

What made Bahrain, a tiny country, the center of such a convulsion?
Was the upheaval mainly the work of local activists and politicians, as
reported by the media, or did it have transnational dimensions? If there
were external players, who were they, and what were their motivations?
Why did MBC shut down the show, incurring substantial financial
losses, if there were "only" a few hundred demonstrators against it? Did
MBC's management not prepare for the eventuality of such a development? Finally, why did Bahrain's parliament witness intense debate
between critics and defenders of *al-Ra'is*? Did busy elected representatives have no more pressing matters to discuss than a reality show? More
broadly, what does this event tell us about politics in Bahrain and other
Gulf countries?

POLITICS, ECONOMY, AND MEDIA IN BAHRAIN: THE SAUDI FACTOR

A small archipelago located in the Persian Gulf between Iran and Saudi
Arabia, Bahrain has been ruled by the al-Khalifa family since 1783, when
the family captured the islands from Persian settlers. For a century after-
ward, Bahrain sought formal British protection from its larger and more
powerful neighbors. Since independence in 1971, Bahrain's declining
oil reserves compelled the government to focus on services, first on pro-
cessing and refining petroleum products, later on banking and finance.
Bahrain is the smallest Arab nation-state, with a surface area of 665
square kilometers and a population of 750,000, including a quarter million nonnationals. Like other Gulf monarchies, this least wealthy member of the Gulf Cooperation Council (GCC) is ruled by Sunni Muslims,

who dominate the country's political and economic elite. But unlike Saudi Arabia, Kuwait, Qatar, the United Arab Emirates, and Oman, the majority of Bahrain's population is Shi'i (estimates range from 60% to 80% of the total population). As a result, though the 1972 constitution established the country as a partial democracy, the political and economic marginalization of the Shi'a spawned a "cyclical pattern of civil dissidence" during most of the twentieth century.[4] Bahrain today has sixteen major political formations. Religious parties include the al-Wifaq National Islam Society and the Islamic Action Association (Amal Islami), both Shi'i; al-Minbar Islamic Bloc Sunni Islamist party (the local chapter of the Muslim Brotherhood); and the al-Asala Islamic Bloc, a Sunni-Salafi party. Nonreligious groups include the National Democratic Action, which is the largest secular leftist bloc (previously the communist party of Bahrain), and the Economists' Bloc, a (neo) liberal party representing the interests of the business community.

After Shaykh Isa Ibn Salman al-Khalifa, the previous ruler, refused to enter negotiations with the Shi'i opposition over social, economic, and political demands, popular demonstrations erupted in 1994, leading to a government clampdown and widespread arrests, including the publicized capture of militants with alleged Iranian sponsorship. When Shaykh Hamad al-Khalifa assumed power from his father in 1999, he adopted an ostensibly reformist policy leading to the National Charter of 2000, which reaffirmed the government's constitutional underpinnings and stipulated an independent judiciary and a bicameral legislature.[5] On October 3, 2000, the new emir (the ruler assumed the title of "king" when Bahrain was declared a kingdom in 2002) gave a speech to Majlis al-Shoura, the upper house of the parliament, in which he called for a wide-ranging national dialogue and a "progress and modernization plan."[6] On July 30, 2001, 98.4 percent of Bahrainis voted in a referendum in favor of the Charter, thus reaffirming the 1972 constitution, but the government reneged on its promises to address socioeconomic disparities that were at the heart of the opposition's demands. More importantly, on February 15, 2002 the government ignored the overwhelming popular support of the Charter and announced a new

---

[4] Peterson, J. E. (2002). "Bahrain's First Steps Toward Reform under Amir Hamad," *Asian Affairs* 33 (2): 216–27. Also see Bahry, L. (Summer 2000). "The Socioeconomic Foundations of the Shiite Opposition in Bahrain," *Mediterranean Quarterly*: 129–43.

[5] Peterson, 2002.

[6] Rabi'a, A. (November 24, 2006). Bahrain: A model of American-style reform. *Al-Quds al-Arabi* [Arabic].

constitution that curtailed legislative and judicial power in favor of the executive branch, in addition to weakening oversight over government agencies.[7] After major promises remained unfulfilled, opposition groups felt betrayed. They – al-Wifaq and the National Democratic Action – boycotted the October 2002 elections, the first that women were allowed to contest (31 ran for office, all unsuccessfully), which enabled Sunni politicians close to the rulers to capture more than half of the seats.[8] As a result, in sharp contrast to the 98.4 percent turnout of the 2001 referendum, the 2002 legislatives drew only 53 percent of voters.[9] With reform efforts stalled, protests erupted again in 2005, and the government attempted to revoke licenses from political parties by passing a restrictive Law of Associations. Opposition forces mounted a robust campaign against the impending law, forcing the government to back down. Nonetheless, these events fueled the chronic "crisis of trust" between opposition and government, which to this day lurks under a surface of relative stability.[10]

Bahrain's economic policies are premised on a dynamic financial services sector. With the lowest oil and gas reserves of any of the Gulf monarchies, Bahrain has focused on economic diversification and the reduction of dependence on petroleum resources since the 1970s. Developing an infrastructure of financial services has been a central element of national policy.[11] According to the Bahrain Economic Development Board, there are more than four hundred licensed financial institutions in the country.[12] Of these, more than thirty specialize in Islamic finance, an area of banking that has been growing globally due to the Gulf oil boom and in which Bahrain is an innovative leader.[13] The kingdom has successfully branded itself as the financial hub of the Middle East, integrating its financial services in the global economy and focusing on attracting foreign investments.[14] Bahraini experts have

---

[7] Ibid.
[8] Peterson, 2002.
[9] Rabi'a, 2006.
[10] Ibid.
[11] Al-Maraj, R. M. (January 10, 2008). Vigorous economic growth in Bahrain. Speech by His Excellency Rasheed Muhammad Almaraj, Governor of the Central Bank of Bahrain, at the Strategic Forum on the Bilateral Trade and Investment Opportunities in Banking and Finance, London.
[12] Bahrain Economic Development Board 2008, http://www.bahrainfs.com (accessed April 28, 2008).
[13] Al-Maraj, 2008.
[14] Siddiqi, M. A. (June 2001). "Bahrain: Financial Hub of the Middle East," *Middle East* 313: 37.

counseled governments worldwide on the intricacies of *hawala* and other Islamic financial products. In addition, Bahrain, which became a member of the General Agreement on Tariffs and Trade (GATT) in 1993 and along with Kuwait was the only GCC founding member of the World Trade Organization (WTO),[15] is considered a strong proponent of free trade in the Gulf region. This is not uncontroversial. When the kingdom's free-trade agreement with the United States became public in December 2004, Saudi leaders publicly voiced their opposition.[16] Bahrain's economic policy and its relationship with Saudi Arabia, we shall briefly see, are important catalysts of the debate that followed the shutdown of *al-Ra'is*.

But why shoot *al-Ra'is* in Bahrain? I asked several directors, producers, and other creative media types who worked on the show, when I visited MBC's Dubai headquarters a few months after the debacle. Because it could not be shot in Saudi Arabia, they answered in unison, where it is unacceptable for unmarried men and women to share living quarters. In today's transnational Arab television industry, programs are shot in one location, broadcast from another, and watched throughout the Arab world. The producers of *al-Ra'is* had a house custom built for the show on al-Amwaj, a man-made island resort off the coast of Bahrain's main island. Less expensive and more liberal than its larger Saudi neighbor, Bahrain is a favorite weekend destination for Saudi men, who cross the King Fahd Causeway (KFC), a 15.5-mile four-lane bridge over Persian Gulf waters in search of a more permissive atmosphere – the KFC is nicknamed "Johnny Walker Bridge" and billboards tout cures for "sexual dysfunction." Why not shoot *al-Ra'is* in Lebanon or Egypt, Arab production centers that are socially more liberal than Gulf societies? Because, I was told, unlike Lebanon or Egypt, Bahrain, though more socially liberal than Saudi Arabia, shares cultural and social characteristics with its bigger and wealthier neighbor, MBC's main market, making it an obvious shooting location for *al-Ra'is*.

Despite a dynamic economic policy, Bahrain's media institutions have lagged behind those of its neighbors. Bahrain has no equivalent to Qatar's al-Jazeera and no major pan-Arab entertainment channel like

---

[15] "The Endeavours of Gulf Countries to Meet WTO Requirements" (2001), *Arab Law Quarterly* 16 (1): 49–51.

[16] See Katzman, K. (March 14, 2005). *Bahrain: Key Issues for U.S. Policy*. Washington, DC: Congressional Research Service; Wallin, M. (December 24, 2004), and "U.S.-Bahrain Accord Stirs Persian Gulf Trade Partners." *New York Times*, W1.

the Saudi-owned MBC. This is partly due to geography: in a diminutive country with a population of half a million, Bahraini authorities did not feel a pressing need to develop a broadcasting system to promote national cohesion. Unlike Qatar, whose rulers developed al-Jazeera to counter Saudi regional influence, Bahrain's ruling family maintains excellent relations with the House of al-Sa'ud. After a national broadcasting structure was eventually developed, Bahrain's media policy echoed, as the veteran scholar of Arab media Douglas Boyd described it, "the basic economic orientation of the country: to attract people to the tourist-associated industries on the islands and to gain income from the petroleum-rich neighbors."[17] In an otherwise undistinguished Bahraini media history, the long-standing relationship between Bahraini media and Saudi viewers is relevant to the *al-Ra'is* controversy. Bahrain television went on air in 1973 with a color signal and a program grid dominated by imports from Egypt, Britain, and the United States, in partnership with U.S. company RTV International (the government took full control in 1976).[18] From 1973 until 1986 – when Saudi Arabia allowed advertisements on its own television screens – companies wishing to reach the Saudi market advertised on Bahrain's television, whose signals reached the geographically proximate Eastern Region and other parts of the kingdom of al-Sa'ud. In a small domestic market, the economic viability of commercial media in Bahrain depended on the Saudi Arabian market.[19]

The idea for MBC stemmed from recognition that there was an untapped and lucrative Saudi media market. The channel was launched with fanfare in 1991 out of swanky London headquarters by ARA Group International, a Saudi conglomerate headed by Walid al-Ibrahim, brother-in-law of then King Fahd Bin 'Abdulaziz, whose media holdings date back to 1985. Its slogan was "The World through Arab Eyes," and its graphic identity focused on gold and blue, dominant natural colors (sand, sky, and sea) in the Gulf countries. As explained in Chapter 1, competition compelled a rebranding of MBC from news and entertainment to mostly entertainment and contributed to the channel's move from London to Dubai Media City in 2001.[20] At the same time, MBC

---

[17] Boyd, D. A. (1999). *Broadcasting in the Arab World: A Survey of the Electronic Media in the Middle East*, 2nd ed. Ames, IA: Iowa State University Press, 181.
[18] Ibid.
[19] Ibid.
[20] Girard, L. (November 6, 2001). MBC, la pionnière des chaînes arabes, quitte Londres. *Le Monde*.

began to grow from one channel to a multichannel conglomerate, the MBC Group.[21] In 2008, the group launched its sixth channel, MBC Persia, following MBC Action in 2007, four other MBC channels, and al-Arabiya, the Arabic-language news channel launched as a Saudi antidote to al-Jazeera. The main channel MBC provided family entertainment, MBC 2 focused on young adults, MBC 3 on "juniors" (3 to 13 years old), and MBC 4, as the channel's Director of Business Development told me, catered to "mature, cosmopolitan, liberal Arabs, interested in staying abreast of developments in the West both in terms of news and entertainment."[22] Since that interview MBC 4 has shifted its focus onto women viewers.

The relationship between Bahrain and MBC goes back to the early days of the institution. Soon after MBC's launch on satellite, Bahrain retransmitted it terrestrially, which, because of geographical proximity, allowed MBC to reach viewers who did not have satellite receivers in Saudi Arabia's Eastern Province.[23] The arrangement worked well for both sides. Bahrain's government was able to broadcast to its population a new and exciting entertainment channel whose Saudi ownership ensured noncontroversial programs and provided training to Bahraini nationals in television production. At the same time, because Bahraini television historically reached Saudi viewers, MBC management surmised that Bahraini rebroadcasts would attract more advertising spending from companies wishing to reach the Saudi market (the Bahraini market came as a nice extra). Hala 'Omran, who in the early 1990s was a high-level employee in the Bahraini Information Ministry and head of Bahrain Television, was hired as MBC's managing director in 1996 and held this position until 1998.[24] One of the MBC Group's channels, MBC 2 targeted the youth audience.[25] Unlike MBC 1, the group's

---

[21] Kraidy, M. M. and Khalil, J. (2007). "The Middle East: Transnational Arab Television," in *The Media Globe: Trends in International Mass Media*, ed. L. Artz and Y. Kamalipour. Lanham, MD: Rowman and Littlefield, 79–98.

[22] Author interview with Michel Costandi, Director of Business Development, MBC Group, June 29, 2005, Dubai, UAE.

[23] Boyd, 1999.

[24] Saudi businessmen also have connections with Bahrain because of its leading position in Islamic finance. Shaykh Saleh Kamel, a Saudi mogul who was an initial partner of al-Ibrahim in financing MBC before he left to launch ART, set up a company in Bahrain to manage money according to Islamic principles.

[25] Author interview with Michel Costandi, Director of Business Development, MBC, June 29, 2005, Dubai, UAE. For a more detailed profile, see Kraidy, M. M. and Khalil, J. F. (2009, in press). *Arab Television Industries*. London: Palgrave Macmillan/British Film Institute.

family-oriented flagship channel, MBC 2's viewers were "twenty and thirty something educated Arabs, who are fluent in English."[26] It is on this niche channel that *al-Ra'is* was satcast. When MBC 2 went on air in January 2003, it was revealed that "[M]ost of the investors ... are from Bahrain" and that a Bahraini channel was broadcasting it terrestrially in addition to the main satellite signal.[27] Bahraini investors, with tacit government support, were involved in the channel to such an extent that a newspaper headline stated: "Bahrain launches new TV channel."[28]

In addition to Bahrain's business links with MBC and its political connections with the Saudi establishment, other institutional and political factors contributed to the shutdown of *al-Ra'is*. The episode was not, as Western media and academic reports maintained, merely a clash between Western-inspired popular culture and local moral-religious activists.[29] Surely, this was a reason for the controversy, but only one among several others, which include the influence of Saudi Arabia on Bahraini affairs. In my research I learned that during initial planning for the show, MBC's management approached Saudi authorities seeking "permission" to satcast the show. According to sources within MBC, the matter was examined by a Saudi media committee made up of representatives from the ministries of the interior, information, and religious affairs (the formation of the committee is discussed in Chapter 3). The committee advised against *al-Ra'is*, but some members allowed for an exception if two conditions were met: if it were not shot in Saudi Arabia (Bahrain was suggested) and if a strict separation of men and women was imposed.[30] Deciding to go ahead with the program in Bahrain, Walid al-Ibrahim requested that the studio feature gender-segregated sleeping quarters, prayer rooms, and bathrooms.[31] The main living room was the only space shared by men and women on the set. At the same time, I was told off the record that following a casting decision, all women contestants were divorcées, with the implication that none of

---

[26] "Big Brother Opener Sparks Controversy" (April 2004). *Arabian Business*, 60.

[27] al-Alawi, D. (January 12, 2003). "Bahrain Launches New TV Channel." *Gulf Daily News*.

[28] Ibid., 2003.

[29] Several media accounts are cited in this chapter. For an uncritical academic version, see Sakr, N. (2007). *Arab Television Today*. London: I. B. Tauris.

[30] Author interview with Paul Hitti, Special Projects Manager, MBC, June 22, 2005, Dubai, UAE.

[31] Author interview with Safa al-Ahmad, *al-Ra'is* Story Producer, Middle East Broadcasting Center, June 19, 2005, Dubai, UAE.

them was a virgin.[32] However, because of MBC's contractual obligations to the Dutch format company Endemol as stipulated in the *Big Brother* format, and because of the drive for ratings, production was micromanaged at the highest levels of the institution, with producers *in situ* in Bahrain receiving, as one of them told me, "contradictory and constantly changing instructions: one day, it was 'show more skin;' the next day: 'you're showing too much skin;' the third day: 'you are not showing enough skin.'"[33] Technical glitches also contributed to the snafu: the crew, mostly consisting of Bahrainis without advanced professional training, went on air without adequate preparation. As a producer told me, "one major mistake was committed when the video channel was showing the girls' room while all 8 audio channels were left open (the 4 audio feeds from the boys' room were supposed to be shut off), giving the impression that there were boys in the girls' room" by producing an audiotrack with male and female voices.[34]

This raised concerns over *ikhtilat*, the unsupervised social mixing of men and women unmarried to each other considered illicit by most Islamists, which exploded on the fourth day after the infamous Saudi-Tunisian cheek kissing. The February 27, 2004 demonstrations in Manama, Bahrain's capital, that contributed to the shutdown of *al-Ra'is* were led by Islamists under the banner of protecting Islamic values and morals. The three dominant blocs in Bahrain's legislature, al-Minbar (Sunni, Muslim Brotherhood), al-Wifaq (Shi'i Islamist), and al-Asala (Sunni, Salafi) were united in opposition to *al-Ra'is*, the salafis being most adamant. Though in the past al-Minbar had espoused relatively forward-looking social positions, such as support for women's rights, al-Asala and al-Wifaq regularly cooperated in morality campaigns.[35] These parties' objections to *al-Ra'is*, even though they were not always explicitly articulated as such, focused on the fact that unmarried men and women lived together in one house, creating potential for illicit flirting, physical contact, and even sexual intercourse. On this, the three main religious parties agreed.

[32] Author interviews with creative staff, Middle East Broadcasting Center, June 2005, Dubai, UAE. Obviously, the company did not formally publicize this; rather, it appeared that this information was leaked to appease religiously conservative opponents of the show.

[33] Author interview with Safa al-Ahmad, *al-Ra'is* Story Producer, Middle East Broadcasting Center, June 19, 2005, Dubai, UAE.

[34] Ibid.

[35] Understanding Bahrain's Third Parliamentary Elections (November 2006). Durham, U.K.: Center for Iranian Studies, 5. This source states that al-Asala and al-Wifaq perceive al-Minbar to be exceedingly relaxed on social issues.

In spite of this consensus, according to members of the *al-Ra'is* production team who were present at the scene, demonstrators consisted of only a couple of hundred men, and not one thousand demonstrators, the figure advanced in some press accounts. There was also a demonstration of a few dozen women in front of the Ministry of Information.[36] But the controversy soon found a broader audience. Several days after the show was shut down, 'Adel Mu'awida, the Salafi Vice-President of Bahrain's legislature, called al-Jazeera studios to intervene in *Bila Hudud*'s episode dedicated to the reality TV controversy (discussed in Chapter 1). On the air, he said

> **'Adel Mu'awida:** In truth, I regret not to have watched this program from the beginning, but someone alerted me to it, and since we are experiencing this issue in Bahrain these days, after God almighty got rid of the nightmare [of *al-Ra'is*], those who sought to get us rid of it asked me to call and contribute to your discussion.
>
> **Ahmad Mansour:** Please, no need for this introduction ... if you have an opinion, please go ahead and express it ...
>
> **Adel Mu'awida:** Our problem now, with those who defend these types [reality TV] of programs, is that they speak a different language. There are people who reject imperialism and Westernization, and there are those who say it is a reality that we must accept happily ... imperialism is behind this program and free persons cannot accept imperialism. Are the imperialists in this case Arabs or are they people manipulating Arabs? Are they from among us or from the outside? ... in our midst the end does not justify the means. If we let them do that, we lose our values, morals and principles. ... [37]

The trope of "imperialism," which had not surfaced in initial clerical objections to *al-Ra'is*, was tailor-made for secular-Arabist and Islamist segments of al-Jazeera's audience. It also put forth the notion that reality TV shows, even when shot in Arabic, with Arab participants, and in an Arab country, are foreign, nonauthentic, and pernicious – the hybrid as subversive. The culmination of this argument was that reality TV was incompatible with Arab reality.

[36] Bouhaji, S. (February 28, 2004).
[37] Mimicking Western Programs and Imposing Them on Arabs, Episode 1 (March 3, 2004). Bila Hudud (Ahmad Mansour, Host). Doha, Qatar: al-Jazeera [Arabic].

Two days earlier, in interviews published in the Bahraini press, the same 'Adel Mu'awida spelled out his reasons for opposing *al-Ra'is*: "This program showed an abnormal way of living, which is totally opposed to our thoughts, culture, everything. . . . *It is not reality TV at all, especially in our part of the world.*"[38] This and other similar statements indicate that the claims made on reality TV programs that they represent "reality" are contentious in themselves (as explained in detail in Chapter 1).[39] The dispute around whether reality TV does or does not represent reality connects to broader issues of modernity and authenticity. Contesting the "realness" of an Arab television show adapted from a Western format can be understood as a maneuver by the opposition to negotiate Western modernity on its own terms. In Bahrain, this often means adopting Western modernity's economic practices wholeheartedly and its political institutions haphazardly (spearheaded by the government), while vehemently opposing Western cultural and social mores (led by the opposition). In this context, the debate that engulfed Bahrain in the wake of the *al-Ra'is* shutdown reflected broader struggles in the Arab world between rival narratives of what it means to be Arab-Muslim and modern.

BARGAINING FOR REALITY: NATIONAL REPUTATION AND INSTITUTIONAL BRAND

The complexity of the *al-Ra'is* episode comes into full view when we consider that many members of the Bahraini parliament rose in defense of the program, and especially when we examine the arguments they used: defenders of *al-Ra'is* publicly argued that the program would boost tourism, promote foreign investment, and create new jobs, therefore contributing to national growth.[40] Because Bahrain, a small country with dwindling energy reserves, bet its postoil prosperity on its status as a financial hub, arguments couched in the language of economic pragmatism appeal to a section of the elite whose members are emboldened publicly to oppose the Islamists. A special parliamentary committee discussed the impact of *al-Ra'is* on Bahraini society and considered

---

[38] MacFarqhar, N. (March 5, 2004). "A Kiss Is Not Just a Kiss to an Angry Arab TV Audience." *New York Times*, emphasis added.

[39] Reality television's claim to be "real" is an issue that has received significant scholarly attention, e.g., in Mark A., *Reality TV: The Work of Being Watched.* Lanham, MD, 2004 and Hill, A., *Reality TV: Audiences and Popular Factual Television.* London, 2005.

[40] MacFarqhar, March 5, 2004.

"ways to protect investments and preserve Bahrain's Islamic ethics"[41] –
a balancing act, we shall see throughout this book, which is a recurring
feature of Arab experiences with modernity. Statements by the head of
the committee, Member of Parliament (MP) Ahmed Ibrahim Bahzad,
reflect that the debate went beyond an opposition of Islamists to the
culture industry. Rather,

> There are three distinct opinions about *Big Brother*, and they reflect
> the vivacity of our society. . . . There are people who reject the pro-
> gram completely; the second section does not show any interest in
> the issue, while the third group says that the focus should not be
> on the program but on the participants. . . . There are people who
> want to cancel the contract with the producing companies, but
> this is opposed by the businessmen who fear that such a decision
> would hurt Bahrain's reputation and undermine potential invest-
> ment agreements.[42]

In the Arab context, references to "national reputation" arise in the
context of government suppression of political dissent. This catchall
notion is frequently used against activists or journalists critical of government policies. As the Egyptian media critic Amina al-Khairy noted
ironically in an *al-Hayat* column entitled "National 'Reputation'":

> Vulgar movies harm national reputation; taking pictures of gar-
> bage piling up on side streets harms national reputation; pub-
> lishing reports on bad economic performance harms national
> reputation; sexy music videos harm national reputation; hosting
> opposition figures on television talk shows hurts national repu-
> tation. . . . And so it is that national reputation has become an
> autonomous theme. . . . [T]here are two kinds of people, the first
> kind harms national reputation, and the second kind is interested
> in pointing out who is harming national reputation.
>   The strange thing is that the proliferation of satellite channels
> in the last decade intensified the "national reputation" phobia that
> we inherited a long time ago in our Arab world. . . . This accu-
> sation plays on the chords of powerful feelings that constitute a
> winning card and a strong justification in the hands of "some" . . .
> [including] . . . regimes that feel extreme embarrassment, and

---

[41] "The Reality of Reality TV in the Middle East," www.albawaba.com/news/print
Article.php3?sid=271966&;lang=e, March 7, 2004 (accessed April 15, 2005).
[42] Ibid.

maybe a threat to their power and strength, every time there is a report that they feel is critical, or a program that they feel is biased, or even a news item that they feel confuses public opinion. And all of these are clearly put in the basket of media material that is harmful to national reputation.

. . .

Luckily, the accusation of harming national reputation has been "democratized." Today everybody uses it, not only the regimes. The dancer who presents a music video that some consider has too much nudity harms national reputation. The singer who dodges military service harms national reputation, and the people behind a film about prostitutes harm national reputation. And advertisements that feature bikini-wearing girls to promote tourism harm national reputation; the list is long, even endless.

Though the accusation is now accessible to everyone, punishment is still the exclusive domain of regimes that are able to derail the operations of a satellite channel that "harms national reputation." At the same time, satellite channels resort to another form of punishment, more intelligent because indirect, which is the "pull and release" style, for example not letting some faces appear on the screen, or exposing facts that regimes do not want exposed. Punishment could be extreme when exposure comes at critical times. What is remarkable in all this is that corruption, a bad [socioeconomic] situation, daily suffering, the decay of education, pollution, the collapse of values, the rise of unemployment are not considered harmful to national reputation. . . . Poor nation indeed![43]

The ability of some Arab media institutions strategically to focus the spotlight on some issues while keeping others in the dark even as they risk state reprisal reflects the new kinds of visibility engendered by media proliferation. Al-Khairy takes advantage of it in this column to expose the instrumental and repressive nationalism practiced by Arab governments. Turning the most nefarious excuse for state repression – "national reputation" – on its head, al-Khairy contrasts the never-ending list of actions and behaviors that allegedly harm national reputation with a litany of real social, economic, and political problems riddling Arab countries.

The same bread-and-butter issues were raised in reaction to the ostensibly moral-religious panic that met *al-Ra'is* in Bahrain, leading

---

[43] al-Khairy, A. (December 8, 2006). National "Reputation." *Al-Hayat* [Arabic].

to appeals to government efficiency and responsiveness to the practical needs of citizens. In their opposition to the shutdown of *al-Ra'is*, liberal Bahraini parliamentarians countered the Islamists with socioeconomic arguments. Abdullah al-Dossary, an "independent" member of the Majlis who is close to the al-Khalifa ruling family, asked: "[T]here are other important issues to be tackled by the deputies. Why all the fuss over a TV show? What happened to the citizens' problems such as housing, salary improvement and education?"[44] This attention to the everyday life concerns of the citizenry, with bigger economic arguments in the background, indicate that a purely "culturalist" (in this case Islamicist) explanation of public debates about the impact of reality TV does not suffice. Such an approach provides us with only a partial understanding of an overall picture in which nonreligious forces contend with speakers in the name of Islam.[45] More than a reflection of cultural factors, the contest between proponents of public morality and advocates of bread-and-butter pragmatism is another echo of the struggle to define what it means to be modern in the contemporary Arab world.

More broadly, invoking the trope of national reputation in reference to Bahrain's fitness for foreign investment reflects a shift in Arab public discourse toward free-market ideals, unfettered trade, and the search for competitive advantage to lure global capital – modernity as neoliberal governance. Critics of the *al-Ra'is* shutdown warned of its dire consequences for foreign investment and economic growth. A recurrent theme among those who opposed the shutdown of *al-Ra'is* was the impact of such an action on Bahrain's economy. A prominent businessman stated that the show would bring in more than U.S.$15 million in direct investment and provide work to two hundred nationals. "What the MPs are doing will only discourage potential investors," the businessman said.[46] The columnist Ahmad Jum'a criticized legislators for "trying to score political and election points at the expense of national

---

[44] "The Reality of Reality TV in the Middle East," www.albawaba.com/news/print Article.php3?sid=271966&;lang=e.

[45] The socioeconomic arguments could be described as "emergent" while Islamist claims can be said to be "established," a distinction admittedly in need of elaboration. Although in this case the show was canceled, the fact that Gulf Arab politicians opposed public claims grounded in religion is significant, as is MBC's rhetorical gesture to use "Arab" as "opposed" to "Islamic" in its corporate statement, even when there is connotative overlap between the two adjectives.

[46] "Bahrain MPs Seek to Grill Minister on Reality TV Show" (February 26, 2004). *Gulf News*, www.gulf-news.com. See also Davies, F. (2004). "Al-Rais Has Fallen Silent," Geneva: European Broadcasting Union.

policies that encourage investments and an open economy."[47] Defenders of *al-Ra'is* articulated strictly economic arguments, while its opponents attacked it on moral bases. This reflects the multiple sources of public arguments over national policy, symptomatic of the pluralism inherent in modernity. Recognizing this multiplicity allows us to avoid what the historian Ibrahim Kaya, after the political theorist Bernard Yack, called the "fetishism" of modernity, which "unifies many-sided social processes and phenomena into a single grand objective."[48] Bahrain's internal diversity embodies an apparent paradox, expressed by a journalist in this column:

> Manama [Bahrain's capital city] is the capital of Gulf paradoxes par excellence. This is the city that demonstrated in order to kick out *Big Brother*, which belongs to the reality TV genre. This is the city that also voted for its Bahraini candidate Ahmad Salah in *Star Academy*, saving him from expulsion more than once. This is also the city who refuses to welcome the lovely singer Nancy 'Ajram, a topic debated by Parliament the next day, and at the same time, the British singer Brian Adams gives concerts and Manama streets are buzzing with the news of the imminent arrival of the US band Westlife. Night in Bahrain is full of various forms of entertainment; morning sees Parliament discussing the establishment of a Commission to Promote Virtue and Combat Vice.[49]

The last sentence uses the words *night* and *morning* not only as contexts for fundamentally different practices, but also as a metaphor for the two extreme poles in Bahrain's public life and the ubiquitous Saudi neighbor: On the one hand, we have a relatively freewheeling nightlife, which attracts locals and Saudi tourists in high numbers, a product of economic policy and relatively relaxed social mores; on the other hand, there is a vocal moral police, heavily represented in the legislature, whose members take Saudi Arabia's clerics as a model for combating vice.

Arab and Western media accounts left out the powerful intrainstitutional forces that worked to undermine *al-Ra'is* even before the show went on the air. Several people involved in the production shared with

[47] Ibid.
[48] Kaya, I. (2004). "Modernity, Openness, Interpretation: A Perspective on Multiple Modernities," *Social Science Information* 43 (1): 35–47.
[49] Jaza'iri, M. (April 9, 2005). Al-Manama: Capital of youth contradictions. *Asharq al-Awsat* [Arabic]. Author note: Westlife is actually an Irish pop band.

me that they were alarmed at the apparent lack of preparation. For one thing, to use the words of one of *al-Ra'is'* producers, MBC "sat on" the *Big Brother* format for three years after it purchased it from Endemol.[50] At the same time, the channel aired infrequent promotional clips for the show, and mainly on MBC 2, with a few on the more widely watched MBC.[51] In the words of an *al-Ra'is* producer, who at the time of our interview still worked for MBC, "promotion was nill, logistics ill-prepared, staff not ready."[52] Also, there was no public relations strategy for dealing with potential controversy.[53] At least a half-dozen directors, producers, and managers who worked on the show agreed, mostly off the record, that an internal power struggle at MBC undermined *al-Ra'is.* They pointed to a former head of production who had left the channel on bad terms but retained enough clout among decision makers to be a key spoiler. One high-level MBC manager told me that after MBC did not adhere to the Saudi media committee's recommendation not to air the show, powerful players associated with the committee were bent on undermining *al-Ra'is.*[54] More than one source at the channel believed that Saudi clerics enlisted cleric-politicians in Bahrain to "make a fuss" about the show. One even believed that Saudi-Bahraini complicity in undermining *al-Ra'is* went to the "highest [royal] level." Even with the significant breaks from the *Big Brother* format agreed to by Endemol in the name of cultural sensitivity (one MBC manager told me "*we destroyed the format* . . . no touching, no kissing, no sex . . . two separate prayer rooms!"), MBC could not find sponsors for the show before the satcast because advertisers were concerned about potential controversy. After the first episode was aired and no vocal objections were voiced during the first couple of days, Pepsi signed on as a sponsor.[55]

MBC's official explanation suggests that religion was not the dominant factor in their decision; the channel's management explicitly claimed other reasons. Even after deciding to cancel *al Ra'is,* MBC argued that the program "was more realistic in reflecting the reality" of

[50] Author interview with al-Ahmad, Safa, *al-Ra'is* Story Producer, Middle East Broadcasting Center, June 19, 2005, Dubai, UAE.
[51] MBC launched MBC 2 in order to avoid airing potentially controversial programs like reality shows on the flagship "family" MBC channel.
[52] Author interview with al-Ahmad, Safa, *al-Ra'is* Story Producer, Middle East Broadcasting Center, June 19, 2005, Dubai, UAE.
[53] Author interview with Mroue, Leila, *al-Ra'is* Story Producer, Middle East Broadcasting Center, June 25, 2005, Dubai, UAE.
[54] Author interview with Hitti, Paul, Special Projects Manager, MBC, June 22, 2005, Dubai, UAE.
[55] Ibid., emphasis added.

Arab youth than other reality TV programs, adding a business-like explanation to the controversy:

> All new products need time to be accepted. In certain cases, they can be wrongly interpreted. . . . By this sacrifice, MBC does not want to risk, through its programs and broadcasting, being accused of harming Arab traditions and values, because it considers the channel one for the Arab family.[56]

This corporate statement reflects the importance of business considerations in MBC's decision to shut down the program. Its "family channel" brand risked losing its luster if it kept a program on the air that a probably small but nonetheless vocal minority considered subversive of "family values." Unlike its Lebanese competitor LBC, known for its ostentatious social liberalism, MBC was constrained by the Saudi value sphere in which it operated.[57] (Ironically, al-Rai's was conceived as a major foray into reality TV and a main asset in MBC's ratings war with LBC.) The mention of "sacrifice" finds its explanation in a self-declared loss of U.S.$6 million because of the shutdown of al Ra'is. This was an enormous sum by regional standards at the time, though the real figure is impossible to ascertain. The invocation of "Arab traditions and values," but not of "Islam," is significant because opposition to the program was mainly under the banner of its putative violation of Islamic values.

In my first interview with Michel Costandi, MBC's director of business development and the channel's lead public relations person on the al-Ra'is issue, I heard an oral version of MBC's press release and an admission that "reality TV may not be suited for the Arab world."[58] Coming to this conclusion as a result of a program shutdown was embarrassing to the channel, whose reaction was haphazard. One producer told me she learned of the shutdown not from MBC but on her way to the studio when a friend who worked for Associated Press' Manama office called her.[59] Another producer intimately familiar with the al-Ra'is debacle told me with a request for anonymity, "MBC just buried the show, pretending it never existed, as reflected in the short statement [released to Associated Press] and the sealed lips of people

---

[56] "The Reality of Reality TV in the Middle East," www.albawaba.com/news/print Article.php3?sid=271966&lang=e.

[57] Author interview with Michel Costandi, Director of Business Development, MBC, June 3, 2004, Dubai, UAE.

[58] Ibid.

[59] Author interview with Safa al-Ahmad, al-Ra'is Story Producer, Middle East Broadcasting Center, June 19, 2005, Dubai, UAE.

involved."[60] This lack of information, according to the same source, "caused great harm to the contestants because people believed the version of the newspapers and al-Jazeera which stated that 'morally wrong' things had happened. This was especially the case for a young Bahraini woman who was ostracized, lost her friends and her job when she left the show amidst the scandal. Contestants were just given $300 in consolation."[61] Contractual directors and producers on the staff of al-Ra'is signed "very strong" nondisclosure agreements, which made it difficult to reconstitute the story.

When Mr. Costandi and I met for a second time a year later, MBC's position was more nuanced, focusing on socially and religiously acceptable reality TV shows.[62] "Real TV [in English] shows have to be associated with values," he said. Star Academy's success was due to the fact that it was "hip, young, edgy," so "Pepsi sponsored it completely and exclusively." In MBC's case, the channel had to find reality shows that fit its focus on the Arab family. The show Starting Over "suits MBC as a family channel and suits the sponsor [Nestlé] especially Klim milk. As a result, Klim was our exclusive sponsor; other Nestlé products as advertisers."[63] Even after the stinging failure of al-Ra'is, the lure of reality TV's high ratings was irresistible, even for a Saudi-owned channel purporting to "see the world with Arab eyes," chastened after its first experiment with the reality genre went awry. Needless to say, Starting Over was neither a ratings sensation nor a source of controversy. The episode, however, signaled the onset of a quest for culturally resonant reality shows, with the significance of such a pursuit to be discussed in subsequent chapters.

The controversy surrounding al-Ra'is indicates that business interests are able to contest ostensibly religious arguments in public debate in the Arab Gulf countries – one of the main alliances in the Bahraini parliament is called the Economists' Bloc. The shutdown of al-Ra'is and ensuing debates cannot be understood as a linear succession of causes and effects. Rather they involve a complex bundle of issues including Saudi-Bahraini relations, Bahrain's economic policy, the increased instrumentalization of popular culture by Islamists and governments alike, and MBC's institutional agenda in the competitive pan-Arab

---

[60] Author interview (Anonymous Source, al-Ra'is), MBC, July 1, 2005, Dubai, UAE.
[61] Ibid.
[62] Author interview with Michel Costandi, Director of Business Development, MBC Group, June 3, 2004, Dubai, UAE.
[63] Author interview with Michel Costandi, Director of Business Development, MBC Group, June 29, 2005, Dubai, UAE.

media market. The debate in the Bahraini parliament between arguments by Islamist parliamentarians (Shiʻi and Sunni) and counterargu-
ments by their liberal colleagues about what constitutes a positive
national reputation is but one visible consequence of various social,
political, and economic forces operating nationally and regionally.

Unlike *Big Brother*'s numerous worldwide renditions, *al-Raʼis* is significant not in what it told us about human nature and social relations
under physical sequestration. This was a telling case because it inaugurated a transnational, pan-Arab contest over social and political reality
triggered by reality TV's ability to stir up unstable social relations. The
media scholar Nick Couldry's argument, in the context of *Big Brother*
UK, that "ten people locked in a compound competing for money is not
in itself of public significance"[64] meets a hard landing when traveling to
the Arab world. So does the related argument about the uncontroversial
banality of surveillance in the United Kingdom.[65] The cases laid out in
this book, like the few studies of the social and political implications of
reality TV in the non-West, moves the United States and Western
Europe away from the center of reality TV studies.[66] In Arab countries,
like in Africa and Malawi, the impact of reality TV cannot be understood merely by debating the genre's historical antecedents, investigat-
ing its impact on civic engagement, or focusing on its neoliberal
underpinnings. Rather, there are existential political, economic, and
ideological issues that come to the fore. In contrast to previous analyses
of the phenomenon, which focus on the display of the individual, the
private, and the emotive,[67] the social reproduction of Arab reality
TV has invested new meanings in the social, public, and, yes, rational.
Compelling studies that understand reality TV in the West as an avenue for neoliberal conditioning notwithstanding,[68] reality TV in the
Arab world triggered a debate about viewers' habituation to contested
liberal values and practices. *Al-Raʼis* was an early episode in a reality

---

[64] Couldry, N. (2002). "Playing for Celebrity: Big Brother as a Ritual Event," *Television
and New Media* 3 (3): 283–93.

[65] Palmer, G. (2002). "Big Brother: An Experiment in Governance," *Television and New
Media* 3 (3): 295–310.

[66] See Jacobs, S. (2007). "*Big Brother*, Africa Is Watching," *Media, Culture and Society*
29 (6): 851–68.

[67] Corner, J. (2002). "Performing the Real: Documentary Diversions," *Television and
New Media* 3 (3): 255–69.

[68] See most recently McCarthy, A. (2007). "Reality Television: A Neoliberal Theater of
Suffering," *Social Text* 25 (4): 17–41 and Ouellette, L. and Hay, J. (2008). *Better Living
Through Reality TV: Television and Post-Welfare Citizenship*. New York: Blackwell.

TV–provoked transnational contest over the power to define social reality that would engulf most Arab countries, illustrating the potential of popular culture to stir public contention, fomenting struggles that pit "reality" against "image," morality against bread-and-butter issues, business against religion, small country against big nation, woman-as-artistic performer against woman-as-body-of-the-nation. The mercurial combination of religion, politics, gender, and money, this book will show, is at the center of fundamental existential dilemmas facing Arabs in the modern era. Undergirding this heady mix is the convoluted "Saudi-Lebanese Connection," untangled in the next chapter.

CHAPTER THREE

The Saudi-Lebanese Connection

All these [reality TV] programs...depend on two things:
money from big Saudi investors and businessmen, and
Lebanese expertise. Those who propagate conspiracy
theories say that the sons of the Arab nation are being
destroyed by Saudi money and Lebanese know-how.[1]

Ahmad Mansour, al-Jazeera

Were you to switch on your television set in Lebanon in the first days of August 2005, and zap from one channel to another, you would be puzzled to see the country's normally fractious television landscape featuring variations of the same scene: a picture of Fahd Bin 'Abdul'aziz, king of Saudi Arabia for twenty-three years until his death on August 1, 2005, with Islamic prayers chanted and inscribed on screens dominated by the colors black, green, and white. In a rare display of unison, Lebanese channels paid homage to the departed royal. Hours after Fahd's death, reporting shifted to the Arabic equivalent of "The King Is Dead; Long Live the King," broadcasting Saudi royal conclaves, known as the *bay'a*, to anoint Crown Prince 'Abdullah as the new king of Saudi Arabia. Lebanese media, like their Arab counterparts, covered the developments live, with the transition slogan "Khayru Khalaf li-Khayri Salaf" (A good successor to a good predecessor) resonating on the airwaves.

That Fahd's death – important but expected, as the king had a debilitating stroke in November 1995 – would be ubiquitous on Lebanese

---

[1] Mimicking Western Programs and Imposing Them on Arabs, Episode 1. (March 3, 2004). Bila Hudud (Ahmad Mansour, Host). Doha, Qatar: al-Jazeera.

television screens is confounding. At first glance, Lebanon and Saudi Arabia do not have much in common. Lebanon is a small, resource-poor, fragmented society where numerous groups live cheek-by-jowl, episodically battling for political control. Many Lebanese think of themselves as the Arab world's most socially liberal community. The country's relatively open social mores and entrepreneurial tradition have made Beirut the Arab world's style capital. Lebanese television flaunts women's bodies and glamorous lifestyles, the country's pop stars have a regional following, its chefs and fashion designers are sought by wealthy Gulf Arabs, and its clinics make it the regional capital of plastic surgery. In contrast, Saudi Arabia is the Arab world's most conservative society, ruled by the strictest interpretations of Islamic doctrine. Women face severe social and legal constraints, including a ban on driving. And yet, though Lebanon and Saudi Arabia occupy the extremes of the Arab sociocultural spectrum, together the two countries are instrumental in shaping pan-Arab media.

This chapter unravels the all-important Saudi-Lebanese connection – the combination of Saudi capital and Lebanese talent at the center of pan-Arab entertainment media. Explaining this liaison fills important gaps in the correct but incomplete story of Saudi dominance of pan-Arab media. Whereas Saudi entrepreneurs with royal connections finance Arab media, Lebanese journalists, producers, and managers populate the industry's ranks. Links can be traced as far back as 1908, when many Lebanese, along with Syrians and Turks, operated Saudi Arabia's first newspapers in the Western province of Hijaz, the site of Islam's holy cities of Mecca and Medina.[2] In the following decades, there were strong political-economic ties between Saudi Arabia and Lebanon, illustrated most conspicuously in Hussein 'Uwayni, a Lebanese national who became Saudi Arabia's representative in Lebanon before he became prime minister in 1951, a striking precedent to Rafiq al-Hariri.[3] But it is really in the 1970s that the Saudi-Lebanese media connection was forged. Since then, the convergence of Saudi capital and Lebanese talent has driven major pan-Arab media developments. How have these two markedly different countries, with distinct media histories and sharply different social arrangements, come jointly to shape the regional Arab

---

[2] Rugh, W. A. (1980). "Saudi Mass Media and Society in the Faisal Era," in *King Faisal and the Modernization of Saudi Arabia*, ed. W. A. Beling (Boulder, CO: Westview Press), 125–44.

[3] See Traboulsi, F. (2008). "Saudi Expansion: The Lebanese Connection, 1924–1952," in *Kingdom without Borders: Saudi Arabia's Political, Religious and Media Frontiers*, ed. M. al-Rasheed. New York: Columbia University Press, 65–78, for more on 'Uwayni.

media order? What are the historical and current forces shaping the Saudi-Lebanese nexus? What are the regional social and political implications of this intriguing liaison? In order to answer these questions, first we have to consider Lebanon and Saudi Arabia not as two separate nation-states but rather as a dynamic pair whose complex interactions shape the pan-Arab media environment – especially satellite television entertainment, the area that concerns us most. Only after we understand the intricacies of the media junction between Lebanon and Saudi Arabia can we grapple with a more relevant query: why and how does the Saudi-Lebanese connection fuel the Arab reality TV controversies?

"New" media technologies have historically met stiff resistance in Saudi Arabia, because they were regarded as vehicles of foreign influence. A pact forged in 1744 between the al-Sa'ud and al-Shaykh families, which gave political power to the former and religious authority to the latter, continues to be the fulcrum of power in the kingdom (Muhammad 'Abdulwahhab, the founder of what became known as Wahhabiyya, hailed from the al-Shaykh family). This alliance of princes and clerics has contained tensions between the enshrinement of Islamic values and the modernization drive espoused by Saudi kings since the 1930s. The telegraph in the 1920s, radio in the 1930s, television in the 1960s, video cassette recorders in the 1970s, satellite dishes and the Internet since the 1990s, and mobile phones and digital cameras in the 2000s triggered disputes about the virtuous society, proper behavior, gender relations, and Western influence.[4] King 'Abdulaziz Ibn 'Abdulrahman al-Faisal al-Sa'ud, known as Ibn Sa'ud, the founder of modern Saudi Arabia in 1932, was convinced that media and information technologies were crucial to his modernization policy. He devised an original but highly effective approach to win over the clerics. To convince them that wireless communication would further God's word, he had Qur'anic verses read and transmitted back and forth between Riyadh and Mecca.[5] Consider the king's masterful rhetorical maneuvers as he convinced the religious scholars to accept photography:

> Painting and sculpture are idolatry, but is light good or bad? The judges pondered and replied that light is good; Allah put the sun in the heavens to light man's path. Then asked the King, is a shadow

[4] See Kraidy, M. M. (2006). "Governance and Hypermedia in Saudi Arabia," *First Monday*, 11 (9), http://firstmonday.org/issues/special11_9/kraidy/index.html (accessed December 30, 2006).

[5] Boyd, D. A. (1999). *Broadcasting in the Arab World: A Survey of the Electronic Media in the Middle East*, 2nd ed. Ames: Iowa State University Press.

good or bad? There was nothing in the Qur'an about this, but the judges deduced and ruled that shadows are good, because they are inherent in light, and even a holy man casts a shadow. Very well then, said the King, photography is good because it is nothing but a combination of light and shade, depicting Allah's creatures but leaving them unchanged.[6]

Ibn Saʿud succeeded in introducing new media like photography and the telegraph without suffering great consequences. His son Faisal, who would become Saudi Arabia's prime minister twice (1958–60 and 1962–4), and then its king from 1964 to 1975, would not be as fortunate.[7]

SAUDI MEDIA IN THE FAISAL ERA (1962–75): NATIONAL GROWTH

When Prince Faisal Bin ʿAbdulʿaziz became prime minister for the second time in October 1962, there were no magazines, only one radio station, and three daily newspapers in Saudi Arabia. Though the U.S. Air Force had been operating a station, AJL-TV, since 1955,[8] and the Arabian American Oil Company (ARAMCO) ran another since 1957,[9] Saudi Arabia did not have a national television service. Radio Mecca, the only radio station in existence, which, since 1948, had broadcast religious programs, was audible only in the province of Hijaz, where two hundred thousand radio receivers existed at the time. The three newspapers together distributed twenty-five thousand copies.[10] When Faisal became king in 1964, he presided over the systematic expansion of Saudi media institutions. This had the heaviest of costs: vehement clerical opposition to television triggered a sequence of events that led to Faisal's assassination in 1975. By that time, there were seven Saudi dailies with a combined distribution of 100,000, Saudi radio could be heard across the kingdom, and Saudi television reached 1.5 million viewers (out of a population of around 7 million).[11] Regulatory and

---

[6] Eddy, W. (1963). "King Ibn Saʿud: Our Faith and Your Iron," *Middle East Journal* 17 (3): 258, quoted in Boyd, 1999, 154.
[7] Faisal was embroiled in a power struggle with his brother Saʿud, who ascended to the throne in 1953, when Faisal was named crown prince. Faisal resigned the prime minister post in 1962 in protest against his brother and gathered political and clerical support to return to the job in 1962. He was appointed regent in March 1964 and king on November 2 of the same year. He was assassinated in March 1975.
[8] Boyd, 1999.
[9] Rugh, 1980.
[10] Ibid.
[11] The Saudi population in 1975 was around 7 million; see Saudi Arabia Country Profile, http://earthtrends.wri.org (accessed June 23, 2008).

supervisory institutions were also created under Faisal: the Ministry of Information in 1962; a new press code in 1964; and the Saudi News Agency in 1971.[12] Under Faisal the Ministry of Information sent Saudis abroad to study communication at the graduate and undergraduate levels.

Faisal's media policies integrated Saudi Arabia in the Arab region and the global economic system by coordinating the Kingdom's clocks with world time. Before radio and television came to the kingdom, William Rugh explained, "clocks were set at 12.00 every sundown, but listeners to the East or West of the transmitter would be confused because their sunset occurred before or after sunset at the transmitter."[13] Program grids of foreign radio broadcasts habituated many Saudi listeners to begin thinking in terms of global time: Saudi Arabia is at Greenwich mean time plus three hours (GMT + 3). This new notion of time enabled King Faisal to announce that Saudi radio would officially make the switch to GMT + 3, in order to increase the number of listeners outside Saudi borders. In effect, traditional time was abandoned because it was incompatible with modern electronic media.[14] These developments underscore the instrumental role of the mass media in bringing about Saudi modernity.

Other considerations drove media expansion in the Faisal era. In the early 1960s, Revolutionary Egypt subjected the House of al-Sa'ud to a relentless onslaught of propaganda that abated only after Nasser's defeat in the 1967 war. Egyptian accusations of Saudi treason and reaction reverberated in Saudi households tuned to Egyptian leader Gamal 'Abdulnasser's Voice of the Arabs and Radio Cairo.[15] It was therefore imperative to develop a Saudi media capacity to retaliate. Faisal's strategy was to establish international media focused on a global Islamic audience, in line with the king's Islamic Solidarity Policy initiated in 1966.[16] At the same time, Faisal's media plan followed the modernization path initiated by King Ibn Sa'ud. A comprehensive media infrastructure was essential to transform a tribally fractured and geographically dispersed population into a national community ruled by the House of al-Sa'ud. This became all the more important when inhabitants of the Eastern Province started receiving television signals from Kuwait and Iran, and

[12] Rugh, 1980.
[13] Ibid., 143.
[14] Ibid., 139.
[15] Boyd, D. A. (2001) "Saudi Arabia's International Media Strategy: Influence through Multinational Ownership," in *Mass Media, Politics and Society in the Middle East*, ed. K. Hafez. Cresskill, NJ: Hampton Press, 43–60.
[16] Rugh, 1980.

later from Qatar and the United Arab Emirates.[17] The mass media were therefore an essential tool for building modern Saudi Arabia.

As they unified the country, the mass media deepened Saudi Arabia's contacts with Western modernity. A growing national economy and nascent government bureaucracy needed an adequate communication infrastructure. With the spread of radio transistors and the lure of a "Western-style consumer economy,"[18] the business community and middle class, used to Egyptian and Lebanese television, demanded a national service that reflected modernizing trends in other sectors. As Rugh wrote,

> The "modern" sector was growing rapidly and increasing numbers of Saudis – particularly those technocrats in the new middle class who had studied or travelled abroad – were anxious for Saudi Arabia to have interesting radio, television, and public entertainment such as cinema and night clubs along with the other attributes of modern society.[19]

These desires would soon clash with another constituency whose members risked being marginalized by the country's modernization drive: the clerics of establishment Wahhabiyya and their allies in the royal family. Saudi rulers faced a double bind. On the one hand, as Douglas Boyd put it, rulers were compelled to deliver to the people "an innovation that was *at least symbolically modern*."[20] On the other hand, the al-Sa'ud needed to placate the *'ulama* from whom they drew their political legitimacy. These rival forces would come to a head in the struggle to establish Saudi television.

One month into his second term as prime minister in October 1962, Faisal announced a ten-point program, including the provision of "innocent means of recreation for all citizens."[21] Because motion pictures were projected in large, dark rooms in which nonmarried men and women could engage in illicit mixing, movies were not considered innocent; therefore they were banned. Television, however, was watched by families at home, so Faisal reasoned it would not pose the same social hazard. But when he announced plans for a national television service in 1963, Faisal could not have known that he was signing his death sentence. Within a year, facilities and equipment were established

17 Ibid., 133.
18 Ibid., 45.
19 Ibid., 130.
20 Boyd, 1999, 152, emphasis added.
21 Rugh, 1980.

with American assistance.[22] Because of vocal opposition to television, authorities claimed a protracted "test" broadcasting period.[23] This caution proved prescient though ineffective: in September 1965 opponents of television led by Prince Khalid Bin Musaʿid marched in anger on Saudi television facilities, and Bin Musaʿid lost his life at the hands of the Saudi police.[24] Redoubling efforts to convince the clerical establishment that television was a formidable tool for spreading the faith, Faisal filled Saudi airwaves with Wahhabi publicity. Ten years later, in 1975, Bin Musaʿid's vengeful brother assassinated King Faisal.

The Faisal era (1962–75), which began during his second term as prime minister, established trends that culminated in the Saudi-dominated pan-Arab media order of the early twenty-first century. It is during Faisal's reign that the systematic utilization of television for religious proselytizing began, in order to win over a clerical establishment opposed to the new medium and to other reformist policies initiated by Faisal – chiefly the education of girls. The first *tele*-imam, Shaykh ʿAli Tantawi, went on Saudi television in 1968. A naturalized religious scholar of Syrian origin, he appeared two evenings a week on Saudi television for a half hour, read letters carrying questions from viewers, and proffered answers.[25] Whether Faisal actually believed in religious propaganda, or whether giving the ʿulama a large presence on television was a strategic ploy to soften the clerics' vehement objections to the education of girls and women,[26] the ultimate result was

[22] Initial contacts between then Crown Prince Fahd and U.S. authorities led to a 1963 field visit by a Federal Communication Commission engineer who drafted a blueprint to build Saudi broadcasting facilities. In 1964, an official agreement was reached between the U.S. and Saudi governments, charging the U.S. Army Corps of Engineers with construction of Saudi television facilities; the corps in turn contracted two American companies: RCA for the equipment and NBC International for operation and maintenance. For details, see Boyd, 1999.

[23] Rugh, 1980.

[24] There are various versions of what happened next, but there is no dispute that Bin Musaʿid was killed as a result of the demonstration. Whether demonstrators intended to simply take over the station, as Abukhalil (2003) asserts following al-Qahtani's account of the struggle between various factions within the Saudi royal family, or whether they wanted to destroy the tower and transmission equipment, as Boyd (1999) claims, remains unclear. The aftermath is equally nebulous: was Bin Musaʿid involved in an altercation with a policeman, who shot and killed the prince, after which the king ruled that the officer's action was appropriate (Boyd, 1999)? Or was the prince actually executed by the government along with other demonstrators (Abukhalil, 2003, following al-Qahtani)?

[25] Rugh, 1980.

[26] Parssinen, C. (1980). "The Changing Role of Women," in *King Faisal and the Modernization of Saudi Arabia*, ed. W. A. Beling. Boulder, CO: Westview Press, 145–70.

the quasidisappearance of women from Saudi television. During the first two years of television in the kingdom, only non-Saudi women would appear on Saudi television; in 1967 there was at least one Saudi woman presenting a children's program. By 1968, however, clerical complaints had dramatically reduced all women's presence on the screen.[27] In subsequent decades, as Chapter 4 makes clear, television censorship would focus predominantly on controlling depictions of women on the screen.

As prime minister, Faisal had been troubled by the relatively high number of Egyptian journalists and technicians working in the Saudi press, at a time of heightened tension between Saudi Arabia and Egypt. Though in those days Faisal's brother King Fahd's lavish lifestyle and conspicuous spending attracted the lion's share of Egypt's anti-Saudi propaganda, throughout 1962 Faisal found himself unwittingly starring with his brother in a program called "Enemies of God" on Nasser's Voice of the Arabs.[28] As a result he was disinclined to tolerate Nasserist sympathies in Saudi newsrooms, all the more so given that Saudi Arabia was by then waging a proxy war against Egypt in neighboring Yemen. When armed hostilities in Yemen began in 1962 between republicans backed by Egypt and royalists backed by Saudi Arabia, some Egyptian journalists at Saudi newspapers went on strike in solidarity with Egypt.[29] The Saudi media-political establishment needed to find another group of journalists who mastered the same technical skills but had different political orientations. Thus the Egyptian-Saudi rivalry set the ground for the Saudi-Lebanese connection.

SAUDI MEDIA AFTER FAISAL (1975–91): REGIONAL EXPANSION AND THE LEBANESE FACTOR

When Faisal died in 1975, the convergence of Saudi media institutions and Lebanese human resources was already in motion. In the same year, the Saudi brothers Hisham and Muhammad 'Ali Hafizh launched the Arab world's first English-language daily, *Arab News*. The sons of a Jeddah publisher, the two brothers would go on to establish the Saudi Research and Marketing Company as one of the largest Arab media

---

[27] Rugh, 1980; James, L. (2006). "Whose Voice? Nasser, the Arabs and 'Sawt al-Arab' Radio," *Transnational Broadcasting Journal* 16, http://www.tbsjournal.com (accessed November 1, 2008).

[28] Ibid.

[29] Rugh, 1980.

conglomerates.[30] The Hafizh brothers faced a big challenge: How to assemble a qualified team of journalists and editors fluent in English and with knowledge of Saudi Arabia and the Middle East? The Lebanese civil war would soon provide the solution. In late 1975, the war forced the Lebanese publisher Kamel Muruwwah to shut down the respected Beirut-based English-language newspaper *Daily Star*, leaving in its wake a group of unemployed journalists and editors experienced in publishing an English-language daily in the Middle East. *Arab News* recruited the group led by Jihad al-Khazen.[31] A former reporter at Reuters, al-Khazen was editor-in-chief of the *Daily Star* from 1968 to 1976,[32] and went on to become one of the most prominent players in the Saudi-Lebanese connection, editing *Arab News* (1976–7) before going on to lead the two major Saudi-owned, London-based pan-Arab papers, first *Asharq al-Awsat* (1978–86) and then *al-Hayat* (1988–98). Al-Khazen also supervised the joint news venture *al-Hayat*-LBC when it was set up in 2002.[33]

As Lebanese journalists rose to leadership positions in the Saudi offshore media, developments on Saudi soil would lead the House of al-Sa'ud to change national media policy. Technologies new to the kingdom – the transistor and the video cassette recorder – had weakened state control over information.[34] In that context, Saudi rulers faced the most weighty challenge to their rule when the militant Juhayman al-'Utaybi and his armed followers took over the Grand Mosque of Mecca on Tuesday, November 20, 1979, in a messianic attempt to restore the true path of Islam, which he accused the royal family of abandoning. At first, authorities were confounded: official Saudi media did not

---

[30] Loqman, F. (1997). *Internationalizing the Arab Press: Hisham and Muhammad 'Ali Hafizh*. Jeddah: Saudi Distribution Company [Arabic].

[31] Lebling, R. (April 22, 2005). "From Beirut to Jeddah: A Desk Editor Reminisces." *Arab News*.

[32] Though the paper closed in late 1975, al-Khazen's biography lists 1976 as the last year of his editorship, probably reflecting contractual arrangements.

[33] Author interview with Jihad al-Khazen, *al-Hayat*, Media and Communication Group, June 7, 2005, London; Jihad al-Khazen's 2006 biography in *Arab Media in the Information Age*. Abu Dhabi: The Emirates Center for Strategic Studies and Research, 601–2. Al-Khazen was born in a Palestinian family that moved to Lebanon in the early twentieth century. See also Schleifer, S. A. (2002). "Super News Center Setting Up in London for al-Hayat and LBC: An Interview with Jihad Khazen and Salameh Nematt," *Transnational Broadcasting Journal* 9, http://www.tbsjournal.com/Archives/Fall02/LBC.html (accessed September 10, 2005).

[34] After the spread of radio transistors increased the information available to average Saudis in the 1960s, the VCR found an enthusiastic reception in a country where most entertainment is home based. See Boyd, 1999 and 2001.

announce the incident on the day it occurred, and the government jammed the signal of Radio Monte Carlo Middle East, a popular source of information for Saudis at the time.[35]

Al-'Utaybi's challenge was particularly threatening to royal authority because he couched his demands in religious doctrine. The House of Sa'ud promptly requested a ruling from senior religious scholars, the 'ulamas, sanctioning a government military attack on the mosque's holy grounds to dislodge the rebels. After evaluating the legitimacy of the rebels' claims, the 'ulamas decided to support the royal family but exacted a price in return: the reversal of the relatively liberal media and women's policies initiated by Faisal. Demands included prohibiting women from appearing on television and tightening media policy to ban even the most minor digressions from Wahhabiyya's diktats.[36] As the journalist Yaroslav Trofimov tells it in his book about the siege of the mosque, some royals later felt that "the ulemas essentially asked al-Sa'ud to adopt Juhayman's agenda in exchange for their help in getting rid of Juhayman himself."[37]

On November 21, with the scholars supporting the king, Radio Riyadh aired an unscheduled religious program, followed at 5:00 A.M. by a short statement from the Minister of the Interior Prince Nayef Bin 'Abdul'aziz about the attack.[38] The next day, Thursday, November 22, Minister of Information Muhammad 'Abdu Yamani gave a speech broadcast on Radio Riyadh, announcing that "matters are now under control" only to contradict himself later and acknowledge that authorities were still struggling to assert dominion.[39] On Friday, November 23, 1979, the usual broadcast of the Friday prayer and sermon from the Grand Mosque in Mecca to a worldwide Muslim audience did not occur, undermining claims that Saudi authorities were in command.[40] In the meantime, other media uncovered details of what had transpired. When al-Nadwa, a Mecca newspaper, published photos of firearm battles between government troops and the rebels, rulers forced a recall of the newspaper – too late.[41] After French commandos invited by the

---

[35] Boyd, 2001.

[36] Trofimov, Y. (2007). *The Siege of Mecca*. New York: Doubleday, 100.

[37] Ibid.

[38] Ibid., 101.

[39] Ibid., 136. According to Trofimov (139), a U.S. consular statement issued the day of the attack uncovered the lack of government sway and irritated Prince Nayef, Minister of the Interior, who complained about U.S. indiscretion in an interview with a Lebanese daily.

[40] Ibid., 142.

[41] Ibid., 158.

rulers finally cleared the Grand Mosque, a reporter from Jeddah's *Arab News* who was allowed inside the compound reported on the extensive destruction that the battle had left in its wake.[42] Finally, on the night of December 4, Saudi television carried a speech by Prince Nayef, featuring footage of some of the rebels taken prisoners. When al-'Utaybi appeared, the voiceover said: "before you is Juhayman bin Seif al Uteybi [as spelled in Trofimov], one of the most evil people of this world in our age. . . . We will not forget him and history will not forget him."[43] In the weeks that followed, Nayef dictated that female announcers be taken off the screen of Saudi television, reflecting a rising tide of conservatism that restricted women's employment opportunities and even hobbled the presence of Westerners in the kingdom.[44] In July 1981, a reshuffled Higher Media Council was announced by royal decree, putting the Minister of the Interior, none other than Prince Nayef, at the helm of Saudi information policy.[45]

With internal control of the media tightened, princes could focus on expanding their external media operations. In the 1980s, Saudi influence over pan-Arab and Europe-based Arabic publications strengthened, steadily dislodging rival media "sponsors" like Iraq, Libya, Kuwait, and the United Arab Emirates. There again, Saudi capital and Lebanese know-how would enter into mutually beneficial alliances. In the second half of the 1970s, Lebanese journalists fleeing hostilities in their native country launched publications in Paris. Two weekly newspapers appeared there in 1977. The first, *al-Mustaqbal*, was created by Nabil Khoury; the second, *al-Watan al-'Arabi*, was the brainchild of Walid Abi Dahr. The former, though featuring a heavy dose of advertisements financed by Gulf monarchies, ceased publication in 1989. The latter was known to be close to the Iraqi regime of Saddam Hussain, but in 1991 it switched sides to join the growing pro-Saudi European media contingent.[46] Growing Saudi clout replaced Paris with London as capital of the offshore Arab press. In 1978, the Hafizh brothers launched *Asharq al-Awsat* under the editorial leadership of Jihad al-Khazen and with the financial support of Prince Turki al-Faisal and Shaykh Kamal Adham, then head of Saudi intelligence. Modeled after the *International Herald Tribune*, the new London-based daily was

---

[42] Ibid., 220–1.
[43] Ibid., 222.
[44] Ibid., 241.
[45] Boyd, 2001.
[46] Elias, H. E. (1993). *La presse arabe*. Paris: Maisonneuve et Larose.

conceived as a newspaper for Arabic readers in the Middle East and worldwide. According to a sympathetic biographer, this was the first newspaper to use satellite technology to print at several locations in Saudi Arabia, the Middle East, and Europe.[47] To give the new daily a distinct identity, *Asharq al-Awsat* used green newsprint, earning the sobriquet of "the green newspaper."[48] Jamil Muruwwah's relaunch of the venerable Lebanese daily *al-Hayat* on October 30, 1988 from London with financial backing from Prince Khaled Bin Sultan further fortified the Saudi-Lebanese connection. By one expert estimate, the Lebanese represented at least 30 percent of staff in Europe's Arabic newspapers, and they constituted more than half of the employees at some institutions.[49] Because the new *al-Hayat* had a largely Christian (Lebanese and Palestinian) management and because it opened its pages to Kurds and Shi'is opposed to Saddam Hussain, its critics called it "a newspaper of minorities in the service of a prince."[50]

In the meantime, the unfolding Lebanese civil war spawned a national media explosion. Unlike its neighbors, the Lebanese state had until recently never fully owned a television station. The national channel Télé-Liban was created by private businessmen who approached the government for a broadcasting license in the 1950s and remained a hybrid, half-private, half-state-owned institution until the early 2000s. By debilitating state jurisdiction, the Lebanese civil war (1975–90) created a media scene as fractured as Lebanon's political landscape. Political parties and warring factions launched several dozen unlicensed radio and television stations as mouthpieces: conservative and radical, Christian and Muslim, secular and religious, capitalist and communist.[51] Just as Télé-Liban was symptomatic of a weak state, its unlicensed competitors symbolized the strength of civil society and sectarian politics. The new channels outperformed Télé-Liban in the ratings and became the most visible indication of the collapse of the Lebanese state.

---

[47] Loqman, F. (1997). *Internationalizing the Arab Press: Hisham and Muhammad 'Ali Hafizh.* Jeddah: Saudi Distribution Company [Arabic].

[48] Ibid.

[49] Elias, 1993, 123.

[50] El-Oifi, M. (December 2006). Voyage au coeur des quotidiens panarabes. *Le Monde Diplomatique.*

[51] Kraidy, M. M. (1998). "Broadcasting Regulation and Civil Society in Postwar Lebanon," *Journal of Broadcasting and Electronic Media* 42 (3): 387–400. See also Kraidy, M. M. (2000). "Television Talk and Civic Discourse in Postwar Lebanon," in *Civic Discourses in the Middle East and Digital Age Communications,* ed. L. Gher and H. Amin. Norwood, NJ: Ablex, 1–17.

A pressing postwar regulatory challenge consisted in restoring state authority while preserving a politically representative media system. The Document of National Understanding, underwritten by Saudi Arabia, brokered by then Saudi special envoy to Lebanon Rafiq al-Hariri, and signed in the Saudi resort city of Ta'if on October 22, 1989, put an end to military conflict in Lebanon and called for the reorganization of the Lebanese media within a "modern" regulatory framework. The resulting 1994 Audio-Visual Media Law (AVML) was hailed as the first broadcasting law in the Arab world, but the licensing process was nakedly political. The AVML implementation in 1996 favored media institutions owned by leading politicians and cut down the number of privately owned television stations from sixty to four.[52] Licensing followed the customary Lebanese sectarian formula. Licensed were a Maronite station (LBC), a Sunni station (Future TV), a Shi'i station (National Broadcasting Network, or NBN) and a Greek Orthodox station with Druze influence (Murr Television, or MTV). Additional licenses were later given to al-Manar, Hizbollah's outlet, Télé-Lumière, a Christian station operated by the Maronite clergy, and New TV, formerly owned by the Lebanese communist party.[53] Télé-Liban, whose monopoly ended with the AVML, fell into a protracted decline.[54] The equilibrium achieved by licensing stations on sectarian bases, though periodically shaken by inflammatory broadcasts or state harassment,[55] lasted until the tumultuous events of 2005 to be discussed in Chapter 7 – with the notable exception of the shutdown of MTV by the Lebanese-Syrian security apparatus in September 2003.

The Lebanese civil war was an incubator of the Saudi-Lebanese connection. The proliferation of unlicensed radio and television stations during the war developed a large pool of creative and managerial media talent, who, cutting their teeth in times of war, had ample opportunities to learn from their mistakes and develop their expertise. The timing could not have been more propitious. Less than a year after the Ta'if agreement officially ended the Lebanese war, preparations were underway for Operation Desert Storm to rout Iraqi troops from Kuwait under

---

[52] Ibid., 1998.
[53] Ibid., 1998.
[54] Ibid., 1998.
[55] See Kraidy, M. M. (1999). "State Control of Television News in 1990s Lebanon," *Journalism and Mass Communication Quarterly* 76 (3): 485–98, for a discussion of the various ways in which the Lebanese state tried to control the media in the first five years after the passing of the AVML.

U.S. leadership. It was then that the Arab satellite television revolution was set in motion. In 1990, Mubarak's government launched the Egypt Satellite Channel to reach Egyptian troops deployed in Iraq under coalition command and inoculate them from Saddam Hussain's propaganda.[56] More significantly, in 1991, Saudi moguls Saleh Kamel and Walid al-Ibrahim inaugurated MBC in London.[57] It is there that the convergence of the Lebanese "media brain drain" and Saudi media moguls made a qualitative leap.

The first Lebanese were recruited to MBC in the early 1990s, followed by dozens who moved to Orbit, the Saudi-owned pay channel at first headquartered in Rome, and MBC in the early to mid-1990s when the drastic enforcement of Lebanon's AVML reduced professional media opportunities in Lebanon. As successive episodes of violence shook Lebanon, waves of journalists, anchors, directors, producers, and managers found their way to higher wages in safer outposts (e.g., Dubai, London, and Rome) of the sprawling Saudi media empire. In particular, MBC's transformation from a news channel to a family entertainment channel increased the influx of Lebanese because they were prominent in entertainment production. By the early 2000s, an MBC official estimated that 50 percent of the channel's staff was Lebanese.[58] MBC's flagship program, *Man Sa Yarbah al-Malyoun* (the Arabic adaption of *Who Wants to Be a Millionaire?*) was hosted by George Qordahi and initially produced by Salwa Souayd, both Lebanese, and was initially shot in a Beirut studio. The creative staff of the infamous *al-Ra'is*, discussed in Chapter 2, and later of *al-Mustathmer* (*The Investor*), another MBC reality show, was predominantly Lebanese.[59] This reflected a trend: in the early 2000s, MBC established Beirut as an entertainment production center and the channel's game, variety, and reality shows featured Lebanese hosts speaking in the Lebanese accent to their guests who were, in disproportionate number, Lebanese.

---

56 Amin, H. and Boyd, D. A. (1994). "The Development of Direct Broadcast Satellite Television to and within the Middle East," *Journal of South Asian and Middle East Studies* XVIII (2): 37–50.

57 See Kraidy, M. M. (2002). "Arab Satellite Television between Regionalization and Globalization," *Global Media Journal* 1 (1), http://lass.calumet.purdue.edu/cca/gmj/new_page_1.htm (accessed January 15, 2003).

58 Le Pottier, G. (2003). Le monde de la télévision satellitaire au Moyen-Orient et le rôle des libanais dans son développement, in *Mondialisation et nouveaux médias dans l'espace arabe*, ed. F. Mermier. Paris: Maisonneuve et Larose, 43–72.

59 The show's executive producer, creative director, set designer, and all but one of its story producers were Lebanese.

The Lebanese influence went beyond the number of employees who held that nationality; it extended to a kind of cultural hegemony that spread over Arab satellite television entertainment. At MBC in the late 1990s, for example, the majority of programs were presented in Lebanese Arabic rather than Egyptian Arabic (the two being dominant in Arab media), as "numerous non-Lebanese individuals in London [had] a tendency to adopt the Lebanese accent when they [went] on the air."[60] Perhaps more than Cairo or Dubai, Beirut remains a trendsetter in Arab culture, media, and fashion. The Lebanese creative class, at the social-liberal extreme of the Arab spectrum (though some of its members are politically conservative), has spawned pop stars whose provocative demeanor, alluring fashion, and engaging songs have made them pan-Arab household names. Ubiquitous in music videos on Arab screens from Morocco to Iraq, these starlets have raised the ire of clerics and parliamentarians in Bahrain, Egypt, and Kuwait. An Arab columnist coined the phrase "Nancy 'Ajram's parliamentarians" to describe a group of Egyptian legislators who attempted to enact laws to ban the Lebanese pop star from performing in Egypt.[61] Another Lebanese diva, Haifa Wehbi, who was featured on *People* magazine's 2006 "Most Beautiful People" list, recurrently provokes parliamentary debates and moral campaigns throughout the Arab world. Male celebrities from Lebanon are also visible but not controversial. These are extreme examples of a prevailing trend of informality, titillation, and glamour that pervades the Lebanese and, by extension, the pan-Arab, satellite industry. As a Saudi journalist wrote, summing up an investigative report about the leading Arab media conglomerates in the Arabic *Forbes*:

> The look that has come to dominate the new wave [of Arab satellite television channels] is derived primarily from Lebanese TV channels; they attracted a vast number of viewers as soon as they entered the arena . . . having a Lebanese element in a program's production and presentation can be a major contributor to the program's success.[62]

References to a "Lebanese look" invariably invoke two channels: Future TV and LBC. Future TV was the brainchild of Rafiq al-Hariri,

[60] Le Pottier, 2003, 47.
[61] About Future TV, http://www.futuretvnetwork.com/Default.aspx?page=aboutus (accessed May 20, 2008).
[62] Mishkhas, A. (January 27, 2005). "Who's Who Out There?" *Arab News*.

who launched it in 1993 as the flagship of his growing media empire, which included Radio-Orient and *al-Mustaqbal* newspaper. A school teacher who left his native Sidon to make a fortune in construction in Saudi Arabia, al-Hariri developed a close relationship with Saudi royals, especially King Khaled (reigned 1975–82) who bestowed Saudi citizenship on al-Hariri after the Lebanese contractor completed a hotel in record time in the 1970s. After accumulating enormous wealth, al-Hariri parlayed his role as a peace broker in the Ta'if agreement to return to Lebanon as prime minister in 1992. Future TV had two objectives: promoting the agenda of its founder and his reputation as the "rebuilder" of Lebanon and, on its satellite channel launched in 1996, promoting Lebanon as a destination for Gulf Arab tourists and investments. Hence its onetime motto: al-Balad Mashi wal-Shughl Mashi (The Country Is Fine and Business Is Good). Supported by al-Hariri's deep pockets, the channel rapidly earned a reputation as a major player in Lebanon and the Arab world. In the words of its own Web site, Future TV developed "an eccentric funky look, extensive family programming, an Oriental-Western promotional blend and . . . an optimistic view of the future."[63] Though Future TV succeeded in establishing a strong brand identity with pan-Arab audiences, nowhere is the "Lebanese element" – said to be a recipe for success in the Arab media industry – as visible as in LBC.

THE CROWN JEWEL AND THE PRINCE: LBC AND AL-WALEED BIN TALAL

In 1985, fifteen years before it became the crown jewel of the Saudi-Lebanese connection, LBC went on the air as a platform for the Christian-nationalist Lebanese Forces militia and rapidly became the most watched station in Lebanon. As the longest-running privately owned Arab television channel, LBC reflects the rise of American-style commercial broadcasting over the older European system: the station's name was a three-letter acronym, it focused on entertainment programs, and it relied on advertisements. Even as a partisan voice in the war, LBC from its early days was run like a business, for example broadcasting special Ramadan programs for Muslim viewers during the civil war. Since then, LBC has grown into a dramatically more complex institution – the LBC Group. Today, the terrestrial station, LBC International (LBCI) is registered in Lebanon and subject to Lebanese law.

---

[63] About Future TV (2008).

Its satellite operation, al-Fada'iyya al-Lubnaniyya (the Lebanese Satellite Channel, known as LBC-Sat), is a multinational corporation registered in the Cayman Islands, primarily to circumvent Lebanese media-ownership laws.

Saudi moguls have been major investors in LBC since the company launched a satellite channel in 1996. Saudi businessman Saleh Kamel initially owned 49 percent of the shares of LBC-Sat, but his involvement did not endure. Kamel's personal religious convictions made him ambivalent about his stake in the socially liberal and Christian-managed Lebanese channel. When he was asked how he reconciled his "dedication to Islamic principles" with his "investment in LBC," Kamel equivocated:

> Our investment in LBC involves the delivery system; we are not responsible for content. Whoever subscribes to it does so of his own free will. We have, nevertheless, *been able to influence the choice of programming at LBC, especially that having to do with their aims concerning the Islamic faith.*[64]

Nonetheless, before long Kamel sold his shares to another Saudi mogul, Prince al-Waleed bin Talal, Saudi royal prince and global investor extraordinaire. Al-Waleed, who earned global fame when he bailed out Citicorp in 1991 and purchased 25 percent of Euro Disney in 1994, is no ordinary Saudi royal prince. His father, Talal Bin 'Abdulaziz, advocated constitutional reforms in Saudi Arabia and rebelled against his brothers and cousins in the 1960s, briefly partaking in Nasser's radio campaign against the House of Sa'ud. His mother, Mona al-Solh, is the daughter of independent Lebanon's first prime minister. Most importantly, unlike his numerous cousins, al-Waleed is an ambitious workaholic not content to live a life of passive luxury on a royal stipend.

His peculiar parentage, business acumen, and vast media holdings make al-Waleed bin Talal the poster boy of the Saudi-Lebanese connection. In 2000 his purchase of Kamel's stake in LBC-Sat for U.S.$100 million, or half of the total shares, injected massive equity in the company and enabled it to bolster its position as market leader in entertainment. It also afforded LBC a measure of political protection because Bin Talal was close to Lebanese President Emile Lahoud, a major ally of the Syrians in Lebanon. This was crucial because LBC had a history of opposition to Syrian interference in Lebanon and was vulnerable in 2000 when the Syrian-dominated Lebanese state was clamping down on

---

[64] Sheikh Saleh Kamel (1998). Featured interview, *Transnational Broadcasting Journal* 1 (1), http://www.tbsjournal.com (accessed September 15, 2005), emphasis added.

media dissenting from Pax Syriana.[65] Al-Waleed's investment in LBC upheld his status as a towering personality in the Arab media business (he had already been named Man of the Year by the trade magazine *Arab Ad* in 1999) and capped a series of investments in the sector that started a decade earlier. In 1993, his company, Kingdom Holding, bought two major Saudi companies and 30 percent of Arab Radio and Television, the latter for U.S.$240 million. In 1995, he bought 25 percent of Rotana Audio Visual, "the largest Saudi soundtrack and music producer,"[66] 50 percent of Wire and Wireless, a Saudi telecom company, and 3 percent of Mediaset S.P.A, an affiliate of Italian Fininvest, for more than U.S.$100 million. This was followed in 1997 by acquisitions of stocks in Apple computers, Planet Hollywood, advertising giant Saatchi and Saatchi, Sony Entertainment, Netscape, and, most famously, 5 percent of Rupert Murdoch's News Corporation Limited for U.S.$400 million.[67]

Insisting on defining himself as a "Muslim businessman," the twice-divorced prince makes no secret of being "committed to Lebanon and his people."[68] A Lebanese citizen through his mother, the prince emerged as a potent if unlikely critic of Rafiq al-Hariri's economic policies in postwar Lebanon. His close ties with al-Hariri's archrival Emile Lahoud, president of the Lebanese republic, fueled persistent rumors of prime ministerial ambitions, a post for which he is eligible as a Sunni Muslim, according to Lebanese political tradition. In addition to LBC, his Lebanese media assets have included stakes in Lebanon's MTV, shut down by Lebanese authorities by Syrian orders in September 2003 and relaunched in April 2009, and *Annahar* newspaper, which covers the activities of the prince and his Lebanese wing of the family.[69]

In the following years, al-Waleed focused on building a horizontally and vertically integrated music television conglomerate that became

---

[65] Most importantly, LBC was in position to "retaliate" to the challenge posed by MBC's launch of *Man Sa Yarbah Al-Malyoun*, the Arabic version of *Who Wants to Be a Millionaire*, the first Arabic television format-adaptation and the most popular Arab satellite television program in the pre-*Star Academy* era. (This Saudi-funded program featured Lebanese host George Qordahi and Lebanese executive producer Salwa Soueid, another product of the Saudi-Lebanese connection.)

[66] Prince al-Waleed Bin Talal: Man of the Year (1999). *Arab Ad* 9: 1.

[67] Ibid.

[68] Ibid.

[69] al-Waleed's Lebanese ventures were not trouble-free across the board: in the late 1990s, the prince was locked in a bitter lawsuit, which he eventually lost, with the Frayha family, owners of al-Sayyad publishing house in Lebanon, over what he claims was a 50% share of their company.

akin to "MTV, Atlantic Records, and Ticketmaster merged in one entity."[70] To do that, the prince increased his stake in Rotana from 25 percent in 1995 to 48 percent in 2002 to 100 percent in 2003.[71] He also bought Arab Radio and Television's music channel and its vast Arabic music archive, which included 2,500 music videos and 5,000 recorded concerts. This enabled him to launch four specialized music channels under the name of Rotana, a company worth U.S.$1 billion.[72] The deal cemented al-Waleed's position as the dominant player in the pan-Arab music industry, a clout compounded by Rotana's exclusive production, distribution, and marketing contracts with leading Arab singers. Rotana's headquarters were in Riyadh, but production was centered in Beirut (until 2008) and to a lesser extent in Cairo, allowing it to sign the Lebanese and Egyptian pop singers who dominate Arab airwaves and concert halls. In contrast to a Saudi Arabian location, Beirut provides a more liberal feel to Rotana programs, which have systematically attempted to graft Arab sensibilities on a Western style, by including poetry programs, announcing prayer times five times a day, and ordering its video jockeys to dress conservatively during the holy month of Ramadan.[73] Rotana's business strategy, like LBC's foray into reality TV, relied heavily on the commercial promises of hypermedia space: ring tones for mobile phones, interactive text-messaging, Web downloads, and multimedia services, which generate revenue directly or indirectly by promoting other Rotana products.[74] By early 2007, the increasingly similar business strategies of the two companies fed rumors of an imminent joint venture between Rotana and LBC.[75]

The grapevine was accurate. On August 8, 2007, Rotana's announcement that it was merging with LBC-Sat was treated as a major event in the Arab media. The press release included mutual praise between

[70] Braude, J. (October 5, 2006). "Rock the Casbah," *Radar Magazine*, http://www.radar online.com/features/2006/10/the_prince_of_pop.php (accessed November 1, 2007).

[71] See Agnew, R. (August 21, 2005). "The Arabian kings of cash," *Arabian Business*: n.p., and Khan, R. (2005). *Al-Waleed: Businessman, Billionaire, Prince*. London: Harper Collins.

[72] Kraidy, M. M. and Khalil, J. F. (2008). "Youth, Media, and Culture in the Arab World," in *International Handbook of Children, Media and Culture*, ed. S. Livingstone and K. Drotner. London: Sage, 330–44.

[73] Ibid.

[74] Ibid.

[75] Michel Murr, previously head of MTV and after its closure head of the production studio Studiovision, based in Naqqash, a Northern suburb of Beirut, helped Rotana launch its music channels.

al-Waleed Bin Talal and LBC General Manager Pierre el-Daher, with the latter stating that "In today's media landscape only groups able to offer a comprehensive package of targeted channels to advertising markets are expected to grow two to three fold over the next five years and we intend to be part of that growth."[76] In the Saudi press, al-Waleed spoke of more altruistic objectives such as contributing to social and cultural development and raising Arab media to the "highest international levels."[77] In the following days, commentators noted that the partnership fell short of an actual merger. Speaking in the Saudi-owned *Asharq al-Awsat* (al-Waleed had purchased 25 percent of this newspaper's mother company earlier in 2007), Lebanese ad man Ramsay Najjar described the proclaimed merger as "moving in together" rather than "a marriage,"[78] while the Lebanese opposition daily *al-Akhbar*, which tends to be critical of the Saudi role in Lebanon, mused:

> The [press release] added that the two companies will remain independent structurally and financially . . . so how is this a merger then? . . . [T]he focus is on giving full prerogatives to el-Daher, known for being a visionary, to change Rotana's programming strategies.[79]

Although the deal placed Rotana under the purview of a renowned Lebanese media manager, it did not change much for LBC-Sat. What the "merger" effectively accomplished was to consolidate the influence of the Lebanese element in the operation of a Saudi-owned pan-Arab channel. In this, the Saudi-Lebanese connection reached a new level of entanglement.

A fundamental expansion in the Saudi-Lebanese connection was underway by the time Rotana and LBC joined forces in August 2007. In addition to ongoing Saudi recruitment of Lebanese producers, directors, and hosts, Lebanese channels began hiring Saudi presenters. The Beirut channels were not alone in this trend. The "Saudi programs phenomenon," as the pan-Arab press dubbed it, started in 2002 when 'Abdelrahman al-Rashed presented *Sa'at Diyafa* on Future TV and was in full swing in Dubai by 2004 and 2005 when prominent

[76] "LBCSAT and Rotana Television Channels Merge to Form Media Powerhouse" (August 9, 2007). Riyadh, Saudi Arabia: Company Press Release.
[77] LBCSAT and Rotana channels merge in one entity (August 9, 2007). *Al-Riyadh* [Arabic].
[78] 'Akoum, C. (August 13, 2007). Has the era of Arab media alliances arrived? *Asharq al-Awsat* [Arabic].
[79] LBC finally merged with Rotana! (August 9, 2007). *Al-Akhbar* [Arabic].

Saudi journalists hosted their own shows on Gulf channels – Hussain Shobokshi in *al-Taqrir* (*The Report*) on Abu Dhabi TV, Turki al-Dakhil in *Ida'at* (*Illuminations*) on al-Arabiya, and Daoud al-Shiryan in *al-Maqal* (*The Column*) on Dubai TV.[80] In Lebanon, the Sunday evening talk show *al-Hadath* (*The Event*), hosted by Shadha 'Omar on LBC, had already been focusing on issues salient in Saudi Arabia: terrorism, municipal elections, education, journalism, and . . . reality TV. In line with this concern for all matters Saudi, *al-Hadath* featured a growing number of Saudi guests. In the last two or three years, LBC and its chief Lebanese competitor Future TV have increasingly targeted the Saudi market with their game, variety, sports, and talk shows.

These developments reflected commercial calculations in a market where "everyone knows that the Saudi viewer is the target of satellite channels . . . because he is the advertisers' target."[81] In the wake of the 2006 battle between Israel and Hizbollah, LBC started *'Eishu Ma'na* (*Live with Us*), a social talk show hosted by a Saudi couple, Mona Siraj and 'Ali al-'Alyani. Future TV also signaled its interest in the Saudi market: its self-styled "Arab Oprah Winfrey," Zaven Kouyoumdjian, tackled sexual impotence in Saudi Arabia on his talk show *Sireh Wen Fathet* (*Open Conversation*),[82] while Zahi Wehbi regularly hosted Saudi literary and social figures on his show *Khallik bel-Bayt* (*Stay Home*). Then Future TV's general manager Tariq 'Ayntrazi saw the introduction of Saudi faces on Lebanese channels as a necessary step to reach the Saudi market, which according to him stood for 60 percent of the Gulf market, "thus 60% of the satellite television market."[83] Ayntrazi concluded that Future TV's strategy was to "become an Arab channel satcasting from Lebanon and not a Lebanese channel satcasting to Arabs."[84]

In addition to featuring Saudi media personalities, LBC-Sat began airing Saudi productions, most of which reflected lower production values than the channel's customary offerings. This left LBC open to criticism. One Arab media critic related the following story:

Last Thursday . . . I decided to watch LBC [-Sat], starting with a Saudi comedy serial called *Me, You and the Internet*, after which

---

[80] Badi, I. (December 16, 2006). "Gulf Pages" follows "Live with Us" in Beirut . . . Saudis behind the cameras . . . anchors or emigrants? *Al-Hayat* [Arabic].

[81] Ibid.

[82] Haddad, V. (September 17, 2006). Lebanese satellite channels compete for Saudi media personalities. *Asharq al-Awsat* [Arabic].

[83] Ibid.

[84] Ibid. This strategy has not succeeded for various political and programming reasons.

the continuity anchor appeared, with her Lebanese accent and Lebanese style, to announce that the following program would be *Mehn Ghayr* [Saudi Candid Camera]. I watched that primitive, incoherent program, in which a few Saudi youths behave clownishly, featuring poor acting and devoid of ideas, until the LBC anchor appeared again to announce that the following program would be the Gulf drama series *'Uyun Min Zujaj* [Eyes of Glass]!"[85]

By pursuing the Saudi audience so intently, the author argued, LBC was harming itself; by encouraging what the author judged to be mediocre Gulf productions, the channel was also harming the Gulf television industry. LBC, the author concluded, "appears to be more royal than the king" by showing programs that MBC, "a purely Saudi channel," would refuse to air. "Why then," the writer asked, "does LBC endanger its identity by featuring Saudi productions of modest quality?!"[86]

The answer is because of internal Saudi politics, in addition to the lure of the Saudi market. Consider what happened in the aftermath of the Anglo-American invasion of Iraq. In the summer of 2004, Saudi authorities contacted LBC asking the channel to feature Muhammad Hussain Fadlallah, the towering Lebanese Shi'i *marja' al-taqlid* (source of emulation). The Saudis asked the cleric to articulate peaceable message to Saudi Shi'a, who were growing restive in their second-class status as they watched their Iraqi brethren rising to power after decades of repression. It is befitting of the convoluted Saudi-Lebanese connection that Saudi princes who rule in the name of Sunni Wahhabiyya would ask a Christian Lebanese channel to feature a Shi'i Lebanese religious scholar to appease Saudi Shi'a![87]

Such byzantine maneuvers are needed because of the fierce battle between liberals and conservatives in Saudi Arabia and because of the royal family's precarious balancing role in those debates. The clerical establishment has a firm grip on national television, and exerts great influence on religious satellite channels such as Iqra' and al-Majd. This constrains Saudi royals, who often use offshore Saudi channels like MBC or non-Saudi institutions like LBC to convey important messages to the Saudi public. The guardians of Sunni Wahhabiyya would not have tolerated the appearance of a preeminent Shi'i cleric like Fadlallah on a

---

[85] Mansour, M. (December 13, 2007). LBC's welcome to Saudi productions: Media charlatanism harmful to both sides! *Al-Quds al-Arabi* [Arabic].

[86] Ibid.

[87] Author interview with a prominent LBC figure (2004), Lebanon. Name, exact date, and place omitted to protect anonymity.

Saudi channel; LBC provided the needed platform. Tawfiq Rabahi, a media critic for *al-Quds al-Arabi*, captured the roundabout communication practices of the Saudi elite:

> To break the chains imposed by religious institutions, the Saudi approach relies on channels of foreign origin but of Saudi affiliation, the most prominent of which is a Lebanese channel that manages the scheduling and content of its programs according to Saudi timing [an unsubtle hint to LBC]. Here Saudis, hosts and participants, say what is prohibited in their country's channels because of the power of religious groups, or maybe because the ruling institution hides behind the putative power of these groups.[88]

The author went on to call LBC's April 2007 hiring of Saudi filmmaker Haifa Mansour to host a show a "taboo breaker" through which LBC "prepared a 100% Saudi dish on Lebanese land, out of the reach of the Commission to Promote Virtue and Combat Vice,"[89] the feared Saudi religious police. Replaying a role the Lebanese press performed in the 1970s and 1980s, when it provided a pulpit for many Arab dissenters, Lebanese satellite channels today provide a platform for various Arab "reformers." "The difference now," Rabahi wrote ominously, "is that both the Saudi government and the opposition practice reform from the outside,"[90] through channels like LBC.

But why do Saudi princes favor Lebanese media personalities and institutions as proxies? It is here that the root-cause of the Saudi-Lebanese connection comes to the fore. Politically, Saudi Arabia has long supported the Sunni community in Lebanon, represented at the highest level in the office of prime minister, a post by tradition reserved for a Sunni. Saudi interest and involvement in Lebanese affairs has grown in recent years, in parallel to the tightening Saudi-Lebanese connection in the media industry. (On July 5, 2008, al-Waleed Bin Talal increased his stake in LBC-Sat to "more than 85 per cent and less than 90.")[91] Growing Saudi involvement in Lebanon cannot be simply reduced to the kingdom's desire to protect the Sunni community there; if this were the case, the Saudis would be involved in Iraqi politics in

---

[88] Rabahi, T. (July 17, 2007). Saudi loyalty and dissent . . . from abroad, and war of attrition in Qassem and Haddad's topics. *Al-Quds al-Arabi* [Arabic].

[89] Ibid.

[90] Ibid.

[91] Abuzeid, R. (July 6, 2008). Alwaleed expands media empire. *The National*, www.thenational.ae (accessed July 6, 2008).

the same way, which they are not. Rather, as historian of Saudi Arabia Madawi al-Rasheed argued in *al-Quds al-Arabi*:

> [Lebanon] is an intermediary on which Saudi Arabia relies in various fields, a role that no other Arab country, large or small, is able to play. Lebanon, state and people, plays this role in different realms including culture, media, politics, economics, and even religion.[92]

As a touristic destination, Lebanon "provides Saudi Arabia a social and entertainment space, a mediator between internal Saudi isolation and external Western openness."[93] In addition, Lebanese historians, journalists, and media institutions were historically able to promote Saudi agendas, regionally and internationally, and in several languages. As al-Rasheed proceeds to explain, various Saudi "reform" projects about hot-button issues such as women, religion, and politics (discussion of which does not exist in Saudi media) find their way to the Saudi sphere through the Lebanese intercessor. This is why, the author argued,

> [television] programs that focus on the internal Saudi situation have become a Lebanese specialty, while [many] Saudis are kept away from these dialogues by the state. The Saudi person comes to this open, Saudi-owned, media space, carrying his concerns, sharing his private life and the secrets of his society with a Lebanese dialogue partner, on screens that appear to be Lebanese though in fact they are Saudi in both inclination and ownership.[94]

Saudi influence in Lebanon has grown in the last decade. Politically, the kingdom has played an important and direct role in supporting the "March 14" coalition headed by Rafiq al-Hariri's son in a protracted political battle with Hezbollah and its allies.[95] In the same period, Prince al-Waleed Bin Talal increased his stakes in LBC's satellite channel to a near totality of the shares, effectively merging LBC-Sat with Rotana,

---

[92] al-Rasheed, M. (April 12, 2008). The Saudi sect joins Lebanon's seventeen sects. *Al-Quds al-Arabi* [Arabic].

[93] Ibid.

[94] Ibid.

[95] See Abukhalil, A. (2008). "Determinants and Characteristics of Saudi Role in Lebanon: The Post-Civil War Years," in *Kingdom without Borders: Saudi Arabia's Political, Religious and Media Frontiers*, ed. M. al-Rasheed, New York: Columbia University Press, 79–88. Also, the opposition daily *al-Akhbar*, which is sympathetic to Hezbollah, has published several op-eds critical of the Saudi role in Lebanon.

with LBC's Pierre el-Daher becoming general manager of Rotana. At the same time, el-Daher is fending off legal challenges by the Lebanese Forces, the party who founded LBC in the 1980s and whose bosses were trying to reclaim the terrestrial channel LBCI from el-Daher for use as a platform in the summer 2009 legislative elections in Lebanon. Nonetheless, as the battle plays out in Lebanese courts, the Saudi-Lebanese connection continues to serve both its actors well because it is particularly symbiotic. It enables Saudi media moguls to staff their institutions with qualified personnel whose skills are particularly needed at a time when the ascent of television formats requires professionals adept at negotiating across cultures, something that the multilingual Lebanese creative class offers. Lebanese editors and journalists have also been reliable spokespersons for the political and economic agendas of Saudi princes. At the same time, access to Lebanese screens has provided a platform for "reformist" princes and "liberal" activists to reach the Saudi public. On the Lebanese side, the Saudi media empire injects capital in cash-starved Lebanese institutions operating in a small domestic market and provides professional opportunities to numerous Lebanese journalists, editors, directors, producers, and managers, driven out of their native country by episodic violent conflicts or lured away from Lebanese companies by higher salaries. Because it is beneficial to the parties involved, the Saudi-Lebanese connection is poised to endure and be deployed in some of the Middle East's major geopolitical and social conflagrations, playing critical roles in the intense polemic over *Star Academy* in Saudi Arabia (Chapter 4) and getting embroiled in the Beirut demonstrations in the spring of 2005 (Chapter 7).

CHAPTER FOUR

Contesting Reality: *Star Academy* and Islamic Authenticity in Saudi Arabia

H isham 'Abdulrahman was anonymous in December 2004 when he left his native Saudi Arabia to participate in the second season of *Star Academy*, the widely popular pan-Arab reality show. When he returned from Lebanon four months later, after winning *Star Academy 2*, Hisham had become an adulated superstar in his homeland. Upon landing in the Jeddah airport, he was greeted by a crowd of adoring fans waving his picture and begging for autographs. But the next day, April 22, 2005, when young Saudi girls touched him in public at a shopping mall, the religious police, tasked with enforcing strict behavior in the name of Wahhabiyya, arrested Hisham and threw him in jail. However, within hours of the arrest, the Saudi prince and media mogul al-Waleed Bin Talal secured Hisham's release and later invited him to a much-publicized visit at his office.

'Abdulrahman's dizzying transformation from average person to pop idol to prison inmate to royal guest was courtesy of the Saudi-Lebanese connection. In its first year, LBC's *Star Academy* shattered pan-Arab television rating records and spawned heated public debates in Saudi Arabia, despite the fact that the Saudi contestant, Muhammad al-Khalawi, had been voted off the show at an early stage. When Hisham emerged as a front-runner in *Star Academy 2*, Saudi airwaves, pulpits, and opinion pages were ablaze with vehement disputes about *Star Academy*'s vices and virtues, focusing on the show's impact on Saudi identity and authenticity. 'Abdulrahman's victory led to late-night celebrations throughout the country and to front-page coverage the next morning. It also poured fuel on the fire of a controversy that had been raging for a year in the kingdom.

The notion of authenticity is a sacrosanct matter in the eyes of Wahhabiyya, Saudi Arabia's official and ultraconservative version of

Sunni Islam. The doctrine's founder, Muhammad Ibn 'Abdulwahhab, was a fiery preacher whose alliance with the al-Sa'ud clan in the mid-eighteenth century remains the basis of power to this day in Saudi Arabia. Propagated by Ibn 'Abdulwahhab's descendents, the al-Shaykh family, Wahhabiyya is, in al-Rasheed's words, "religiously dogmatic, socially conservative and politically acquiescent."[1] It validates royal authority over political and economic issues in exchange for clerical control over the social, educational and cultural spheres. In those realms, Wahhabi clerics focus on preserving Saudi cultural and religious purity and maintaining strict separation between men and women.

In the name of authenticity, state Wahhabiyya provides religious sanction for political control. Saudi Arabia has no public institutional mechanisms for contesting and negotiating with rulers, because Wahhabi doctrine advises that rulers can only be contested discreetly and deferentially. There were no significant challenges to the alliance between al-Sa'ud royals and al-Shaykh clerics until the 1970s, when oil wealth and urbanization spawned new political formations.[2] In the ensuing decades, several groups have contested prevailing political arrangements.[3] Two of these are germane to this analysis. On the one hand, activists of *al-Sahwa al-Islamiyya* (The Islamic Awakening) believe Saudi Arabia to be insufficiently Islamic and accuse establishment clerics of selling out to the royal family.[4] On the other hand, activists known in Saudi Arabia as *al-libraliyyun* (The Liberals) – a motley crew of academics, novelists, business owners, journalists, lawyers, and former

---

[1] al-Rasheed, M. (2007). *Contesting the Saudi State: Islamic Voices from a New Generation.* Cambridge: Cambridge University Press, 5.

[2] al-Rasheed, 2007; Moaddel, M. (2006). "The Saudi Public Speaks: Religion, Gender, and Politics," *International Journal of Middle Eastern Studies* 38: 79–108.

[3] The religious spectrum begins on the right with the Jihadi-Salafis, to the Sahwist (with establishment Wahhabiyya in the middle), to various "centrist" or "moderate" Sunni and Shi'i variations. Lacroix (2008) describes the emergence and decline of a centrist "Islamo-Liberal" formation. Clearly, the Saudi ideological spectrum is wide and unstable.

[4] The Jihadi-Salafi current that contributed to the 1979 siege of the Grand Mosque in Mecca and continues to inspire radical violence in the name of Islam is to the ideological right of the Sahwis and is of no direct concern for this book. For more on Saudi Islamist dissenters, see al-Rasheed, 2007; and Fandy, M. (1999). *Saudi Arabia and the Politics of Dissent.* New York: Palgrave Macmillan. A broader view of the struggle between Islamists and liberals is found in Lacroix, S. (2005). "Islamo-liberal politics in Saudi Arabia," in *Saudi Arabia in the Balance: Political Economy, Society, Foreign Affairs,* ed. P. Aarts and G. Nonneman. New York: New York University Press, 35–56.

leftist dissidents – advocate a more inclusive system that enshrines political, minority, and women's rights.[5] Boundaries between these groups are porous: Sahwi firebrands occasionally undergo ideological makeovers, emerging from prison terms in televised repentances; likewise liberals are occasionally jailed or co-opted by the monarchy.

THE BATTLE FOR SAUDI MODERNITY: ISLAM, WOMEN, AND MEDIA AS BATTLEGROUNDS

In the 1980s and 1990s, Saudi Arabia witnessed fierce public battles between advocates and adversaries of modernity, resuscitating debates that emerged initially in subdued forms during the formative years of modern Saudi Arabia in the mid-1920s and reappeared throughout the twentieth century in disputes over poetry. For a very brief time in the early 1980s, Saudi television even aired a program called *al-Kalima Taduqqu al-Sa'a* (*The Word Strikes the Hour*), widely followed by the Saudi intelligentsia, featuring modernist Arab authors and poets from Egypt, Iraq, and Lebanon, but shied away from showcasing Saudi modernists, a move that would have been provocative. But the modernity wars lasting from 1985 to 1995 were more intense, exacerbated by the 1991 Gulf War that brought thousands of American troops to the holy Islamic grounds of Saudi Arabia and involved a wider circle of participants. The publication of *al-Khati'a wal-Takfir* (*Sin and Excommunication*) by the literary theorist 'Abdullah Muhammad al-Ghaddhami was a formative event in the Saudi modernity wars. After provoking strong reactions in the country's clerical and intellectual circles, the book was widely discussed in Saudi society. As described by al-Ghaddhami, the upheaval uncannily foreshadowed the *Star Academy* scandal explained in this chapter. The book

> became a topic to which were attributed all the problems of the nation and all the dangers of the future, till it reached mosques' pulpits, animated Friday sermons, and became material for preachers, missionaries, *fatwa* makers, cassette-tapes, publications and

---

[5] See Dekmejian, R. (2003). "The Liberal Impulse in Saudi Arabia," *The Middle East Journal* 57 (3): 381–99. "Liberal" in this context refers broadly to Saudis who advocate civil rights, in opposition to both Sahwa clerics and the Wahhabi establishment. Some of the Saudi and other Gulf countries' liberals' positions on geopolitical issues, however, may be described as "neo-conservative." According to Dekmejian, academics and writers constituted the majority of the signatories of the January 2003 petition to the king titled "Strategic Vision for the Present and the Future."

posters; Books were published and *fatwas* were issued, and [*Sin and Excommunication*] became the talk of councils and societies, and was the talk of Saudi society for five full years.[6]

The book, a theoretical treatment of the modernist poet Hamza Shahata, who came to prominence in the mid-twentieth century, generated a barrage of attacks beginning with a widely circulated cassette tape, *al-Hadatha fi Mizan al-Islam* (*Modernity in the Scale of Islam*) that was later published as a book prefaced by 'Abdulaziz Bin Baz, a prominent arch-conservative cleric who would become Grand Mufti of Saudi Arabia in 1993. From that experience, al-Ghaddhami developed the notion of the "symbolic event" (*al-hadath al-ramzy*) when new ideas threaten the prevailing order by challenging what he calls the "conservative mode" (*al-nasq al-muhafizh*) and spawning heated polemics.[7] The Saudi modernity wars became unruly to the point that the minister of information banned the use of the word *modernity* in print and audiovisual media, though the prohibition was implemented only temporarily.[8]

The battle over Saudi modernity overlapped with post-1991 political activity in which Sahwi, liberal, and other activists submitted petitions to the king advocating various reforms.[9] These "Memoranda of Advice" nudged the royal family to acknowledge diverging opinions, eventually leading the then regent and now King 'Abdullah to launch the National Dialogue Forum in June 2003, two years before he became the sixth king of Saudi Arabia in August 2005. Participation in the National Dialogue Forum is restricted to a group of individuals handpicked by the king periodically to discuss issues framed by the royal agenda and under the auspices of the King 'Abdulaziz Center for National Dialogue, whose president is the king. This reflects the secrecy endemic in Saudi politics: when in September 2005 King 'Abdullah met with a group of business and intelligentsia women, the tenor of their discussion was not revealed.[10] During the years the Dialogues have become more public – some sessions were even televised, C-SPAN style, by state-owned news satellite channel al-Ekhbariyya – heretofore, as a Saudi columnist put it, only "hundreds of Saudi men and women have engaged in six National

---

[6] al-Ghaddhami, A. M. (2005). *The Tale of Modernity in the Kingdom of Saudi Arabia (Third Edition)*. Beirut and Casablanca: The Arab Cultural Center [Arabic], 207.

[7] Ibid, 100. In addition to "mode," *Nasq* can be translated as "system," "order," "disposition," or "alignment."

[8] Ibid.

[9] See al-Rasheed, 2007; Dekmejian, 2003; and Fandy, 1999.

[10] al-Rasheed, 2007.

Dialogue forums."[11] In contrast to this highly selective forum, the polemic around *Star Academy* suggests that controversies over popular culture can become protracted public contests that draw a large number of clerics, intellectuals, journalists, and even members of the royal family. Two related questions emerge from these polemics: Why has *Star Academy* been so intensely controversial in Saudi Arabia? After all, this is an Arabic-language program, produced by a Lebanese network whose satellite channel is half-owned by a Saudi prince, featuring Arab contestants. That this "Arab" cultural production would trigger a controversy shriller than previous outcries about "foreign" programs is therefore perplexing. And what does the *Star Academy* controversy reveal about Saudi politics?

To answer these questions, we need to recall the remarkable consolidation of pan-Arab media ownership in Saudi hands and the Saudi-Lebanese connection. In addition to the twenty-one million relatively wealthy consumers (not counting 5 to 6 million resident foreigners, many of whom are Arabic speakers) who make the Saudi market the holy grail of pan-Arab advertising, Saudi holdings include two London-based pan-Arab daily newspapers, *al-Hayat* and *Asharq al-Awsat*, the multichannel MBC Group based in Dubai, and several religious radio and television stations, in addition to stakes in various Egyptian and Lebanese channels.[12] As explained in Chapter 3, Lebanese professionals occupy key industry ranks in advertising, journalism, and particularly dominate entertainment television production.[13] The socially liberal ethos of Lebanese productions – what in LBC's case I call "conspicuous liberalism" – has stirred polemics in Saudi Arabia, but interelite struggles and business interests have prevented Saudi media owners and investors from dictating homogenously conservative programs.[14] The

---

[11] Qusti, R. (April 20, 2007). National Dialogue chief says no boundaries in forums. *Arab News*.

[12] See Kraidy, M. M and Khalil, J. (2007). "The Middle East: Transnational Arab Television," in *The Media Globe: Trends in International Mass Media*, ed. L. Artz and Y. Kamalipour. Lanham, MD: Rowman and Littlefield, 79–98.

[13] With the exception of drama, chiefly an Egyptian and Syrian province.

[14] Diversity of outlooks within the Saudi elite has spawned channels airing various programs ranging from titillating music videos (Rotana) to puritanical religious sermons (al-Majd). For that perspective, dissimilarity in programs on Saudi-owned channels is not as paradoxical as some have argued, for example Mellor, N. (2008). "Bedouinisation or Liberalisation of Culture? The Paradox in the Saudi Monopoly of the Arab Media," in *Kingdom without Borders: Saudi Arabia's Political, Religious and Media Frontiers*, ed. M. al-Rasheed. New York: Columbia University Press, 353–74.

Saudi upheaval over *Star Academy* indicates that the Saudi-Lebanese connection polarized Saudi opinion because it subverted Wahhabi notions of social order and individual piety that have long shaped Saudi media policy.

Saudi national identity is deeply imbued with Wahhabiyya's focus on purifying Saudi Islam from "foreign" influence.[15] Anxieties about the social impact of technology, with its ability to move ideas and images across national boundaries, are commonplace in Saudi history, regularly causing contention since "modernization" was declared a national objective in the 1930s.[16] As discussed in Chapter 3, television and camera-equipped mobile telephones among other media have caused various controversies in the country.[17] We saw that the rulers introduced television in the 1960s with the twin aims of modernizing a vast country with a tribally and regionally fractious population and having a propaganda tool at a time when the al-Saʿud were reeling from a hostile Egyptian media campaign. Saudi clerics dropped initial objections to television when they gained a media policy-making role, tightening censorship and aligning it with the tenets of Wahhabiyya. Prohibitions have included "scenes which arouse sexual excitement," "women who appear indecently dressed, in dance scenes, or in scenes which show overt acts of love," "women who appear in athletic games or sports," "alcoholic drinks or anything connected with drinking," "derogatory references to any of the 'Heavenly Religions,'" "treatment of other countries with praise, satire, or contempt," "references to Zionism," "material meant to expose the monarchy," "all immoral scenes," "references to betting or gambling," and "excessive violence."[18]

Media regulations focus on women, alongside political and religious issues, because the separation of men and women lies at the heart of social order in Saudi Arabia. In the Wahhabi worldview, the pious woman is the bearer of authentic Islamic principles and as such it is

---

[15] Which includes not only the West but also non-Sunni Saudi Muslims – notably the Shiʿa. See al-Rasheed, M. (1998). "The Shiʿa of Saudi Arabia: A Minority in Search of Cultural Authenticity," *British Journal of Middle Eastern Studies* 21 (5): 121–38.

[16] See al-Ghaddhami, 2005.

[17] Kraidy, M. (2006). "Governance and Hypermedia in Saudi Arabia," *First Monday* 11 (9), http://firstmonday.org/issues/special11_9/kraidy/index.html (accessed December 30, 2006).

[18] Shobaili (1972), cited in Boyd, D. A. (1993). *Broadcasting in the Arab World: A Survey of the Electronic Media in the Middle East*, 2nd ed. Ames: Iowa State University Press, 164.

central to Saudi identity. Saudi social space is therefore compartmental-
ized in order to prevent *ikhtilat* (illicit mixing between men and women),
and a sharp boundary between private and public space governs male-
female interactions.[19] Women are allowed in public space only in the
company of a male guardian; they are banned from driving automobiles
and until recently they were banned from traveling outside of the country without the company of a male relative. When imported country-
western movies are shown on Saudi state television, kissing scenes are
crudely censored, with a couple's faces coming close to each other for a
romantic kiss, then abruptly retreating from each other before the
occurrence of physical contact. Movie theaters are prohibited.[20] For
proponents of Wahhabiyya, Saudi Arabia derives its moral superiority
from having the world's most rigid separation of women from men.[21]

By focusing on protecting the ideal Islamic woman as bearer of the
nation's identity, television censorship reflects the importance of gender segregation as a public display of Islamic piety. Wahhabi dogma
focuses on daily aspects of femininity like clothing, makeup, and hair
removal, revealing, in the words of al-Rasheed, the "*the centrality of
ritual practices in Wahhabi thought and expertise, used to control the
social sphere.*"[22] Television is thus crucial to the House of al-Sa'ud, who
uses it to exalt the royal family's piety through broadcasting religious
rituals like the Hajj prayers in Mecca or ceremonies of royal power transfer. "The repetitiveness and regularity" of these programs, al-Rasheed
explains, "confirm Saudi society as obsessively concerned with the
ritualistic aspect of Islam . . . [reducing] a world religion to a set of
prohibited and permissible actions for the sake of demonstrating the

---

[19] Two cautionary notes are in order here. First, gender separation can be found worldwide, but is more intense in Saudi Arabia. Second, there were also concerns over
privacy that echo those raised in the West, though they were overshadowed by social-
religious worries.

[20] Saudis flock to neighboring Bahrain to attend movie theaters, an experience captured in "Cinema 500 Km," a Saudi docudrama about the 300-mile, movie theater–
seeking journey from Saudi Arabia to Bahrain. Saudi film production is nascent: the
first Saudi-produced movie, *Keif al-Hal* (*How Is It Going?*), was shot in Dubai and
released in non–Saudi Arab locations in 2006. A project of Prince al-Waleed Bin
Talal, the film featured Hind Muhammad, the first Saudi film actress, in a leading
role. See Saudis become refugees cinematically as they celebrate *Keif al-Hal* as the
first popular release movie (November 12, 2006). *Al-Riyadh* [Arabic]. A more recent
treatment can be found in Fawwaz, 'A. (August 25, 2008). Saudi cinema gambles on
the future. *Al-Akhbar* [Arabic].

[21] Doumato, E. A. (1992). "Gender, monarchy and national identity in Saudi Arabia,"
British Journal of Middle Eastern Studies 19 (1): 33.

[22] al-Rasheed, 2007, 54–5, emphasis added.

religiosity of power."[23] Television is a potent ritual tool in the hands of the rulers.

Since the early 1990s, Saudi Arabia's entanglement in pan-Arab media has dulled the effectiveness of the monarchy's television rituals. Saudi media tycoons have pursued commercial and political agendas with their own idiosyncratic censorship guidelines, which might or might not agree with official rules; for instance, religious and political conversation is banned on *Star Academy*, but mingling between the sexes is not.[24] At the same time, the important Saudi advertising market is targeted by programs from Beirut, Dubai, and Cairo without official Saudi approval. Saudis are avid viewers of transnational television: An October 2007 Gallup poll found that 93 percent of Saudis "rely on pan-Arab television to keep up on events in other countries" and 82 percent do so to stay informed about events in their own country.[25] Contradicting media agendas continue to weaken the ritual bases of power in Saudi Arabia and lay the ground for controversy: *Star Academy* is so intensely controversial because ritualistically it reflects the liberal extreme of Lebanese social mores, which clashes with Wahhabiyya's vision of the virtuous society.

ANATOMY OF A CONTENTIOUS MEDIA EVENT

When LBC adapted *Star Academy* from a Dutch original television format, it marketed it as "reality TV." As mentioned earlier, *Star Academy* entered the scene in 2003 with a regional casting campaign that netted sixteen contestants from several Arab countries who agreed to be sequestered as *tullab* (students) in "The Academy" from December 2003 to April 2004. There sixty cameras captured every moment in every corner of the building except the restrooms, and viewers could peek inside the academy 24/7 for four months by watching *LBC Reality*, a dedicated satellite channel.[26] LBC emphasized the show's pedagogical aspects. It was an "academy" where contestants, who were officially

[23] Ibid., 60.
[24] A policy reportedly due to al-Waleed Bin Talal's personal preferences.
[25] Rheault, M. (October 11, 2007). *International Television Receives High Marks in Saudi Arabia*. Washington, DC: Gallup. The same poll found that al-Jazeera is the top-rated channel in Saudi Arabia with 30% of the Saudi audience, followed by two Saudi-owned outlets, MBC at 24% and al-Arabiya at 23%, the Saudi government's Channel 1 and LBC *ex-aequo* at 5% each, followed by Hizbollah's al-Manar at 4%, and Dubai TV and the U.S. government's al-Hurra at 2% each.
[26] Author interview with Rula Sa'd, Director of Promotion and Marketing, Lebanese Broadcasting Corporation International, July 4, 2004, Adma, Lebanon.

called "students," were coached to achieve personal and professional growth. Each week, viewers voting determined who was dismissed from the show.

Star Academy was a national event in Saudi Arabia, where Friday "primes," aired during the weekly peak viewing time, emptied the streets of major cities like Jeddah and Riyadh. Men gathered at cafés to watch *Star Academy* on large screens and women stayed at home to presumably do the same. Mosque sermons, opinion pages, and talk shows featured passionate discussions as *Star Academy* achieved record ratings.[27] But with popularity came controversy, and widespread reactions made *Star Academy* a highly visible and contentious episode used by rival activists to advance agendas dissenting from the status quo and by religious, social, and business institutions to reassert the status quo. The upheaval publicized usually secretive Saudi political dynamics.

In the winter of 2004, as *Star Academy* became the talk of the country, Sahwi activists began peddling on city streets a cassette tape titled *Satan Academy*, for one riyal a piece, or a quarter of a U.S. dollar, which they claimed sold a million copies.[28] The tape featured a thirty-six-minute and forty-one-second sermon by Muhammad Saleh al-Munajjid, a Syrian-born cleric who has a weekly Saturday afternoon show on Qur'an Radio and is active on the Internet. The *Satan Academy* sermon presents the most analytical, conceptual, and systematic critique of reality TV from a Wahhabi perspective, which will be discussed later in this chapter. Another cleric recorded a tape titled *SARS Academy*, in reference to the deadly (Severe Acute Respiratory Syndrome) virus of the same name, in which he told the story of a little girl who lost her innocence and decided to become a pop star after watching *Star Academy*, at which moment the sound of an explosion can be heard. Both *Satan Academy* and *SARS Academy* tapes were cleared by the Ministry of Information, indicating official approval.[29] Nonetheless, ordinary Saudis who were drawn to *Star Academy* but concerned by the fierce opposition to the show, asked clerics to rule on whether it was religiously *haram* (prohibited) or *halal* (permitted) to watch and participate in *Star Academy*. The commotion reached such a proportion that establishment Wahhabiyya

---

[27] Author interviews with Jihad Fakhreddine, Director of Research, Pan-Arab Research Center (PARC), June 1, 2004, Dubai, UAE; and Shadi Kandil, Director of Research, IPSOS-STAT, June 2, 2004, Dubai, UAE.

[28] Abbas, F. (June 8, 2005). Satan's academy. *Asharq al-Awsat* [Arabic]. The tape features a speech by Shaykh Muhammad Saleh al-Munajjid, in which he presents a systematic case against *Star Academy* grounded in Wahhabi doctrine.

[29] Ibid.

had to weigh in unequivocally. The "Permanent Committee for Scientific [or Academic] Research and the Issuing of Fatwas" – a subcommittee of the Higher Council of 'Ulamas supervised by the Ministry of Religious Affairs – issued a dedicated *fatwa*. It prohibited watching, discussing, voting in, or participating in *Star Academy* and exhorted businessmen not to finance this type of program. The committee's main charge was that *Star Academy* violated and subverted Islamic principles because it carried "a number of serious evils" such as:

> *Free mixing of the sexes* . . . the main idea of [*Star Academy* and similar shows] is mixing between the sexes and removing all barriers between them, as well as the wanton display and unveiling on the part of women displaying their charms, which leads to much evil . . . *Blatant promotion of immorality* . . . by making [Muslims] get used to seeing these shameful scenes that provoke desires and by distancing them from good morals and virtue.[30]

Like Saudi censorship rules, the *fatwa* was most concerned with women and their interaction with men.[31] But unlike media regulations, which apply to institutions, the *fatwa* called upon believers directly and as individuals to actively oppose *Star Academy*: "It is not sufficient for you to abstain from watching these shows," the 'ulamas stipulated, "[y]ou should also advise and remind those whom you know watch them or take part in them in any way, because that comes under the heading of cooperating in righteousness and piety, and forbidding one another to engage in sin and transgression."[32]

Anger against *Star Academy* was widespread. An Imam at Mecca's Great Mosque called it a "Weapon of Mass Destruction."[33] Even the relatively liberal newspaper *al-Riyadh* published guest op-eds such as "Destructive Academy Is Harmful to the Family"[34] and "Star Academy . . . the Other Terrorism," whose author wrote that "modesty and morals

---

[30] Fatwa on *Star Academy* (2004). Standing Committee for Scientific Research and the Issuing of Fatwas. Saudi Arabia [Arabic].

[31] Two verses from the Qur'an focus on women's dress code to preempt the sexual temptation of men: verse 31, Sura 24 (The Light); and verse 59, Sura 33 (The Clans). For more see Dabbous-Sensenig, D. (2006). "To Veil or Not to Veil: Gender and Religion on Al-Jazeera's Islamic Law and Life," *Westminster Papers in Communication and Culture* 3 (2): 60–85.

[32] Fatwa on, 2004.

[33] *Star Academy* "Weapon of Mass Destruction" (April 3, 2004). Middle East Online, http://www.middle-east-online.com/english/?id=9498=9498&format.

[34] al-Dakhil, M. M. (February 27, 2005). Destructive academy is harmful to the family. *al-Riyadh* [Arabic].

vanish when . . . young men and women get together, wearing clothes that provide modesty for very few parts of their bodies . . . [and] reflect confusion about . . . authentic identity and culture." Deriding *Star Academy's* pedagogical pretensions, the author concludes:

> The objectives of this so-called *Star Academy* . . . are progress and knowledge!! . . . which means . . . trampling the dearest thing that you have . . . your timeless (religious) beliefs and principles!! . . . [T]here is a hand grabbing morals and tossing them aside and offering us modern art reeking of the smell of moral terrorism!![35]

Viewing *Star Academy* as a harbinger of foreign values and therefore a threat to Saudi authenticity, the column is typical of conservative attacks, which begin with concerns about cultural decline and social confusion, and then invoke religion as a conclusive argument against the show's imputed moral defects.[36]

In sharp contrast, other writers in Saudi newspapers praised *Star Academy* as an alternative to extremist dogma and an invitation to dialogue.[37] Some even glimpsed political lessons, like Badreiah al-Bishr, a female Saudi journalist who in a column titled "Star Academy's Democracy," wrote that

> Arabs shied away from voting because . . . [of fraud] . . . until satellite television . . . corrupted us by inciting us to vote: "vote, you are the referee" . . . "nominate your favorite candidate," "do you support?" "do you think?" . . . the [Arab] viewer has become obsessed with voting chiefly because voting results resemble election results in the United States, and unlike Arab elections, nobody wins by 99.99%, but rather by logical proportions.[38]

Writing during the first local elections in Saudi Arabia, which were held between February and April 2005, the author concludes that "the fire of

[35] al-'Enezi, H. A. (March 19, 2005). Star Academy . . . the other terrorism. *Al-Riyadh* [Arabic].

[36] Also see al-Dabib, M. A. (March 11, 2005). These programs aim to destroy the social tissue, especially the youth. *Al-Riyadh* [Arabic]; al-Dakhil, M. M. (February 27, 2005). Destructive Academy is harmful to the family. *Al-Riyadh* [Arabic]; al-Dawyan, W. M. (March 22, 2005). *Star Academy*: A sincere invitation to *ikhtilat*. *Al-Riyadh* [Arabic].

[37] Nasrallah, M. R. (February 9, 2004). The extremists' generation . . . and Star Academy's generation! *al-Riyadh* [Arabic]; al-Jabban, M. (February 20, 2004). Star Academy channel . . . ideas for dialogue. *Asharq al-Awsat* [Arabic].

[38] al-Bishr, B. (April 19, 2005). Star Academy's democracy. *Asharq al-Awsat* [Arabic].

voting is ablaze among . . . Saudi citizens, men and women, old and young, who enthusiastically voted in the *Star Academy* show. . . . I say this as I keep an eye on the [Saudi] municipal elections, which can benefit from the experiment of *Star Academy*, using procedures that demonstrate to voters that their vote has value."[39]

Other liberals were exasperated by conservative and radical reactions to the show. A columnist in the Jeddah-based *Arab News*, also a woman, exclaimed: "How vulnerable we must be if a TV program can 'destroy our moral standards', and teach our children bad things. If our society is that weak, then we have every reason to stop all TV programs, close our doors and windows and stay at home." She then told an anecdote:

> A mother of three boys who are avid watchers of *Star Academy* told me: "I know it's a silly program, but kids need some fun. Society does not provide them with much to do, so what do they do with their spare time? Can they go to clubs? No. Can they go to public libraries? No. So what are they supposed to do? I saw her point. . . . What do we give our teenagers? We give them everything except the right guidance and venues to expend their energies? So if we stop *Star Academy* . . . will our problems end? Will we turn into a utopian society?"[40]

In contrast to Wahhabiyya's focus on censorship and prohibition, liberal columnists used the *Star Academy* polemic to criticize Wahhabi-inspired social policies and to discuss and promote alternatives for Saudi youth.

A notable Saudi-liberal voice in the debate hailed from within the royal family. Prince al-Waleed Bin Talal was clearly one of the "businessmen" alluded to in the anti–*Star Academy fatwa* discussed earlier, to which the prince's spokesperson said "our comment is no comment." During the show's second season, al-Waleed actively supported *Star Academy 2*. He sent his private plane to Beirut to bring Hisham 'Abdulrahman back to Saudi Arabia after the young Saudi won *Star Academy 2*. Bin Talal's commercial interests were on display in photographs of 'Abdulrahman brandishing the *Star Academy* trophy while standing next to a large logo of Rotana, the prince's Arabic music label and television conglomerate. It is in this context that on April 22, 2005, when the Saudi religious police jailed 'Abdulrahman after spotting him mingling

---

[39] Ibid.
[40] Mishkhas, A. (March 9, 2004). Do we give our children what they want? *Arab News*.

with teenage girls in a Jeddah mall, the prince secured his release, invited him to his palace, and made sure that pictures of the meeting appeared in Saudi newspapers.[41]

Two weeks later, on May 10, 2005, sixty Saudi clerics issued a statement against *Star Academy*, criticizing its "exploitation of teenagers for commercial gain by individuals at the expense of corrupting young men and women and cheating the nation" and its "commercialization of women's bodies," singling out *ikhtilat*. The statement carried a barely concealed rebuke of al-Waleed bin Talal by calling his Rotana company (and *al-Riyadh* newspaper and – of course – LBC) "channels of sin" for "promoting" *Star Academy*.[42] Unruffled, the prince went on to offer 'Abdulrahman a lead role in the first indigenously produced Saudi movie[43] and to merge his company Rotana with LBC in August 2007 (refer to Chapter 3), flaunting his disregard of establishment Wahhabiyya.

Bin Talal's behavior reflects long-standing disputes within the Saudi leadership. The prince's own father Talal Bin 'Abdul'aziz led the so-called Red Princes movement in the 1960s whose members agitated in favor of turning Saudi Arabia into a constitutional monarchy. As a result, Talal was ostracized by his brethren who argued that the Qur'an was Saudi Arabia's only constitution. He was forced into exile in Egypt between 1960 and 1962, where he used Nasser's Voice of the Arabs radio to criticize the Saudi regime. Talal was later permitted to return to Saudi Arabia with the condition that he refrain from making public statements. Decades later, he returned to the spotlight in a well-publicized interview aired on January 12, 2007 on al-Arabiya, a liberal – non-Islamist, pro-Saudi rulers, pro–U.S. Middle East policy – Dubai-based, Saudi-owned satellite channel. Then in a September 5, 2007 interview in London, Talal announced the founding of Saudi Arabia's first political party, with a progressive agenda echoing its founder's beliefs; a few days later he backpedaled, saying that King 'Abdullah's permission was necessary for the formation of any political group.[44]

Even after the formal end of the modernity wars in 1995, Saudi intellectuals remain at the forefront of public debate about culture, politics,

---

[41] Hisham is arrested in Riyadh (April 22, 2005). *Assafir* [Arabic].

[42] More than sixty clerics in Saudi Arabia issue a joint statement attacking Star Academy 2 (May 10, 2005). *Al-Quds al-Arabi* [Arabic].

[43] Saudis become refugees cinematically as they celebrate *Keif al-Hal* as the first popular release movie (November 12, 2006). *Al-Riyadh* [Arabic].

[44] Prince Talal bin 'Abdulaziz: Politics of exclusion pushes us to found a party to participate in public governance (September 7, 2007). *Al-Quds al-Arabi* [Arabic].

and religion in the kingdom. In *Arab Culture in the Era of Globalization*, the critic and novelist Turki al-Hamad, a prominent liberal[45] in the continuing debate over Saudi authenticity, argued that "getting rid of that obsessive fear over the loss of our identity and culture, is the way to survive in a merciless world of unstoppable transformations."[46] His call for openness to foreign influence clashed head on with Wahhabiyya's obsession with protecting Saudi purity and authenticity from alien cultural invasions. The clearest expression of al-Hamad's views can be found in a column he wrote for the Dubai daily *al-Bayan*:

> The concept of cultural invasion is premised on [the] concept . . . of "authenticity," assuming that there is a complete or pure authenticity that needs to be preserved in the face of "intellectual invasion". . . . [I]f everyone adopted that definition of authenticity and therefore the concept of cultural invasion, humans would not have gone beyond the stone age. . . . Pure authenticity is an illusion equal to the illusion of the pure race. . . . It is usually the weakest party in intercultural . . . relations that invokes the concept of cultural invasion. . . . [I]t expresses its fear, anxiety and weakness in terms like cultural invasion, similar to a military invasion, and it takes up the cause of authenticity. . . . [A]ll these are defense mechanisms . . . [that] do not reflect the dynamic nature of culture. . . . Isolation is in truth the weakest protection . . . even if it appears to be the strongest. History tells us that.[47]

Because of al-Hamad's challenge to Wahhabi norms of authenticity, he was declared a *kafir* (apostate) by radical preachers, though King 'Abdullah took him under his protection and reportedly offered him his own pen – a symbolically potent gesture that protects but also co-opts the intellectual. Predictably, al-Hamad eschews Saudi politics in the column he currently publishes in *Asharq al-Awsat* – now frequently consisting of toothless expressions of sympathy with the suffering of the Iraqi people, grand-scale geopolitical analysis, impressionistic essays, and so forth. Nonetheless, the Saudi culture wars continue with

---

[45] According to Dekmejian (2003), al-Hamad vocally persisted in criticizing his Islamist opponents in the few years after the 1991 Gulf War, at a time when most liberals acted like "muted critical observers" (404).

[46] al-Hamad, T. (2001). *Arab Culture in the Era of Globalization*. Beirut and London: Al-Saqi [Arabic], 13.

[47] al-Hamad, T. (June 19, 2005). It is in the concept that all the meaning resides. *Al-Bayan* [Arabic].

al-Hamad voicing concerns for his safety after another *fatwa* declared that liberals were not true Muslims.[48]

For a period of time, the *Star Academy* controversy became an important forum for the ongoing struggle for the future of Saudi Arabia. Not only did conservatives and liberals duel on op-ed pages, but also the approval of the radical taped sermons by the Ministry of Information and the anti–*Star Academy fatwa* underscored that clerics and some members of the royal family (presumably the conservative Prince Nayef, the powerful Minister of the Interior) were opposed to the show, while others, like al-Waleed Bin Talal, supported it. In a country devoid of political institutions where such issues could be publicly deliberated, the *Star Academy* battle royal publicized rival visions of national identity and cultural authenticity, and reflected dissent from official Wahhabiyya. More importantly, *Star Academy*'s widespread popularity and the ensuing polemic suggest that Saudis are ambivalent toward conservative and liberal ideologies.

THE AMBIVALENCE OF THE SAUDI PUBLIC

On March 7, 2004, as the first season of *Star Academy* was entering its final month, Shadha 'Omar, the charismatic young woman who hosts LBC's Sunday night talk show *al-Hadath*, led a discussion of *zhahirat telfizion al-waqi'*, the "reality TV phenomenon." Her guests were Rashed al-Rashed, director of the Beirut office of the Saudi daily newspaper *al-Riyadh*, Marwan Gharzeddin, a Beirut-based psychoanalyst, Elie Khoury, from the Lebanese advertising industry, and Rula Sa'd, Director of Marketing and Promotion at LBC and "Director of the Academy." The discussion broached familiar themes and carried predictable arguments: Sa'd and Khoury were supportive of *Star Academy*, and LBC clearly used the talk show as a promotional opportunity. More interesting than the discussion were short reportages about the public reception of *Star Academy* in several Arab countries. The one from Saudi Arabia makes for particularly interesting television.

In the background, the camera shows a spacious coffeehouse where Saudi men are seated, sipping coffee and smoking *shishas* or snacking while watching *Star Academy* on a wide screen. In the foreground, the

---

[48] Saudi fatwa against liberals raises fears of their exposure to attacks (July 9, 2007). *Al-Quds al-Arabi* [Arabic]; Struggle between liberal and religious movements over mass media . . . Turki Al-Faisal in 'Amman to participate in reform conference (April 10, 2007). *Al-Quds al-Arabi* [Arabic].

LBC reporter declares that "opinions differed on the Saudi street which appeared to be more opposed to than supportive of *Star Academy*," and explains that "Saudi society is conservative and its customs and traditions may not be compatible with the program." Then, one by one, the men walked to the foreground to answer the reporter's queries:

Man in coffeehouse 1: *Star Academy* is successful with the public in all criteria, but it has some defects and some points of contention, especially the transfer of Western culture, like kissing and *ikhtilat* (gender mixing).

Man in coffeehouse 2: *Star Academy* has supporters and opponents. I am an opponent because in all sincerity *Star Academy* has *ikhtilat* between male and female students.

Reporter: The participation of the Saudi youth Muhammad al-Khalawi in the program [first season] stirred interest among Saudis, who followed the program and nominated contestants, in solidarity with their compatriot.

Man in coffeehouse 3: Of course, there was Muhammad al-Khalawi, [but] there was exaggeration in showing immoral things. However, I cannot say that the program is not successful, and I hope it will continue and that there will be a part two, and I hope that the number of participants from Gulf countries will increase.

Reporter: The program has created conflict within families, where fathers and mothers are worried that their sons and daughters are exposed to behavior that is not compatible with their convictions.

Man in coffeehouse 4: Frankly *Star Academy* is a successful program . . . on all criteria, but there are some reservations. [The camera pans back and forth on the all-male audience watching the show, including previous interviewees.] Because people watch it every day, it creates problems between parents and the fans of the program, especially teenagers; at home there are problems between my two parents and my brothers and sisters, "Watch it! Do not watch it!" . . . Surely, however, frankly, as an idea and as a program *Star Academy* is successful.

Man in coffeehouse 5: I am among the opponents of this program, and I do not support it. Obviously we know the view of Islamic Shari'a [Islamic law] on *ikhtilat*. [*Star Academy* contestants] are live on air, 24 hours a day, and there are love relationships. I cannot see myself in that program.

Reporter: There is a lot of controversy over *Star Academy* on the Saudi street, to the extent that we can say that this program "filled the world" and preoccupied people, both those who reject it and those who accept it. For *al-Hadath*, Myassar al-Shanmary, al-Hayat-LBC, reporting from al-Riyadh [the Saudi capital].[49]

Though several women writers published criticism and praise of *Star Academy*,[50] the fact that no Saudi women were interviewed in the segment in the preceding text reflects the fact that public space in Saudi Arabia remains largely a male domain (or that the male reporter was not allowed to interview Saudi women). Nonetheless, the *al-Hadath* report featured a slice of the male Saudi public that is clearly ambivalent about *Star Academy*. When these young men take turns in front of the news camera, say "I like it, but it I have moral reservations," then regain their seat and resume watching, are they simply voicing moral objections to play "as if,"[51] pretending to follow Wahhabi prescriptions? Or are they watching *Star Academy*, in spite of genuine moral reservations, because "everyone else" is watching the show?

Partial answers reside in recent surveys that found the Saudi public ambivalent about social issues. A 2006 survey found that though "[r]eligion, women, and democracy are among the most contested categories in the intellectual debates about the future of the kingdom," 71 percent of Saudis, the survey revealed, were in favor of democracy, and 59 percent agreed that a working mother can establish as warm a relationship with her children as can a stay-at-home mother. In contrast, 23 percent of Saudis disagreed that men make better political leaders than women, and 81 percent of Saudis agreed that a woman must always obey her husband. Only 5 percent disagreed on that last question. Among the survey's rather unexpected findings was that overall "The Saudi public appears to be *less* religious than Egyptians and Jordanians."[52] More recently, a December 2007 Gallup poll found the Saudi public to be even less conservative, with majorities supporting various freedoms for women: 55 percent of Saudi men and 66 percent of Saudi women support women's right to drive a car (which has been legally forbidden since 1991), and 75 percent of men and 82 percent of women support women having

---

49 *al-Hadath* (March 7, 2004). "The Reality TV Phenomenon," Marwan Matni, Producer; Shadha 'Omar, Host. Adma, Lebanon: Lebanese Broadcasting Corporation [Arabic].

50 al-Bishr, 2005; Mishkhas, 2004 and Mishkhas, A. (January 13, 2005). Tilting at the wrong windmills. *Arab News*; al-Dabib, 2005, and al-Dakhil, 2005.

51 I borrow the "playing as if" notion from Wedeen's (1999) study of power and compliance in Syria.

52 Moaddel, 2006, 92.

jobs outside of the home, a gender gap of seven compared to twenty-one points in Egypt.[53]

If Saudis are less religious than is commonly assumed, then attitudes and official policies toward women are inspired by social norms that overlap but are not subsumed into religious beliefs and practices. These norms are couched in religious language, but they hark back to a time when women marked tribal boundaries – a political, not religious, matter. As the historian Joan Scott argued in a landmark essay, the connection between controlling women and wielding authoritarian power is manifest throughout history, inside and outside of the West. "Gender," Scott wrote, "is a primary field within which or by means of which power is articulated."[54] In the Saudi past piety was measured by men's action, behavior, and dress. The shift to women's piety as a symbol of the virtuous society occurred because of political expediency, because it appealed to Saudis across religions, regions, and social classes. In short, women's invisibility makes religion visible.[55]

Patriarchy and political expediency, rather than strictly religion, explain gender segregation, a central tenet of an ostensibly religious discourse that is a political idiom of governance: "[T]he Wahhabi 'ulama," wrote al-Rasheed, "contributed to the consolidation of a state that is politically secular and socially religious."[56] Policies toward women – including supportive policies such as health and employment benefits – are framed in religious terms to win legitimacy. More importantly, gender separation is a royal emblem of religiosity. In the turbulent years of 1979 and 1980, during the armed takeover of the Grand Mosque in Mecca by Juhayman al-'Utaybi and his companions, and then again in the 1990s when Saudi rulers had to validate the presence of non-Muslim American troops on Islam's holy grounds for the conduct of the 1991 Gulf War, many *fatwas* and police actions focused on gender separation, illustrating how such an emphasis is used to deflect political tensions.[57] However, satellite broadcasts are virtually impossible to control, so shutting down *Star Academy* was not a viable option. Many other Arab and foreign television programs broadcast in Saudi Arabia fail to respect Wahhabiyya's draconian rules; yet none provoked as intense a

---

[53] Rheault, M. (December 21, 2007). *Saudi Arabia: Majorities Support Women's Rights.* Washington, DC: Gallup.

[54] Scott, J. W. (1986). "Gender: A Useful Category of Historical Analysis," *American Historical Review* 91 (5): 1053–75.

[55] Doumato, 1992, 45.

[56] al-Rasheed, 2007, 57.

[57] al-Rasheed, 2007; Doumato, 1992; See also Dekmejian, 2003.

controversy as the one spawned by *Star Academy*.[58] So the question remains: What specifically about this program struck such a sensitive chord in Saudi Arabia? Why were clerics, princes, journalists, and activists compelled to weigh in on the merits of a Lebanese reality TV show?

SUBVERSIVE RITUALS: VIOLATING BOUNDARIES OF GENDER AND CULTURE

Seeds of the controversy reside in the special relationship between Saudi Arabia and LBC – a focal point of the Saudi-Lebanese connection discussed in Chapter 3. Ever since LBC began satellite broadcasting in 1996, Saudi investments have enabled it to be a top-tier channel, in addition to a news-gathering joint operation with the pan-Arab daily *al-Hayat*, owned by Saudi prince Khaled Bin Sultan Bin-'Abdul'aziz. LBC's association with al-Waleed bin Talal culminated in July 2008 when al-Waleed raised his stake up to 85 percent (see Chapter 3). Saudi funding notwithstanding, LBC's screen aesthetic reflects the socially liberal extreme of the Lebanese ethos, characterized by an ostensible mimicry of Western consumer lifestyles, slick production values, informality in newscasts and talk shows, language switching between Arabic, French, and sometimes English, and, most importantly, the ubiquity of alluringly dressed women – LBC's signature *conspicuous liberalism*.

If the Islamic ideal of the pious woman is central to Saudi Arabia's national identity, the consumer ideal of the "Western-looking," uninhibited woman is central to LBC's corporate identity. When I asked LBC's General Manager Pierre al-Daher to distill his channel's profile, he said, "We are a general entertainment channel without social inhibitions."[59] An unsubtle social liberalism was manifest since the channel's launch in 1985, with variety shows featuring provocative fashion and behavior and commercial breaks full of suggestive advertisements for lingerie and cosmetics. Commoditized femininity became central to LBC's pan-Arab brand in the satellite era. Saudi tourists have reportedly driven to LBC headquarters northeast of Beirut to meet Haifa, an aerobic and exercise television star whose long-running morning

---

[58] The Saudi comedy show *Tash Ma Tash* and the Arabic-dubbed Turkish drama series *Nour* provoked major controversies that nonetheless were less all-encompassing than the upheaval triggered by *Star Academy*.

[59] Author interview with Pierre el-Daher, General Manager, Lebanese Broadcasting Corporation, June 30, 2004, Adma, Lebanon.

show consists of close-up shots of various body parts with a few longer shots of her and two acolytes exercising in a warehouse or on the beach (not to be confused with pop star Haifa Wehbi). In a revealing double entendre, Arabs refer to LBC as *elbessee*, Arabic for "get dressed." LBC's commoditization of the female form is central to its ability to create programs mixing high production values, lightheartedness, boldness, and titillation because these characteristics lure audiences, most importantly the prized Gulf and Saudi viewers. Controversies ensue in Saudi Arabia because the hypervisibility of women's bodies on LBC clashes head on with Wahhabiyya's compulsive invisibility of the female body in public space.[60]

But unlike past instances when broadcasts offensive to Wahhabi sensibilities were censored, interrupted, or shut down, *Star Academy* persists on the air (*Star Academy 6* aired in spring 2009, though the controversy subsided during the years). The scandalous shutdown of *al-Ra'is*, the Arabic *Big Brother* whose story is told in Chapter 2, indicates that LBC is able to produce shows that are off-limits to its competitors, a leeway the channel owes partly to its Christian management and Lebanese location. As a reporter quipped, "*Star Academy* ... [did not] generate ... quite the horror of *Big Brother*, in part because [it was] broadcast from Lebanon, which much of the Arab world considers depraved anyway."[61] To critics, this Lebanese exceptionalism makes LBC a Trojan horse that insidiously introduces unwelcome Western values; to its admirers, it reflects cosmopolitan savvy. Regardless, LBC reality shows have remained pan-Arab rating boosters, a commercial success that has brought them a measure of protection and longevity in a pan-Arab media industry where business calculations sometimes trump political considerations and religious sensibilities.

The paradoxical relation between the Arab world's most socially liberal media institution (LBC) and its most socially conservative clerico-political regime (Saudi Arabia) has been one catalyst of the Saudi debate over authenticity. Featured nightly on *Star Academy*, images of young Arab and mostly Muslim men and women, alluringly dressed, dancing, hugging, and singing together on stage or in their common house, have

---

[60] *Star Academy* producers do not show Saudi contestants (all male) dancing or touching female contestants; neither do they show them in the swimming pool introduced in later seasons.

[61] MacFarqhar, N. (March 5, 2004). "A Kiss Is Not Just a Kiss to an Angry Arab TV Audience." *New York Times*.

provoked controversy because *Star Academy* displays a lifestyle that breaches the Saudi prohibition on *ikhtilat*. Women not only dress immodestly, but also they touch men physically and sing and dance; they also publicly disagree and argue with the men on the show, compete with them, and even sometimes beat them in various competitions. By being, in the words of one Saudi critic, "A Sincere Invitation to *Ikhtilat*,"[62] *Star Academy* offers an alternative social reality with fluid gender boundaries and imbued with women's agency, albeit contrived and commoditized, and thus inimical to Wahhabi definitions of social order.[63] As discussed earlier, this is compounded by LBC promotions touting the "real" aspect of the "*reality* TV" show, which provoked vehement objections from clerics infuriated by the claim that *Star Academy* represents reality.

Inasmuch as it claims to represent reality, *Star Academy* reflects a blend of multiple realities. It is a highly public and therefore controversial, a cultural hybrid. *Star Academy* confounds the boundaries between the "domestic" and the "foreign," between what is "Arab" or "Islamic" and what is alien. It violates Wahhabi diktats on gender segregation and cultural purity, enforced through ritualistic behavior in prayer, dress, and social relations. A culturally ambiguous category that muddles notions of identity and authenticity, *Star Academy* threatens the core of Wahhabiyya in two specific ways. It reflects a radically pluralistic world and compels participants to enact alien social norms.

As the Arabic version of a European television "format," *Star Academy* is a mixture of multiple cultural predilections. The contestants' demeanor reflects the socially liberal extreme of the Lebanese spectrum; it is significantly more relaxed than Saudi customs (I am *not* arguing that there is something "authentically Lebanese" about *Star Academy*). In the show, several North African and Lebanese contestants spoke

---

[62] al-Dawyan, W. M. (March 22, 2005). *Star Academy*: A sincere invitation to *ikhtilat*. *Al-Riyadh* [Arabic].

[63] Clearly, I am not using "gender" to mean "women" but rather to connote the constructed reality of femininity and masculinity and the way the relationship between them is socially organized. In interviews with *Star Academy* staff I was told that during production every attempt was made not to show male contestants dancing or acting in ways that could be seen as "effeminate" or "gay." Opponents in Saudi Arabia and elsewhere in the Gulf often criticized *Star Academy* for promoting *muyuʻa*, which means "unsteadiness," "effeminacy," and "softness," from the verb *maʻa*, which means "to become soft" and "to be indulgent," connoting concerns about masculinity. Clearly, anxieties related to gender concern the instability of both femininity and masculinity.

an Arabic peppered with French words, and during Friday primes they frequently performed French and English, and occasionally Spanish, songs. (In *Star Academy 4*, prime 3, January 30, 2007, one contestant from Oman even performed a Bollywood tableau in Hindi.) English is the show's logistical *lingua franca*, as the terms "star academy" and "nominee," and the notion of "star" is American. Friday primes are carnivalesque spectacles, with music and dance tableaux alternating Lebanese Rahbani musicals, *khaliji* (Arabian Gulf) songs, Bollywood performances, Broadway musicals, French Cancan, Russian circus numbers, and Chinese dance. Various generic elements from distinct cultural registers recombine in individual performances. From the point of view of Wahhabiyya, this radical and hybrid eclecticism invokes the *jahiliyya* – literally the "age of ignorance" – the chaotic pre-Islamic era on the Arabian peninsula characterized by fragile tribal orders and fluid gender boundaries; therefore *Star Academy* must be strenuously opposed.

By grafting an Arabic-language program on a Western format, *Star Academy* is what the literary theorist Mikhail Bakhtin calls an "intentional" hybrid. Unlike organic hybridity, which is an unintentional product of intercultural contact, intentional hybridity is "*concrete and social*," resulting from the perception of one cultural system through the language of another culture, the latter being "*taken as the norm.*"[64] Because Western standards set production norms for Arab reality TV programs, *Star Academy* depicts not merely a fantasy world that viewers watch but also a social world that viewers re-create through rituals like nominating and voting for contestants. Because reality TV claims to represent reality, *Star Academy* posits a *normative* social world. As a cultural hybrid, the show exposes within the Arab world what the media scholar Jesús Martín-Barbero, writing about Latin America, describes as "the sense of continuities in discontinuity and reconciliations between rhythms of life that are mutually exclusive"[65] – another way of saying that reactions to the show reveal the coexistence of different ways of feeling and being modern. To its critics, *Star Academy* is culturally invasive precisely because it asks contestants ritualistically to perform a social world

---

[64] Bakhtin, M. (1981). *The Dialogical Imagination: Four Essays*. M. Holquist, ed., C. Emerson and M. Holquist, trans. Austin: University of Texas Press, 359–60, emphasis added.

[65] Martín-Barbero, J. (1993). *Communication, Culture and Hegemony: From the Media to Mediations*. London: Sage, 188.

not only alien but also profoundly threatening to Wahhabiyya's values. In that social world, "Lebanese" social norms ostensibly act as a pernicious intermediary between the Western format and its Saudi viewers.

The Western media and popular culture literature articulates authenticity for the most part as a minority discourse.[66] In contrast, invocations of authenticity in Saudi Arabia appear to be a majority discourse. The influence of Wahhabiyya means that an extreme version of the discourse of authenticity, one that emphasizes purity and separation from an outside world that is postulated as morally inferior, sits at the core of national identity and policy. As a widely popular program that is culturally hybrid, *Star Academy* exposes the tension between the official dogma of cultural purity and the effective reality of cultural fusion. *Star Academy* draws Saudi viewers to participate in rituals (e.g., watching and voting) that enact a syncretistic identity, subverting the notion of cultural purity cardinal to Saudi identity. The ensuing polemic exposes Wahhabiyya's fear and rejection of the outside world, all the more so because the show ritually enacts, and therefore upholds, alien norms, values, and behaviors.

Star Academy undermines the prevalent notion of authenticity in a more fundamental way due to formal elements of the reality TV genre, whose success largely depends on its ostensible liveness. The claim to represent reality is based on the premise that what viewers see on the screen is spontaneous and unrehearsed. Like many other reality shows, the key moments in *Star Academy* are the points in time when participants are caught (by cameras) being their authentic selves. It is precisely when contestants allegedly lose sight of the cameras that reality TV reaffirms its claims to liveness and reality. Although from the audience's point of view, this feature represents one of reality TV's main attractions; these "moments of truth," in the context of reality television's claim to the real, signal a redefinition of the notion of authenticity from obedience to Wahhabi diktats to an individual performance through which the contestant reveals his or her "true," authentic self, validating the whole reality TV enterprise. *Star Academy* not only conjures up a social order inimical to Wahhabiyya, but also it feats the individual

---

[66] Mcleod, K. (1999). "Authenticity within Hip-Hop and Other Cultures Threatened with Assimilation," *Journal of Communication* 49 (4): 134–50; Molina Guzmán, I. (2006). "Mediating Frida: Negotiating Discourses of Latina/o Authenticity in Global Media Representations of Ethnic Identity," *Critical Studies in Media Communication* 23 (3): 232–51.

body – which Wahhabiyya sees primarily as an instrument of sin – as the locus of identity.[67]

This personally experienced, individually performed authenticity lies at the heart of reality TV's presumptive connection to reality. Clerics fiercely contested *Star Academy*'s reality claims because establishment Wahhabiyya seeks to preserve its monopoly on representing social reality. In contrast, *Star Academy* turns viewers into witnesses of a reality created by a television genre that claims to represent reality. This was a central theme in al-Munajjid's *Satan Academy* sermon:

> These programs do not consist of acting, lying and pretending; rather they are in the realm of reality. . . . [*Star Academy* is] a real thing practiced realistically . . . not a written script that actors have rehearsed, but a real thing whose events occur in reality. It is also live. . . .[68]

Witnessing involves searching one's memory to extract the details of that eventful moment, when the witness was present in space (there) and time (then), and then rendering the event to an audience that was not present when the event occurred. Media institutions derive a great deal of their social authority from their role as witnesses. Unlike news or documentary, however, reality TV ostensibly relinquishes some of the power-to-witness to its viewers. Al-Munajjid succinctly captured this when he sermonized that:

> In the past events used to be reported . . . to those who did not see or live them. In contrast today [in reality TV shows] events are witnessed and attended [*mashhuda* wa *mahdura*].[69] The media have shifted from "it happened" to "it is happening" [*min hadatha ila yahduthu*]. . . . The public and the viewers intervene to determine

[67] This is accomplished by exhortations to participate, call, nominate, etc., as al-Munajjid argued in the *Satan Academy* sermon: "Learning and preaching with images is more potent than face-to-face. If you are told '. . . be corrupted, be corrupted, be corrupted; take this [phone] number, take this number, take this number; call, call, call;' you will be influenced somewhat; but when you see the scenes yourself and interactivity occurs, its impact on the self is more potent." See al-Munajjid, M. S. (March 19, 2004). *Satan Academy* [akademiyat al-Shaytan wal-Superstar], http://www.islamway.com/?iw_s=Lesson&;iw_a=view&lesson_id=28385.

[68] al-Munajjid, M. S. (March 19, 2004). *Satan Academy* [akademiyat al-Shaytan wal-Superstar], http://www.islamway.com/?iw_s=Lesson&iw_a=view&lesson_id=28385.

[69] *Mahdura* comes from the verb *hadara*, which means "attended" or "watched," connoting presence. *Hadar* refers to sedentary or settled peoples (as opposed to nomads); *hadaara* means "civilization."

things, so it is an interactive process. Viewers did not intervene in films or televisions serials except by watching; but today [reality TV] programs entail contributions from viewers who nominate, comment, and send text-messages or emails that appear immediately on the television screen....[70]

Viewers experiencing *Star Academy* as a 24/7 flow await the eventful moment – the moment of authenticity – with anticipation. They are, in a sense, witnesses in reverse. Unlike witnessing, which the communication scholar John Peters reminds us is "retroactive,"[71] the ritualized watching of *Star Academy* is proactive. Whereas witnesses are compelled to produce a verisimilar rendering of a past event, reality TV viewers are enthralled by the future possibility of the program going "off script." The former calls for a narrowing of alternatives to come as close as possible to a necessary "truth," the latter proliferates alternatives whose "authenticity" rests on their liveness, hence their contingency. Viewers wait for contestants to forget the cameras and "come out" as their true, authentic self, the moment when authenticity comes into being (though some contestants become adept actors with contrived "spontaneous" outbursts). Reality TV viewing in this case is a kind of intense, vigilant, intentional – albeit reverse – witnessing.

Reality TV's treatment of viewers as witnesses to manufactured situations is controversial because a witness makes a version of an event more legitimate than other versions. *Star Academy* viewers therefore are complicit in a social reality that clashes head on with regnant Saudi definitions of authenticity. Viewing as witnessing entails the ritual diffusion of the power to define social reality. Ritualistic Islam is a dominant preoccupation in Saudi Arabia because Saudis as a community engage in conspicuous worship rituals that are punctiliously regulated and intolerant of variation. *Star Academy* depicts alternative rituals of engagements on a popular television show at a time when Wahhabi clerics, in al-Rasheed's description, have turned "[p]rayer, fasting and pilgrimage ... into spectacles regularly dramatized on local and satellite television channels."[72] By establishing alluring rituals that rival those described in the preceding text, reality TV poses a threat to Wahhabi governance.

[70] al-Munajjid, 2004.
[71] Peters, J. D. (2001). "Witnessing," *Media, Culture and Society* 23 (6): 703–23.
[72] al-Rasheed, 2007, 59.

GRAPPLING WITH MODERNITY

The Saudi controversy over *Star Academy* is a particularly contentious episode in ongoing Saudi debates about national identity, authenticity, gender relations, and political participation that began with the founding of modern Saudi Arabia. In al-Ghaddhami's telling, the debate evolved in several stages, from poetic modernity, to theoretical-critical studies, to the broader social application of literary criticism and the spread of the novel as social commentary.[73] The battle over *Star Academy* can be understood as another stage in the evolution of the debate, widening the circle of participation in it and illustrating the important public role that popular culture can take in the absence of public institutions for debate and deliberation.[74] In addition to being a catalyst and platform for debate, the *Star Academy* controversy revealed political and social fault lines not only within the Saudi intellectual and media elite but also within the ruling establishment. As such, the controversy helps to shed light on political struggles in one of the world's most secretive political systems.

Star Academy articulates an alternative social reality by undermining the core principles of the prevalent social order. The prohibition on *ikhtilat* lies at the center of the Saudi social system, and the preservation of an unadulterated Saudi authenticity is a core concern of Wahhabiyya. By creating an environment of unbridled gender and cultural mixing, *Star Academy* posed a direct affront to the most vital components of Saudi authenticity – the country's existential center – defined by the political-religious establishment. Instead of prayer, fasting, and pilgrimage, *Star Academy* lures Saudi viewers into fandom, mobilization, and voting. Though no Saudi female participated in *Star Academy*, the fracas over the show made visible the displacement of that center.[75] *Star Academy*'s popularity and controversy are therefore explained by the show's articulation of a "reality" that not only clashes with the Saudi social order, but also subverts its most elemental building blocks.

---

[73] al-Ghaddhami, 2005.

[74] Wedeen (2008) develops a concurrent view in her book on the performance of politics in Yemen, where she argues that the absence of state institutions can actually foster popular democratic practices.

[75] Throughout the show's five seasons, female contestants were predominantly from Egypt, Lebanon, Morocco, Syria, and Tunisia. The only woman from a Gulf country was a Bahraini who was voted out early on in *Star Academy 4*. A Saudi female fashion designer participated in the first season of *Mission Fashion* on Future TV, on which she wore the *niqab*.

It would be a mistake to view the vociferous objections to *Star Academy* as the battle cry of tradition against modernity. It is rather symptomatic of a struggle between rival versions of modernity: the Saudi debate over authenticity reflects a struggle to accommodate change without relinquishing one's identity. Proponents of Wahhabiyya want to preserve their stranglehold on power in the kingdom and have used the power of media technologies to install a dominant and ritualistically based version of Islam as an idiom of control. Grappling with modernity is not a choice, but the ways in which modernity is defined and managed – like Saudi censorship guidelines demonstrate – are a matter of constant negotiation. For establishment clerics and radical Sahwi activists, invocations of authenticity are tools for bargaining with external (e.g., Western culture and the United States) and internal proponents of rival versions of modernity. Even the liberal camp in the Saudi culture wars is essentially a local movement that struggles to articulate a modern *and* Muslim society, "a purely indigenous collectivity without external sources of support."[76] Prince al-Waleed Bin Talal said to his biographer: "Saudi Arabia Westernized – never; modernized – definitely!"[77] and went on to launch the "soft-Islamist" channel al-Risala as an expression of his commitment to Islam. In addition to scoring political points, publicizing their ideas, and placating their opponents, for all protagonists in the controversy, invoking authenticity is a negotiating tool that helps them to domesticate various elements of modernity.

The broad participation in the *Star Academy* debate reflects deep hopes and anxieties related to social and political change. Liberals glimpsed in *Star Academy* fleeting visions, even if contrived, of a more participatory and inclusive society, one with less clerical influence and a wider margin of individual autonomy. In contrast, Wahhabiyya's engagement with the formal characteristics of reality TV – discussing and rejecting its claims to representing reality – suggests that clerics and activists understand the new kinds of agency that become possible when viewers become avid and participatory fans of programs that are based on ritualistic viewer engagement in an environment that stifles participation in public life – because the clergymen maintain their hegemony through similar media rituals. Opponents of reality TV discern that popular participation in the ritualistic redefinition of authenticity

---

[76] Dekmejian, 2003, 410; the works of Turki al-Hamad (2001) and 'Abdullah Muhammad al-Ghaddhami (2005) are good examples of the quest for a meaningful articulation of modern and Saudi identities.

[77] Khan, R., 2005, 370.

threatens the prevalent social order – in that sense *Star Academy*'s popularity may be a symptom of the decline of Wahhabiyya's grip on Saudi
society. Saudi Arabia, as the French political scientist Stéphane Lacroix
has suggested, may be entering the era of post-Wahhabism.[78]

How would the debate over reality TV evolve if it were channeled by
political, social, and media institutions that are relatively independent
from each other? How would the dynamics of public argument differ in
an environment where women have a more forceful tradition of political activism and media participation? What difference would it make to
have an elected legislature with a history of robust interventions against
executive power? Chapter 5 will show how the presence of functional
institutions, such as a vibrant press, a feisty legislature, and active wom-
en's groups, shaped the debate over reality TV in Kuwait, Saudi Arabia's
smaller neighbor, which came to international fame in 1990 when it was
invaded by Iraqi troops under the command of Saddam Hussain.

[78] Lacroix, S. (Spring 2005). "Post-Wahhabism in Saudi Arabia?" *ISIM Review* 15: 17.

CHAPTER FIVE

Gendering Reality: Kuwait in the Eye of the Storm

As dawn broke over Kuwait on November 16, 2005, the capital city of this small Gulf emirate was hit by a powerful rainstorm whose downpour flooded streets and slowed down the morning commute. By midmorning, a joke dispatched by text messaging had made the rounds of Kuwaiti liberals: "This is not hurricane Katrina," the banter went, "this is hurricane Ma'ssuma." A few months earlier, in early June, Ma'ssuma al-Mubarak, a professor of political science at Kuwait University and an occasional columnist, made history when the emir of Kuwait designated her minister of planning and development. The ruler had paved the way for this consequential appointment when he decreed the political enfranchisement of Kuwaiti women on May 17, 2005. As the first nonmale to hold a major ministerial portfolio – succeeding a member of the ruling al-Sabah family in that position – al-Mubarak was thrust into the national limelight. The day before the rainstorm, November 15, 2005, Kuwaiti newspapers featured pictures of her on their front pages because she had publicly questioned government recruitment practices that, in her opinion, were discriminatory against women. The hurricane analogy reflected the powerful resonance of a woman's appointment to a high-level government job in Kuwait.

As the rain abated, I made my way to the office of 'Aisha al-Rshaid, who was among those who received the text-message quip that morning. A journalist with the daily newspaper *al-Watan* (*The Nation*) and the manager of her own events company, Shorooq, al-Rshaid was a political activist with a declared ambition to run for a seat in Kuwait's 2006 legislative elections. In her fifth-floor office in a nondescript building on Al-Sur street, at walking distance from Kuwait's Ministry of Information, she told me how she got entangled in the Arab reality TV wars. Two years earlier, al-Rshaid rose to national fame when her company staged a concert by finalists of the Lebanese reality show *Superstar*, the Arabic-language *American Idol*, satcast by Future TV from Beirut and reaching two dozen Arab countries. When the powerful Islamist bloc in the Kuwaiti legislature launched a preemptive campaign against the event, al-Rshaid found herself at the center of a political firestorm.

Led by the Salafi firebrand Waleed al-Tabtaba'i, Sunni Islamists controlled eighteen out of a total of fifty elected seats. They orchestrated recurrent attacks on television and popular culture for what they saw as the promotion of debauchery in Kuwaiti society. Central to their campaigns for strict morality in the name of Islam was the status of women and their relation to men. Like their Saudi and Bahraini fellow travelers in Sunni salafism, al-Tabtaba'i and his allies abhorred *ikhtilat*. For years, they blocked attempts to give women full political rights, on the premise that such a policy would be "un-Islamic." In their worldview, women's bodies, movements, and speech must be tightly controlled to avoid social disorder. By bringing men and women on the same stage, holding competitions between them, airing the whole thing on television, and calling on viewers to vote, *Superstar* promoted *ikhtilat* and wide-scale debauchery. The Islamists' nickname for the reality show was *super-fasad* – super-corruption.

Al-Rshaid's attitude, I was told by Hamed Sultan, Future TV's representative in Kuwait, poured fuel on the fire. In his opinion, she was overly blunt and eager for a fight.[1] During my meeting with al-Rshaid in her office on that unusually rainy morning, her pugnacity was noticeable. Earlier when she had come under attack, she defied those she called *al-muta'aslemeen* (those who claim to be true Muslims), promptly asserting that the concert would go ahead as scheduled (she told me that she enjoyed support in the highest places). This was not the only public battle she would wage in the context of *Superstar*. As a journalist from the liberal tradition in Kuwaiti politics, al-Rshaid wrote extensively about the Arab reality TV controversies. In a famous column titled "Who is Super Star of the Arabs in 2004: Yasir 'Arafat or Mu'ammar al-Qaddhafi?," she boldly accused Arab leaders of interfering in the results of Arab reality TV competitions.[2] She was swiftly taken to court by Libya's Qaddhafi through the Libyan embassy in Kuwait, and robustly defended herself in the pages of *al-Watan*, a Kuwaiti daily founded in 1962 and known for its criticism of the government.

---

[1] Author interview, Hamed Sultan, Media PS, November 17, 2005, Salhiyya, Kuwait.
[2] al-Rshaid, A. (August 12, 2004). Who is Super Star of the Arabs in 2004: Yasir 'Arafat or Muammar Al-Qaddhafi? *Al-Watan* [Arabic].

Al-Rshaid was an indomitable character who would ultimately prevail over Islamist parliamentarians. Popular sentiment in Kuwait was on her side. As she told me:

> When contestants arrived, there was a crowd waiting for them at the airport. They arrived at 7 pm and we could not get out of the airport until 11 pm. It was like a huge wedding at the Meridian Hotel by the sea where they stayed.

When the concert was finally held, policemen dispatched to the venue found few protesters and many concertgoers. Al-Rshaid's continued telling me her story:

> The concert was extremely successful and got front page coverage the next day. I started crying, because I won the battle. After they left, I held another press conference stating I was going to try to bring Shakira, Jennifer Lopez, and *Star Academy* for concerts . . . then I backed out of that.[3]

In that press conference, al-Rshaid boastfully berated the Islamists: "You aptly failed!!" she said, continuing: "What [you Islamists] have done has no relation to Islam. . . . Kuwait shall not hijacked by you; your attempts to impose your view by force, threats, and promises are rejected."[4]

Al-Rshaid's story is a telling case study of reality TV's ability to articulate religion, politics, gender, and business in the Arab world. It showcases a woman, who is at once a journalist, a business owner, and a declared candidate for political office, using the interconnections between these various roles to battle Islamist legislators. Islamist politicians stir up moral panics over popular culture to score points against their opponents; likewise liberals such as al-Rshaid deftly navigate these controversies to suit their political and economic interests. The publicity brought by her public scuffle with al-Tabtaba'i and his associates gave al-Rshaid's columns a wider readership, generated free publicity for her concert, and gave her the kind of visibility that is essential for seekers of public office in Kuwait. This chapter explores these political dynamics, teasing out connections between reality TV, politics, religion, and gender in Kuwait. In addition to explaining why reality TV was so

---

[3] Author interview, Aisha al-Rshaid, General Manager, Shorooq Exhibitions and Conferences, and Journalist, Dar al-Watan, November 16, 2005, Kuwait.

[4] Baqer, M. (September 22, 2003). Aisha al-Rshaid: I say to *al-muta'aslemeen*: You aptly failed!! . . . and you are not the National Assembly's people. *Al-Watan* [Arabic].

controversial in Kuwait, it seeks to answer several related questions: Why did reality TV become a priority item on the agenda of the National Assembly? How did the Kuwaiti minister of information lose his job over *Star Academy*? In what historical context did women's suffrage become a central contentious issue and how did the reality TV upheaval relate to that issue? What role did the vibrant Kuwaiti press play in the reality TV controversy? How was the Kuwaiti situation different from the Bahraini and Saudi cases discussed in Chapters 2 and 4? Finally and more broadly, what does the reality TV fracas in Kuwait tell us about the role of political and media institutions in focal national debates?

THE PROTRACTED BATTLE FOR WOMEN'S POLITICAL RIGHTS IN KUWAIT

The struggle for women's political rights began shortly after Kuwait gained independence from Britain in 1961. The first elected National Assembly in 1963 restricted the right to vote and hold political office to a select group of male Kuwaiti citizens. Since then, women's political enfranchisement has been a stormy issue for every Kuwaiti parliament. This debate has often occurred in tandem with demands for widening political participation. As the leading Kuwait scholar Mary Ann Tétreault wrote, women's social and political enfranchisement has tracked closely with the democratization of Kuwaiti politics at large.[5] Both processes evolved erratically, subjected to the tug and pull of a combination of political, security, religious, economic, and social forces. The vibrancy of Kuwaiti public life relative to neighboring Gulf states stems partly from the fact that the ruling al-Sabah family has historically accommodated the economic and political interests of Kuwait's powerful merchant class who view the al-Sabah as "glorified house sitters."[6] Since the 1970s, royals and merchants have faced ascendant Islamist and liberal political forces. Along with women, these four groups – rulers, merchants, Islamists, and liberals – are the main actors in the national drama over the right of Kuwaiti women to vote and stand for elected office.

The rise of the modern nation of Kuwait transformed attitudes toward women. Though merchants' concerns about family lineage

---

[5] Tétreault, M. A. (2001). "A State of Two Minds: State Cultures, Women and Politics in Kuwait," *International Journal of Middle East Studies* 33: 203–20.

[6] Crystal, J. and al-Shayeji, A. (1998). "The Pro-Democratic Agenda in Kuwait: Structure and Context," in *Political Liberalization and Democratization in the Arab World*, vol. 2, ed. B. Korany, R. Brynen, and P. Noble. Boulder, CO: Lynne Rienner, 109.

historically made them conservative on women's issues, postindependence merchant families encouraged their women to be active in social and civic associations. In subsequent decades, the merchant class saw an active social role for women as an asset in a modernizing country. The media were crucial in this regard. Since independence, as Hala al-Mughni and Mary Ann Tétreault put it, "there was an almost symbiotic relationship between women and all forms of media."[7] Media coverage of women's issues began timidly in a dedicated "Women's Corner," but quickly expanded to include articles and columns written by women about women's issues. In the 1960s, magazines and newspapers published pictures of women from the country's merchant families.[8] The first women's magazine appeared in 1965 and a woman directed and presented the first women's program on the newly established Kuwait Television.[9] Women's new visibility was noted by a journalist who wrote: "The new woman has arrived. She is educated. She earns. She wants to vote. . . . [T]he new woman is lobbying MPs, getting a lot of press coverage."[10] This visibility can be deceiving: though by the late 1960s, 43 percent of Kuwaiti school students were female, in 1970 women constituted only 2 percent of the workforce.[11]

The 1970s witnessed the rise of two major political movements. Women's growing public role led to the first drive for women's political rights, spearheaded by the Arab Women's Development Society (AWDS).[12] The campaign was pivotal as it initiated a relentless struggle for women's enfranchisement that would animate Kuwaiti politics for decades. At the same time, Kuwait witnessed an Islamist resurgence that had a decisive impact on social life. As Muhammad al-Jasem, a prominent Kuwaiti journalist, told me: "Social life became a political issue when the Islamists gained clout in the mid-1970s. It used to be that Kuwait Airways served alcohol; not anymore. A bottle at a hotel was OK, as long as it was not too conspicuous. This is no longer the case."[13]

[7] al-Mughni, H. and Tétreault, M. A. (2004). "Engagement in the Public Sphere: Women and the Press in Kuwait," in *Women and Media in the Middle East: Power through Self-Expression*, ed. N. Sakr. London: I. B. Tauris, 120–37.

[8] Ibid., 128.

[9] Ibid.

[10] Ibid., 128.

[11] Longva, A. N. (1993). "Kuwait Women at a Crossroads: Privileged Development and the Constraints of Ethnic Stratification," *International Journal of Middle East Studies* 25: 443–56.

[12] al-Mughni, H. (2001). *Women in Kuwait: The Politics of Gender*. London: Al-Saqi.

[13] Author interview, Muhammad al-Jasem, Editor-in-Chief, *Meezan*, November 15, 2005, Kuwait.

In 1971, the Islamic Reform Society, the Kuwaiti branch of the Muslim Brotherhood, launched *al-Mujtama'* (*Society*), an Islamic magazine.[14] One year later, several merchant families began publishing *al-Qabas* (The Light), a liberal newspaper, which four years after its inception became Kuwait's most highly circulated daily.[15] After legislative elections in 1971 and 1975, rising opposition to the rulers' agenda led Emir Sabah al-Salim to suspend the National Assembly in 1976.[16] It is also worth noting that in 1978 Kuwait Television launched a second channel featuring a mix of local and imported productions.[17]

Like elsewhere in the Arab world, the 1970s saw the ascent of Islamism at the expense of Arab nationalism after the devastating Arab defeat in the 1967 war with Israel. The growing influence of Kuwaiti Islamists drew the government to consort with their cause, which by the late 1970s translated into a policy of Islamization.[18] The monarchy was motivated by the increasingly Islamist hue of the opposition galvanized by the suspension of constitution. Also, as Tétreault and al-Mughni explained,

> popular adherence to Islamic values and principles suited the interests of the regime. Unlike Arab Nationalists, who placed a high value on democracy and individual rights, the Islamists called for *intima'* [cultural belonging], discipline, the preservation of traditional family forms and obedience to political authority. These values reinforce the position of the regime. In contrast, the secular opposition challenges it by making persistent demands for democratization.[19]

Now empowered by tacit support from the rulers, the Islamist movement was able to fend off attempts to emancipate Kuwaiti women by turning women's enfranchisement into a permanently active political battleground. At the same time, Islamist calls to bring women back into domestic space resonated with young men facing increasingly dimmer employment prospects as privatization reduced the number of available

[14] al-Mughni and Tétreault, 2004.
[15] Rugh, W. A. (2004). *Arab Mass Media: Newspapers, Radio, and Television in Arab Politics*. Westport, CT and London: Praeger.
[16] Tétreault, 2001.
[17] Boyd, D. A. (1999). *Broadcasting in the Arab World: A Survey of the Electronic Media in the Middle East*, 2nd ed. Ames: Iowa State University Press.
[18] Tétreault, M. A. and al-Mughni, H. (1995). "Gender, Citizenship, and Nationalism in Kuwait," *British Journal of Middle Eastern Studies* 22 (1/2): 64–80.
[19] Tétreault and al-Mughni, 1995.

public-sector jobs that in the past absorbed most young Kuwaiti males.[20] Kuwaiti politics in the 1980s followed 1970s trends of dual growth in women's and Islamist activity, though the Islamists appeared to have the upper hand. One of the acts of the National Assembly after it was restored in 1981 was to defeat a proposed law granting political rights to women. At that time, Islamist women were becoming more visible, and the press focused on division within the women's movement. Liberal legislators invoked these divisions as a reason for the assembly's vote against women's enfranchisement.[21]

The vote can also be attributed to male anxiety about the implications of women's growing visibility for Kuwaiti national identity. In the 1980s women made significant social, economic, and educational advances: in 1985, working women made 20 percent of the labor force, and by 1990 approximately 70 percent of students enrolled at Kuwait University were women.[22] This progress notwithstanding, Kuwaiti women were enfolded in their country's national identity in ways that hindered their struggle for political rights. A 1985 national census revealed that Kuwaiti citizens made only 27.7 percent of the inhabitants of the country.[23] This alarming news exacerbated social imperatives at work since the 1960s to mark the boundary between citizen and noncitizen, which was hitherto accomplished mostly through traditional dress styles: the white *dishdasha* for men and the black *'abaya* for women. As the Norwegian anthropologist Anh Nga Longva argued, rather than a religious symbol, the *'abaya* used to be "a signal of Kuwaitness"[24] meant to motion to the vast community of expatriate men a reverential attitude toward Kuwaiti women.[25] After liberation from Iraqi occupation in the context of the 1991 Gulf War, two contrasting female clothing styles emerged: whereas urban women dressed increasingly in Western attire, tribal women began wearing the full-face cover known as *niqab*, another symptom of what al-Mughni called the "Islamist-tribalist alliance" in postoccupation Kuwait.[26]

The August 2, 1990, Iraqi invasion of Kuwait had a decisive impact on the status of women and Islamists. Under occupation, Kuwait was a

---

[20] al-Mughni, 2001.
[21] al-Mughni and Tétreault, 2004.
[22] al-Mughni, 2001.
[23] Tétreault and al-Mughni, 1995.
[24] Longva, 1993, 448.
[25] Ibid.
[26] al-Mughni, 2001, 151.

"city-state of women"[27] who were "visible, active, and defiant," and published underground *samizdat*-like newsletters promoting national morale and defiance in addition to providing practical information about food and safety.[28] These publications were crucial in maintaining information flowing among Kuwaitis at a time when national media institutions were shut down or operated by the Iraqi invaders and when people's movement was restricted. Donned proudly by undaunted Kuwaiti women, the *'abaya* now projected defiance. Mosques and clerics were also crucial in maintaining networks of communication and mutual aid in the country and in organizing resistance against Iraqi forces. As a result, women and Islamists emerged as postoccupation heroes, their status raised and their causes reinvigorated. Although for women the fruit of their bravery was restricted to basking – all too fleetingly – in the national spotlight, Islamists leveraged their newfound luster into electoral advances. They captured nineteen out of a total fifty seats in the National Assembly in the October 1992 election[29] and began pushing for the infamous law requiring segregation of men and women in postsecondary educational institutions, which was passed in 1996.[30] Postoccupation politics dealt Kuwaiti women, who by 1993, constituted 25 percent of the national labor force,[31] a cruel blow. Although Islamists were rewarded for their opposition to Iraqi aggression, women were, in effect, punished for their wartime fortitude.

When the occupation ended, the media were catapulted to the center of national priorities. In 1991, a minister of information official stated that the country's top priority was to restore broadcasting capacity that was decimated by the Iraqis.[32] Not only were the two national channels promptly resuscitated, but also two new channels, 3 and 4, were launched.[33] In the same year, Fatma al-Hussain launched *Samra* (*Brunette*), which quickly became an influential women's magazine.[34] This revival was fueled by a renewed popular interest in news. Kuwaitis rushed to

---

[27] al-Mughni, H. (2000). "Women's Movements and the Autonomy of Civil Society in Kuwait," in *Feminist Approaches to Social Movements, Community and Power, vol. 1, Conscious Acts: The Politics of Social Change*, ed. R. L. Teske and M. A. Tétreault. Columbia: University of South Carolina Press, 170–87.

[28] al-Mughni, 2001, 152.

[29] Ibid.

[30] Tétreault, 2001.

[31] Tétreault and al-Mughni, 1995.

[32] Boyd, D. A. 1999.

[33] Ibid.

[34] al-Mughni and Tétreault, 2004.

purchase satellite television dishes, betraying a thirst for information brought on by the occupation-time trauma of news blackout. Since liberation, "TV is taken very seriously," an observer said. Satellite television access is considered "a way of preventing future occupation, or a lack of preparedness for invasion, war or security threat."[35] As a result, Kuwaiti media space became increasingly entangled with the then-nascent pan-Arab satellite television industry.[36]

In the following decade, various political and media developments created a fertile ground for the reality TV controversies that would engulf Kuwait in 2003. The integration of Kuwait in the pan-Arab media industry gave Kuwaiti viewers easy access to television programs that were neither vetted by policy makers nor cleared by religious authorities. With Iraqi repression lifted, Kuwaiti media enjoyed a rising degree of autonomy from the government. "Now journalists go to prison only if they criticize religion or the Emir. Before we would be jailed for anything," a prominent journalist told me.[37] Finally, postoccupation the Kuwaiti press turned increasingly inward, focusing on pressing issues such as reconstruction, unemployment, political participation, and, inevitably, women's role in national political life. Auspicious to debate, the Kuwaiti press would soon see experienced columnists of various stripes contributing to the national controversies over *Star Academy* and *Superstar*.

THE KUWAITI REALITY TV MATCH, ROUND ONE: *SUPERSTAR*

The first Kuwaiti battle over reality TV occurred in 2003 with the first season of *Superstar*. Like *Star Academy* in Saudi Arabia (see Chapter 4), *Superstar* generated heated exchanges between Islamists and liberals in Kuwait. These skirmishes culminated in a showdown in the National Assembly in September 2003. Led by al-Tabtaba'i, Islamist parliamentarians attacked Minister of Information Muhammad Abul Hassan for approving the concert by *Superstar* contestants organized by Aisha al-Rshaid. Speaking at a *diwaniyya* – a typically Kuwaiti social and political assembly in a private home – al-Tabtaba'i elaborated critiques of reality

---

[35] Quoted in Tétreault, M. A. (2003). "Advice and Dissent in Kuwait," *Middle East Report* 226: 36–9.

[36] Kuwait Projects Co.'s (KIPCO) partnership with Showtime to launch Showtime Arabia was a pioneering action for Kuwait and the pan-Arab media industry, because it delivered uncensored programs to subscribers.

[37] Author interview, Muhammad al-Jasem, Editor-in-Chief, Meezan, November 15, 2005, Kuwait.

TV that would become standard arguments against *Star Academy*. He denounced reality TV's corrosive impact on Islamic moral values and its fomenting of *ikhtilat*. The Salafi MP also asserted that the idea of the program came from Lebanon, "the source of folly and *muyu'a* [spoiled-ness/effeminacy]."[38] Though the statement is factually wrong – the *Superstar* format is the property of Fremantle Media, a British company – sweeping attacks on "Lebanon" as a source of objectionable television programs became emblematic of Islamist campaigns against reality TV.

A few days later, on September 14, 2003, the liberal counterattack came swinging. In a column titled "Superstar's MPs," Iqbal al-Ahmad, a prominent Kuwaiti woman (she has been an advisor to the United Nations Development Program and editor-in-chief of the Kuwait News Agency), lampooned the Islamists:

> [With] signs of religiosity and gravity on their faces, they give the new Minister of Information one of two options: either yielding to their demands, or going to *al-miqsala* [the guillotine] sorry I mean *al-minassa* [the hot seat]. For what guilt? Because a group of young Arabs who distinguished themselves with their voices and became the center of attention of the Arab world for months, will now give a concert in Kuwait, no more no less – these are *Superstar*'s stars. But . . . statements by the virtuous MPs suggest that those who are poised to visit Kuwait are . . . brazen apostates who came from the streets and alleys of whoredom, from outside the Islamic religion, deviant outcasts rejected by their families. . . .[39]

After casting her opponents as bloodthirsty (through the "guillotine" fake slip-up) and extremist, al-Ahmad moved on to defend Lebanon against Islamist invective, upbraiding al-Tabtaba'i for attacking those that

> we hold in high respect and appreciation like the Lebanese people. . . . How is it possible to describe a brotherly country that stood by us in our greatest crisis on that infamous August 2 [1990, day of the Iraqi invasion of Kuwait] and was the first Arab voice at a time when countries that are more religious and more contiguous to us were silent for days whose harshness is known to al-Tabtaba'i and

[38] al-Barazi, A. and Muhammad, G. (September 11, 2003). A legislative Superstar threatens Information Minister with the platform and al-Tabtaba'i considers Lebanon a "source of silliness and spoiledness." *Al-Rai al-Aam* [Arabic].

[39] al-Ahmad, I. (September 14, 2003). Superstar's MPs. *Al-Qabas* [Arabic].

others. The least we Kuwaitis can do through our deputies . . . is to show respect and appreciation and not throw at others what we would not like to be thrown at ourselves. You, O virtuous deputy Waleed al-Tabtaba'i, in light of your position . . . every word you utter is consequential. . . .[40]

After exculpating Lebanon and implicating Saudi Arabia ("countries . . . more religious and more contiguous"), whose ruling family for three days remained officially silent about the Iraqi invasion, al-Ahmad brought up the issue of women's political rights with a sarcastic swipe at her foe:

I am in no position to guide MP al-Tabtaba'i, since he is superior to me for many reasons, first among them according to him is the fact that I am a woman while he is a man; second is his level of eloquence of which I admit falling short; third he is a deputy with power over my fate while I am powerless.[41]

Following another encomium to warm Kuwaiti-Lebanese ties, al-Ahmad chided liberal legislators in the National Assembly (in theory her allies):

I find strange that our deputies who are counted as part of the liberal orientation . . . did not issue any statement . . . amidst this Islamist push that has not abated since the . . . last elections. . . . I wish that behind this silence there is tactical coordination for a forthcoming phase of contestation, because we expect a lot, a lot of them . . . my fear is that their silence is the beginning of a wintery freeze.[42]

Al-Ahmad's column outlined thorny issues at the heart of the Islamist-liberal struggle: rival visions of the good society, the fight over women's political enfranchisement, and antagonistic views of other Arab countries like Lebanon and Saudi Arabia, the two poles of the influential Saudi-Lebanese connection explained in Chapter 3. The importance of the numerous columns written by representatives of both sides in the Kuwaiti reality TV tussles resided in their timing: they were published at a time when reality TV was a national preoccupation, which gave these columns a wider readership, a broader resonance, and a deeper impact.

[40] Ibid.
[41] Ibid.
[42] Ibid.

The amplitude of the reality TV battle was manifest seven months later, when *Star Academy*, that other Lebanese reality TV import, set Kuwaiti public life ablaze. Consider these two stories from the Kuwaiti press in March 2004. The first highlights the impact of *Star Academy* on family life:

> The boy supports Sophia and his youngest sister supports Bashar. As a result, they both entered the hospital to be treated for wounds they inflicted on each other after . . . an intense battle in which were used all the weapons available in the house. After he discovered the impact of the battle on his dear children's faces, the father had no choice but to take them to the hospital, cursing *Star Academy* and all its contestants. But he did not forget to return home quickly after his children were treated to know who had won: Sophia or Bashar![43]

The second story reflects how *Star Academy* became a social phenomenon, notably among Kuwaiti women. The female journalist shares a personal experience:

> At a wedding party I recently attended, the young mother sitting next to me was exhibiting clear signs of anxiety as she spoke on her mobile phone nearly every two minutes. . . . I am not nosy so I refrained from asking her what was preoccupying her so intensely, even though everyone sitting around her had clearly noticed. After joy suddenly took over her face during her last phone conversation, I smiled at her, which prompted her to say: "It is over . . . now I can rest. Thank God!" "Thank God," I replied.
>
> I learned in the conversation that ensued that that was . . . the day when nominees were announced on *Star Academy* . . . [nominees] to be voted out by the public. The woman sitting next to me at the wedding party was worried sick that her favorite contestant, Baha' the Tunisian, would be nominated. . . . She relaxed once she learned that Baha' was not one of the nominees (for elimination).
>
> Quickly, news of the nominations spread among the mobile phone-clutching ladies at the wedding, and the atmosphere turned into something akin to an open debate about *Star Academy* and the favorite stars of all female wedding attendees, and *I discovered that everyone in attendance, and not just myself, avidly followed the show.*

---

[43] Family battle! (March 6, 2004). *Al-Qabas* [Arabic].

... when the bride finally sat down ... the conversation turned to problematic aspects of the show. .... [O]ne said "frankly, the program is full of prohibited things ... young men and women in one house day and night together, what do you expect? *Matches and gas ... the result is clear.*[44]

Predictably, *Star Academy*'s far-reaching social impact pressed Islamists to respond. On February 17, 2004, the Dean of the Faculty of Islamic Law and Studies at Kuwait University, Dr. Muhammad al-Tabtaba'i, delivered a *fatwa* that prohibited "watching *Star Academy*, shown on LBC, participating in it, whether by calling or sending text-messages [or] ... supporting the program." Heads of households were enjoined to "prohibit their families from watching it ... [and] publics in Arab countries and beyond [to] boycott this and similar shows, because it constitutes a threat to Arab and Islamic moral values."[45] The ruling, which drew extra potency from the fact that the dean is a cousin of Salafi legislator Walid al-Tabtaba'i, galvanized Islamist opposition to *Star Academy*.

Nonetheless, as several media reported, the *fatwa* fell on deaf ears.[46] On March 8, 2004, the liberal newspaper *al-Qabas* published the results of a poll of five hundred citizens that confirmed *Star Academy*'s popularity in Kuwait. To the question "Do you watch *Star Academy*?," 80 percent of Kuwaitis polled answered "yes," 9 percent answered "sometimes," and only 11 percent said "no." When asked "Is *Star Academy* a purposeful program [*barnamaj hadef*]?," 92 percent said "no," 6 percent "yes," and 2 percent answered "don't know." Finally, when quizzed "Why do you watch *Star Academy*?," 60 percent of respondents answered "for excitement," 20 percent "to fill dead time," and 20 percent said "don't know."[47] With nearly 90 percent of Kuwaitis watching *Star Academy* at least sometimes, the show clearly struck a chord in Kuwaiti society.

The problem for the Islamists was that programs coming into Kuwait by satellite are virtually impossible to censor. With the Internet, DVDs, and mobile phones, even banning satellite dishes would not keep *Star*

---

[44] Mufreh, S. (March 7, 2004). *Star Academy*: A detailed reading on paper of details of life on the air (2): The program's critics are its most avid daily followers, in secret. *Al-Qabas* [Arabic], emphasis added.

[45] al-Shatti, S. (February 17, 2004). Muhammad al-Tabtaba'i to "son Bashar": Go back to your parents and do not be an instrument in the hands of religion's enemy with which they strike at Islam. *Al-Rai al-Aam* [Arabic].

[46] E.g., see Fatwas did not affect the popularity of *Star Academy* (April 5, 2004). *Al-Qabas*; and In spite of fatwas prohibiting it Arab youth are saying: Yes to Star Academy (April 4, 2004). *Al-Siyassah* [Arabic].

[47] Baji, A. (March 8, 2004). 80% of citizens watch *Star Academy*. *Al-Qabas* [Arabic].

Academy out of Kuwaiti society. From this perspective, Islamist fury at the reality show was a storm in a teapot. Rhetorical campaigns aside, there was not much al-Tabtaba'i and his followers could do.[48] That is, until the opportunity presented itself when a rumor of a forthcoming Kuwait concert by *Star Academy* finalists began circulating. The Islamists geared up for a replay of the *Superstar* battle that had unfolded a year earlier. Satellite television signals were untouchable; concerts held on Kuwaiti soil, however, were eminently vulnerable to attacks in the National Assembly.

THE KUWAITI REALITY TV MATCH, ROUND TWO: *STAR ACADEMY*

In May 2004 (approximately one month after the conclusion of the first season of *Star Academy*), with rumors of a *Star Academy* concert amplifying, the Ministry of Islamic Endowments Affairs issued a *fatwa* stipulating that "[I]t is not permitted for anyone to organize a concert under the name of *Star Academy* or any other name, as long as that concert includes forbidden practices, such as a woman's voice heard by men not related to her and *ikhtilat* between women and men with the unveiling of pudenda."[49] (*Pudenda* technically refers to female external genital organs, which in this context is used in reference to behavior considered shameful because sexually charged, and not because any sexual organs are actually visible.) For weeks, the Islamist block in the National Assembly threatened to hold hearings with the minister of information in the hot seat.[50] After the concert was held with tight police security and a demonstration opposing it, a statement by MP Faisal al-Muslim summarized the Islamists' perspective on *Star Academy*: "[T]his program is silly and indecent.

---

[48] In the meantime, opposition to *Star Academy* in neighboring Saudi Arabia, whose clerics are influential in Sunni Islamist circles in Kuwait, was expressed at the highest levels. On March 30, 2004, the Permanent Committee for Academic Research and the Issuing of Fatwas issued the fatwa discussed in detail in Chapter 5. Echoing the opinion of the Committee, on April 2, 2004, a prominent Imam in Riyadh, the Saudi capital, called *Star Academy* "Weapon of Mass Destruction."

[49] Kuwaiti fatwa prohibits Star Academy concert in Kuwait (May 25, 2004). *Al-Bayan* [Arabic].

[50] Threats to "grill" the minister of information were taken seriously because in Kuwaiti politics there is a history of ministers submitting to parliamentary questioning, and in 1999 then Minister of Justice Ahmed al-Kulaib's grilling led to a major political crisis in the country.

It promotes corrupt values that undermine the family and Islamic morals."[51]

The issue remained in the public eye into fall 2004, when Islamists finally acted upon their threats and submitted an official motion to "grill" Minister of Information Muhammad Abul Hassan: "There is a defect in the ministry's performance in protecting morality and the minister's supervision over the media is lacking and negative," stated al-Tabtaba'i.[52] In effect, the minister of information was forced out of his job, and one of the first decisions of the new minister, Anas al-Rasheed, was to announce in March 2005 the creation of a Committee to Monitor Video Clips, another controversial genre of popular culture.[53] When I interviewed the head of the committee, Moubarak al-Sahly, Director of Kuwait Television's Channel 4, in his office at the Kuwait Ministry of Information, I concluded that the committee was established to placate the Islamists by filtering what airs on national television, rather than to implement systematic censorship. "The National Assembly is very pleased with us,"[54] al-Sahly told me.

Even if censorship of satellite signals were technically feasible, enthusiastic fans of reality TV would have found a way to watch their favorite son in competition. Kuwaitis were frenzied by the stellar performance of their own Bashar al-Shatti, who rose to the *Star Academy* finale which he lost to a young Egyptian, Muhammad Attiya. Emerging as a national icon, al-Shatti rallied Kuwaitis in a heartfelt display of patriotism. On March 6, 2004 a columnist exclaimed:

> What Bashar accomplished for Kuwait through his participation in *Star Academy* exceeds the accomplishments of all the programs of Kuwait Television for many years. This is what a Lebanese female viewer told me . . . "We rediscovered Kuwait and Kuwaitis." . . . Looking at the text-messages that appear on the ticker at the bottom of the screen on the *Star Academy* channel [LBC Reality], we saw that the majority of viewers support Bashar. . . . Bashar

---

[51] Kuwaiti MPs to question minister over concert (May 9, 2004). *Arab News.* A few days earlier, an Islamist activist had filed a lawsuit against the cabinet for allowing *Star Academy* to hold a concert in Kuwait.

[52] Kuwait minister faces grilling over "failure to protect morality" (October 22, 2004). *Arab News.*

[53] I interviewed Moubarak al-Sahly, the head of the "Committee to Monitor Video Clips" and Director of Kuwait TV Channel 4, on November 15, 2005, at his office in the Ministry of Information in Kuwait City.

[54] Ibid.

solidified Kuwaiti national unity among young people . . . because he always insisted on reminding everyone of his Kuwaiti identity and on speaking with the Kuwaiti accent.[55]

In the last two weeks of *Star Academy*, Kuwaiti society was gripped. As a firsthand witness described it to me, "people in Kuwait were having home parties, a bunch of friends with a large screen in the middle, mobile in hand, voting non-stop; performances, dances, then they . . . vote; a woman told me she spent 350 KD [just under U.S.$1,200] for her cell phone bills for the last two weeks. One million calls went out from Kuwait on the last day of *Star Academy*! If you did not vote, you were an outcast."[56]

The rise of nationalistic sentiments among Kuwaitis overruled clerical injunctions to boycott the show. Ignoring a series of *fatwas* and speeches, Kuwaitis were taken by *Star Academy* mania. Voting for Bashar was seen as a badge of patriotism, a clear indication of national pride. Commenting on the hysteria that took over Kuwait during *Star Academy*'s concluding night and upon Bashar's return to Kuwait a few days later, a journalist opined:

> What happened . . . is that publics followed this program in an unprecedented way, across ages from 7 to 70 . . . and with a passion that we never noticed before especially with Kuwaiti citizens who are usually reserved and in the past would not even salute a singer in a face to face encounter. . . . But now, look at the thousands flooding the airport . . . the hundreds who surrounded Bashar's car as it made its way out of the airport . . . and the dozens who climbed on the roof of the car!!! And look at the thousands who partook in a parade that took to the streets after 9 pm and into the early hours of dawn, in that strange night?![57]

The reporter noted that popular acclamation of *Star Academy* raised questions about the real authority of clerics hostile to reality TV.

[55] Bashar . . . deserves it! (March 6, 2004). *Al-Qabas* [Arabic].

[56] Author interview with Hamed Sultan, Media PS, November 17, 2005, Salhiyya, Kuwait. Other industry people told me of rumors about a Kuwaiti woman who spent more than U.S.$3,200 during the same period, including my interview with Moussa, George, journalist, varieties page, *al-Hayat*, July 20, 2005, Beirut, Lebanon. Though I was unable to track down the woman in question to try and ascertain the amount, the fact that rumors of such wild figures achieve some credibility testifies to the amplitude of the phenomenon.

[57] al-Jasem, W. J. (April 6, 2004). If I were a clergyman. *Al-Watan*.

"If religious *shaykhs* . . . were to . . . correctly read implications . . . they would realize that the attack *fatwas* . . . excessive in their ferocity and exaggerated in their prohibitions . . . contributed to demean clergymen and to decrease people's engagement with religion and its *fatwas*."[58] The rise of nationalism occurred at the expense of religious authority – a nationalism embodied in a youthful, hip, charismatic, and patriotic young reality TV contestant. A few weeks after *Star Academy* concluded, a headline in *al-Qabas* proclaimed Bashar a "national symbol."[59] This is symptomatic of modernity's pull to integrate various ethnic and religious allegiances into the fold of the nation-state, though it is important to underscore that the cumulative impact of such sporadic performances of national identity are difficult to determine. Nonetheless, their recurrence testifies to unfinished nationalist projects.

What Kuwait as a nation should or should not be was at the heart of the debate over reality TV. The dilemma of whether to censor these programs or not is emblematic of the arduous task of negotiating a predominantly Western modernity. This balancing act is taken up first by policy makers. Ali al-Rayyes, Director of Kuwait TV Channel 1, the flagship institution in state-owned media, expressed that dilemma well when I interviewed him in his office:

> Kuwait TV is a pioneer in the Gulf. We aim to preserve Kuwaiti identity while embracing progress and globalization, but within limits and with balance. Yes, we seek to meet globalization but preserve our heritage, traditions and customs. . . . This is very difficult. We are an Islamic country. Balance is key. . . . We show music videos but with strict criteria to preserve morals. . . . We do not cover reality TV, even when they have Kuwaiti contestants. These shows are too bold, so we ignore them. We aim to preserve traditions.[60]

Wide access to privately owned satellite television channels, however, makes state media programming strategies irrelevant. Kuwaitis who gravitated *en masse* to reality TV shows are lost to state channels that refuse to air such shows. The hopelessness of government policies focused on banning or filtering media programs was underscored by

---

[58] Ibid.

[59] Fakher, M. (April 20, 2004). University students: Bashar is a national symbol and his victory is a triumph for Kuwait. *Al-Qabas* [Arabic].

[60] Author interview, Ali H. al-Rayes, General Director, Kuwait TV Channel 1, Ministry of Information, November 16, 2005, Kuwait.

Dr. 'Ali al-Tarrah, Dean of the Faculty of Social Sciences at Kuwait University, the state university. In an interview published in *al-Qabas*, al-Tarrah said that

> in our fast-paced and electronically interconnected world, we can no longer stand against the sweeping waves of globalization. . . . We ought not to fight these [reality TV] shows; rather we should consider airing shows that address young people's concerns, issues and aspirations. . . . The great attachment and broad viewership of these programs confirms that a great number of people wish for openness and interaction with the new world. We have to comprehend the fact that these programs have a strong attraction on young people, who express their repressed desires in their attachment to *Star Academy*.[61]

Arguing that *Star Academy* gives young Kuwaitis something vital that their society does not provide, al-Tarrah expressed bold yet indirect criticism of the Islamists when he said:

> . . . we are sick and tired of abusing talk about the *umma's* immovable values and principles [*thawabet*], as if these values and principles hang in the air, vulnerable to being uprooted.[62]

Clarifying his argument, al-Tarrah concluded:

> We are not advocating surrender to the new phenomenon . . . we have to present our youth new cultural models . . . but those who think of building iron curtains in the Internet era, have to understand that globalization has the power to penetrate borders, and that the era of taboos is gone.[63]

Noteworthy in al-Tarrah's views is his advocacy for "new cultural models" for Kuwaiti (and by extension Arab) youth. The notion that *Superstar* and especially *Star Academy* present a social and cultural model is at the heart of the controversy. As discussed in Chapter 4 in the context of Saudi Arabia, *Star Academy* does not merely depict behaviors or a lifestyle that some Kuwaitis might find objectionable; rather, the show makes contestants participate in interactive rituals that have the potential to subvert prevailing norms and values by socializing fans into alternative ways of thinking and acting. A Kuwaiti columnist expressed direct concerns about this particular issue:

---

[61] Iron curtains are irrelevant in the Internet era (March 8, 2004). *Al-Qabas* [Arabic].
[62] Ibid.
[63] Ibid.

In spite of everything that has been said about this program and the new foreign values that it disseminates on Arab families, even the most open among them, [Star Academy's] influence goes further that what has been said and what might be said. It is not only that it features scenes of interaction between young Arab men and women that contradicts the way we were brought up; it is only because it authenticates [yu'assel] these ways of interaction as an inescapable reality. . . .[64]

This authentication is all the more effective because like all ritual, its success depends on repetition. In *Star Academy*, the same rituals of interaction, competition, nomination, and eviction are repeated every week as they are watched by enraptured audiences. Some news reports told of a spillover effect from *Star Academy* into real life, for example at Kuwait University, where a twenty-one-year-old female student told reporters:

> Male and female students imitate personalities from *Star Academy*, and get attached to them to the point of obsession, to the extent that there is now a "*Star Academy* Part-2" in our faculty, through attire and comportment. . . .[65]

This provides anecdotal evidence supporting the notion of ritual authentication, a link between television watching and social behavior that we explored at length in the case of Saudi Arabia (Chapter 4). In combination, repetition and popularity legitimate the values and behaviors featured in the program, especially the fact that LBC promotions, and subsequently the Kuwaiti and Arab press, emphasized the "reality" aspects of the show. Another columnist succinctly captured the concern that:

> Though many channels are airing bolder programs . . . the danger of some scenes in *Star Academy* that some observers deem to be bold, resides in the fact that they are *real scenes with real people*, and not theatrical scenes that everyone knows are fiction within fiction.[66]

---

[64] Mufreh, S. (March 6, 2004). *Star Academy*: A detailed reading on paper of details of life on the air (1): Star Academy fills the Arab world and preoccupies its people between believing, denying, rejecting and agreeing. *Al-Qabas* [Arabic].

[65] "Reality" programs between rejection, acceptance . . . and embarrassment (February 27, 2004). *Al-Anbaa'* [Arabic].

[66] Reality . . . and fiction (March 6, 2004). *Al-Qabas* [Arabic], emphasis added.

Like al-Munajjid's critical analysis in the *Satan Academy* sermon in Saudi Arabia, the preceding column articulates concerns over the relationship between reality and reality TV by focusing on reality TV's generic characteristics and its claim to represent reality.

In this context, LBC's framing of *Star Academy* as a pedagogical enterprise (the words *academy* and *tullab* [students] to refer to participants) made it vulnerable to attacks by those who fear its influence on Kuwaiti youth. The Kuwaiti case crystallizes the implications of *Star Academy*'s pedagogical pretensions that remained nebulous in the Saudi case. In "Corruption Academy," a column in *al-Watan*, the author wrote:

> In yesteryears when we heard the word "academy" it conjured up . . . meaningful, and productive knowledge, beneficial to both individual and society; but *Star Academy* subverted this high term and brought it down to the ground, as its meaning becomes insolence and corruption . . . propagation and incitement to abandon Islamic identity and violate all the customs and traditions. . . .[67]

MEDIATING WESTERN MODERNITY

As I set out to explain in earlier chapters, a tradition-versus-modernity, Islamists-versus-Western culture framework can lead to, at best, a limited understanding of the Arab reality TV wars. Opposition to reality TV by Kuwaiti Islamists is best understood within the context of the ongoing selective adaptation of Western modernity in Kuwait, which unleashes fierce debates over what constitutes social reality. Critics of *Star Academy* fear that the learning rituals embedded in the show would lead Kuwaiti youth to abandon their traditions wholesale in order to adopt Western modernity wholesale. As one columnist put it, "most of our young people today wear a new garb of blind imitation, selling out their morals and chastity."[68] The implications are summed up rather dramatically in the following column about *Star Academy*:

> This program is more dangerous that pornographic movies, because this program gives young people the wrong education,

[67] al-Shammari, N. S. (March 23, 2004). Corruption academy. *Al-Watan* [Arabic].
[68] al-Mesh'el, M. N. (April 5, 2004). Star Academy . . . An art of moral decadence. *Al-Watan* [Arabic].

while the viewer of pornography knows that it is wrong even if he watches it, and as a result pornography does not cultivate in him values and traditions the way that *Star Academy* does.[69]

Revealingly, the author then sets up the West in a comparative angle, concluding that the process of selecting from Western modernity is flawed:

> The West progressed and prospered not via *Star Academy*, *Superstar*, and their ilk; rather it progressed through its advanced science and technology; unfortunately, we have developed a bad habit of importing Western values instead of beneficial Western science, and this is a very grave matter.[70]

Disregarding whether "values" and "science" are actually inseparable, this argument was made over and over again by Islamist and conservative Kuwaiti columnists, who essentially argued that selections from Western modernity have to be turned upside down – that existing criteria be discarded and new criteria adopted to guide Kuwaitis to selectively adapt aspects of Western modernity. Speaking about *Star Academy*, Nazhem al-Misbah, an Imam and preacher at the Ministry of Religious Affairs and Endowments, argued that

> if Muslims have to import from the developed world, let them import technology, medicine and knowledge in all its fields, and ... do not bring things of no benefit to them.[71]

Even Waleed al-Tabtaba'i, the Islamist leader in the National Assembly, apparently agreed that *Star Academy* does not represent Western culture *tout court*, but only its worst elements. He accused the show of cementing the view

> that the paths to success, creativity and distinction go not through academic and intellectual achievement and accomplishments in sports, but through lightness and spoiledness and satellite television channels.... [T]he argument that participation in those shows is an important representation of Kuwait ... [does not stand]. It is the son [author note: but not the daughter] who comes back home

---

[69] Baqer, Y. A. (April 2, 2004). Star Academy . . . and the Western invasion. *Al-Qabas* [Arabic].

[70] Ibid.

[71] al-Misbah: (Star Academy) against Islamic Shari'a and against human nature (March 8, 2004). *Al-Qabas* [Arabic].

with an academic diploma or a technical discovery prize or a medal for military valor or a distinguished athletic accomplishment. . . . What accomplishments result from gathering young men and women from throughout the Arab world in the interest of a show that serves Western culture at its worst?[72]

The West looms large in these arguments, underscoring the fact that Western modernity is an unavoidable source of norms that inform debates about Kuwaiti values and policies. A columnist who first argued that *Star Academy* was "a dangerous project whose objective is to finish off the morals of this *umma*. . . . This blind imitation of the West will transform Arab Islamic society to an old and weak society, poised to collapse at any moment," went on to cite Montesquieu, Gibbon, Spengler, and Toynbee regarding civilizational decay.[73] Western sources are invoked by critics of Western influence to support the argument that the West is a source of cultural corruption. Even for its opponents, the West is a compulsory detour in debates about their own societies.

One of the noteworthy differences between the cases of Bahrain (Chapter 2) and Saudi Arabia (Chapter 4), on the one hand, and the case of Kuwait, on the other hand, is that Kuwaiti liberals fought Islamist attacks more forcefully and more successfully than their Bahraini and Saudi counterparts. Unlike Bahrain, where *al-Ra'is* was shut down within a week of its launch, and unlike Saudi Arabia, where liberal columnists were for the most part timid and indirect in their criticism of Wahhabi attacks on *Star Academy*, in Kuwait reality TV generated a robust public debate, with liberals fending off attacks by al-Tabtaba'i and his allies against a concert by finalists from *Star Academy 5* in June 2008. (There was never any *Star Academy* concert in Saudi Arabia.) Why does Kuwait, a Gulf oil monarchy like Bahrain and Saudi Arabia, present a distinct case?

The answer lies in the fact that, unlike Bahrainis and Saudis, Kuwaitis have developed operative institutions. Chief among these are the National Assembly, which is stronger than its elected Bahraini counterpart and far more contrarian than the rubber-stamping appointed Shura Council in Saudi Arabia. Another important institution is Kuwait's constitution, which is widely respected, unlike in Bahrain, where the king has

---

[72] al-Tabtaba'i: Celebrating *Star Academy* sends the wrong message to Kuwaiti youth (April 4, 2004). *Al-Qabas* [Arabic].

[73] al-Qahs, M. F. (March 23, 2004). Star Academy made Islamic societies poised to fall and suffering from old age (al-kuhula). *Al-Watan* [Arabic].

manipulated it, and in Saudi Arabia, which does not have an actual constitution because official Wahhabiyya proclaims the Qur'an as the country's constitution.[74]

Also unique to Kuwait is the institution of the *diwaniyya*, a social and political gathering, historically for men, which operates as nodes of political discussion and socialization, information gathering and fact checking, and entertainment.[75] Press reports and field research indicate that many *diwaniyyas* hosted fierce debates about reality TV. News carried by television or the Internet often gains or loses credibility in *diwaniyyas*. In effect, they provide an alternative communication network to national and international media and a vetting process to the information these media distribute. Through the *diwaniyyas*, the advent of satellite television has created a dynamic link between mass and interpersonal communication. As Tétreault described them, "*diwaniyyas* help to mobilize activists, nationalize issues and personalities, and contribute to forming coherent, though far from unitary, perspectives on social and political life."[76] In the early post–independence day, *diwaniyyas* even operated to disseminate government policy initiatives. Each Kuwaiti city now has anywhere between fifteen and thirty *diwaniyyas*, and these are heavily attended: 60 percent of Kuwaitis attend them one to three times a week, and 66 percent of Kuwaitis agree they are essential to society.[77] In the last decade, Kuwaiti feminists like Rula Dashti have launched their own *diwaniyyas*, so this vital sociopolitical institution is no longer exclusive to men.[78]

Another important institution that sets Kuwait apart from its neighbors is the diverse, vibrant, and feisty press whose relative independence from government and clerics enables it to contribute effectively to national debates. As already discussed, the Kuwaiti press played an important role in the reality TV battles. Unlike the reality TV wars in Bahrain and especially in Saudi Arabia, where the debate occurred, for the most part, in terms that were general and broad, in Kuwait the issues at stake were spelled out clearly and consistently, articulating women's

---

[74] Crystall and al-Shayeji (1998) write that "the institutions around which there appears to be at least some consensus, consist of the constitution and a National Assembly (101).

[75] *Diwaniyyas* and equivalent gatherings exist in most Gulf countries, but in Kuwait they are more explicitly political.

[76] Tétreault, 2003, 38.

[77] al-Roomi, S. (2007). "Women, Blogs and Political Power in Kuwait," in *New Media in the New Middle East*, ed. P. Seib. New York: Palgrave Macmillan, 139–55.

[78] Tétreault, 2003.

political rights, relations with Saudi Arabia and Lebanon, the aspirations and frustrations of Kuwaiti youth, and the rival agendas of liberals and Islamists. The language used was significantly more hard-hitting than in Saudi Arabia and somewhat more incisive than in Bahrain. The level of boldness in Kuwaiti columns is rarely found in Bahrain and virtually inexistent in Saudi Arabia. Kuwaiti columns probing the effects of *Star Academy*, like those exploring the subversive ritual aspects of the show, were more specific and probing than in Bahrain and Saudi Arabia. Because of the national press institution, the Kuwaiti episode clarified the full implications of issues that remained vague in the Bahraini and Saudi cases.

Finally, Kuwait University has been a successful national institution in the sense that, unlike many Saudi universities, Islamists do not hold the same level of influence. Witness the sharply opposing opinions voiced by two Kuwait University deans. Whereas Dean al-Tabtaba'i, issued a *fatwa* attacking *Star Academy*, Dean al-Tarrah went on the record in opposition to censoring reality TV programs and advocated the development of alternatives to *Star Academy* for Kuwaiti youth.

These political and social institutions play a crucial role in mediating Western modernity and its attendant philosophies of gender, personhood, and nation. This process of social and cultural translation has three pivotal and interrelated aspects: the status of women, nationalism, and the new kinds of visibility created by people's interactions with the commercial and transnational Arab media landscape. In Kuwait and elsewhere in the region, gender is a lightning rod that attracts and commingles issues like Western influence, changing political and social norms, the Islamist and secular visions of the good society, and power struggles between executive and legislative branches. Gender is also central to the ways in which the new kinds of visibility brought by the pan-Arab media explosion are negotiated. The main objective of the Kuwaiti struggle for political rights is to empower women to step out of the private sphere of home and family into the public realm of discourse and governance. Reality TV adds further strain to the relation between the private and the public by exposing contradictions in that relation. In his interview about the social impact of *Star Academy*, Dr. al-Tarrah laid bare the paradoxes between private selves and public lives, prodding Kuwaitis to recognize that we are peoples who have become habituated to [social] schizophrenia, used to practice all our hobbies/desires in secret, so that individuals in our society carry numerous contradictions.... [79]

The battles over *Star Academy* and *Superstar* exposed the fact that what the Islamists accuse reality TV of bringing into Kuwaiti society was already present there before the advent of reality TV. This exposes the Islamists to ridicule by liberals who point to the fact that Islamists are increasingly divorced from the reality of Kuwaiti society. Muhammad al-Jasem put it to me this way: "If you go looking around in Kuwait, you see girls and boys together. This is not controllable. We still wear the mask of conservatism, but behind that mask, things are different."[80] In stirring the private-public nexus, reality TV is emblematic of the increasingly commercial and less manageable media environment in which Kuwait finds itself. For example, al-Rai TV, Kuwait's first private television channel, caused an outcry in 2005 when it aired a program featuring a transsexual man claiming intimate affairs with members of Kuwait's highest social and political echelons.[81] But whereas these shows air infrequently, reality TV has day by day, week by week, year after year been an accessory in transforming the ways that private life and the public realm interact. The full political implications of the changing boundary between private and public, reality and image, persons and nations, would become manifest during the Syrian-Lebanese media war that unfolded around *Superstar* and culminated during Beirut's "Independence Intifada," the topics of the two following chapters.

[79] Iron curtains, 2004.
[80] Author interview, Muhammad al-Jasem, Editor-in-Chief, *Meezan*, November 15, 2005, Kuwait.
[81] Author interview, Joumana Fehmi, Director of Programming and Production at al-Rai TV, Salhiyya, Kuwait, November 16, 2005.

CHAPTER SIX

A Battle of Nations: *Superstar* and the
Lebanon-Syria Media War

Two small spontaneous riots erupted in Beirut on a summer evening in 2003 over the results of *Superstar*, the Arabic version of *Pop Idol* (and *American Idol*). The first brawl occurred at the Beirut Hall, a concert venue where the *Superstar* semifinals had just concluded. Several people fainted, including the mothers of two semifinalists and the third semifinalist herself, who lost consciousness after learning she had moved on to the finale. The second scuffle unfolded one mile away, when fans of the ousted semifinalist gathered spontaneously in front of Future TV studios in the Spears neighborhood to protest the decision. An hour earlier, Future TV, the Lebanese channel owned by the family of Rafiq al-Hariri, had announced voting results of the semifinal. What gave the two commotions their poignancy was the fact that the Lebanese contestant Melhem Zayn was eliminated while the Syrian candidate Rowayda 'Attiyeh was elevated to the finale. Reactions to the victory of a Syrian contestant over a Lebanese one, on a Lebanese program, betrayed a complex political situation of Lebanese patriotism rising against protracted Syrian dominance. Though *Superstar* drew one of the largest pan-Arab audiences in history, the contentious events of August 11, 2003 would bring specifically Lebanese concerns to the program's forefront.

Events unfolding on and around *Superstar* from its first season in 2003 through its third in 2006 reflect the historic reversal in the Lebanese-Syrian relationship between those years. Syrian domination of Lebanese affairs grew during the Lebanon civil war (1975–1990) until Hafez al-Asad, a magnificent practitioner of divide-and-rule politics, sealed his dominion over Lebanon by joining the U.S.-led coalition that ousted Saddam Hussein's troops from Kuwait in 1991. During the 1990s, the Syrian regime controlled Lebanon indirectly through what became known as the troika system, a relationship between the Syrians on one side and the Lebanese president, prime minister, and speaker of the house on the other side. Because these three positions have traditionally been held by a Maronite Christian, a Sunni Muslim, and a Shi'i Muslim, respectively, the troika system enabled the Syrians at once to manipulate Lebanon's three most important government institutions and its three largest confessional groups.

When Emile Lahoud, then commander-in-chief of the Lebanese armed forces, was elevated to the Lebanese presidency in 1998, Syrian policy, at least officially, relinquished the troika system and established a police state in Lebanon similar to the one in Syria. Lahoud was Syria's strongman in Lebanon. During his tenure, various intelligence and security "services" became all-powerful, reminding the Lebanese of authoritarian slippages during the 1958 to 1964 tenure of President Fu'ad Shihab and leading some observers to conclude that the Syrian regime had cloned itself in Lebanon.[1] Nonetheless, from his headquarters in the Lebanese border city of 'Anjar, the head of Syrian intelligence in Lebanon, Rustum Ghazalah, was in effect the country's proconsul. By summer 2003, when the *Superstar* riots occurred, Syrian control had grown to an extent that many Lebanese believed that the Syrian *mukhabarat*, the feared secret police, decided even the most trivial issues in Lebanon.

SUPERSTAR 1 AND THE FRAUGHT SYRIAN-LEBANESE RELATION

It was in this context that within minutes of the announcement of the *Superstar* semifinal results by Future TV executives, rumors had spread by text messaging that Syrian intelligence officers, seconded by their Lebanese counterparts, had pressured Future TV managers to elevate the Syrian contestant to the finale, though viewers' votes should ostensibly determine which candidate is terminated. Rumors of Syrian intervention were fueled by an ill-timed power cut and widespread disruptions to telephone and Internet communications, which prevented thousands of Lebanese from voting, and by claims of viewers who, after voting for Zayn, received text-message replies thanking them for voting for one of his opponents. Feeding the rumor mill, Future TV's Web site, through which viewers could cast their vote, was down for most of the day on Monday. Nadim al-Munla, then Future TV's general manager, denied

---

[1] Ghassan Salamé, the Paris-based political scientist and former Lebanese minister of culture, used the cloning metaphor in various writings and interviews.

that any political manipulations had taken place and explained Zayn's loss by the small size of the Lebanese population.[2] Other rumors concerned Jordanian intervention through Rafiq al-Hariri's wife Nazik, who is of Jordanian descent. The media contributed to the rumors. During a live interview with Zayn on a morning program on Future TV, juror Tania Mer'eb called to say that "Melhem's elimination was unthinkable" and demanded to "know what happened."[3] In Shmestar, Zayn's hometown in the Beqa' Valley, angry mobs roamed the streets and assaulted Lebanese soldiers with sticks when Zayn lost. The right-of-center Lebanese daily *Annahar* (*The Day*) initiated an online poll as to whether Zayn was eliminated under political pressure. A Kuwaiti paper said Queen Rania of Jordan had ordered free phone lines be dedicated for Jordanians to vote for Carazon but a Jordanian telecommunications official denied the story. It is a testament to the global reach of Arab satellite television that in several Gulf countries there were small protests backing Zayn and that the Lebanese community in Brazil issued statements denouncing *Superstar 1* voting results.[4]

Syria and Lebanon have long been uneasy neighbors. Syrian resentment against the French carving of Lebanon out of historic Syria as a homeland for the Maronite Christians is compounded by geopolitical concerns about Lebanon being Syria's "soft flank," vulnerable to Israeli attacks. Syrian troops entered Lebanon in the 1970s with Arab Dissuasion Forces charged with separating feuding Lebanese militias and stayed on until the 1989 Ta'if agreement legitimated their presence in Lebanon by making the "redeployment" of Syrian troops contingent on negotiations between the Syrian regime and Lebanese governments, which Syria knew it would de facto control. Nonetheless, for six and a half decades after the two countries achieved independence from the French mandate, Syria persistently refused to open an embassy in Beirut, underscoring its view that Lebanon is an illegitimate nation-state. (Relations between the two countries have thawed somewhat, and the two governments decided in late 2008 to exchange ambassadors, but tensions persist.) Short of annexing Lebanon, the Asad regime – *père et fils* – was able to retain significant influence in Lebanon's fractured political landscape. The Lebanese, in turn, have had a complicated

---

[2] "La Future Television dément les accusations don't elle fait l'objet" (August 13, 2003). *L'Orient-Le Jour*.

[3] Ibid.

[4] Jaber, H. (August 17, 2003). "Army Called Out as Pop Idol Starts Battle in Beirut." *Sunday Times*, 25.

relationship with the Syrian leadership, variously soliciting or opposing their bigger, more powerful neighbor. Some Lebanese, especially but not exclusively Christians, have historically fought Syrian influence in Lebanon because they perceive it as an existential threat. Others, especially but not exclusively Muslims, have had strong social and political affinities with Syria, whose self-proclaimed status as the "Beating Heart of Arabism" they admired, Arab "authenticity" they valued, and *mukhabarat* they feared. But after a quarter century of heavy Syrian military presence many Lebanese across confessional and political persuasions felt that Syrian soldiers had overstayed their welcome.

When Future TV adapted the British Fremantle Media–owned *Pop Idol* format into the Arabic *Superstar*, it stirred inter-Arab rivalries and various expressions of nationalism by Arab governments and populations alike. Launched with great success in 2003, *Superstar 1* propelled Future TV to the top of Arab television ratings. Thousands of young Arab men and women auditioned to participate in the program as millions watched, cheered, and voted for their favorite contestants. *Superstar 1*, whose stage design and production style resembled *American Idol*'s, featured singers performing on stage under the scrutinizing eye of three jurors and a studio audience. The program was considered a reality TV show because segments featured putatively spontaneous backstage statements by the contestants and ostensibly unscripted social interactions among them, and viewers voted for their favorite contestants. The reality TV label came to encompass, in the parlance of the Arab media industry and in the mind of many viewers, any show that features amateurs and voting by viewers.

The jury was composed of three Arab show-business personalities led by Elias al-Rahbani, member of Lebanon's most-famous musical family, who donned edgy formal wear to play the role of juror-in-chief, a workable if a bit contrived version of Simon Cowell, the acerbic music producer and jury leader in *American Idol*. Sitting between two lesser Arab musical figures like a reigning patriarch, Rahbani evaluated performances in public pseudodeliberations with his cojurors, the Kuwaiti composer 'Abdullah al-Qa'ood and the Lebanese model and fashion designer Tania Mer'eb in the first season, then Lebanese composer Ziyad Boutros and others in later seasons. Any resemblance to Cowell notwithstanding, the Arabic *Superstar* jurors eschewed the public humiliations that Cowell inflicted on most *American Idol* contestants. In contrast, jurors on *Superstar* were didactically supportive, with lengthy explanations and suggestions for improvements preceding elimination. In addition to two program hosts, one male and one female, a thirty-five-member strong orchestra accompanied contestants live.

Superstar 1 was a pan-Arab event, capturing some of the largest audiences and highest advertising rates in Arab television. A thirty-second advertisement on the program fetched U.S.$12,000, a regional record. Around thirty million viewers watched the finale of *Superstar 1*.[5] Out of the 4.8 million votes, 52 percent went to the Jordanian winner.[6] In addition to contemporary pop songs, the repertoire included Arab classics by Umm Kulthum, Fayruz, 'Abdulhalim Hafez, and Farid al-Atrash, sure to attract older viewers. An intensive television and print promotional campaign preceded the first episode, framing the program as an artistic competition for the title of "Superstar of the Arabs," invoking the fabled pan-Arab imagined community stretching from Morocco to Iraq, an audience of 200 million that in size, if not in purchasing power, rivals the largest linguistically based audiences in the world. Unlike *Star Academy 1*, journalists and the general public perceived *Superstar 1* to feature what media and cultural critics that I interviewed in Beirut, Dubai, and Kuwait called "superb" or "real" voices.[7] In contrast with the contrived, spectacular performances in *Star Academy 1*, where stage antics, out-sized personalities, and erotic tension factored into the competition, in *Superstar*, contestants won or lost based on their voices and the merits of their performances. The critical and public consensus was that *Superstar*

---

[5] Maalouf, L. (January 14, 2004). "Western Television Craze Makes Assured Debut on Region's Networks." *Daily Star*.

[6] Abou Nasr, M. (February 4, 2004). "Who Wants to Be a Superstar? 12,000 Do." *Daily Star*. According to the same source, the fever carried through into the next season: More than 40,000 auditioned for *Superstar 2*.

[7] These author interviews include Ibrahim Mshawrab, Media and Variety Editor, *Al-Bayan*, Dubai, June 17, 2005; Joseph Bou Nassar, Media Editor, *Annahar*, Beirut, August 10, 2005; Rasha al-Atrash, Media Page Editor, *Assafir*, July 20, 2005; Maher al-Shawwa, *Dalil Annahar*, Beirut, August 1, 2005; Aisha al-Rshaid, journalist, *al-Watan*, Kuwait, November 16, 2006; Vicky Habib, *al-Hayat*, Beirut, July 19, 2005; and Hanadi Issa, *Laha Magazine*, Beirut, July 19, 2005. In published interviews, many Arab singers expressed a similar opinion. See: "Walid Tawfiq: Superstar presented distinguished voices and Star Academy did not" (April 30, 2004). *Al-Bayan* [Arabic]; "The Lebanese artist Melhem Zayn: Beautiful voices are absent from Star Academy" (April 23, 2004). *Asharq al-Awsat* [Arabic]; al-Najmi, Hassan (March 24, 2005). "Are you happy now? Muhammad 'Attiya sings for Diana Carzon." *Al-Riyadh* [Arabic]; and "Ruwaida 'Attiya: I cherish singing and do not seek fame or money" (May 27, 2004). *Al-Bayan* [Arabic]. For analysis, see al-Jacques, Sana' (August 13, 2004). The equation merges geography and economics in rumor wars: Superstar 2 between the authenticity of the voice and the majority of votes. *Asharq al-Awsat* [Arabic].

was a more "authentic" singing competition, less tainted by the flashy vicissitudes of show business.[8]

As weeks passed and suspense mounted, however, politics overshadowed artistic authenticity. *Superstar 1* evolved from an artistic competition between individual contestants to an international rivalry in which each contender was performing primarily as a representative of his or her country.[9] From the early weeks of the program, viewers could see frenetic flag waving in the ostensibly multinational studio audience, and text messages feeding into television tickers featured patriotic statements flanked with small national flags. Arab media reported that voting followed national bases: according to Future TV's numbers, Jordan's Carazon won 84 percent of votes cast in Jordan, Syria's Attiyeh won 97 percent of the votes called in from Syria, and Lebanon's Zayn won 79 percent of votes from Lebanon.[10] Newspaper columns throughout the Arab world were abuzz with excitement, speculation, and political allegories. Because viewers could vote as many times as they wanted, wealthy inhabitants of Gulf countries like Kuwait, Saudi Arabia, and the United Arab Emirates wielded disproportionate influence over the fate of *Superstar* contestants. But the jury acted ostensibly as a filter when it eliminated the weakest contestants, ensuring that artistic talent would be rewarded and mitigating the nationality factor in viewers' votes.

Once the Lebanese contestant Melhem Zayn was voted out, competition intensified between the Jordanian Diana Carazon and the Syrian Roweida Attieh. The escalating frenzy surrounding *Superstar*, masterfully stoked by Future TV's marketing campaign, stirred up the historically strained relationship between Jordan and Syria. Jordanian-Syrian tensions go back to debates about Arab unity that preoccupied Arab elites between the two World Wars. Since then, Syrian-Jordanian relations have fluctuated between military threat and strategic collaboration: in 1970, Hafez al-Asad sent two army brigades into Jordan to support the Palestinians against Jordan's Hashemite monarchy, in contrast

---

[8] The popular favorable response to *Superstar* may have something to do with viewers' familiarity with *Studio al-Fann*, a singing competition that started on Télé-Liban in the 1970s.

[9] Among other reports on this issue, see Bassem Mroue, Arab world's version of "American Idol" has nationalistic bent, and vehement fans (April 18, 2003). Beirut: Associated Press; and Arab idol a battle of nations (August 18, 2003). Beirut: Associated Press.

[10] "La Future Television dément les accusations don't elle fait l'objet." *L'Orient-Le Jour*, August 13, 2003.

to the late 1970s when Jordan and Syria cooperated in political, military, and economic matters. The Jordanian-Syrian "cold war" continues today, with Jordan fretting about Syrian control of the waters of the Yarmouq River through a series of dams and Syria's protracted extrajudicial incarceration of around seven hundred Jordanians. In turn, Syrian leaders resent the Hashemite monarchy's historically compromising stance toward Israel and scorns Jordan's peace treaty with Israel, its military cooperation with Turkey, and its close relation with the United States. *Superstar 1* unsettled the Jordanian-Syrian relationship, already one of the most tumultuous between two Arab states.[11] More recently, tensions have escalated since Jordan and Syria have been on opposite sides of the contest between the United States and Iran for supremacy in the Middle East.

With this charged history in the background, *Superstar 1* fever gripped Syria and Jordan. In Syria, telecommunications companies installed billboards on Damascene thoroughfares promoting the Syrian contestant and exhorting Syrians to perform their national duty and vote for her. In interviews with Western press agencies, Syrians on the street were unequivocal: they were voting for her because she was Syrian; the fact that she was a good performer was just fine, but they were primarily motivated to participate because of the contestant's national identity,[12] which was made easier when telecommunications companies dedicated (and subsidized) mobile telephone lines for voting in *Superstar*. The Arab press described rumors of a full-fledged national mobilization in Jordan: King 'Abdullah was rumored to have instructed his military to vote for Carazon, the Jordanian candidate who ultimately was crowned "Superstar of the Arabs." Businesses exploited the situation as a marketing opportunity: an ice cream parlor offered free ice cream for those who voted for Carazon, and a car dealership advertised a 2003 sedan in the daily *ad-Dustour* (*The Constitution*) that it would give to Carazon.[13] Jordan's telecommunications companies Fastlink and MobileCom, poised to make large profits from their share of the voting bills, pledged "full support" in an advertising campaign urging readers to vote for the

[11] Ryan, C. R. (2006). "The Odd Couple: Ending the Jordanian-Syrian 'Cold War.'" *The Middle East Journal* 60 (1): 33 [article 33–56]. See also Brand, L. A. (1994). "Economics and Shifting Alliances: Jordan's Relations with Syria and Iraq, 1975–81," *International Journal of Middle East Studies* 26 (3): 393–413, and Brand, L. A., *Jordan's Inter-Arab Relations: The Political Economy of Alliance-Making*. New York: Columbia University Press, 152–96.

[12] Arab idol a battle of nations. Beirut: Associated Press, August 18, 2003.

[13] Ibid.

Jordanian contestant.[14] A Jordanian newspaper depicted what can only be described as national mobilization:

> Jordanians from all walks of life, as well as companies, state television and the press have all put their weight behind Carzon for the show's final segment Sunday. . . . MobileCom ads show Carzon wearing a long traditional embroidered dress with the caption: "*A beautiful Jordanian dream*" or "Give your vote to Diana for our happiness to be complete." . . . In the run-up to Sunday's finale, Jordanian newspapers and Jordan television have also joined the fray. The latter dedicating an entire programme to Carzon with clips showing her asking for support . . . "*Voting for Diana is a national duty*," particularly after the [prejudice] expressed by some of the other contestants.[15]

Superstar 1 was "a Battle of Nations."[16] Arab regimes, political parties, and businesses rallied around contestants in a symbolic battle made all the more significant by the show's mammoth pan-Arab audience. Unlike the fiery broadcasts of Gamal 'Abdulnasser's Voice of the Arabs radio, which addressed all Arabs as members of a single community, *Superstar 1* viewers and voters followed narrower national affiliations, undermining claims of a satellite television–driven pan-Arab unity "from the [Atlantic] Ocean to the [Persian] Gulf," as the Arab saying goes. For a time, the frenzy of viewing and voting in popular reality television programs eclipsed regionally salient issues like the plight of Palestinians and Iraqis under occupation and filled the airwaves with more provincial affirmations of patriotism. This followed a trend in Arab history, where expressions of national pride and state sovereignty coexist with pan-Arab claims and aspirations. Although national pride was essential to governing nascent Arab nation-states, invoking a broader Arab nationalism gave leaders symbolic capital that they could expend in various political areas.[17]

The political controversy around *Superstar 1* absorbed moral and cultural objections to the show. Though the Islamic Action Front, a Jordanian

---

[14] Pan Arab song contest fuels passions in Jordan (August 17, 2003). *Jordan Times*. In order to vote, viewers call "toll" numbers, with a charge several times higher than the price of a normal phone call. Profits are divided according to preset agreements between television channels and telecommunications companies.

[15] Ibid., emphasis added.

[16] Arab idol, 2003.

[17] See Barnett, M. (1998). *Dialogues in Arab Politics*. New York: Columbia University Press.

group affiliated with the Muslim Brotherhood, issued a "Press Statement Surrounding the Program *Superstar*" condemning the show for "promoting cultural globalization" and the Americanization of Islamic values, the debate around *Superstar* in Jordan was squashed by a groundswell of patriotic pride when a Jordanian won the competition. By the time Future TV began casting for *Superstar 2*, the show had become a pan-Arab legend. According to Future TV figures, sixty thousand hopefuls applied to audition, six times more than applied the first season. Only forty thousand actually auditioned and eighty-three were selected to be part of the final competition (12 were selected in Jordan, 8 in Dubai, 10 in Egypt, 8 in Bahrain, 14 from Syria, 1 from Libya, and 19 from Lebanon, in addition to 12 Lebanese from France).[18]

SYRIA FROM HEGEMONY TO VULNERABILITY

In *Superstar 2*, broadcast in 2004, a young Palestinian from the West Bank town of Salfit, 'Ammar Hassan, quickly became a front-runner. When he performed, the twelve thousand residents of Salfit stayed indoors, glued to their screens: when he rose to the finals against the Libyan Ayman al-A'tar, two thousand people gathered in a Salfit park to watch together on a large screen, chanting "'Ammar, 'Ammar, Superstar." The then Palestinian leader Yasir Arafat reportedly phoned 'Ammar to encourage him[19] and asked his cabinet members to vote for him.[20] The mobile provider Jawwal offered a 20 percent discount on calls to vote for 'Ammar.[21] In reaction to *Superstar 2*'s popularity among the Palestinians, the Movement of the Islamic Resistance known as Hamas issued a statement condemning the Palestinian frenzy around *Superstar*. "Our people," Hamas argued, "are in need of heroes, resistance fighters, and contributors to building the country and are not in need of singers, corruption mongers, and advocates of immorality."[22] The young contestant's father had a different view: "Palestinians," he told the *New York Times*, "wherever they are . . . see Ammar as an ambassador for them. . . . The Palestinian people are not just throwing stones and bombs. In the struggle we have educated

[18] Abou Nasr, M. (February 4, 2004). Competition is intense for slots on talent show's 2nd season. *Daily Star*.

[19] Erlanger, S. (August 22, 2004). "Palestinian Carries a Tune and the Hope of His People," *New York Times*, 10.

[20] "An Arab Idol Is Crowned" (August 30, 2004). *New York Times*, 8.

[21] Erlanger, 2004.

[22] Habeas, A. (August 23, 2004). "Palestinian Singing Finalist Tunes into Nationalism," Associated Press/*Boston Globe*.

people – doctors, intellectuals, musicians – and we have a singer. Ammar, too, is a defender of his people."[23] Yet the young man eschewed such nationalist sympathies, saying "I want to win for my talent, and don't want to win on the back of my people and my cause."[24] Speculations that 'Ammar would win because of Arab sympathy toward the Palestinians were countered by rumors that Libya's Mu'ammar al-Qaddhafi was investing millions in advertising, free telecommunications services, and other enticements in support of Ayman al-A'tar, the Libyan who faced 'Ammar in the finale. During the final week of *Superstar 2*, when more than 3.2 million votes were cast, the eccentric Libyan leader invited the two finalists to have dessert with him in his traditional tent. In the end, presumed pan-Arab sympathy for the Palestinians was not enough, and 'Ammar lost with 46 percent of the votes to the Libyan Ayman al-A'tar, who garnered 54 percent.[25]

Like the *al-Ra'is* and *Star Academy* controversies, the commotion surrounding *Superstar* was a battle between various political, clerical, and business actors, rather than a simple antagonism between controversial forms of popular culture and doctrinaire speakers in the name of Islam. Reactions to *Superstar* favored political and national anxieties over moral concerns because *Superstar*'s production format featured candidates performing on a stage facing a jury from a distance, and, unlike *al-Ra'is* or *Star Academy*, it did not entail the kinds of physical interaction between men and women that provoked outrage among Gulf Islamists. That groups as disparate as Hamas, business owners, and governments felt compelled to intervene testifies to the power that these groups ascribe to popular culture and to the political and economic advantages they believe they can reap from participating in the debate over Arab reality TV. As a highly visible, immensely popular media event, *Superstar* was a magnet for social and political actors who knew that having a voice in the debate would give them greater media coverage and better opportunities to mobilize their supporters.

Though rhetorical struggles over *Superstar 1* and *Superstar 2* reflected long-standing tensions within and between Arab countries, *Superstar 3*, broadcast in 2006, occurred in the newly polarized climate of the aftermath of Rafiq al-Hariri's assassination in Beirut on February 14, 2005, and was therefore caught in the recently heightened turbulence of Lebanese-Syrian politics. The radical political changes that occurred in

[23] Erlanger, 2004.
[24] Ibid.
[25] An Arab Idol, 2004; Erlanger, 2004.

Lebanon between *Superstar 1* and *Superstar 3* form the backdrop of the 2005 Syrian-Lebanese media war. When Lebanese viewers demonstrated against what they perceived to be the Syrian-coerced elimination of their contestant in August 2003, *Superstar* entered the fray of Lebanese-Syrian relations. Differences between the 2003 and 2006 seasons of *Superstar* clearly and publicly reflect the reversal in Lebanese-Syrian relations. In 2003, Syrian hegemony over Lebanese affairs was uncontested given Syria's political and military domination. The Syrian-forced unconstitutional extension of President Emile Lahoud's mandate in 2004 confirmed Syrian hegemony but also marked its peak. Imposed on the Lebanese political class by Syrian fiat, the extension triggered public expressions of opposition to Syria, notably moving Rafiq al-Hariri, Lahoud's nemesis, into undeclared opposition to Syria's role in Lebanon. Al-Hariri's assassination intensified anti-Syrian sentiment and contributed to the withdrawal of Syrian troops from Lebanon in April 2005 under combined pressure from the United States, France, Saudi Arabia, and Lebanese street demonstrations. (Chapter 7 focuses on reality TV's embroilment in the "Independence Intifada.")

The assassination of al-Hariri, Lebanon's billionaire ex–prime minister, brought Lebanese resentment toward Syria to a boiling point as a Syrian role in the assassination was widely assumed. More importantly, it pushed the majority of Lebanon's Sunni Muslim community, which al-Hariri represented at the highest level in the Lebanese polity, into opposition to Syria. A media war ensued between the two countries, fomented by street demonstrations in Beirut and by the internationalization of the crisis made evident by multiple official statements by the United States, France, and Iran. In Lebanon, Future TV and its sister publication *al-Mustaqbal* (*The Future*), both owned by the al-Hariri family, joined LBC and the right-of-center Lebanese daily *Annahar* in attacking the Syrian regime and its interference in Lebanese affairs. *Annahar* already had a history of criticism of Syria, regularly publishing columns by Michel Kilu and other Syrian dissidents. Its erstwhile editor-in-chief Gebran Tuayni penned a famous "Open Letter to Dr. Bashar al-Asad" in 2000 asserting that "Lebanon is not a Syrian province," thus breaking the taboo against public criticism of Syria's control of Lebanon. Tuayni was elected to the Lebanese Parliament in 2005 only to be assassinated in December of that year. He was the second *Annahar* journalist to be killed in 2005 after his colleague Samir Qassir was liquidated by a car bomb. A systematic critic of the Syrian regime and a Lebanese with Syrian-Palestinian parentage, Qassir had played a leading role in organizing the anti-Syrian Beirut demonstrations earlier that year.

With the Arab media "revolution" in the middle of its second decade, Lebanese television talk shows posed a more concrete threat to the rulers of Damascus than columns in *Annahar* and *al-Mustaqbal*, which were easily banned from being distributed in Syria. LBC and Future TV have influential satellite channels and are not easily kept out of national borders. Like many Arab viewers, Syrians gravitated to LBC's entertainment programs though they were aware of LBC's historically anti-Syrian politics. Since its founding in 1985 as the mouthpiece of the Lebanese Forces, a Christian-Nationalist wartime militia, LBC had been critical of Syrian influence in Lebanon. The Arab world's oldest private and continuously broadcasting television channel was subjected to continuous harassment and several attempts to shut it down by Syria's Lebanese clients, but, through shifting political alliances and financial partnerships with Saudi tycoons, LBC survived. To Syrian viewers, the surprise came from Future TV when the channel's hitherto accommodating editorial line toward Syria turned vitriolic in the aftermath of al-Hariri's assassination. In its newscasts, talk shows, patriotic music videos, and virtually all other programs, Future TV became a full-time critic of the Syrian regime, unifying its terrestrial and satellite operations for that purpose. A new nightly talk show, *The Crime against Lebanon*, hosted by pro-al-Hariri journalist Faris Khashan, featured intense criticism of Syrian intelligence officers and politicians, who, as a result, were compelled to phone in to Lebanese talk shows to defend their actions toward Lebanon. Syrian figures that only a few months earlier enjoyed full hegemony over Lebanon were now on the defensive.[26]

It is therefore no surprise that newspapers talked of a "divorce" between Future TV and the Syrian public, who expressed dismay and disappointment at Future TV's campaign in a couple of demonstrations (likely government orchestrated) and public statements to the media.[27] In the meantime, the intelligentsia at the nexus of the Saudi-Lebanese connection (see Chapter 3) gleefully commented on Syrian president Bashar al-Asad's appeals to Egyptian and Saudi leaders to muzzle Lebanese

---

[26] Syrian Interior Minister Ghazi Kan'an, previously commander of Syria's *mukhabarat* in Lebanon, called Christian-owned Voice of Lebanon to defend his record and apologize to the Lebanese for "any harm done," hours before "committing suicide" in his Damascus office.

[27] Author interview, 'Ayntrazi Tariq, General Manager, Future TV, December 20, 2005, Dubai, UAE.

media attacks on the Damascus leadership. The Syrian government press, led by the daily *al-Ba'th* [Resurrection], was replete with columns accusing the anti-Syrian Lebanese of ingratitude and betrayal. Even on the few satellite channels relatively sympathetic to Syria such as al-Jazeera, New TV, and Iran's Arabic-language satellite channel al-'Alam, Syrian journalists and politicians were defensive. The Syrian-Lebanese media war became a pan-Arab news story distinct from the political events and positions at its foundation. That the media war became a story in and of itself leads us to ask why the Syrians reacted with such intensity to the Lebanese media campaign. After all, Lebanon posed no military threat to Syria, and the Iraq quagmire had dimmed prospects of a U.S.-led "regime change" in Damascus. Why, then, did the Syrian leadership take the Lebanese media attacks so seriously?

The answer lies first in the Arab political environment, where the ability to deploy the symbols of Arabism has historically been an instrument of power and influence in inter-Arab relations. "Arab politics," wrote the political scientist Michael Barnett, "was symbolic politics,"[28] an observation that remains largely true – in the Arab world and elsewhere – even after the demise of Arab nationalism. Syria's leaders have consistently legitimated their rule by invoking their commitment to Arabism. Accusations by Lebanese media that the Syrian regime was behind the assassination of al-Hariri – a Sunni Arab, a self-made billionaire, and, in the eyes of many, an icon of Arab success – challenged Syria's view of itself as the heart of Arabism and made Syria vulnerable to rhetorical sanctions. Even more dangerous was the prospect that the Lebanese media campaign, which had a wide reach into Syria, could undermine the regime from within. The Syrian regime is, by its very nature, particularly vulnerable to media attacks. If, as the political scientist Lisa Wedeen argued, Hafez al-Asad's cult was in itself a strategy of domination "generating a politics of public dissimulation in which citizens act *as if* they revere the leader,"[29] then the Lebanese media campaign directly undermined al-Asad's grip on power. In this case it even posed an existential threat to the regime by denigrating the person of Bashar al-Asad in addition to his policies. Besides, at the time of his death al-Hariri had extensive connections with the urban Sunni Syrian bourgeoisie. Sunnis outnumber 'Alawis six to one in Syria and of Syria's various groups pose the only serious threat to the minority 'Alawi

---

[28] Barnett, 1998, 42.
[29] Wedeen, L. (1999). *Ambiguities of Domination: Politics, Rhetoric and Symbols in Contemporary Syria*. Chicago: University of Chicago Press, 6.

regime. As a regionally visible and geographically proximate symbol of Arab Sunni power, al-Hariri was from Asad's perspective a potential troublemaker.

The Syrian leadership's sense of vulnerability was heightened by its inability to mount an effective campaign to counter Lebanese media attacks. Syrian media were in the midst of a profound schizophrenia. Syrian *musalsalat* (television serials) were considered among the best in the Arab world, eclipsing even their famed Egyptian counterparts, largely due to the 1991 Syrian Investment Law Number 10, which eased restrictions on the production and distribution of television drama. The law enabled partnerships between the state and private writers and directors, who received assistance in return for rights of first broadcast on state television. Television drama boomed also because it attracted "investors" associated with key regime figures such as a son of the erstwhile vice-president and now-exiled opposition figure 'Abdulhalim Khaddam, who owned several production and distribution companies.[30] In spite of regime-associated owners, the less-restrictive atmosphere drew filmmakers and writers whose training in Soviet film realism led to stunning videography, solid dialogue, and engaging treatment of historical themes. This in turn attracted television programmers from the oil-rich Gulf countries, who filled their Ramadan schedules with Syrian drama. Increased profits and recognition emboldened the industry to tackle controversial contemporary issues such as government corruption, terrorism, and AIDS. In recent years, for example, drama series about terrorism directed by the Syrian Najdat Anzour became pan-Arab events, airing on several terrestrial and satellite channels and animating editorial pages across the region. This success rattled the Egyptian television industry but compelled venerable figures like Muhammad 'Ukasha, Egypt's leading drama writer and director, to collaborate with Syrian actors and producers.

In sharp contrast with the remarkable success of Syrian television drama, Syrian news and public affairs have suffered a protracted crisis. The Syrian Broadcasting Organization was founded in 1946 as the official state-owned radio service and in its first decade developed broadcasts in English, French, Hebrew, and Turkish. Syrian television, launched in 1960, benefited from the ill-fated union with Egypt called the United Arab Republic (1958 to 1961) when Egypt had the most developed media in the Arab world. Syrian radio and television followed the Nasserist propaganda model, which

---

[30] See Kawakibi, S. "Le Rôle de la télévision dans la relecture de l'histoire. *Monde arabe Maghreb Mashrek* 158 (Oct.–Dec. 1977): 47–55.

persisted after the United Arab Republic ended in 1961. There were no expansions in television broadcasting in the 1960s and 1970s because of economic problems compounded by Syria's costly participation in the 1967 and 1973 wars. When signal spillover from Jordanian, Israeli, and Turkish television compelled the Syrian regime to launch color broadcasting in 1979, the U.S. International Communication Agency (later the U.S. Information Agency) lent Syrian television a lighting expert because Syrian technicians did not know how to light the news set for color television.[31] Though Law 10 eased restrictions on television drama production in 1991, the Syrian Satellite Channel went on air in the late 1990s, and various privately owned Syrian satellite channels attempted to attract viewers, by 2009 the overall structure of Syrian television remains unchanged.

That the Syrian press, in its three official organs *Tishreen* (*November*), *al-Thawra* (*Revolution*) and *al-Ba'th*, remains largely immune to this debate speaks volumes about the arduous road ahead for would-be media reformers. Syrian journalists have written about the issue in pan-Arab or Lebanese newspapers such as *al-Hayat*, *al-Quds al-Arabi*, and *Annahar*. As a result, those among them living in Syria have been harassed or imprisoned, like Ibrahim al-Hamidi, a prominent Syrian journalist and *al-Hayat* Damascus bureau chief, who was later released under a presidential pardon dressed up as a court decision. Headlines about Syrian media are revealing: "Will Syrian Media Get Out of the Cave?," "It Wishes It Could Go Back to the Pre-Print Era: How Do Syrian Media Confront Reality," or "Syrian Media Out of (Touch With) Its Epoch."[32] Consider this article by Anwar al-Qassem, a Syrian writing in the London-based *al-Quds al-Arabi* daily newspaper:

> Have you ever seen a man coming from the jungles of Africa carrying a mobile telephone that he is unable to operate? This is the current situation of Syrian terrestrial and satellite media. ... How far is the distance between July 23, 1960, the day of the launch of the first Syrian television broadcast from the flanks of the Qassioun mountain, using a small 10 Kilowatt transmitter, and 2005 when we have mountains of technology and progress, in addition

---

[31] Boyd, D. (1999). *Broadcasting in the Arab World: A Survey of the Electronic Media of the Middle East*. Ames: Iowa State University Press.

[32] See, e.g., al-Baba, H. (March 17, 2005). Wishing for a return to the preprint era: How do Syrian media confront Syrian reality? *Al-Quds al-Arabi* [Arabic]; Badr, A. (2005). Mehdi Dakhlallah himself was considered to sing beyond the group! Syrian media out of its epoch . . . and banning publications continues. *Al-Quds al-Arabi* [Arabic]; and al-Qassem, A. (February 24, 2005). Will Syrian media get out of the cave? *Al-Quds al-Arabi* [Arabic].

to more than 6000 employees who cannot equate the effectiveness and influence of those 10 Kilowatts. . . . Why does the Syrian media sector, with its three television channels and its three newspapers, [remain] backwards and in perpetual crisis, so that Syrian viewers have forsaken it, and 90% of the Syrian audience has turned to other Arab channels? I go as far as to affirm that there isn't a single Syrian citizen who awaits the Syrian television newscast, with the exception of news writers themselves, since watching Syrian Television has become a burden and the option of last resort.[33]

His stereotyping of Africa notwithstanding, the author argues that Syrian television "does not reflect a constructive and honest dialogue about what is happening in the viewer's country" and concludes that "Syrian media did and still does play the role of the Chinese toy made of three monkeys, and its motto: I see not, I hear not, I speak not."[34]

Realization of the dismal performance of Syrian media had been making headway among Syria's political and media elite. Before the 2005 Ba'th Party Congress, then Information Minister and former journalist Mehdi Dakhlallah publicly stated that Syrian newspapers were "unreadable," pressured Syria's chief censor to resign, and called on journalists to insist on "freedom of expression" and abandon "the vocabulary of confrontation."[35] Dakhlallah also declared that Syrian media were in a planned transition from "dirigiste media" to "media with a purpose."[36] Structural reforms in the plan included establishing a Syrian Media City on the outskirts of Damascus, allowing privately owned Syrian satellite television channels to operate within restrictions, permitting privately owned FM radio stations, and appointing an increasing number of women in key positions in the sector. At the time the newly appointed director of Syrian television, Diana Jabbour, a Christian woman and not a Ba'th member, announced that her mission was to "make the screen a bridge between citizens and the state."[37] Bolder steps have included allowing limited and controlled access to

---

[33] al-Qassem, 2005.

[34] Ibid.

[35] Minister of information calls on journalists to hold on to "freedom of expression" and to relinquish "the vocabulary of confrontation" . . . Syria toward "controlling" electronic publishing in a new media law (April 15, 2005). *Al-Hayat* [Arabic].

[36] Dakhlallah: Syria has a promising future and its media in transition from dirigiste to purposeful (November 16, 2004). *Al-Hayat* [Arabic].

[37] Hajj-'Abdi, I. (April 28, 2005). Diana Jabbour: Why don't we turn the screen into a bridge between citizens and the state? *Al-Hayat* [Arabic].

official newspapers by Syrian opposition writers – typically critics of institutional corruption but not individual politicians, the regime, the military, or the intelligence services.

Despite a relative loosening of restrictions, the Syrian media remained under tight state control, legitimating the regime at all times and mobilizing the population in times of crisis. This *modus operandi* did not serve Syria well during the Lebanese-Syrian media war. Syria's hitherto airtight mobilization against the Lebanese media campaign would be undermined by the outstanding performance of a young aspiring Syrian singer participating in *Superstar 3*. If the falling out between Future TV and the Syrian public was akin to a divorce, as the Arab press described it, then Shahd Barmada, the Syrian *Superstar 3* finalist, was the child whose presence makes divorces gut-wrenching.

WOMEN'S BODIES AS NATIONS' BATTLEFIELDS

February 5, 2006, was a difficult day for Shahd Barmada. The seventeen-year-old Syrian woman faced Ibrahim al-Hekmi, a twenty-five-year-old Saudi, for the title of "Superstar of the Arabs." A gifted performer with a warm voice and an impressive stage presence, Barmada had the misfortune of performing in the finale of *Superstar 3* during one of the tensest moments in Lebanese-Syrian relations. Though Syrian troops had withdrawn from Lebanon nine months earlier, Barmada was caught in the crossfire of the Lebanese-Syrian media war. She was a Syrian national competing on the television channel owned by the al-Hariri family one week before the first anniversary of the al-Hariri assassination, which, it should be recalled, had been blamed widely on the Syrian regime. Barmada had spent the previous week fending off interviews in the Arab press, asking people to vote for her "as an artist," and insisting that politics should be left out of *Superstar*.[38]

Then the fatidic moment arrived. As Barmada descended the spiral staircase and glided to the front of the stage in a long shimmering beige dress, performing a song by the Arab diva Warda al-Jaza'iriyya, the camera zoomed into a medium shot showing Barmada from the waist up. Suddenly the screen was obscured by a man's back in a grey suit jacket topped with a head of graying hair. As he moved away from the singer to take back his seat among the studio audience, the man, who

[38] al-Hekmi, I. (February 4, 2006). Shahd Barmada: I am participating in an artistic program unrelated to politics. *Al-Quds al-Arabi* [Arabic].

turned out to be Barmada's father, revealed a large Syrian flag that he had just wrapped around his daughter's body. With a forced smile following a brief moment of what clearly was intense unease, Barmada disentangled herself and laid the flag on her left shoulder, never interrupting her stunning rendition of Warda's song. The young woman who had spared no effort in portraying her participation as a personal, artistic achievement unrelated to politics had found her body hijacked by Syrian patriotism. Getting rid of the flag was an untenable proposition, so laying it on one shoulder was the next best option.

Watching the episode, there was a sense of doom hovering over Barmada. As a reporter who attended the studio shooting wrote:

> During the evening... the Syrian contestant looked like a bird about to be shot down.... The gigantic contestant with the "sweet voice" [in reference to al-Hekmi, the oversized Saudi contestant] won over his small colleague with the gigantic talent [Barmada].[39]

According to the same reporter, Barmada's father put the flag on her shoulders in reaction to a Saudi in the studio audience who draped Hekmi with the Saudi flag. That incident, however, did not make it onto the screen of Future TV.

Until the Lebanese media campaign further soured Lebanese-Syrian relations, it was assumed in Arab and Syrian media circles that more Syrians watched Future TV than viewed Syrian Television.[40] *Superstar* was extremely popular in Syria. In Damascus, on evenings when *Superstar* was on the air, "the only movement comes from a stream of lights emitted by a large apartment complex across the way," the source of which turned out to be all the television sets tuned in to Future TV.[41] By another account, Syrian government officials, business owners, and the general public engaged in a "populist carnival" in support of the Syrian contestant in *Superstar 1*.[42] Despite minimal coverage by Syrian media of Barmada's participation in *Superstar 3* and calls by the Ba'th press to boycott Future TV entirely, the Syrian "street" was abuzz. Can Barmada receive a fair treatment on Future TV? Can she withstand the combined

---

[39] al-Qabah, R. (February 8, 2005). Victory goes to the Saudi ... And to the Syrians the thanks of voters. *Al-Hayat* [Arabic].

[40] al-Khudr, M. (February 4, 2006). .... And Syrians are unfazed. *Al-Hayat* [Arabic].

[41] MacKenzie, T. "The Best Hope for Democracy in the Arab World: A Crooning TV 'Idol'?" *Transnational Broadcasting Studies* 13, Fall 2004, http://www.tbsjournal.com/Archives/Fall04/mackenzie.html (accessed October 15, 2005).

[42] al-Khudr, 2006.

power of a strong Saudi contestant and his deep-pocketed compatriots' zealously patriotic voting in pan-Arab reality television shows? And what about the al-Hariri family's intimate ties to Saudi royalty? In interviews published in *al-Quds al-Arabi*, *al-Hayat*, and *Assafir* (*The Ambassador*), ordinary Syrians poured scorn on Future TV but expressed hope that Barmada would prevail, while others were concerned that official calls to boycott the program would hurt Barmada's chances. The same newspapers published accounts that some Lebanese were worried that the al-Hariri family would crown Barmada as "Superstar of the Arabs" to mend its fraught relationship with the Asad regime.

The result, announced the following night, was close: Hekmi won with 53 percent and Barmada lost with an honorable 47 percent of the votes. As the camera showed her father crying, Barmada said that she was "above all the political and racist arguments, otherwise she would have withdrawn from the program a long time ago."[43] Nonetheless, a statement she made in an interview published two days earlier in *al-Quds al-Arabi* betrayed her own ambivalence about the politicization of *Superstar*. Asked about her opinion of "those in Syria who do not want to vote for you so that Future TV does not win," she answered: "Those who think logically will not be swayed by those requests. We are in an artistic show unrelated to politics. Otherwise I would have had to withdraw from the show earlier. These people are superficial. Let those who love me vote for me. *I am a daughter of Syria after all*."[44] After spending weeks disassociating the competition from nationalist affiliations and sentiments, Barmada's ambivalence underscored the tightness of the rope on which she walked.

As a mythical figure like France's Marianne demonstrates, the connection between women's bodies and national identity is not restricted to the Arab and Muslim worlds. Women are reproducers of the nation and at the same time markers of boundaries between the nation and its others. This privileged symbolic status is also a liability because, as the feminist international relations scholar Jan Jindy Pettman put it, "women's movements and bodies are policed, in terms of their sexuality, fertility and relations with 'others.'"[45] As a potentially permeable cultural and social boundary, women's bodies are imbued with symbolic

[43] al-Hekmi is Superstar for 2006 (February 7, 2006). *Assafir* [Arabic].
[44] Mer'i, Z. (February 4, 2006). Shahd Barmada: I participate in an artistic program unrelated to politics. *Al-Quds al-Arabi* [Arabic], emphasis added.
[45] Pettman, J. J. (1992). *Women, Nationalism and the State: Towards an International Feminist Perspective*, Occasional Paper 4 in Gender and Development Studies, Asian Institute of Technology, Bangkok, 5–6.

significance that increases when the woman is publicly visible. In the context of the Lebanese-Syrian media war, Barmada's presence on *Superstar 3* meant she had perilously crossed the boundary between self and other, because Future TV was demonized in Syria as a traitor of the Arab cause. Her comments that there was nothing political about *Superstar 3*, and that people should vote for her based on vocal performance, not nationality, paradoxically threatened the Syrian nation because Barmada underplayed her belonging to Syria in order to gain approval from others but still claimed her identity as "a daughter of Syria."

By sheathing Shahd with the Syrian flag, her father took it upon himself to police the boundary and bring his daughter back into the national fold, even at the cost of endangering her prospects of becoming "Superstar of the Arabs." Her loss to al-Hekmi in effect restored the boundary: rejected by the "Other" to whom she wanted to endear herself, Barmada had no choice but to reintegrate her national community. Whether or not the announced results truly reflected viewers' votes, Barmada's loss stitched her back into the fabric of the Syrian nation. A Barmada victory would have raised uncomfortable questions about the porosity of national boundaries and the fluidity of national identity, questions that would have complicated the polarization resulting from al-Hariri's assassination and sustained by the Syrian-Lebanese media war – in short, questions that at this historical juncture were unfathomable. Tragically, Barmada's experience illustrates that women, in the words of literary scholar Anne McClintock, are "typically constructed as the symbolic bearers of the nation but are denied any direct relation to national agency."[46] Clearly, her exit from the stage had a symbolic echo that resonated beyond her loss in a reality TV contest.

Arab reality TV contestants are drafted into the performance of international rivalries, sometimes with deleterious consequences. As public events pitting contestants from multiple Arab nationalities against each other, Arab reality shows become idioms of contention, providing an arena and a vocabulary for waging political battles whose scope and implications are completely beyond the contestants' control.[47] As other contestants before her, Shahd Barmada fell victim to this game of nations, as her own body was used as a display space for nationalism; in

[46] McClintock, A. (1997). "'No Longer in Future Heaven': Gender, Race and Nationalism," in *Dangerous Liaisons: Gender, Nation and Postcolonial Perspectives*, ed. A. McClintock, A. Mufit, and E. Shohat. Minneapolis: University of Minnesota Press.
[47] See Kraidy, M. M. (2007). "Idioms of Contention: *Star Academy* in Lebanon and Kuwait," in *Pan-Arab Media, Democracy, and the Public Sphere*, ed. N. Sakr. London: I. B. Tauris, 44–55.

one brief moment politicizing the *Superstar* journey that she spent weeks arguing was "unrelated to politics."

The French philosopher Ernest Renan, a pioneering writer on collective identity, pithily wrote centuries ago that "[t]he existence of a nation is a plebiscite of everyday, as the existence of the individual is a perpetual affirmation of life."[48] In this sense the continued participation of the Syrian contestant in *Superstar* was an affirmation – albeit ambivalent and contested – of the life of the Syrian nation in the Arab community of nation-states, symptomatic of the definition of reality television by the cultural studies scholar John Hartley as a "plebiscitary industry."[49] Episodes of nationalist fervor surrounding reality TV competitions evince Wedeen's argument that "the nation is a contingent category rather than a substantial thing."[50] In that sense, the contention surrounding reality TV operated as a constitutive rhetoric. As a project-in-the-making, the nation needs constantly to be re-created, hence the desire of some Arab leaders to be seen with reality TV contestants from their country. In this vein, against the Western ethos of the individual as the locus of identity and authenticity, Barmada's story is a poignant demonstration of how nation-states can compel the individual body to relinquish its status as what communication historian John Peters called "the bastion of communicative authenticity"[51] in the name of the imagined community of the nation.

Just like the nation enlists its citizens to represent it in contests with its rivals, citizens in turn can stage events to exalt the nation. National crises awaken dormant national sentiments, stoked by politicians and extolled by the media. *Superstar*'s embroilment in the convoluted Lebanese-Syrian relation was a mere prelude to more-significant developments. After rhetorical skirmishes in Bahrain led to protracted contention in Saudi Arabia, Lebanon, and Syria and activated political and social institutions in Kuwait, the Arab reality TV battles descended to the street, entering the fray of massive geopolitical upheaval tearing up the region as the United States trumpeted its vision of a "New Middle East." The massive Beirut demonstrations that followed al-Hariri's slaying were some of the most dramatic nonviolent political events in recent

---

[48] Renan, E. (1996). *Qu'est-ce Qu'une une Nation? What Is a Nation?* Charles Taylor, intro., Wanda Romer Taylor, trans. Toronto: Tapir Press, 3.

[49] Hartley, J. (2007). "'Reality' and the Plebiscite," in *Politicotainment: Television's Take on the Real*, ed. K. Riegert. New York: Peter Lang, 21–58.

[50] Wedeen, 2008, 28.

[51] Peters, J. D. (1999). *Speaking Into the Air: A History of the Idea of Communication.* Chicago: University of Chicago Press, 190.

Arab history, and generated vivid media coverage by national, pan-Arab, and global media. In those street protests, political activists, media corporations, and journalists used the language and style of *Star Academy* and *Superstar* explicitly, dramatically illustrating links between media, modernity, and nationalism, and consummating the exploitation of reality TV as an idiom of contention. The following chapter tells that story.

CHAPTER SEVEN

The "New Middle East"? Reality Television and the "Independence Intifada"

A t 12:56:26 P.M., on February 14, 2005, a massive explosion resounded throughout Beirut. At first, many Beirutis assumed from experience that Israeli air-force jets had crossed the sound barrier in a mock raid over the Lebanese capital. Others in the city felt the ground shaking and thought that it was an actual Israeli air bombing. Then people saw black smoke billowing from the seaside road alongside the famous St. George Hotel, a prewar hangout for socialites, spies, and intellectuals. Minutes earlier, Rafiq al-Hariri, Lebanon's erstwhile prime minister and a towering personality in postwar Lebanese politics, had left the Lebanese Parliament building located at Place de l'Étoile, driving his own car wedged within his security convoy to his mansion in the Quraytem neighborhood of Beirut. Out of three possible itineraries, Hariri's security detail selected the route that was likely to have the least traffic at that hour of the day, which passed by the St. George. As it rode past the hotel, a white Mitsubishi van cut through the convoy and exploded, killing al-Hariri and twenty one others.[1]

Al-Hariri had spent the morning participating in legislative debate over a controversial electoral law that was engineered by Syrian military intelligence to favor pro-Syrian candidates in the 2000 elections. Discussions of the law were heating up ahead of the 2005 parliamentary elections on which Hariri pinned his hopes to regain the prime minister's seat. Under the 1926 Lebanese Constitution amended by the Ta'if Agreement in 1989, the President of the Republic has to conduct binding consultations with deputies [members of parliament] to appoint a prime minister. Presiding over a "list" that wins legislative elections was

---

[1] The time line is borrowed from Blanford, N. (2006). *Killing Mr. Lebanon: The Assassination of Rafik Hariri and Its Impact on the Middle East*. London and New York: I. B. Tauris.

therefore a ticket to the prime minister post. Al-Hariri had built a vast coalition throughout Lebanon's regions and sectarian communities and by many estimates was poised to make a strong comeback. He had done it once before in 2000, when a landslide electoral victory brought him back to the prime minister's office in spite of a protracted struggle with Emile Lahoud, Lebanon's president, who had engineered al-Hariri's ouster in 1998. In late 2004, al-Hariri insisted that he would win the election no matter which version of the electoral law prevailed.

Lahoud's constitutional single term (1998–2004) in office was forcibly extended for three years on September 3, 2004, when Lebanese deputies amended the constitution under Syrian orders. The historic and contested vote took place one day after the United Nations Security Council passed Resolution 1559, which called for the withdrawal of all foreign troops from Lebanon (clearly aimed at Syria), the disarmament of all militias (clearly aimed at Hizbollah), and the holding of free and fair elections. The coerced extension of Lahoud's term until November 2007 was a tipping point. It pushed al-Hariri further away from Syria, whose heavy-handed control of Lebanese public life had become unbearable, and closer to the Lebanese opposition. Al-Hariri's allies in the opposition accused the Syrian regime and its Lebanese partners of being behind the assassination – a direct and unprecedented challenge to the Damascus leadership. As prime minister for most of the preceding thirteen years, al-Hariri was a partner of the Syrians. After his death, al-Hariri's allies propelled him as an icon of resistance to Syria. Whether Syria was behind it or not, al-Hariri's brutal death shifted the balance of power in Lebanon and inaugurated a protracted showdown between competing Lebanese groups and their supporters in Damascus, Paris, Tehran, and Washington, a clash that would keep Lebanon and the Middle East in turmoil for years to come.

Television assumed a central political role in the wake of al-Hariri's murder. Future TV reacted immediately to the late-morning bombing that killed its founder. A diagonal black band on Future TV's logo signaled mourning and an on-screen digital calendar marked the days since February 14, 2005. The channel became a full-time propaganda machine, celebrating al-Hariri's legacy, attacking the Syrian regime widely perceived to be behind the assassination, keeping a focus on the UN investigation initially headed by German judge Detlev Mehlis, and clamoring for Lebanese sovereignty. Future TV talk shows featured a parade of anti-Syrian speakers while political music videos and promotional clips asking for "The Truth" (about the assassination) flooded the program grid. This situation prevailed until December 2005, when a new general manager was hired to bring Future TV back to a semblance of normalcy to stop the gaping financial losses of the previous eleven months.[2] LBC, whose political bosses were allies of al-Hariri's block in parliament but whose management insisted on profitability, focused exclusively on the assassination only for a few days before going back to regular programming on LBC-Sat, thus avoiding the crippling financial repercussions of "opening the air" completely to the al-Hariri story, while keeping the terrestrial LBCI focused on unfolding events.[3] Both Future TV and LBC's editorial lines were highly critical of the Syrians and favorable to U.S. and European intervention against Syria.

On the opposite side, New TV, owned by al-Hariri foe Tahsin Khayyat, and Hizbollah's al-Manar (The Beacon) articulated a different narrative, which was opposed to Western interference in Lebanon and concerned about "U.S.-Israeli plans" for the region. Although they did not explicitly support Syrian interference in Lebanon, both stations were critical of the UN Mehlis investigation, which they perceived to be a tool of U.S. foreign policy. New TV, which was critical of the Syrian-Lebanese security apparatus, and al-Manar questioned the version of events given by the other side, oftentimes in a tit-for-tat direct questioning of facts (to be described later in this chapter). In the looming political battle, television news and talk shows were poised to play a predictably partisan role. Less expected was entertainment television's embroilment in Lebanese politics. Notably, by giving protagonists an idiom of contention and journalists a lexicon of interpretation, reality TV would play a role in shaping rival versions of political reality unfolding in the streets of Beirut.

A "PATRIOTIC NIGHT"

Moments after Rafiq al-Hariri's demise, Rula Sa'd, the Director of Marketing and Promotions at the LBC, made a curt on-screen appearance in *Star Academy*, broadcast live on the LBC Reality channel and again during that evening's prime on the terrestrial channel LBCI and the satellite channel al-Fada'iyya al-Lubnaniyyah, or LBC-Sat. This was a rare instance when outside events intruded upon life in the building called simply "the Academy," located near LBC headquarters in Adma, a coastal town twenty

---

[2] Author interview, 'Ayntrazi Tariq, General Manager, Future TV, December 20, 2005, Dubai, UAE.

[3] At that time there were growing tensions between Pierre el-Daher, LBC's general manager, and Samir Ja'ja', leader of the Lebanese Forces party released from jail in the summer of 2005, which culminated in a legal struggle still underway.

miles north of Beirut, which otherwise was completely cut off from the outside world, following the rules of the "live-in" reality TV genre (see Chapter 1).

When she entered the set on February 14, 2005, Sa'd was acting in her capacity as "Director of the Academy" to inform the *tullab* of al-Hariri's death and to announce that "Lebanon was mourning," heralding a ten-day hiatus in *Star Academy* broadcasts. Like other Lebanese channels, LBC suspended its regular schedule to focus on the aftermath of the assassination but returned to its normal program grid within days. *Star Academy* resumed with a prime on Friday, February 25, 2005, that the Arab press dubbed "The Patriotic Night."[4] Hilda Khalifé, the show's hostess, appeared on stage clad in a black evening gown and dark makeup. As she solemnly introduced *Star Academy*'s first postassassination prime, Khalifé alluded to "the painful event that hit Lebanon." Then the prime started with a patriotic song called "No, the Story Has Not Ended," performed by a cast of pop stars including Wa'el Kfoury, Haifa Wehbi, Nawal al-Zoghbi, Amal Hijazi, Sabah, Nancy 'Ajram, and Melhem Zayn, the one-time Lebanese contestant in *Superstar* whose eviction from the show caused an uproar in Beirut (see Chapter 6). Dressed in black, *Star Academy* contestants (including some from the program's first season who were brought back for the occasion) solemnly performed patriotic songs with a large Lebanese flag hanging in the background. Then the *tullab* intoned *Star Academy*'s theme song, *Jayee al-Haqiqa* (*The Truth Is Coming*). Melodically the song is an Arabic version of *Let the Sunshine In*, drawn from the soundtrack of *Hair*, the famous play and film about the American counterculture in the 1960s, itself a political text. The song's lyrics are critical of the Arab status quo, using words like *darkness* and *cold* and proclaiming that "the truth," which was on the verge of coming, would change the situation for the better. The song concludes:

> Let us get out of this darkness
>
> And let freedom shine on people
>
> And let us say, let us say to the people
>
> The Truth is coming, coming to speak out, another story

---

[4] Articles using this terminology include al-Shawwa, M. (2005). "Star Academy 2": A patriotic "prime" and the exit of Syrian Joey Bassous. *Mulhaq-Annahar* [Arabic]; Haydar, D. (February 28, 2005). A "painful event" produces "patriotic night." *Assafir* [Arabic]; Moussa, G. (February 27, 2005). "Star Academy" also … takes a "patriotic stand." *Al-Hayat* [Arabic].

The song's music video, which played heavily on LBC and other channels in the preceding year, visually echoed the lyrics' political connotations. It was directed by Nadine Labaki, a young filmmaker whose music
videos for the likes of Lebanese pop diva Nancy 'Ajram had turned
Labaki into a star.[5] Released in December 2003 to coincide with the
launch of the show's first season, *Jayee al-Haqiqa*'s video is dominated
by hues of blue, grey, and black. In what at times looks like a solemn
commercial for The Gap, *Star Academy* contestants march through
streets, dressed in urban chic black, grey, and olive green clothes and
scarves, some sporting "dog tags" around their necks, shaking their fists,
and waving the flags of Arab countries from Morocco to Iraq, the Lebanese flag fluttering most visibly. Toward the end of the video, the camera angle abruptly shifts as the marchers are joined by children, an
unsubtle hint about the change needed for the sake of future Arab generations. The video ends with a long shot of the group, joyous, hopeful,
and defiant. More than a year before the spring 2005 demonstrations in
Beirut triggered by al-Hariri's killing, the video's depiction of young
demonstrators bore an uncanny resemblance to the massive spring 2005
Beirut rallies known as the "Independence Intifada," where, echoing the
song's lyrics, "The Truth" would become one of two main slogans – the
other being "Freedom, Sovereignty, Independence." The intriguing
prescience of the music video foreshadowed the degree to which Lebanese popular culture would tune into political developments in the following years.

On the evening of February 25, 2005, when many Lebanese had not
had the time to absorb the shock of al-Hariri's assassination nor to begin
to comprehend its broader repercussions, the atmosphere was charged
in *Star Academy*'s studios. An *al-Hayat* reporter who attended the production wrote:

> The atmosphere at LBC studios in Adma during the "prime" was
> not ordinary. . . . Instead of carrying pictures of their favorite con-
> testants, fans present in the studio waved Lebanese flags . . . with
> the exception of some pictures supporting Samer, the Lebanese
> contestant who was in danger [of being voted off the show]. . . .
> [T]he prime was stuffed with sentiments, and emotion played a
> visible role in an episode that enjoyed high ratings.[6]

[5] Since LBC's inception, patriotism has been a regular feature of LBC videos, whether
they are explicitly political or institutional self-promotional.
[6] Moussa, 2005.

Though the atmosphere of the prime was dictated by al-Hariri's assassination, not once was the word *al-Hariri* uttered during the evening.[7] Rather, the prime was a folkloric celebration of a resurgent patriotism that brought Lebanon's most-venerable singers and its hippest pop idols side by side with *Star Academy*'s cast. The episode also celebrated Kuwait's national day, a gesture of solidarity between small Arab countries like Lebanon and Kuwait that are threatened by larger and more powerful neighbors like Syria and Iraq. "On the eve of its 44th national holiday Kuwait was a special guest on *Star Academy*," proudly wrote the Kuwaiti daily *al-Ra'i al-Aam*, concluding that the prime offered "an evening of contradictions, where sadness and separation mixed with joy, patriotism, brotherhood and unity."[8] This gesture toward Kuwait, though political, was also commercially motivated: Kuwait is a small but lucrative market for LBC's advertisers. Aside from this brief nod toward Kuwait, the focus stayed on Lebanon.

The week's nominations implicated *Star Academy* deeper in Lebanon's political upheaval. The "nominees" that faced expulsion were a Bahraini man, Ahmad Salaheddin, a Syrian woman, Joey Bassous, and a Lebanese man, Samer Doumit. According to the rules of *Star Academy 2*, the contestant who garners the highest number of votes from the public is "saved" and remains on the show. The remaining nonnominated contestants then vote, live on-air, to "rescue" one of the two remaining nominees; the third nominee then permanently exits the show. That evening, the Bahraini nominee won the popular vote by 34.99 percent, while the Syrian ranked second with 33.2 percent of the votes, followed by the Lebanese who garnered 32.06 percent. The contestants' vote in the studio resonated with the tense situation on the streets. Of the seven remaining *tullab*, only one voted for Joey from Syria, while six opted to rescue their Lebanese colleague Samer, who therefore remained on the show even though he ranked third and last in the public vote. The *dénouement* was pure political spectacle. The Syrian contestant was voted out, and an eerie silence wrapped her humiliating exit from the stage.[9]

The ousting of Syrian contestant Joey Bassous from *Star Academy* echoed the political atmosphere. The assassination of al-Hariri brought tensions between Syria and Lebanon to a boiling point, with widespread

---

[7] See al-Shawwa, 2005 and Haydar, 2005.
[8] Saleh, H. (February 27, 2005). Dishdasha, Ghutra and 'gal in Star Academy's celebration of Kuwait's holidays. *Al-Ra'i-al-Aam* [Arabic].
[9] *Star Academy* Prime (February 25, 2005). Adma, Lebanon: Lebanese Broadcasting Corporation International and Al-Fada'iyya al-Lubnaniyya [Arabic].

suspicion, in Lebanon and in Arab and Western capitals, of Syrian implication. News stories abounded about threats to al-Hariri from the Syrians, and about U.S. and French warnings to Syria throughout the preceding autumn not to cause harm to Lebanon's one-time prime minister. Reports of Bashar al-Asad threatening to "break Lebanon over al-Hariri's head" and of Rustum Ghazalah, chief of Syria's military intelligence in Lebanon, storming furiously out of a meeting with al-Hariri in January were now interpreted as a sequence of events leading to the February 14, 2005 car bomb. Developments in *Star Academy 2* reflected the growth of Lebanese discontent with Syria into outright anger. Contrary to the applause and dancing that usually accompanies exiting contestants, *Star Academy*'s amphitheater was eerily silent as the Syrian contestant stepped off stage, a scene that would play itself out again during the *Superstar 3* finale (see Chapter 6). As if Joey's expulsion was a foregone conclusion, a Lebanese journalist wrote, a tad ironically:

> Of course she had to leave because it was not possible for someone called Joey-the-Syrian to stay at the expense of Samer-the-Lebanese, with the audience in that amphitheater yearning for Lebanon's rise. . . . One moment, she was the daughter of an Arab academy; next thing she knows she is the daughter of a Lebanese prime.[10]

In *Assafir*, a Lebanese daily sympathetic to Syria, media critic Sahar Mandour wryly reported that:

> A joke made the rounds that this was the first Syrian withdrawal and the first Lebanese victory in history over the brotherly country [Syria], and it occurred through democratic voting. A funny idea; but there is no running away from the symbolic dimension: Freedom, sovereignty, independence.[11]

The Arab press commented that politics loomed large in *Star Academy*'s "patriotic evening." Overall, pan-Arab media were sympathetic to the Lebanese and critical of Syria, reflecting the House of al-Saʿud's anger at the killing of a Sunni Lebanese politician whose family enjoyed a close bond with Saudi royals. In the meantime, street demonstrations, heated rhetoric, and a fierce media battle pitted rival Lebanese groups against one another and their foreign backers Syria, Iran, and the United States. France and Saudi Arabia intensified diplomatic efforts; so did the Arab

---

[10] Haydar, 2005.
[11] Mandour, S. (February 28, 2005). The "Jumblatti" moment in "the Academy." *Assafir* [Arabic].

League and the United Nations. Arab newspapers and satellite television channels echoed the all-consuming battle raging among Lebanese media institutions and their internal sponsors and external supporters. For weeks, the Beirut demonstrations and counterdemonstrations commanded the lion's share of pan-Arab media coverage.

ZOOM IN, ZOOM OUT: DEMONSTRATIONS AND COUNTERDEMONSTRATIONS

In the early hours after the assassination, demonstrators flocked spontaneously to the al-Hariri family compound in Quraytem. Then on February 21, around twenty-five thousand people staged a sit-in at the explosion site, holding signs such as "Hey Syria! Who's Next?"[12] Quickly thereafter, journalists, advertising executives, and politicians from the opposition began managing and "branding" the demonstrations to focus on ousting the Syrians from Lebanon. In the building of the Chamber of Deputies on Place de L'Étoile, vehement arguments between Syria's friends and foes echoed the tumult on the streets. Then a major surprise came on February 28, when pro-Syrian prime minister 'Omar Karami abruptly announced his resignation in Majlis al-Nuwwab (Chamber of Deputies) during a debate on al-Hariri's assassination. The announcement stunned Karami's supporters and his opponents. After opposition MPs stood up and applauded, making victory signs with their hands, Chamber of Deputies president Nabih Berri publicly admonished Karami for not informing him of the impending resignation.[13] Watching the speech on large screens positioned at the edges of Martyrs Square, participants in the opposition's largest rally to date cheered at what they saw as the first sign of collapse of the resented Syrian-installed police state. The event had a regional echo as al-Jazeera's and al-Arabiya's viewers watched – live – a sitting Arab prime minister resign under popular pressure. Meanwhile in Washington, D.C., not cognizant of the Christian-Nationalist connotations of Lebanon's green cedar, Undersecretary of State Paula Dobriansky held a press conference in which she coined the term "Cedar Revolution."[14] (In contrast, "Independence Intifada" resonates with the Palestinian cause and connotes pro-Arab leanings

---

[12] Blanford, 2006, 153.
[13] Karami's resignation: Celebrations in Beirut and anger in Tripoli (March 1, 2005). *Al-Quds al-Arabi* [Arabic].
[14] Morley, J. (March 3, 2005). "The Branding of Lebanon's 'Revolution.'" Washington Post.com, http://www.washingtonpost.com/ac2/wpdyn/A1911–2005March2?lan.

that preempt Syrian accusations of betrayal of the Arab cause.) By the end of February, more than 100,000 Lebanese were permanently demonstrating in the center of Beirut without clashing with the armed forces or the police.[15] Buoyed by Karami's resignation, the demonstrators clamored harder for Syrian withdrawal.

Pressure was ratcheting up on the Syrian regime. A potent combination of public discontent, growing street demonstrations, a massive Lebanese media campaign, and mounting external pressure from the United States, France, and Saudi Arabia left Damascus with few options. On March 5, 2005, President Bashar al-Asad addressed the Syrian Majlis al-Sha'b (Council of the People) in its chambers, announcing his decision to withdraw his troops to the Lebanese-Syrian border. Like Karami's one week earlier, Asad's speech was covered widely by the Arab and Lebanese media, and the Beirut demonstrators watched it live on wide screens, booing and taunting the Syrian leader as if he were physically present. Asad punctuated his delivery with impromptu comments and chuckles, and criticized the performance of Lebanon's television channels, accusing them of inflating the size of the demonstrations by using narrow camera angles. "Zoom out," he said (using the English expression), challenging unnamed Lebanese channels sympathetic to the opposition rallies, and it would become clear that the demonstrations were small. Many Lebanese throughout the country and the world celebrated the news of a Syrian withdrawal thirty years after Syrian troops had first entered Lebanon.

At the same time, the English expression "Zoom Out" entered the political lexicon. At a press conference the next day, Hizbollah Secretary-General Hassan Nasrallah humorously implored reporters to "zoom out" when they cover Hizbollah's demonstration planned for March 8.[16] The Beirut demonstrators were jubilant and responded tit-for-tat, brandishing signs asking Syrian leaders to "Zoom Out and Count," and Syria's troops to "Zoom Out." The incident was noted by Lebanese journalists from various political persuasions.[17] In the Saudi-owned *Asharq al-Awsat*, pro-al-Hariri Lebanese journalist Diana Muqalled mocked Asad by pointing to the narrow camera angles used by Syrian TV to cover Asad's entrance to Majlis al-Sha'b before his speech, artificially

---

[15] Rizq, G. (March 1, 2005). When did screens see a such a scene? New (bikr) television coverage for Arab crowds made by youth in downtown Beirut. *Assafir* [Arabic].

[16] Muqalled, D. (March 12, 2005). The Zoom war! *Asharq al-Awsat* [Arabic].

[17] See among others al-Atrash, R. (March 9, 2005). In defense of "Zoom In," *Assafir* [Arabic]; al-Atrash, R. (March 8, 2005). "Freedom Square": "Zoom In" on Arab viewers. *Assafir* [Arabic]; Muqalled, March 12, 2005.

magnifying the small number of Syrians cheering for their president.[18] In *Assafir*, Rasha al-Atrash published a column titled "In Praise of 'Zoom In'" noting "the camera's hypocrisy as it plays."[19]

The "Zoom Out" episode signaled the appearance of a new language with which Arab citizens contested political authority, a political vernacular predicated on bodily performance rather than rational deliberation.[20] Demonstrators massed on the streets of Beirut challenged Asad's version of the reality on the ground – immediately, corporeally, and publicly. Syrians, who risk repression if they publicly challenge their ruler, were treated by Arab satellite channels to his public dressing down. By using the lingo of television production to chastise his opponents, Asad handed them a golden opportunity to return the favor in a media environment that was sympathetic to the demonstrators' cause and suspicious of Asad's motives. In addition to Future TV and LBC, the Saudi-controlled satellite channels and pan-Arab newspapers sided clearly with the then Lebanese opposition.[21] Even al-Jazeera, no ally of the Saudis or of their friend al-Hariri, covered the demonstrations extensively. No matter which version of Arab political reality they espoused, Arab journalists could not avoid reporting on the historic events unfolding on the streets of Beirut and echoing throughout Arab airwaves and households. The magnitude of the event imposed itself across the ideological and political spectrum.

As they witnessed these dramatic developments, Arab journalists began interpreting the Independence Intifada through the prism of reality TV. The liveness, avowed realism, managed unpredictability, production style, and technical lingo associated with reality TV helped journalists make sense of the new dynamics of social and political communication manifest in the unfolding spectacle. Hussain Shobokshi, a columnist in *Asharq al-Awsat*, was among the first journalists to invoke reality TV. In a March 6, 2005 column titled "Academy Politics," he wrote:

> The Lebanese have specialized in presenting Arabized copies of reality TV in the past years, and now here they are presenting a new Arab model for effective popular political change, which can be called "Academy Politics!" It is a peaceful expression of anger

---

[18] Muqalled, March 12, 2005.

[19] al-Atrash, March 9, 2005.

[20] For conceptual discussions of language and political performativity, see Kohn, 2000 and Wedeen, 2008.

[21] Sa'd al-Hariri (Rafiq's son) and his allies, then the opposition, are now the ruling coalition, with Hizbollah, Michel 'Awn's Free Patriotic Movement and their allies in the opposition.

and a peaceful assertion of desire for change. Not a single bullet was fired, nor a single person was killed or even wounded, in a country with a large number of sects, groups, parties and players.... Lebanon, which was the Arabs' touristic destination, is today their political destination, as they follow what happens there with surprise and admiration, riveted as they watch events on Lebanese reality/realistic television [*al telefizion al-waqi'i*].[22]

The relationship between media coverage and political reality was hotly debated in the Arab media. Were television channels sympathetic to the Independence Intifada using narrow angles to make the demonstrators appear more numerous than they really were? Or were opponents of the demonstrators, including Syria's Asad, merely resorting to criticizing the media because the demonstrators' political position, there and then, looked unassailable? These questions would soon compel rival Lebanese forces to "resort to the street" to demonstrate their popular legitimacy, playing a highly mediatized "numbers game." During the following fortnight, these forces would heed the French sociologist Pierre Bourdieu's argument that in order to be effective, demonstrations have to be deliberately made for television.[23] Lebanese and pan-Arab channels played footage of the rallies *ad infinitum* for several months, etching the demonstrations in the national imagination. The two major political blocs that emerged in the aftermath of Rafiq al-Hariri's murder, "March 8" and "March 14," obtained their names from the dates on which they held major rallies in downtown Beirut.

In response to the growing number of people demonstrating against Syrian control, Hizbollah called for a massive demonstration of its supporters on March 8 in Riyad al-Solh Square, a few block from Martyrs' Square. The party framed the event as an expression of gratitude to Syria and rejection of U.S. intervention. The March 8 demonstrators focused their ire on UNSCR 1559, which, by calling for the disarmament of all militias in Lebanon, posed an imminent existential threat to Hizbollah. Among numerous signs rejecting American and Western interventions

[22] Shobokshi, H. (March 6, 2006). Academy politics. *Asharq al-Awsat* [Arabic].
[23] Bourdieu, P. (1996). *Sur la télévision*. Paris: Raisons d'Agir Éditions, 22. Bourdieu writes: "Ceux qui en sont encore à croire qu'il suffit de manifester san s'occuper de la télévision risquent de rater leur coup: il faut de plus en plus produire des manifestations pour la télévision, c'est-à-dire des manifestations qui soient de nature a intéresser les gens de télévision étant donné ce qui sont leurs catégories de perception, et qui, relayées, amplifiées par eux, recevront leur pleine efficacité."

in Lebanon, some said: "No to American Interventions. No to 1559." One English-language sign simply said: "1559. No." Media outlets affiliated with the Party of God had a similar focus on the Security Council resolution. During al-Manar's coverage of population movements converging onto Beirut for the demonstration, the studio anchor posed a loaded question to the channel's correspondent stationed on the coastal highway linking the southern city of Saida to the capital: "Wouldn't it be possible to call all this spontaneous crowd formation a referendum around UNSCR 1559?"[24] Rather than asking Syria to remain in Lebanon, the event – unfolding one day after Syrian troops began "redeploying" from various Lebanese regions to the Beqaaʿ Valley, which is adjacent to Syrian territory – was an assertion of Hizbollah's strength, post–Pax Syriana. "No to American-Zionist Intervention. Yes to Lebanese-Syrian Brotherhood," one banner proclaimed.[25]

Among the Lebanese channels, Hizbollah's al-Manar was first on the scene, covering the events since dawn, while al-Hariri's Future TV was last.[26] Among the pan-Arab networks, al-Jazeera began coverage first, and al-Arabiya showed up much later, followed only by the U.S. government's al-Hurra.[27] The names that the different channels gave to their coverage of the March 8 street rallies reflected their political positions. The most descriptive was al-Jazeera's caption: "Hundreds of Thousands of Lebanese Are Demonstrating in Support of Syria and Rejection of U.S. Pressures." Lebanon's state-owned Télé-Liban simply relayed Hizbollah's al-Manar's sympathetic coverage, and New TV referred to the event as "Demonstration of Lebanese Parties and Forces in Riyad As-Solh Square Rejecting Foreign Intervention and in Loyalty to Syria." On the other side of the fence, for LBC it was "The Loyalty to Syria and Lebanon's Independence Demonstration Called for by Lebanese Parties and Associations Loyal to Syria," while Future TV curtly called it "Demonstration of Loyalty to Syria." The U.S.-owned al-Hurra acted as if the rally was not taking place and declined to give it a name.[28]

In a surprise appearance that galvanized the crowd, Secretary-General Hassan Nasrallah, standing amidst dozens of Lebanese flags,

---

[24] Haydar, D. (March 9, 2005). Al-Manar is mother of the bride and Future TV last well-wisher. *Assafir* [Arabic].

[25] Fattah, H. (March 8, 2005). "Pro-Syria Party in Beirut Holds a Huge Protest." *New York Times*, A1.

[26] Haydar, March 9, 2005.

[27] Ibid.

[28] Ibid.

told his supporters: "Today, you decide the future of your nation and your country; today, you answer the world." Then, defying Israeli leaders, he stated: "Forget about your dreams for Lebanon. What you did not win in war, I swear, you will not win in politics." He then turned his attention to the Bush administration: "You are wrong in your calculations in Lebanon. Lebanon will not be divided. Lebanon is not Somalia; Lebanon is not Ukraine; Lebanon is not Georgia."[29] The opposition, in the voice of Gebran Tuayni, publisher of *Annahar* and a principal organizer of anti-Syrian demonstrations who would be assassinated by car bomb on December 12, 2005, dismissed the March 8 demonstration as a "farewell party" to Syria – not an inappropriate characterization.[30] Unequivocally partisan, Future TV news focused on ferreting out Syrians participating in the demonstrations to prove that March 8 was not "purely Lebanese." Equally partial, Hizbollah's al-Manar responded in kind. Two young demonstrators who were designated "Syrian" in Future TV's newscast later appeared on al-Manar, defiantly brandishing their Lebanese identity cards on the screen.[31]

Hizbollah scored several political points. It demonstrated that it had a large popular constituency ready to answer the call to take over the streets of Beirut – estimates ranged from 300,000 to 1,000,000 demonstrators. The Party of God also showcased its sophisticated organizational skills, gathering hundreds of thousands of people without any fights breaking out. At the same time, the March 8 demonstration reminded Lebanese, Arab, and world public opinion that a major segment of the Lebanese, perhaps half the population, did not support U.S. policies in Lebanon and the region. In an editorial titled "Hezbollah and the Cedar Revolution," the *New York Times* was perplexed by Hizbollah's peaceful action:

> It was disorienting to see supporters of Hezbollah, the militant Shiite movement, flooding Beirut last week with Lebanese flags and signs reading: "No to foreign interference." The movement usually marches under a yellow banner with a fist brandishing an AK-47, and the rally supported the biggest foreign interlopers in Lebanon – the Syrian troops who have imposed Syrian control since 1976. . . . It remains a long shot, but exchanging his banner

[29] Fattah, March 8, 2005.
[30] Ibid.
[31] Future TV showed them and they went to al-Manar to clarify: Two youths confirm they are Lebanese (March 12, 2005). *Assafir* [Arabic].

for Lebanon's flag suggests that Sheikh Nasrallah is not above changing his stripes if it is politically expedient.[32]

More importantly, Hizbollah compelled the Lebanese opposition to enter into street politics and the "numbers game." A direct result was the March 14, 2005 demonstration – the iconic event of the Independence Intifada.

In a gesture of one-upmanship designed to demonstrate that the opposition enjoyed broader popular support than Hizbollah and its allies, a massive demonstration was organized on March 14, 2005, by a motley crew of opposition forces, including al-Hariri's Future Movement, the Free Patriotic Movement (Michel 'Aoun), the Progressive Socialist Party (Walid Joumblatt), the Lebanese Forces (led by Samir Ja'ja'), the Democratic Left Gathering (Elias 'Atallah), and others, united by their opposition to what they termed the "Lebanese-Syrian Security Apparatus." This gathering of Christian, Sunni, Druze, and self-described secular forces from across the political landscape reflected the depth and breadth of the Lebanese population's frustration with Syrian control. The demonstration, which was estimated by some admittedly sympathetic sources to have topped one million, making it possibly the largest demonstration in Lebanese history, took place in Martyrs' Square, a few blocks from the al-Solh square where Hizbollah gathered its constituency on March 8. The numbers game reflected competing popular legitimacies, and betrayed anxieties about each community's demographic weight that have been kept hidden since the last national census was conducted in 1932.

FROM THE SCREEN TO THE STREET: REALITY TV AS IDIOM OF CONTENTION

If initial responses to Hariri's assassination confirmed that media institutions in Lebanon remained primarily political instruments in the hands of their owners, the demonstrations that ensued indicate that the participatory activities called for in *Star Academy*, like nominating and voting by mobile phone, using text messaging to build alliances and promote contestants, can in some cases have concrete political applications. The ways in which demonstrators used mobile phones, television, and vocabulary from reality TV shows suggests that the combination of

---

[32] "Hezbollah and the Cedar Revolution" [Editorial] (March 13, 2005). *New York Times.*

digital media's technical capacities and popular culture's affective appeal may broaden spaces of citizenship and lure into the political processes groups otherwise disenchanted by conventional politics – especially youth – and as a result may foster civic engagement.[33]

The March 14, 2005 demonstrators brandished numerous signs using the language of television and popular culture to express their main demands: the withdrawal of Syrian troops from Lebanon and the resignation of Lebanon's leading politicians and security officers. One sign featured the picture of the Justice Minister 'Adnan 'Addoum, a particularly loathed Syrian tool, with the English-language caption "Wanted, Dead or Alive." A more daring signboard carried the portraits of Syria's president alongside the late Hafez al-Asad, with a sarcastic inscription (also in English) "Papa Don't Preach, I'm in Trouble Deep," drawn from a song by U.S. pop star Madonna. Advertising slogans were used to political effect: Johnny Walker Scotch Whiskey's "Keep Walking" (English again) invited Syrian troops to walk out of Lebanon, and Persil laundry detergent's "Removes Stains," played on the words "Beqaa'," the valley in the Lebanese hinterland directly controlled by the Syrians, and "Boq'a," the Arabic world for stain. "1559 removes them from the Beqa', all the Beqa'," a placard said in Arabic, trumpeting UNSCR 1559 as a means to get rid of the Syrians.[34] Popular culture provided demonstrators with what the media scholar Justin Lewis described as "semiotic resources to draw on for describing categories of real life."[35]

Signs using the argot of reality TV went further in fusing entertainment and politics. Reality TV's ritual of nominating someone to be "voted off the island" or "voted out of the academy," resonated with demonstrators' demands to oust leading figures in the Lebanese-Syrian security state. Consider a handmade, English-language sign carried by a demonstrator (Figure 7.1): the words "Lahoud Nominee" (referring to Lebanese President Emile Lahoud, whose term was illegitimately extended by Syrian fiat) sit atop the exhortation "call 1559" (in reference

---

[33] See Bennett, W. L. (2008). "Changing Citizenship in the Digital Age," in *Civic Life Online: Learning How Digital Media Can Engage Youth*, ed. L. Bennett. Cambridge, MA: MIT Press, 1–24, for a succinct discussion of this issue. Also see the special issue of *European Journal of Cultural Studies* edited by J. Hermes and P. Dahlgren (2006).

[34] I owe several of these descriptions to Khatib, L. (2007). "Television and Public Action in the Beirut Spring," in *Arab Media and Political Renewal: Community, Legitimacy and Public Life*, ed. N. Sakr. London: I. B. Tauris, 28–43.

[35] Lewis, J. (2004). "The Meaning of Real Life," in *Reality TV: Remaking Television Culture*, ed. S. Murray and L. Ouellette. New York: New York University Press, 288–302.

Figure 7.1 During rallies marking the one-month anniversary of the assassination of Rafiq al-Hariri in downtown Beirut, demonstrators brandish political signs inspired by reality television. *Source*: Arab Documentation Center (Assafir), Beirut.

to the UN resolution calling for the withdrawal from Lebanon of Syrian troops and intelligence operatives). The sign is effective because it replicates weekly reality TV rituals like nomination, mobilization, and voting, which a vast number of Arab viewers know well. With reality TV's entrance into daily discourse throughout the Middle East and North Africa, Arab youth was *fluent* with *Star Academy's* idiom while older generations were *familiar* with it. Because of reality TV's extreme "publicness," this generational difference is less sharp than in other areas of popular culture about which older Arabs might know little or nothing. Reality TV helped create, even if temporarily, a broad multigenerational public.

When those rituals are transposed onto a sign carried by a Beirut demonstrator and captured by the cameras of myriad Arab satellite television channels and individual mobile phones equipped with digital cameras, the banner articulates a political agenda concisely and effectively. It uses a vocabulary that most Arabs, familiar with *Star Academy*, recognize and understand. The message on the sign, consisting of a few words and four digits, is eminently media savvy in an age of image, sound bites, and attention scarcity. Expressing a complex political issue in a snapshot rich with meaning, it is perfect material for the frantic and repetitive news cycle of channels such as al-Arabiya and al-Jazeera in addition to CNN and other Western networks. Because the text messaging of nominations and votes are part of reality TV rituals worldwide, the message has a potentially global audience. Satellite television financed by Saudi Arabian tycoons brought Lebanese politics to pan-Arab audiences, and popular culture made it widely palpable.

In the wake of the al-Hariri assassination and the political forces it unleashed, television feverishly pursued reality. News channels struggled to keep up with street events and to make sense of demonstrations as they unfolded in real time. In contrast, reality TV appeared to be ahead of reality, foreshadowing momentous political developments. In hindsight, the unceremonious dismissal of the Syrian contestant from *Star Academy* on February 25 looked like a logical preamble to the resignation of Prime Minister 'Omar Karami on February 28. In a rare moment in Arab politics, popular demonstrations had compelled a leader to resign, an event watched live throughout the Arab world. The importance of this event should not be underestimated. With thousands of Syrian troops still on Lebanese land and their colleagues in the *mukhabarat* (secret police) still haunting Lebanese streets and psyches, hundreds of thousands of demonstrators called for and obtained the resignation of a sitting prime minister backed by Syria. Of course, without U.S., French, and Saudi backing, the Beirut demonstrations may have been quelled. Nonetheless the television cameras of pan-Arab and Western channels, feeding live pictures to a worldwide audience, played a crucial role in sustaining the demonstrations.

As it struggled to make sense of reality, television was "pursued" by the media savvy Beirut demonstrators. They did not take U.S.-French-Saudi support for granted but courted and nurtured it, staging attractive visual spectacles to lure television cameras. The "branding" of the Independence Intifada was not completely improvised but was built on previous preparations. Months before the fatal car bomb, several political operatives had begun meeting with journalists and advertising professionals to design a media strategy for that spring's parliamentary elections in which the opposition expected to contest Syrian-supported candidates in a country that everyone assumed would still be dominated by Syria's troops and intelligence services. Samir Qassir, the *Annahar* columnist who would be assassinated on June 1, 2005, was a key figure in those preparations. A Francophone journalist who founded the short-lived *L'Orient L'Express*, a highbrow French-language magazine, Qassir wrote a bold column in Arabic in *Annahar* in which he regularly attacked Syria's domination of Lebanon. Hailing from a mixed Palestinian-Syrian family and often writing about the Palestinian cause, Qassir could not be easily dismissed by opponents as a Lebanese nationalist. After holding long discussions about what colors the opposition would adopt (orange would be seen as an imitation of the Ukraine's "Orange Revolution"; different shades of blue connoted the United Nations, the European Union, or even Israel; rainbow would connote the international gay rights movement) the group opted for red and white.[36] Both colors were on the Lebanese flag and both would be visible on television screens. Green was eschewed, likely due to its association with Islamism and to its being the color of the cedar at the center of the Lebanese flag, which to some parties within the opposition connotes Lebanese nationalism with a Christian hue.[37] The color selection was therefore meant to convey the broad range of religious, ideological, and political affiliations within the opposition.

As popular rallies began to form after al-Hariri's murder, the opposition transposed plans prepared for the spring elections to the current, unexpected political action triggered by al-Hariri's dramatic death. Walid Joumblatt's spouse Nora ordered forty thousand red-and-white scarves that the Intifada's leaders would soon wear around their necks.[38] Red and white was a photogenic color combination, and red symbolized "the blood of the martyr Rafiq al-Hariri." On February 26, they organized

---

[36] Wilson, S. and Williams, D. (April 17, 2005). "A New Power Rises across Mideast." *Washington Post*, A01.

[37] The banners of the Phalange Party and of the Lebanese Forces both carry a green cedar. A far-right party was called Guardians of the Cedar. According to Blanford, 2006, the scarves intended for al-Hariri's spring election campaign were to be green and white.

[38] Wilson and Williams, 2005.

a human chain made up of thirty thousand people that linked the site of al-Hariri's assassination in front of the St. George Hotel to Martyrs' Square downtown. On March 12, the opposition staged a huge human flag created by ten thousand people holding red, white, or green panels. For the mammoth March 14 demonstration, opposition leaders instructed their followers to wave Lebanese flags exclusively in order to underscore their main message of "national unity." The Lebanese flag, with two horizontal red bands framing a green cedar set against a white background, saturated downtown Beirut and, in turn, television screens. Fabric flags were waved, cardboard flags brandished, and faces were adorned with flags of paint. Young women painted small Lebanese flags on their cheeks like English soccer fans, and the less inhibited among them painted the tricolor flag on chests partly exhibited by *décolleté* shirts or skimpy tank tops, a move certain to attract media attention. The ubiquity of the Lebanese flag and the absence of sectarian banners was a new development in Lebanese politics. It had an unmistakable impact on public opinion in a country ordinarily marred by multiple political, religious, and social cleavages.[39] This strategy also preempted state repression under the guise of banning sectarian activities and preserving national unity.

The Independence Intifada witnessed what the political communication scholar Lance Bennett calls a *news reality frame*, one that works in "an information-restricted dimension of social space ... [to] ... obscure or distort the larger situation to which they refer."[40] This was manifest in the opposition's "branding" of the rallies to entice favorable media attention and in news coverage of the demonstrations. The opposition attempted to project a newly found national unity at a time when the demonstrations merely expressed converging political and sectarian interests animated by the desire to terminate Syrian hegemony. The initial, spontaneous rallies featured "a battle of the flags," underscoring that Lebanon remained a deeply fractured, radically pluralistic polity.[41]

[39] See Rizq (March 1, 2005). For secondary sources, see Khatib, 2007 and Kraidy, M. M. (2007). "Saudi Arabia, Lebanon, and the Changing Arab Information Order," *International Journal of Communication* 1 (1): 139–56, http://ijoc.org/ojs/index.php/ijoc/article/view/18/22 (accessed February 10, 2008).

[40] Bennett, W. L. (2005b). "Beyond Pseudoevents: Election News as Reality TV," *American Behavioral Scientist* 49 (3): 371.

[41] The quote is attributed to al-Hariri supporter Ghattas Khoury, in Blanford. Nicholas, 2006, 154. The Free Patriotic Movement headed by former Army Commander, General Michel ʿAwn, was a major participant in the March 14 rallies, but later broke with "March 14" and concluded a memorandum of understanding with Hizbollah on February 6, 2006.

More importantly, the fact that al-Hariri had been a partner of the Syrian regime for more than a decade in postwar Lebanese politics – Joumblatt once reportedly called al-Hariri Syria's real foreign minister – was obliterated by the vehemence of the new anti-Syrian discourse among al-Hariri's supporters, many of whom had benefited politically and personally from Syria's hegemony over Lebanon between 1990 and 2005. Listening to the slogans clamored by street demonstrators, reading their handheld signs, or watching news on Future TV and other sympathetic channels, one would be compelled to believe that Rafiq al-Hariri had spent his career militating against Syrian control of Lebanon. This demonstrates that political alliances are fluid and national loyalties are intermittent.

Paradoxically, his murder immortalized al-Hariri by making his picture ubiquitous and his personality larger-than-life – literally when one sees his enormous portrait decked on the wall of the imposing al-Amin mosque he built on Martyrs' Square, where al-Hariri was ultimately buried. As a Saudi columnist put it, rather lyrically,

> The killers of Rafiq al-Hariri transformed his personality from a businessman and politician to an immortal legend. Today Hariri's personality is a blend of Bill Gates and Che Guevara and Khalid Bin al-Waleed and 'Omar Bin al-Khattab and the awaited Mehdi and 'Omar al-Sharif in one person![42]

Though this blend of guerilla allure, Hollywood glamour, corporate prestige, historical charisma, and religious mysticism is a bit strained, the Independence Intifada crystallized al-Hariri's personality cult. A media critic writing in *Annahar*, a daily sympathetic to al-Hariri, captured Future TV's role in that endeavor:

> Since the assassination of Rafiq Al-Hariri, Future TV lives, and we live with it, in another world. . . . It is as if, in a world of pictures, humans create a . . . parallel world populated by copies of us. Though technically these copies do not precede us in presence, they transcend and outlast us. On Future TV the image . . . framed a reality that outdid reality, giving birth to a world whose cardinal rule is "you are present on television, therefore you exist," your television presence transcends your biological existence. As for us, in real life, our image is marginalized and we live in the shadow; featureless creatures, bodies outside of the frame, shadows of a

---

[42] Shobokshi, H. (March 6, 2005). Academy politics. *Asharq al-Awsat* [Arabic].

truth we dared to call hypothetical until it took its revenge by creating a "real" world from which it excluded us. The picture became truth and we became hypothetical, it became the reality and we the illusion, it the original and we the copy![43]

The incessant recurrence of al-Hariri on Future TV in memorial clips edited like news segments created the impression that he was a driving force – very much alive, albeit visually – of the revolution to regain Lebanon's freedom and independence. This was reinforced by Sa'd al-Hariri's (Rafiq's political heir) habit of placing a large portrait of his father on an empty chair beside him in meetings with Lebanese and foreign officials. The ubiquity of al-Hariri's image defied the fact of his death. Image overran reality.

A HYPERMEDIA EVENT

Nonetheless, the Independence Intifada can be described as a pseudo-event only in part.[44] Street rallies were, to use Bennett's words, "constructed by communication consultants . . . to disconnect an event from an underlying complicating or contradictory reality,"[45] but the demonstrations expressed genuine feelings of grief and popular anger at the system, and journalistic coverage was not entirely passive or acquiescent. Nonetheless, in the polarized Lebanese environment, rival politicians and media outlets robustly contested the opposition's framing of the events. This occurred most dramatically during the March 8 "loyalist" demonstration discussed earlier and in the nightly newscasts of New TV and Hizbollah's al-Manar. Contesting the opposition's – at the time dominant – frame of the Independence Intifada, these television channels provided competing information, therefore introducing a rival interpretive scheme. The size and scope of the demonstrations meant that only television, through roof-top and helicopter-carried cameras operating at the widest angles, could depict the event as a whole.[46]

---

[43] al-Khoury, S. (March 18, 2005). The original and the copy/image. *Annahar* [Arabic].

[44] In addition to Boorstin, D. (1961). *The Image – Or What Happened to the American Dream*. London: Weidenfeld and Nicholson; the term "pseudoevents" was used by Bennett, 2005b, 371, and Meyer, T. (2002). *Media Democracy: How the Media Colonize Politics*. Cambridge: Polity.

[45] Bennett, 2005b, 371.

[46] Not unlike what Lang and Lang's study of the MacArthur Day parade, reprinted in Lang, E. G. and Lang, K. (1984). *Politics and Television Reviewed*. Beverly Hills, CA: Sage.

The Independence Intifada might be described more accurately as a *hypermedia event*. The term *hypermedia* captures the technological convergence and media saturation that characterize many contemporary societies, while emphasizing the speed and convergence of communication processes.[47] Unlike pseudoevents and media events,[48] hypermedia events are not entirely staged by the communication industry or officialdom. They have a bottom-up element represented by genuine popular feelings of frustration, grief, and anger that lead to popular contestation. Even the most competitive type of media events described by media scholars Daniel Dayan and Elihu Katz, which they term "contests," operate under generally agreed upon norms and rules, pitting "evenly matched individuals or teams against each other and bid them to compete according to strict rules."[49] From that perspective, even contests are moments of social solidarity. In contrast, hypermedia events, like the Saudi controversy over *Star Academy* explicated in Chapter 4, the Syrian-Lebanese media war analyzed in Chapter 6, and the Independence Intifada, are contentious episodes of political turbulence and social fragmentation. Most importantly, hypermedia events are literally constructed by actors who use "small" media to access public space. These events do not reinforce the status quo as do Dayan and Katz's; rather than being concerned with ceremonial politics, they express the rise of contentious politics.

This type of events is enabled by the rise of *hypermedia space*, a symbolic field created by interactions between multiple media, from mobile telephones to satellite television. By facilitating connections among multiple media devices, convergence creates a symbolic territory with multiple access points that are personalized, mobile, and nonconspicuous, and therefore makes possible multiple forms of engagement.[50] This hypermedia space redefines conventional understandings of liveness by fostering what Couldry called "group liveness . . . a mobile group of friends who are in continuous contact via their mobile phones through

---

[47] I borrow this from Deibert, R. J. (1997). *Parchment, Printing, and Hypermedia: Communication in World Order Transformation*. New York: Columbia University Press.

[48] The notion of media events was developed in Dayan, D. and Katz, E. (1992). *Media Events: The Live Broadcasting of History*. Cambridge, MA: Harvard University Press.

[49] Dayan and Katz, 1992, 33.

[50] For a detailed theoretical discussion, see Kraidy, M. M. (2006). "Governance and Hypermedia in Saudi Arabia," *First Monday* 11 (9), http://firstmonday.org/issues/special11_9/kraidy/index.html (accessed December 30, 2006).

calls and texting."[51] In so doing hypermedia space decentralizes political communication and increases the likelihood of contestation by widening avenues for public engagement. Television may be the only means to capture the event in its visual entirety, but to do so it relies on several points of access enabled by smaller mobile media.

The commercial and dramatic logics of reality TV activate hypermedia space and show "group liveness" in action. To mobilize support and vote for favorite contestants, viewers conjoin mobile phones, e-mail, and television in fluid and interactive communication processes that form hypermedia space. This contributes to making Arabs aware of the political impact of media convergence, aided by journalists who analyze the role of new media in Arab politics through the prism of the reality TV debates. Clearly, the actual use of hypermedia space depends on political context, availability of technology infrastructure, and, most importantly, people willing to use various connected media for specific social or political purposes. Though its direct impact ought not be overstated, reality TV is an accessory in creating that willingness. When viewers read and watch information about reality TV shows, produce information about contestants on blogs and fan sites, mobilize and create voting coalitions by using e-mail and mobile phones, they set up networks of social engagement. In sum, reality TV activates hypermedia space because it promotes participatory practices like voting, campaigning, and alliance building by using mobile telephones and related devices.

These "operational" tactics can be applied in the political realm. When the Lebanese army established checkpoints around central Beirut to prevent demonstrators from reaching public spaces, soldiers at some checkpoints were clearly unwilling to use force to send demonstrators back on their tracks, a nugget of information that was immediately "blasted" using text messages, allowing demonstrators to converge on checkpoints where soldiers or commanding officers appeared sympathetic to their cause.[52] At other checkpoints, young women put flowers in soldiers' hands, thus "disarming" them and helping flows of men and women alerted through text-messaging "blasts" to reach designated

---

[51] Couldry, N. (2004). "Liveness, 'Reality,' and the Mediated Habitus from Television to the Mobile Phone," *The Communication Review* 7: 353–61. He defines traditional liveness as "individual communication to a socially legitimated point of central transmission" (357).

[52] Personal communications with several participants in the demonstrations, Beirut, Lebanon, June–Aug. 2005.

protest areas.[53] Demonstrators used mobile phones to mobilize and organize and utilized reality TV's lexicon to attract cameras and propagate their message.

The Beirut demonstrators exploited hypermedia space to their full political advantage. They took pictures with their mobile phones' digital cameras, which they promptly transmitted to news organizations or to friendly bloggers who uploaded them on Web sites dedicated to their cause. These "citizen-correspondents," as *Assafir* media critic Rasha al-Atrash called the people who took the first pictures of the July 2005 bombings in the London tube, ensured that their cause would be seen across the world. Unlike the conspicuous CNN and al-Jazeera cameras, the invisible cameras of thousands of demonstrators acted as an unobtrusive and inconspicuous surveillance system that went a long way in preempting repression by the security apparatus. The proliferation of cameras is likely to have contributed to preventing clashes between demonstrators and counterdemonstrators, no easy feat when one considers that between one-quarter and one-half of the total Lebanese population descended on the streets of Beirut in the span of a week in March 2005.[54]

Knowledge and experience gained through social engagement in the context of reality TV shows can be tapped by political activists who plug into networks of friends and acquaintances engaged or familiar with reality TV, converting them partially into instruments of political mobilization. In doing so, they turn social involvement into civic engagement and political contestation. This was evident in the signs using reality TV's lingo to make political statements. The resulting large numbers of demonstrators, once on television news, became a potent tool of political pressure on the Lebanese and Syrian regimes, whose leaders knew that in a media-saturated environment, clamping down on demonstrators would create a public relations nightmare.

The flags, cameras, and mobile phones did not, on their own, prevent the Syrian-Lebanese security apparatus from repressing the demonstrators, but their combination with pressure from the United States, France, and Saudi Arabia did. Saudi Arabia, whose princes and moguls control most Arab media, was on the side of the Independence Intifada, so Saudi

[53] Ibid.
[54] See al-Nakt Rahme, Z. (March 17, 2005). Audiovisual media cover the opposition in its independence uprising (Independence Intifada) and "spaces" more heated than demonstrations [Investigation]. *Annahar* [Arabic]. At least one prominent journalist said she believed the presence of the cameras of the Arab and foreign press protected Lebanese journalists.

officials did not attempt to limit coverage of the demonstrations. As this chapter has shown, Future TV and LBC supported "March 14." The alignment of the political economic structure of Arab media with the cause of the Lebanese demonstrators and against the Syrian regime gave political teeth to the rallies. The potency of hypermedia space depends on the ability of activists to use digital media but also on the political decisions of "big" media owners, a dependence that is nonetheless not complete because al-Jazeera, opposed to the Saudi regime and to U.S. policies in the Middle East, gave sustained and overall positive coverage to the Beirut demonstrations. In this case, the judicious use of hypermedia space contributed to a transformation of the field of contention in Lebanon.

By the summer of 2007, the Independence Intifada was in shambles. The massive red-and-white popular display of unity had given way to internecine sectarian struggle and Byzantine political bargaining, abetted by foreign intervention from the United States, Syria, Iran, and France, in a country wrecked by Israel's military onslaught on Lebanon in the summer of 2006. In the preceding two and a half years, a series of car bombs had dispatched key symbols of the Independence Intifada such as Samir Qassir and Gebran Tuayni. The atmosphere is tense, people disillusioned; across the political spectrum, there is growing resentment against foreign intervention in Lebanese politics and against local politicians eager to enlist outside help. The momentum of the spring of 2005 has turned into a political stalemate between "March 8" and "March 14." As the Independence Intifada becomes a fleeting memory, reality TV helped people make sense of the situation. In a column entitled "What If?" Ibrahim al-'Aris, al-Hayat's chief media critic, imagined a political conversation between a Beirut barber and his customer in the summer of 2007:

> ... a light bulb went on in the barber's head as he kept talking ... on the one hand angry at what happened, on the other hand amazed at the surprising idea that came to his mind. ... Then he said: Do you remember *Star Academy*? [The client replied] "And what does *Star Academy* have to do with the matter?" he [The barber] waited ... [then said] "in *Star Academy*, contestants were kept together and each one of them attempted to beat the others ... they were all put in front of dozens of cameras ... and microphones. ... That enabled virtuous, god-worshipping, viewers to follow what occurred and what was said moment by moment, and then decide who they preferred over whom.
>
> "So, neighbor, what you are proposing is ..." And as if the barber did not hear that last question, he continued: "What if top level

politicians – not second or third tier – were put in a locked house, with dozens of cameras, and they were asked to debate. Wouldn't the people at that moment know who is lying and who is telling the truth? Who is the steward of people's interest and the future of the country? And who serves foreigners, their interests, and their wars? "Completely isolated?" asked the journalist. The barber answered: With the insistence that telephones be available so that each one of them can call to consult and be enlightened every once in a while . . . with one condition. "What is the condition?" Simply that all telephone lines be local, incapable of calling abroad![55]

Two lessons can be drawn from the Independence Intifada. First, shifts from sectarian politics to an unstable national unity to a period of reconfigured political fragmentation evinces the mercurial character of nationalism. The "March 8" and "March 14" political blocks that dominate Lebanese politics today feature striking aberrations from traditional Lebanese political orientations, including the new anti-Syrian line of the al-Hariri-led Lebanese Sunnis and the alliance between the predominantly Christian Maronite Free Patriotic Movement and Hizbollah. Second, the Beirut events during spring 2005 call for a new understanding of Arab politics grounded in political peformativity rather than exclusively in elite bargaining or deliberative rationality. Reality TV's intrusion in the Independent Intifada indicates that the Arab reality TV wars have contributed to creating an idiom of contention on the street and screen and a glossary of interpretation on op-ed pages, in addition to proliferating opportunities for potentially defiant political performance.

[55] al-'Aris, I. (July 17, 2007). What if. . . ? *Al-Hayat* [Arabic].

Conclusion: Performing Politics, Taming Modernity

This book set out to understand why, how, and with what consequences the Arab reality TV battles mixed politics, religion, business, and sexuality, setting Arab public discourse ablaze in times of
political crisis, military strife, and religious tension. As we come to the
end of the story, it is useful to recall some of the big questions that animated this book. The pretense of reality TV to represent reality inspired
the first question: What is the relation between reality TV and social
reality? Many Arab journalists, we have seen, grappled with the answer,
which goes to the heart of the social authority of the media; a couple of
years into the Arab reality TV polemics and two months after al-Hariri's
assassination, a columnist captured the situation as follows:

> After reality TV programs occupied an important part of social
> "reality" during the last two years, reality TV's status has begun a
> decline, bowing to the shocks of the real "reality." . . . Real reality
> won the gamble, outshining the program that had to leave the
> limelight for a time . . . which seems to have killed the notion of
> "real TV" [in English]. . . . As if these shows lost their luster, and
> their realism, and rushed towards the real reality whose realism
> they sought to appropriate. . . . Didn't *Big Brother* shake and stir
> Bahrain? . . . The realism of that show provoked the real reality
> and became part of social reality, and not the other way around.
> In contrast, today we see that these programs are themselves in-
> fluenced by reality to the point of self-denial. . . . Which of these
> two realities is reality? It is as if real reality discovered the fake-
> ness of reality TV, the fragility of its logic. . . . We have an emer-
> gent, noisy reality [represented by reality shows] that is more
> than what we can handle. . . . Real reality is completely different:

it contains no dancing and no voting through text-messages in a democratic experiment, and the sadness it brings is by far deeper than the passing tear shed when a friend leaves the studio.[1]

The competition between reality TV and "real reality" for public relevance at a time of crisis reflects the special role that reality TV played in the battle for Arab viewers. *Star Academy* competed with a car-bomb assassination not by providing an alternative to on-the-ground reality but by engaging deliberately with security and political developments – the screen in symbiosis with the street. Reality TV stirred contention in public life because it mobilized people, crystallized issues, and incessantly stressed the question "what constitutes reality?" while simultaneously preempting the formation of consensus on that question.

"It is only with the coming of modernity," wrote the sociologist Shmuel Eisenstadt, "that drawing the boundaries of the political becomes one of the major foci of open political contestation and struggle."[2] Arab reality TV is contentious because its claim to represent reality spurs wide-ranging political battles to distinguish the real from the nonreal. Politicians, clerics, journalists, and ordinary people argue over what is real and what is not; what is socially acceptable and what is not; and what is worthy of political action and what is not. They offer rival visions of the good society and the role of religion, the state, and the West therein. Like chemical developer bringing latent patterns into crisp view, contention over reality TV brings simmering social and political tensions to the surface of public life.

Heated polemics awaken long-standing debates on Arab-Western relations. With its Western provenance, its claim to the real, its plebiscitary ethos, its individualist premises and its popularity with Arab viewers, reality TV activates Arab memories of the West's historical power to define their societies. This motivates Arabs to enter broad public debates on hot-button issues like the place of women in society, religion and political power, and individual achievement versus social harmony. Though couched in the language of cultural resistance, the debate converges on one question: because the West presents both despised and desirable features, how can Arab societies selectively integrate Western influence? Stated otherwise: how can you be Arab and modern at the same time, without one of these identities usurping the other?

---

[1] Hazin, G. (April 19, 2005). When reality collides with reality TV. *Al-Hayat* [Arabic].

[2] Eisenstadt, S. N. (2000). "Multiple Modernities," *Daedelus* 129: 1, 6.

Media institutions play a crucial role in this process of cultural translation. In particular, television contributes to cultural hybridization, the selective incorporation of foreign values and styles that I explored at length in a previous book.[3] The public contest over reality TV offered a platform to debate the virtues and vices of a modernity perceived to be Western. At various times during the polemic, "real" meant "truthful," "authentic," or "self-defined." These definitions revolve around the role of the West, mooring arguments about reality in long-standing grievances by Arabs vexed by their inability to define their social, economic, and political realities on their own terms. The concentration in Western hands of the power to define the world is a chief source of the Arab malaise, and it clearly comes to the fore in Arab public life. Rival demonstrators in Beirut's squares rejected both American definitions of the event as the "Cedar Revolution"[4] and the Syrian president's attempt to belittle Lebanese activists by criticizing media coverage of their cause. The Beirut protesters pushed their cause while national politicians and outside powers manipulated street protests to fit their own agendas. In their effort to represent themselves, the foot soldiers of the Independence Intifada fought symbolic battles with backers and opponents; all parties attempted to manipulate the fundamental nexus of the battle for Arab viewers: the gap between reality and image. This brings us to the next question.

What do the reality TV controversies reveal about the power to represent reality and about the implications of such power? Criticism of reality TV's claim to represent reality stems from a widely shared sentiment that the reality put forth in *al-Ra'is* and *Star Academy* was alien to local norms and values, and as such its pretense to be real in the Arab context is akin to Western symbolic violence that robs Arabs of the ability to construe their own reality. This unfulfilled desire for self-definition cripples propaganda attempts to reach Arab "hearts and minds." Assuming erroneously that Arab animosity toward the United States was a problem of communication, the Bush administration created several Arabic-language media outlets including Radio Sawa and al-Hurra Television. A loud megaphone sending one-way messages to a tiny sliver of the Arab audience who tunes in, this media apparatus is physically

---

[3] Kraidy, M. M. 2005. *Hybridity, or the Cultural Logic of Globalization*. Philadelphia: Temple University Press.

[4] Though some of members of the March 14 group paid lip-service to it, the moniker "Cedar Revolution" did not gain wide popular acceptance. On the opposite side, I have already mentioned that Hizbollah's Hassan Nasrallah humored the media to "zoom out" to show the real size of pro-Hizbollah demonstrations.

formidable but effectively useless. Not only do Arabs view it as another Western attempt to define Arab societies, but also the U.S. government's mass communication is disabled by its framing as a weapon in the U.S.-declared "Global War on Terror" – an unfortunate rhetorical concoction. Through that frame, Radio Sawa and al-Hurra Television define Arab viewers, albeit indirectly, as potential terrorists. Cutting through the fog of patronizing talk about freedom and democracy, Arab viewers see dichotomies between "moderate Arabs" who support U.S. policies in the Middle East and "bad Arabs" who do not. At the same time, debates over reality TV show that Arab viewers' understanding of what they watch is filtered by intense debates about the impact of the media that occur on the airwaves but also in the context of social and political institutions. This punctures the myth of a monolithic "Arab street." To recapitulate: U.S. government–sponsored media are impaired not only because Arabs are at the same time hostile to U.S. policies in the Middle East and highly discriminating viewers of an ideologically eclectic television industry[5] but also because of al-Hurra's and similar institutions' long-standing grievances about dominant Western power to represent Arabs. *The problem is one of power, not one of communication.* The Arab reality TV controversies attest to the depth and intensity of the Arab longing for self-representation and suggest that such a yearning continues to be a potent factor in Arab politics.

Feelings of nationalism manifest during the Arab reality TV contests also emanate from Arab striving for self-definition – for what is nationalism, but the embodiment of a people's will to be and represent themselves? When young Arabs compete against each others in *Superstar* and *Star Academy*, they are ambassadors of their nation-states – willingly or begrudgingly. The ubiquity of national flags in reality show studios and among fans swarming Arab streets, waving national banners, and blaring car horns every time a compatriot wins, testifies to the potency of state-based nationalism (as opposed to pan-Arab nationalism). The rise of various strands of Islamism and Western concerns about it notwithstanding, this book reveals that nationalism remains a major force in the Arab world.[6] In this context it is important to understand that popular

---

[5] Kraidy, M. M. (January 2008). *Arab Media and U.S. Policy: A Public Diplomacy Reset*, Policy Brief. Muscatine, IA: The Stanley Foundation, http://stanleyfdn.org/publications/pab/PAB08Kraidy.pdf (accessed December 30, 2008).

[6] The primacy of nationalism over Islamism is argued by Olivier Roy, most recently in Roy, O. (2008). *The Politics of Chaos in the Middle East*. New York: Columbia University Press.

outbursts of nationalism are episodic and not always predictable. They depend on momentary political performance more than on stable political affiliations. The young Kuwaiti Bashar al-Shatti was elevated to a national icon, triggering a feverish patriotism and exposing the limited influence of Kuwait's Islamists, whose attacks on reality TV did not dampen its popularity but rather made them look extreme and out of touch. Though *Star Academy*'s and *Superstar*'s Lebanese provenance triggered the ire of al-Tabtaba'i, the shows' positive resonance among liberals outweighed Islamist invective.[7] However, as Wedeen recently argued, nationalism does not necessarily rise at the expense of religious identification.[8] This book suggests that the entanglement of women figures with the surge of nationalist sentiments is more pronounced than the connection between nationalism and secularism. This brings forth the next question.

Why did women emerge as powerful and contested symbols in the Arab battles over reality TV? The Syrian *Superstar 2* finalist Shahd Barmada, the Syrian Joey Bahous who was evicted during *Star Academy 2*'s "patriotic night," the Iraqi *Star Academy 4* winner Shadha Hassoun, and the mythical women figures that embody national identity in Saudi Arabia and Kuwait: all were poignant faces of the dilemma women face as icons of their nations. Perceived as markers of identity, women's bodies are thrust into the public eye in celebration of the nation. As the seventeen-year-old Barmada discovered, this put women in a double bind. On the one hand, they are celebrated as icons of nationhood; on the other hand, they are forced to relinquish their individual identities and sacrifice their ambitions. The case of Shadha Hassoun in Iraq is also revealing of a resurgent nationalism that temporarily trumped sectarianism and the Sunni-Shi'i divide awakened by the disintegration of Iraq under American occupation. That a young woman with an Iraqi father and Moroccan mother, who had never visited Iraq, would be seized as an icon of Iraqi unity illustrates the heightened vulnerability of women to symbolic appropriation in times of war. Equally, such events underscore the fragility of the nation at the same time as they shore up feelings of belonging to imagined national communities.

---

[7] Kuwaiti nationalism, galvanized by the brutal Iraqi invasion and occupation, is sympathetic to Lebanese nationalism's struggle against a more powerful neighbor. Iraq and Syria, respectively, have long refused to recognize the legitimacy and sovereignty of Kuwait and Lebanon. *Star Academy*'s tribute to Kuwait's Independence Day (February 25) and Liberation Day (February 26), during the famous February 25, 2005, "Patriotic Prime," was a master strike combining commercial concerns with political affinity.

[8] Wedeen, 2008.

Arab women's predicament is compounded by a collective memory of colonial attempts to change their legal status, as a result of which any change in women's status is viewed as forced Westernization. This fraught history returned with recent expressions of concern in the West for Muslim women in the prelude to the invasions of Iraq and especially Afghanistan. In Leila Ahmed's pithy coinage, Arab women are subjected to "colonial feminism" – ostentatious colonial attempts to improve the lot of brown women undercut by regressive attitudes toward women in the colonial metropole.[9] Perceptions that Arab women are susceptible to Western conspiracies that undermine local societies play up the vulnerability of women who publicly appear to endorse values and behaviors that are defined as "Western." Women reality TV contestants place themselves in jeopardy by challenging social and religious frontiers. Rising to the finale of a reality show and becoming a national symbol meant entering the protracted debate over reality; doing all that through singing, dancing, and living performances was an unmistakable break with Islamist notions of sequestration that energize reactionary guardians of invented authenticity. As the Turkish sociologist Nilüfer Göle put it, "Islamism, in its pursuit of the establishment of religious boundaries, gives priority to *the visual, corporal,* moral regulation of social relations" between men and women.[10] Women who rise to advanced stages in Arab reality TV shows cut a particularly tragic figure in an economy of visibility in which they are at once market commodities, national idols, and icons of religious subversion – sequestered once again, albeit symbolically. At the same time, this book presented a complex picture of women and gender. The reality TV wars have seen instances of women's victimization as symbolic pawns of nations or as repositories of traditions created by men; but in the same context women made and defended public claims, agitated politically, participated in demonstrations, and in some cases confronted self-appointed custodians of tradition. Furthermore, accusations by Saudi and Kuwaiti Islamists of *muyu'a* reflect concerns about effeminate male behavior in reality shows and underscore that the matter of sexuality in the Arab reality TV polemics exceeded the woman question. The lesson to be drawn from this book is a reconfirmation of the centrality of gender as a field for the deployment of power.

---

[9] Ahmed, L. (1992). *Women and Gender in Islam: Historical Roots of a Current Debate.* New Haven, CT: Yale University Press.
[10] Göle, N. (2000). "Snapshots of Islamic Modernities," *Daedelus* 129: 1, 112, emphasis added.

Women are not the only figure thrown in the limelight of the new visibility. By subjecting the notion of "reality" to scrutiny, reality TV made political reality more visible. What does the new visibility of power mean for Arab politics? Their actions and foibles on public display, Arab leaders face new constraints. With state-owned media systems attracting dismal ratings, leaders and governments find it more and more difficult to control their image. This forces them into compromises with media institutions that hold sway over the economy of visibility. With its pretense to be real, backstage front-stage dynamics, and voting rituals, reality TV provided a fitting vocabulary to describe the new visibility, even nakedness, of Arab political leaders. As one Arab journalist commented:

> In spite of all the criticism that were leveled at *Star Academy* and similar programs ... triviality ... negative influence on youth ... with which I agree, I see an important benefit in this program and its ilk: It gave us a truthful picture of the process of manufacturing stars and public personalities charged with social and political leadership and influence over public opinion.[11]

Citizens and leaders see the process of manufacturing publicness exposed on television, Web sites, magazines, and blogs that orbit reality TV shows. The creation of stars has shed light on the process of governance, all the while puncturing the media's claim to social authority.

Does this mean that reality TV has contributed to the democratization of the Arab world? Some of the evidence presented in this book points to an affirmative answer. After all, as the political theorist Jon Elster has argued, conflict resolution in pluralistic polities can occur through variations on three practices that constitute the essence of democracy: arguing, bargaining, and voting.[12] This book has shown that the Arab reality TV polemics activated these practices and inspired a lexicon of political analysis visible in the Arab press and an idiom of political expression manifest in the 2005 Beirut demonstrations. There is no doubt that *Star Academy*, *Superstar*, and *al-Ra'is* made Arabs argue, bargain, and vote. But if we were to adopt a narrow definition of democracy as regular contested elections with unpredictable results, then clearly reality TV has not democratized Arab politics at large. If,

---

[11] al-Fatwaki, S. (August 30, 2005). A technique for manufacturing leaders. *Al-Quds al-Arabi* [Arabic].

[12] Elster, J., ed. (1998). *Deliberative Democracy*. New York: Cambridge University Press.

however, we were to adopt a broad definition of democracy as popular contention, deliberation, and performance, then reality TV can be said, albeit cautiously, to have a "democratizing" effect. As Wedeen argued, "democratic persons are . . . produced through quotidian practices of deliberation. These acts are not embellishments of a democracy independently existing. They are the thing itself."[13] The gap between the two definitions of democracy – as formal elections in the context of institutions of government or as informal deliberations in the context of popular performance – does not necessarily reflect the existence of two distinct spheres, one of decision making in politics and the other of deliberation, what Habermas called "weak" and "strong" publics.[14] It is nearly impossible to measure, for example, the extent to which the *Star Academy* polemic contributed to policy changes in Saudi Arabia; it is equally arduous to pinpoint the agency of the Beirut demonstrators (as opposed to U.S., French, and Saudi pressure) in effecting the withdrawal of Syrian troops. Nonetheless, it is beyond dispute that in both cases, actors took advantage of reality TV – its language, the debates it generated, the social imaginary it spawned – in momentous political activity to advance their arguments against rivals. In brief, reality TV has contributed to modifying the field of contention by amplifying the resonance of some political agendas and blunting others.[15]

Arab regimes are determined to prevent their opponents from exploiting this new media environment. Weary of the proliferating opportunities for political deliberation and performance offered by popular culture, and of the unforgiving news cycle that relishes images of blatant crackdown, the authoritarian state now resorts to new regulations that provide legal cover for repression. To bolster the fiction of justice – few make rhetorical gestures toward democracy anymore, so much has the notion been tainted by the Bush administration's attempts to remake the Middle East – regimes create an image of the rule of law. The Arab Satellite Television Charter of February 2008 tried to export Saudi and Egyptian media policies.[16] But frustrated by the political

---

[13] Wedeen, 2008, 3.

[14] Habermas, J. (1998). *Between Facts and Norms.* Cambridge, MA: MIT Press.

[15] McAdam, Tarrow, and Tilly (2001) would describe this as a change in "political opportunity structures." See also Lynch (2008). Medium theory refers to the same phenomenon as "distributional changes" (see Deibert, 1997).

[16] Kraidy, M. M. (2008d). "Arab States: Emerging Consensus to Muzzle Media?" *Arab Reform Bulletin* 6 (2). Carnegie Endowment for International Peace, Washington, DC, http://www.carnegieendowment.org/publications/index.cfm?fa=view&id=19968&prog=zgp&proj=zdrl,zme-kraidy (accessed June 1, 2008).

quagmire of integrating two dozen countries under one regulatory framework, Egypt's minister of information secretly drafted a national media law, which was leaked by the independent paper *al-Masry al-Youm* in July 2008, with a blunt editorial arguing that the law was poised to "slaughter satellite television . . . and Facebook."[17] As crude propaganda gives way to image management in an uncontrollable hypermedia environment – Egypt's prime minister recently stunned the opposition when he contributed to an opposition blog[18] – it becomes clear that Arab leaders are forced to enter the battle to define reality without guarantees that their version of reality would prevail. At the same time, governments made sure that potentially embarrassing reality shows like *To Catch a Predator* would not be aired, for they would puncture claims that social pathologies are peculiar to Western societies. This shift from the propaganda state to the public relations state heralds the rise of a polished, media-savvy "neo-authoritarianism."

Various episodes of contentious politics instigated by reality TV have crucial implications when it comes to political participation and democracy: first, they suggest that a deliberative-performative approach is better suited to understanding the impact of Arab media on public life than the deliberative-rationalistic model developed by Habermas and explicitly or implicitly guides most studies of al-Jazeera's impact on Arab politics. A deliberative-performative model goes beyond a discursive understanding of participation to include the body and related performative activities – holding signs referencing popular culture or making jokes at the expense of politicians, using popular culture as a lexicon for social and political criticism, and singing and dancing in a politicized context. The latter model implicitly excludes entertainment, popular culture, and women from the sphere of politics. The former, used in this book, stems from the recognition that entertainment is political. In this I hope to have provided some evidence to answer my colleague Kai Hafez who recently wrote that "slogans like 'entertainment is political' need to be substantiated."[19] Second, the case studies analyzed in this book bolster existing research that underscores the Arab public's selective enthusiasm for democracy: broad acceptance of democracy when it comes to social justice and political accountability and

---

[17] al-Jallad, M. (July 9, 2008). The Law to "slaughter" satellite television . . . and Facebook! *Al-Masry al-Youm* [Arabic].

[18] Responding to harsh criticism of his government's policies: Egypt's prime minister contributes for the first time to a blog amidst bloggers' astonishment (August 9, 2008). Alarabiya.net [Arabic].

[19] Hafez, 2008, 5.

intense contention over democracy when it means liberal values.[20] The contentious debate about liberal values analyzed in this book invites reality TV scholars to go beyond the established neoliberal template of Anglo-American reality TV studies to consider a wider gamut of social and political processes.

How does Arab youth fare in the new hypermedia environment? Young Arabs find opportunities in hypermedia space that are denied them in "real" social space. By promoting interactivity through mobile phones and the Internet, reality TV has abetted Arab hypermedia space. The popularity of Facebook also contributed to the growing visibility of the personal, the resulting politicization of which triggered harsh government reactions in Syria and Egypt. More widespread are mobile phones, whose initial acceptance as culturally neutral business tools morphed into vocal objections with the rise of multimedia applications. In Saudi Arabia, where gender interaction is strictly regulated, concerns arose with the introduction of text messaging, digital cameras, and especially Bluetooth technology.[21]

Youths have long interacted in malls, where they sneakily threw a piece of paper with their phone number at the feet of their object of attraction as their paths crossed.[22] Bluetooth gave a new twist to this well-established flirting ritual, enabling users to know whether a person of interest is amenable to conversation. Bluetooth activation signals a readiness to socialize. "Using Bluetooth is much better than trying to throw the number to the girls through car windows, or in the shopping center," said a Saudi teenager. "Through Bluetooth I guarantee that the other party chose to accept my number or the file I sent. In other words, I don't impose myself on anyone."[23] This is not without peril: a commercial for the Saudi Telecommunications Company showed a young man trying to reach a young woman sitting with her family in the family section of a coffee shop, who accidentally connected to her father's Bluetooth-activated phone instead of the young woman's. Like a

---

[20] Scholars using different theories and methodologies have reached this conclusion. See Wedeen, 2008; also Jamal, A. and Tessler, M. (2008). "Attitudes in the Arab World," *Journal of Democracy* 19: 1, http://www.arabbarometer.org/reports/democbarometers .pdf (accessed December 1, 2008).

[21] See, e.g., "Bluetooth" in Saudi Arabia prospers in lost time. *Al-Hayat* [Arabic], March 26, 2005 and 'Abbud, G. (February 10, 2005). Teenagers sinking their teeth into new technology. *Arab News.*

[22] See Wynn, L. (1997). "The Romance on Tahliyya Street: Youth Culture, Commodities and the Use of Public Space in Jeddah," *Middle East Report* 204: 30–1.

[23] 'Abbud, G. (February 10, 2005).

stern father, the Saudi government imposed stiff sanctions on peddlers of "phone pornography." Like most such measures, this has not stamped out the targeted behavior, with mobile phone "misuses" breaking scandals regularly. By featuring open male-female interactions and inviting viewers to interact using a mobile phone, reality TV teaches new private behavior in public space.[24] These behaviors are not always contrarian to the status quo: because of the cost of the devices involved, they mostly concern wealthier Arabs, disproportionately located in the Gulf; they include conspicuous consumption, sharing pornography, spreading the faith, and political activism.

Beyond the duality between reality and image, how do the reality TV polemics relate to modernity? The story of Arab reality TV is best understood as a process of taming modernity, a "modernity academy" where actors deliberate and contest the meaning of modernity. From this perspective, the heated polemic over *Star Academy* and others is an episode of modernity's "endless trial" in which various segments of the Arab public – or more accurately, various Arab publics and counterpublics – play the roles of defendant, plaintiff, prosecutor, defender, and judge. As the trial proceeds in mitigating the unwelcomed facets of Western modernity, Arab reality TV is less debasing and more didactic than its Western counterparts. The absence of humiliation rituals familiar to viewers of U.S. and U.K. reality shows and MBC's naming the Arabic version of *The Biggest Loser*, al-Rabeh al-Akbar (*The Biggest Winner*) reflect a cultural compromise, a bargain struck by institutions who act as mediators of modernity. Shifting patterns of Arab reality TV production reflect the struggle to figure out how to be Arab and modern. Whereas in 2004 most Arab reality TV shows were formats licensed from European or American companies and adapted to the Arab market, by 2008 a majority (15 out of 26) of Arab reality TV shows were original local creations.[25] This shift involved experimentation by television companies and their staff with foreign ideas and practices before creating their own shows. Once a badge of modernity, outright mimicry of the West has grown less enticing after the polemics over *Star Academy*

---

[24] Those shunned from public space can surreptitiously gain access to it through hypermedia space: it is no coincidence that women make up two-thirds of Saudi Internet users. Country profile: Saudi Arabia, http://news.bbc.co.uk/go/pr/fr/-/1/hi/world/middle_east/country_profiles/791936.stm. London: British Broadcasting Corporation (accessed December 30, 2006).

[25] Snobar, A. (May 2008). *Arab Reality TV Shows*. Amman, Jordan: Arab Advisors Group.

and *al-Ra'is* criticized cultural imitation.[26] The substitution of adapted European formats with locally created shows reflects maturation in the process of absorbing modernity and echoes broader processes of cultural translation.

The media policies of most Arab states mirror the reality TV industries, focusing on taming modernity rather than embarking on the fool's errand of rejecting modernity wholesale. The challenge – coming forth in my interviews with policy makers, in op-eds, and even in *fatwas* – is to strike a balance between "joining the rest of the world" without relinquishing one's distinctiveness. In Bahrain, Kuwait, Saudi Arabia, and elsewhere, the reality television polemics enabled rival groups to articulate their own versions of modernity. The experience of modernity in its economic, political, and cultural aspects, is unavoidable. Contention in public life therefore focuses on defining and managing modernity. Protagonists invoke authenticity not only to publicize their ideas and placate their opponents, but also they do it as a negotiating strategy for localizing various elements of modernity and enshrining them in laws and policies.

All of this unfolds at a time when the Gulf region is experiencing a dizzying transformation. If Latin America is often said to have, in García-Canclini's eloquent summation, "exuberant modernism with a deficient modernization,"[27] then the Gulf countries, with their loud architecture, imported universities, new infrastructures, on the one hand, and their feudal politics, bound servants, and sequestered women, on the other hand, can be said to have exuberant modernization with a deficient modernism. Nonetheless, phenomena like the erotic women's literature wave in Saudi Arabia and the recent widely publicized arrests and prosecutions of public sexual behavior in Dubai, are reminders that what we call "modernism" and "modernization" have a way of stirring each other. This is evident when one looks elsewhere in the region. Unburdened by black gold, other Arab countries exhibit less stark differences between modernism and modernization.

That the Lebanese media and fashion industries set trends in the Gulf countries is not surprising, for the Lebanese are trapped in a fervent, but often shallow, embrace of Western modernity. After all, Lebanon's political system mixes feudal patronage with a sectarian but relatively representative democracy. Women face difficulties when trying to

---

[26] Expressed most dramatically by Ahmad Mansour as quoted in the opening of this book, criticism of cultural and social imitation of the West is regular in the Arab press.

[27] García-Canclini, 1995, 41.

bestow Lebanese citizenship to children they have with non-Lebanese men, but these same women can obtain bank loans for cosmetic surgery. The years that saw the reality TV battles (2003–8) have been particularly turbulent, witnessing war, political assassinations, political turmoil, and economic hardship. "How do you cope with living in Lebanon?" asked a *Times* reporter recently. Her answer: "Get a nose job."[28] "Doctor, give me the lips of Angelina Jolie," is a request often heard by Beirut plastic surgeons.[29] Their clientèle consists not only of Lebanese middle- and upper-class women but also of medical tourists from the Gulf states, sometimes mother-and-daughter teams who go under the scalpel together. Increasingly, men undergo plastic surgery. Though such press accounts are clearly simplistic and somewhat orientalizing, changing one's appearance to fit the beauty norms of the global and Western-dominated fashion industry seems to be at the heart of many people's desire to be modern. An aggressive, albeit in many cases trivial dabbling with modernity, which can be described less charitably as a willingness and ability to imitate all things Western, explains the stylistic influence of the Lebanese creative class over pan-Arab television, embodied most dramatically in the Saudi-Lebanese connection.

What role do media institutions play in the process of negotiating Western modernity? As they juggle commercial interests with political imperatives and social constraints, media institutions set the parameters for localizing modernity. Leading firms like LBC and MBC are arbitrators of relations between markets, politics, religion, and sexuality. Through their production and programming strategies, they manage the pan-Arab economy of visibility. A comparison between these two corporations, both of them implicated in the Saudi-Lebanese connection, illustrates the different roles that media institutions can play as they domesticate elements of Western modernity. From its early days, LBC chose to court controversy with its conspicuous liberalism, offering Lebanese and – after going on satellite – Arab viewers a lifestyle of hedonistic play and ostentatious consumption mixed with Lebanese nationalism; in other words, a skin-deep version of modernity where local culture shines through a Western patina. Because of its Lebanese location, LBC can afford airing titillating shows that command loyal audiences as they stir controversies in the Gulf countries. This is a highly profitable strategy because it provides free advertising in

---

[28] Fordham, A. (August 15, 2008). Bombs and Botox in Beirut. *Times Online*, http://www.timesonline.co.uk/tol/comment/columnists/guests_contrib (accessed August 15, 2008).

[29] Radi, L. (October 26, 2007). Le Liban, Mecque régionale de la chirurgie esthétique. *L'Orient-Le Jour* (Agence France Press).

Arab countries with wealthy viewers who not only spend considerably on consumption in their own countries but also whose visits to Lebanon sustain entire towns who live off the summer Gulf tourist spending.

In sharp contrast, MBC's Saudi cultural anchoring puts constraints on programming choices. Mindful that *al-Ra'is* lasted for one week before it shut down in a storm of controversy while LBC's *Star Academy* is still going strong in its sixth (2009) season, in spite of or maybe due to the polemics, MBC has put out a rich but generally noncontroversial programming grid. Nonetheless, the knowledge that the most popular programs tend to combine local relevance with Western elements has driven even MBC into the land of controversy. The wildfire success of the Turkish television drama broadcast under the Arabic name *Nour* (*Light*), dubbed in Arabic and aired by MBC, has triggered controversy throughout the Arab world, especially among women, its most numerous viewers. Accused of causing divorces and leading women to abandon work and family to follow the adventures of a loving, modern yet Middle Eastern couple who share decision making and treat each other respectfully and romantically, *Nour* has elicited the usual newspaper columns, media coverage, and *fatwas* in Saudi Arabia and its neighbors. Controversy awaits programs that showcase a viable bargain with modernity by coupling local resonance and global longings.[30] This spawns the following question.

What are the implications of this study to the field of global communication studies? This book deliberately attempts to broaden the theoretical repertoire of global communication studies. It seeks implicitly to energize a south-to-south theoretical dialogue.[31] To my central argument that the pan-Arab reality TV wars are best understood as a social laboratory where rival visions of modernity are elaborated, modernization theory has little to offer. Arabs today scorn Daniel Lerner's stark choice "Mecca or mechanization,"[32] toting "Islamic mobile phones"

---

[30] See Turkish serials pushes Arab drama to break taboos (August 5, 2008). *Al-Quds al-Arabi* [Arabic]; Turkish serials . . . stole people's minds (July 7, 2008). *Al-Riyadh* [Arabic]; Al-Sweel, F. (July 26, 2008). Turkish soap opera flop takes Arab world by storm. Riyadh: Reuters.

[31] South-to-south intellectual exchanges have concerned Patrick Murphy and I for several years. See the introduction in Murphy, P. and Kraidy, M. (2003). *Global Media Studies: Ethnographic Perspectives*. London: Routledge, and more recently, Kraidy, M. and Murphy, P. (2008). "Shifting Geertz: Toward a Theory of Translocalism in Global Communication Studies," *Communication Theory* 18: 335–55.

[32] Lerner, D. (1964). *The Passing of Traditional Society: Modernizing the Middle East.* New York: Free Press, 405.

with a compass pointing to Mecca and with alarms going off at prayer times. More illuminating to contemporary Arab culture is the *tiempos mixtos* framework of Nestor García-Canclini, Jesús Martín-Barbero, and others who grappled with the dynamics and dilemmas of Latin American modernities. But helpful as they are, applying these ideas in the Arab world *mutatis mutandis* would reiterate modernization theory's ethnocentrism. Contextualized in Arab societies, however, these ideas resonate, conceptually and historically. The centrality of the West as a potent normative space to be scorned, emulated, or negotiated – modernity as an "elsewhere," as Arjun Appadurai once put it – binds the postcolonial Arab-speaking and Spanish-speaking worlds in equivalent, though dissimilar, historical experiences, marked by ambivalent relationships with the Western imperial-colonial metropolis. Concerns over *ikhtilat*, the illicit interaction of unmarried and non-blood related males and females that emerged in the Arab reality TV polemics, resonate with *la malinche*, the iconic woman figure who represents colonial contamination in Mexico. Both notions are animated by a historical memory of colonial subjugation, but they differ in how they approach the trope of miscegenation, with *mestizaje* becoming official ideology in much of Latin America, while cultural impurity remains anathema to the most conservative elements in Arab societies, Saudi Wahhabiyya being an extreme case in point.

Reality TV and Arab Politics does not pretend to provide answers to the myriad questions bedeviling scholarship on global media and communication. Rather, it begins to address issues that challenge the field to live up to the "global" in its name. For both global communication studies and media studies at large, this book raises more questions than it can answer. Is it time for us to go beyond globalization as a guiding framework[33] and give due attention to regional, national, and local mediations?[34] This book establishes the importance of the national-regional nexus, with national media, social and political actors, and institutions contending within a regional, satellite-enabled, public arena, while it suggests that the global dimension is significant only indirectly. How to retool the comparative media systems methods whose adoption of the nation-state as a bounded unity of analysis has grown increasingly less attuned to realities of geopolitics and transnational media

---

[33] Rosenau, J. N. (2003). *Distant Proximities: Dynamics beyond Globalization*. Princeton, NJ: Princeton University Press.

[34] Joseph Straubhaar explores these connections in *World TV: From Global to Local*. London: Sage.

industries, as my analysis of the Saudi-Lebanese connection dramatically illustrates?[35] What steps do we take to move the study of media events from ceremonial, centralized, television-dominated politics to contentious, fragmented, and hypermediated politics? How do we reintegrate issues of global power while accounting for mediations and gradations in how that power is manifest in local and national settings? More narrowly, are the models and central concerns of reality TV studies – liveness, individual authenticity, neoliberal "schooling" – in the English-speaking world specifically and more broadly in the West, differences within these spheres notwithstanding, universally salient? Ongoing research suggests otherwise.[36] Clearly, the most productive path is one of mutual engagement rather than theoretical chauvinism – nonetheless, making non-Western theories central to our field is required for the "global communication studies" mantle to be credible. At the same time, this book is a conscious effort to move away from broad, theoretically ambitious but empirically tenuous debates about media power. I deliberately eschewed the literature on media imperialism and media globalization and used an empirically grounded concept of modernity in an attempt to provide a strongly contextualized analysis of transnational media power in all its complexity.

As a social laboratory where rival versions of modernity are elaborated, how have the Arab reality TV disputes affected individuals? Key in taming modernity is a reconfiguration of the relationship between the personal and the social, the private and the public. The Arab reality TV wars scrambled this relationship by boosting the ongoing transformation of visibility. Reality TV supplies fresh, though contrived, templates for self-fashioning. Reality TV's underlying premises center on individuals – the exacerbation of desire and emotional conflict, exaltation of individualism, and promotion of self-revealing behavior.[37] Demonstratively unscripted and often broadcast live, daily, and for hours at a time, reality shows like *Star Academy* create intimate bonds with viewers who

---

[35] One creative way of doing global, comparative research can be found in Curtin, M. (2007). *Playing to the World's Biggest Audience: The Globalization of Chinese Film and Television.* Berkeley: University of California Press.

[36] See among others, Jacobs, S. (2007). "Big Brother, Africa is Watching," *Media, Culture and Society* 29 (6): 851–68; and ongoing work by Aswin Punathambekar on *Indian Idol*, in addition to my own work, Kraidy, M. M. (2009). "Reality TV, Gender and Authenticity in Saudi Arabia," *Journal of Communication* 59: 345–66.

[37] Le Guay, D. (2005). *L'empire de la télé-réalité: ou comment accroître le "temps de cerveau humain disponible."* Paris: Presses Universitaires de France.

constantly await one of the contestants saying or doing something outrageous, sensational, or subversive. By luring large audiences for long periods of time and predicating the outcome of each episode on voting, reality TV turns viewers not only into participants in controversial public events but also into witnesses to rituals that validate alternative social and political visions.[38] Within this changing social context, young people recycle reality TV's participatory rituals to communicate outside of the heavily policed familial or social space, or alternatively, for leisure, consumption, and sometimes activism. Because these developments clash with established power structures, reality TV touches on the most sensitive social, political, and even economic issues in the Arab world.

In the United States and Europe, reality TV programs compel participants to unveil the most intimate personal details, thus aiding in the creation of ideal consumers for niche marketing.[39] Likewise, Arab reality TV contributes to the creation of modern composite citizen-consumers. This refashioning is manifest in *Star Academy*, *Superstar*, and *Big Brother*, but also in other, less controversial shows, where primitive survivalism (*Survivor* Arabia), luddite self-sufficiency (*Al-Wadi/ Celebrity Farm*), and plastic surgery (*Beauty Clinic*, the Arab *Extreme Makeover*) transform Arab bodies literally, taking the makeover to its extreme, almost farcical, manifestation. In some recent reality shows, original creations and not format adaptations, European and North American inspiration is discernible in the makeover theme based on personal metamorphosis. Reality TV's promise of individual transformation has some resonance in the Arab world.

But in contrast with many American and British shows, Arab reality TV provides a platform to reclaim things social and political. This book showcased contentious debates over liberal values and practices – individual liberties, gender equality, political pluralism – triggered by Arab reality TV, in stark contrast with the focus on *neoliberal* values and practices – survival-of-the-fittest social behavior, willing submission to surveillance, individual assumption of the state's role – that characterizes scholarship on reality TV in Western countries. Though neoliberal practices are ascendant as a result of the growing impact of globalization on Arab societies, these practices are tempered and sometimes trumped by

---

[38] For an excellent discussion of the notion of witnessing, see Peters, J. D. (2001), "Witnessing," *Media, Culture and Society* 23 (6): 707–23; and (2005) *Courting the Abyss*. Chicago: University of Chicago Press.

[39] See, e.g., Andrejevic, M. (2004). *Reality TV: The Work of Being Watched*. Lanham, MD: Rowman and Littlefield.

nationalism, Islamism, social traditions, and related local contests over liberal values. This may denote that Arab social fabrics are not as thoroughly penetrated by capitalism as some Western, particularly U.S. and British, societies, but it definitely indicates that neoliberalism is not a universally applicable trope; rather it must be understood comparatively and contextually.[40] Several Arab reality shows reaffirm social norms but with a twist: *Millionaire Poet* reenacts traditional oral poetry contests in Arabian Gulf countries and in *Green Light* contestants perform good deeds according to religious customs.[41] *Star Academy* has been reappropriated as a competition in Qur'anic recitation. This mutual pilfering between reality TV and social and religious customs reenchants modernity by imbuing it with local resonance.

Increasingly, Arab reality TV affirms tradition, but within a modern frame. Poetry competition shows on Abu Dhabi TV, *Amir al-Shu'ara* (*Prince of Poets*) and *Sha'er al-Malyoun* (*Millionaire Poet*) have met with considerable success. They promote individual prowess and self-fulfillment in a socially resonant venture. Poetry has a unique status in Arab public life, at once art form and political idiom, a meeting place of literati and the masses. Poets have given voice to taboo desires, scorned the venality of leaders (or sung their praises), and captured the Arab malaise like no other chroniclers of Arab life. Not only is poetry a quintessentially Arabic tradition, but also it combines aesthetic transcendence and political instrumentality, individual creativity and social relevance. Historically a kiln where Arab modernity was forged, poetry claims as its own some the most influential Arab modernists in the twentieth century, including the Syrian-Lebanese Adonis, the Moroccan Muhammad Bennis, and the Saudi Ghazi al-Qusaybi.[42] The Syrian poet Muhammad al-Maghout's famous lament that "there is only one perfect crime, to be born an Arab" captured the depth of Arab feelings of powerlessness. The death of the Palestinian poet Mahmoud Darwish lead to a national funeral, a popular outpouring of grief, numerous op-ed columns, and front-page coverage – the broad resonance that poetry enjoys in Arab culture

---

[40] Even though Australia is linguistically and culturally "proximate" to the United States and Britain, Australian reality television shows tend to display less aggressive behavior than their U.S. and U.K. counterparts, e.g. in *The Biggest Loser*. I am grateful to Tania Lewis for this information.

[41] Green Light: A reality show of another kind (June 1, 2005). *Al-Riyadh* [Arabic].

[42] See al-Ghaddhami, 2005.

is to my knowledge unparalleled elsewhere.[43] By garnering what a market study described as "massive audiences,"[44] Abu Dhabi's poetry reality shows demonstrated the continued resonance of poetry in Arab culture. Televised reality TV style, these poetry competitions connected past and present, repackaging a local tradition in a modern form and passing the taste for poetry to the hypermedia generation. *Amir al-Shu'ara* and *Sha'er al-Malyoun* result from a bargain with modernity, through which media institutions and government bridge the gap between reality and image. At the same time, these shows have featured few female poets, reflecting the persistence of gender as a field of power.[45]

Poetry-themed reality TV indicates that in the era of the new visibility the personal and the social are mutually complementary rather than antagonistic. Shows premised on outward combative and selfish behavior, such as *Survivor Arabia*, enjoyed relatively modest ratings and did not enter public debates. Reality programs that focused excessively on tradition and community, like *Green Light* and *al-Wadi*, received lukewarm responses as well.[46] In contrast, shows that explored active links between the personal and the social, between individual ambition and social norms, were the most popular. Whether on *Star Academy* or *The Biggest Winner*, individual transformations echo desire for social or political change – recall the *Star Academy*'s "patriotic night." Charles Taylor argues that what he calls "acultural" theories of modernity (those believing in a single Western-centered modernity) overemphasize individualism, which he sees as the flipside of "new modes of social imaginary."[47] As he explains:

> Individualism is not just a withdrawal from society but a reconception of what human society can be. To think of it as pure

---

[43] In *al-Hadatha al-Ma'touba* [*Fractured Modernity*, 2004], the Moroccan modernist poet Muhammad Bennis wrote that in the Arab world more poetry than fiction is published.

[44] Snobar, 2008. What the report does not note is that *Prince of Poets*, which featured mostly classical Arabic poetry, was not as successful as *Millionaire Poet*, which focused on Gulf poetry, which suggests that cultural resonance is highly localized.

[45] Poetry shows also reenacted rivalries between Saudi Arabia, the United Arab Emirates, and Qatar.

[46] Another possible reason for the relative unpopularity of *Survivor Arabia* and *al-Wadi* [*Celebrity Farm*] is that by featuring life in a rural or survival setting, they lacked glitziness, glamour, and "lure of the West" power that one finds in *Star Academy*.

[47] Taylor, C. (1999). "Two Theories of Modernity," *Public Culture* 11 (9): 172.

withdrawal is to confuse individualism, which is always a moral ideal, with the anomie of breakdown."[48]

A meaningful relationship between individual and society is, according to Taylor, "the essence of a cultural theory of modernity."[49]

Taylor's focus on the moral strivings of individualism, and the deep connections between morality and religion, leads us to the final question. What does the evolution of Arab reality TV tell us about the role of religion in Arab public life? Doesn't modernity mean the withdrawal of religion to the private domain? Since the late 1960s, public displays of religiosity have permeated Arab public life, making use of various media from the audio cassette tape to the Internet. The popularity of reality TV made it a target for religious "recuperation." In late July 2008, plans were unveiled for an "Islamic *Star Academy*" in Algeria. Slated to air on Algerian television during Ramadan (which in 2008 coincided with September), a peak television viewing period akin to the "sweeps" in the U.S. industry, the show appropriates the *Star Academy* format to promote recitation of the Qur'an. An original creation of Algerian television inspired by *Star Academy*, *The Holy Qur'an Caravan*, pits sixteen contestants who compete in Qur'anic recitation under the critical eye of a jury made of famous Qur'anic orators from several Arab countries in addition to Indonesia and Turkey. In keeping with the plebiscitary nature of reality TV, viewers vote to determine the winner. The new program is a result of a deliberate media policy seeking "balance" in the offerings of the national television channel.[50] A few years earlier, the Lebanese-produced *Star Academy* was pulled off the schedule of national television in a political battle between Algerian president Boutelfiqa and the Islamist-dominated legislature whose members accused *Star Academy* of promoting "nudity" and other sins Islamists ascribe to reality TV.[51] Algerian television in 2006 replaced the widely popular *Star Academy* with a local and more conservative knockoff called *Alhan Wa*

---

[48] Taylor, 1999, 172; two pages later, Taylor is even less equivocal, asserting that "There is never atomistic and neutral self-understanding; there is only a constellation (ours) which tends to throw up the myth of this self-understanding as part of its imaginary (174).

[49] Ibid., 174.

[50] On the screen (July 30, 2008). *Al-Akhbar* [Arabic].

[51] See Algerian television forced to shut down *Star Academy* after widespread criticism in mosques (February 4, 2006). *Al-Quds al-Arabi* [Arabic]; Senoussi, 'Ayyash (April 14, 2006). Algerian television director to al-Hayat: *Star Academy* violated the contract and threats are our daily bread. *Al-Hayat* [Arabic].

Shabab (*Tunes and Youths*).[52] The progression from a controversial Lebanese-produced adaptation of a Dutch format, to a locally produced "secular" but nonetheless conservative variation, ending with an unabashedly religious adaptation of *Star Academy* offers a striking example of the role that media institutions play in mediating modernity.[53] Localization, however, does not necessarily entail adding religious themes. In April 2009, the Qatar Foundation for Education, Science and Community Development announced the launch of *Nujum al-'Ulum* [Stars of Science], a show produced by the Qatar Foundation for Education, Science, and Social Development. Billed by the press a "*Star Academy* for Scientists," the show is another example of meaningful and presumptively uncontroversial appropriation of the reality genre.[54]

By being culturally hybrid, challenging regnant social and political norms, and compelling viewer participation, reality TV has pushed the boundaries of the permissible in Arab public discourse. Throughout the region the reality TV wars contributed to opening a space for suppressed desires, dissenting views, and taboo topics. Most importantly, by bringing a clash between rival worldviews to a wider circle of people, including women and youth, and hosting a debate on momentous issues facing Arabs, the heated polemics I have analyzed bring forth examples of experimentation with different versions of modernity. The debates did not reflect a binary choice between accepting or rejecting modernity; rather they considered a spectrum of selective appropriations. This book told vivid stories of how that struggle expanded the range of permissible speech, actions, and identities, invigorating Arab public life and helping to elaborate what being modern means in the Arab world today. This elaboration is constantly in progress because, as Néstor García-Canclini put it eloquently, modernity is an "unending transit in which the uncertainty of what it means to be modern is never eliminated. To radicalize the project of modernity is to sharpen and renew this uncertainty, to

---

[52] In Tunisia, Nessma TV launched *Star Academy Maghreb*, supervised by Janan Mallat, who was a producer on the LBC show.

[53] Other Algerian television shows following a similar pattern include poetry and soccer reality TV programs, the first banking on the resonance of poetry with Arab viewers, the second relying on soccer being a popular sport that is – at least as far as men's soccer is concerned – socially unobjectionable. It also betrays the Algerian government's desires to burnish its Islamic credentials and to not leave religious broadcasting into private hands (a private Qur'anic recitation radio station exists in Algeria). Finally, Qur'anic recitation, unlike fiery sermons, is politically nonthreatening.

[54] Mustafa, M. (April 18, 2009). "Scientists" also like stardom. *Al-Akhbar* [Arabic].

create new possibilities for modernity always to be able to be something different and something more."[55] *Reality TV and Arab Politics* shows, however imperfectly, that by activating the volatile mix of religion, politics, sexuality, and commerce, Arab reality TV contributed to this project of radicalization.

[55] García-Canclini, 1994, 268.

List of Interviews

The following list comprises most of my interviews – many interviewees requested anonymity, agreeing to be listed here but preferring not to be quoted directly in the book; some requested not to be listed at all. The following list includes, in alphabetical order, names, titles at the time, date and place, keeping in mind that in some cases I conducted several interviews with some individuals: Abbas, Faisal, Media Pages Editor, *Asharq al-Awsat*, June 9, 2005; Abbasi, Jawad, CEO, Arab Advisors Group, Washington, DC, December 2007 and Amman, Jordan, April 26, 2009; Abdo, Rosy, Reporter, al-Jazeera, June 21, 2004, Zouk Mikael, Lebanon; al-Ahmad, Safa, Story Producer, Middle East Broadcasting Center, June 19, 2005 and December 19, 2005, Dubai, UAE; Alavanthian, Sebouh, Director of Programming Department, LBC, June 30, 2004, Adma, Lebanon; Alazmi, Entesar, Head of Section, Foreign Correspondents, Ministry of Information, Kuwait, November 15, 2005; al-Bassam, Mariam, Editor-in-Chief, New TV, July 19, 2004, Beirut, Lebanon; al-Hage, Nakhle, Director of News and Current Affairs, al-Arabiya, June 29, 2005, Dubai, UAE; al-Jasem, Muhammad, Editor-in-Chief, *Meezan*, November 15, 2005, Kuwait; al-Jubeh, 'Abed, Senior Producer, al-Jazeera, June 9, 2005, London; al-Khalidi, Abdallah Zaid, Director, Foreign and International Media, Ministry of Information, Kuwait, November 15, 2005, Kuwait; al-Khazen, Jihad, *al-Hayat*, Media and Communication Group, June 7, 2005, London; al-Kurdi, Walid, Oil Analyst, Platt, previously Chief Editor, CNBC-Arabia, June 7, 2005, London; Alnowaiser, Mowafaq, Director of Offices, *Asharq al-Awsat*, June 10, 2005, London; al-Rashed, 'Abdelrahman, General Manager, al-Arabiya, June 27, 2005, Dubai, UAE; al-Rayyes, Ali H., General Director, Kuwait TV Channel 1, Ministry of Information, November 16, 2005, Kuwait; al-Rshaid, Aisha, General Manager, Shorook Exhibitions and Conferences, and Journalist, Dar al-Watan, November 16, 2005, Kuwait; al-Sahly, Moubarak Faleh, Director, Kuwait Television Channel 4, Kuwait; al-Sayegh, 'Abdullatif, CEO, Arabian Radio Network, June 30, 2005, Dubai, UAE; al-Shawwa, Maher, Media Journalist, *Annahar* and *Nadine*, August 1, 2005, Beirut, Lebanon; 'Assi Azzam, Tania,

Program Manager, New TV, July 19, 2004, Beirut, Lebanon; Atrash, Rasha, Media Pages Editor, *Assafir*, July 20, 2005, Beirut, Lebanon.

Baltaji, Dana, Siraj Marketing Research and Consultancy, June 21 and June 26, 2005, Dubai, UAE; Baltaji, Rania, Senior Graphic Designer, Dubai TV, June 28, 2005, Dubai, UAE; Bibi, Abdelkader, Head of Marketing and Sales, Dubai Media Inc., June 5, 2004, Dubai, UAE; Bou Nassar, Joseph, Editor-in-Chief, *al-Dalil* (*Annahar*), August 1 and August 10, 2005, Beirut, Lebanon; Chayban, Badih, Reporter, *Daily Star*, November 1, 2001, Beirut, Lebanon; Costandi, Michel, Business Development Director, Middle East Broadcasting Center, June 3, 2004 and June 29, 2005, Dubai, UAE; Couri, Fares, Program Editor, MBC News, Middle East Broadcasting Center, June 29, 2005, Dubai, UAE; Dabbous, Dima, Assistant Professor, Communication Arts, Lebanese American University, October 29, 2002, Beirut, Lebanon; Dajani, Nabil, Professor, Social Behavioral Sciences, American University of Beirut, November 2, 2002, Beirut, Lebanon; Dajani, Nabil, Professor, Social Behavioral Sciences, American University of Beirut, July 12, 2004, Beirut, Lebanon; Darouny, Kamal, President, Infomarkets, July 15, 1994 and July 9, 2001, Zouk Mosbeh, Lebanon; Darwish, Noha, Head of Programming Department, NBN, July 13, 2004, Jnah, Beirut, Lebanon.

El-Daher, Pierre, CEO, LBC, June 30, 2004 and August 21, 2005, Adma, Lebanon; Eltahawy, Mona, Columnist, *Asharq al-Awsat*, May 25, 2005, New York; Fadel, Rosette, Reporter, *Annahar*, June 26, 2004, Jounieh, Lebanon; Fakhreddine, Jihad, Research Manager, Pan Arab Research Center, June 1, 2004 and June 25, 2005, Dubai, UAE; Fehmi, Joumana, Programs and Production Director, Al-Rai TV, November 16, 2005, al-Salhiyya, Kuwait; Frayha, Nemr, Professor of Political Science, Lebanese University, July 17, 1994, Zouk Mosbeh, Lebanon; Ghaibeh, May, Branding Consultant, One TV and Dubai TV, June 28, 2005, Dubai, UAE; Ghanem, Marcel, Host, Kalam al-Nass, LBC, July 10, 2004, Zouk Mikael, Lebanon; Ghattas, Mary, previously reporter, al-Hayat-LBC, June 6, 2005, London; Giraguossian, Thomas, Correspondent, *Al-Gumhuriya* (Egypt), April 12, 2005, Washington, DC; Habib, Vicky, Journalist, media and television page, *Al-Hayat*, July 19, 2005, Beirut, Lebanon; Hayek, Georges, Television Critic, *Annahar*, July 27, 2005, Beirut, Lebanon; Henoud, John, Account Executive, Riyadh, Saudi Arabia, November 1, 2002, Zouk Mikael, Lebanon; Hitti, Paul, Special Projects Manager, Middle East Broadcasting Center, June 22, 2005, Dubai, UAE; Hroub, Khaled, al-Jazeera Talk Show Host and Director of the Cambridge Arab Media Project, Cambridge University, June 9, 2005, London.

Ismail, Hisham, Director, CNBC-Arabia, June 3, 2004, Dubai, UAE; Issa, Hanadi, Journalist, media and varieties, *Laha* and *al-Hayat*, July 19, 2005, Beirut, Lebanon; Izzaldin, Fadi, Director of Graphics, CNBC-Arabia, June 3, 2004 and June 21, 2005, Dubai, UAE; Jazzar, Rony, General Manager, Starwave and AVM, July 2, 2004, Beirut, Lebanon; Kamel, Carina, Assistant Producer,

CNBC-Arabia, June 3, 2004, Dubai, UAE; Kamel, Carina, previously CNBC-Arabia, June 19, 2005, London; Karam, Maroun Albert, Studio Director, al-Arabiya, June 29, 2005, Dubai, UAE; Kitmitto, Naji, Consultant, Dubai TV, June 23, 2005, Dubai, UAE; Khalil, Joe, Director, MTV, July 15, 1996, December 14, 1997, October 27 and 29, 2002, Beirut, Lebanon; Executive Producer, CNBC-Arabia, November 28, 2004 (telephone interview), and Creative Director, Middle East Broadcasting Center, June 25, 2005, Dubai, UAE; Khatib, Lina, Lecturer, Royal Holloway, University of London, June 6, 2005, London; Khatib, Nabil, The Executive Editor, al-Arabiya, June 29, 2005, Dubai, UAE; Khayyat, Bushra, Assistant Program Manager, New TV, July 19, 2004, Beirut, Lebanon; Khoury, Khalil, Director, National News Agency, July 14, 2004, Beirut, Lebanon; Khoury, Nadyne, Producer, LBCI, July 8, 2001, Byblos, Lebanon; Kibbi, Ziad, Executive Producer, Al-Wadi (LBC), August 10, 2005, Jounieh, Lebanon; Kinj, Marwan, Head of Animation and Graphics, NBN, July 13, 2004, Jnah, Beirut, Lebanon; Klopper, De Wet, Director, Inobits (IT Consultancy), June 21, 2005, Dubai, UAE; Koukjian, Ronald, Sales Manager, CNBC-Arabia, May 31, 2004, Dubai, UAE; Kouyoumjian, Zaven, Talk Show Host, Sireh-We-Nfathet, Future TV, July 27, 2005, Beirut, Lebanon.

Mahfouz, Abdelhadi, President, National Council for Audio-Visual Media, July 14, 2004, Hamra, Beirut, Lebanon; Maksoud, Clovis, Veteran Journalist, September 6, 2004, Washington, DC; Mchawrab, Ibrahim, Arts and Varieties Editor, *al-Bayan*, June 17, 2005, Dubai; Merhej, Nada, Senior Business and Media Correspondent, *al-Anwar*, November 1, 2002, Beirut, Lebanon; Moqalled, Diana, Reporter, Future TV, and Columnist, *Asharq al-Awsat*, July 21, 2005, Beirut, Lebanon; Moussa, George, Journalist, Varieties Page, *Al-Hayat*, July 20, 2005, Beirut, Lebanon; Mroue, Leila, Task Producer, MBC, June 25, 2005, Dubai; Mtayni, Rashid, Vice-President, Sales and Marketing, CNBC-Arabia, May 31, 2004, Dubai, UAE; Nematt, Salameh, Washington Bureau Chief, Al-Hayat, May 20, 2005, Washington, DC; Omian, Khouloud, Producer, CNBC-Arabia, June 2, 2004, Dubai, UAE; Qandil, Ghaleb, Lebanese Journalist, June 16, 2004, Beirut, Lebanon; Qandil, Ghaleb, Member, National Council of Audio-Visual Media, August 1, 2005, Beirut, Lebanon; Qandil, Shadi, Media Manager, IPSOS-STAT Dubai, June 2, 2004 and Director of Research and Insights, OMD, June 22, 2005, both in Dubai, UAE; Raad, Mimi, Styling Supervisor and Producer, Dubai TV, June 29, 2005, Dubai, UAE; Raad, Nada, Reporter, *Daily Star*, July 6, 2004, Beirut, Lebanon; Radi, Fadi Rida, Creative Services, Graphics Manager, MBC Group, June 29, 2005.

Sa'd, Roula, Director, Programming and Promotions Department, and "Director of the Academy," *Star Academy*, LBC, July 5, 2004, Adma, Lebanon; Saade, Joe, Editor, Lebanon Opportunities, August 8, 1997, Daroun, Lebanon; Sabbagh, Rima, Head of Promotions Department, NBN, July 13, 2004, Jnah, Beirut, Lebanon; Sadek, Haydar, Director, French Newscast, Télé-Liban, June 24, 2001, Tyre, Lebanon; Salibi, Elie, Director of News Department, LBCI, May 3,

1991, Jounieh, Lebanon; Samaha, Michel, Minister of Information, July 7, 2004, Hamra, Beirut, Lebanon; Sbeih, Fady, Creative Director and Partner, 360, November 14, 2005, Kuwait; Sfeir, Sami, Owner, Transgulf Media, May 31, 2004, Dubai, UAE; Stratford, Deborah, Creative Director, CNBC-Arabia, May 31, 2004, Dubai, UAE; Sultan, Hamed, Media PS, November 17, 2005, Al-Salhiya, Kuwait; Trad, Philippe, Technician, Cony (al-Jazeera Kids), November 11, 2005, Paris, France; Yazbeck, Ghayath, General Manager, Arab News Broadcast, July 10, 2004, Naccache, Lebanon; Zeidan, Sami, Executive Producer, Global Leaders Group, June 26, 2005, Dubai, UAE; Zuraiqat, Hala, Director, Jordan Television, Amman, Jordan, April 30, 2009.

Further Readings

There are plenty of English-language sources discussing modernity and multiple modernities. A special issue of *Daedelus* 129 (1) features essays by Shmuel Eisenstadt (2000). "Multiple Modernities," 1–29, Nilüfer Göle, "Snapshots of Islamic Modernities," 91–117, and Dale Eickelman, "Islam and the Language of Modernity," 119–35. A special issue of *Public Culture* featured a seminal essay by Taylor C. (1999). "Two Theories of Modernity," *Public Culture*, 11 (9): 153–174, and an insightful piece by Dilip Gaonkar, "On Alternative Modernities," 1–18. See also Timothy Mitchell's edited volume *Questions of Modernity* (Minneapolis: University of Minnesota Press, 2000). Some of the best works about plural modernities are grounded in the Middle East, including Aziz al-Azmeh's *Islams and Modernities* (1993) and Timothy Mitchell's *Colonizing Egypt* (1988), published by Cambridge University Press.

The book cites excellent sources on Arab media hosting national debates related to modernity, like Lila Abu-Lughod's *Dramas of Nationhood* (Chicago: University of Chicago Press, 2005) and Walter Armbrust's *Mass Culture and Modernism in Egypt* (Cambridge and New York: Cambridge University Press, 1996). For a more deliberate focus on representation in Arab-Western relations, see Melani McAlister, *Epic Encounters: Culture, Media, and U.S. Interests in the Middle East since 1945* (Berkeley: University of California Press, 2005) and Lina Khatib, *Filming the Modern Middle East: Politics in the Cinemas of Hollywood and the Arab World* (London: I. B. Tauris, 2006). For a general reference about Arab television, see Kraidy, M. M. and Khalil, J. F. *Arab Television Industries* (London: Palgrave Macmillan/British Film Institute, 2009, in press).

On the politics–popular culture nexus, classics like Peter Dahlgren's *Television and the Public Sphere* (1995), Toby Miller's *The Well-Tempered Self: Citizenship, Culture and the Postmodern Subject* (1993), and John Street's *Politics and Popular Culture* (1997) (Philadelphia, PA: Temple University Press) remain helpful. More recent works include Liesbet Van Zoonen, *Entertaining the Citizen: When Politics and Popular Culture Converge* (Lanham, MD: Rowman and

Littlefield, 2005), and the special issue of *European Journal of Cultural Studies* (vol. 9, 2006) on cultural citizenship.

For engaging theoretical discussions of performance in politics, see Margaret Kohn (2000). "Language, Power and Persuasion: Toward a Critique of Deliberative Democracy," *Constellations* 7 (3): 408–29 and J. Kulynych (1997). "Performing Politics: Foucault, Habermas and Postmodern Participation," *Polity* 30 (2): 315–46. For a detailed treatment incorporating television and the Internet, see P. Dahlgren, *Media and Political Engagement: Citizens, Communication and Democracy*. (Cambridge and New York: Cambridge University Press, 2009), especially Chapter 4. For a study of political performativity grounded in the Arab world, see Lisa Wedeen's *Peripheral Visions: Publics, Power and Performance in Yemen* (Chicago: University of Chicago Press, 2008).

The literature on reality television keeps on growing. In addition to pioneering English-language works like Mark Andrejevic's *Reality TV: The Work of Being Watched* (2003) and Annette Hill's *Reality Television: Audiences and Factual Television* (2005), see Laurie Ouellette and James Hay's *Better Living Through Reality TV: Television and Post-Welfare Citizenship* (2008). There is an exciting French-language body of work about reality TV, including François Jost's *L'empire du Loft* (Paris: La Dispute, 2007a) and his *Le culte du banal: De Duchamp à la télé-réalité* (Paris: CNRS, 2007b). See D. Schneidermann's *Le cauchemar médiatique* (Paris: Denel/Folio documents, 2004) and D. Le Gay, *L'empire de la télé-réalité, ou comment* accroître le *"temps de cerveau humain disponible"* (Paris: Presses de la Renaissance, 2005). The collection edited by Yves Cartuyvels, *Star Academy: Un objet pour les sciences sociales?* (Bruxelles, Belgique: Publications des Facultés universitaires Saint-Louis, 2004), provides a systematic multidisciplinary approach to *Star Academy*. For a broadly critical perspective in Arabic, see 'Abdulhalim Hammoud, *Reality TV: Humans in the Cage of the Image* (Beirut: Dar al-Hadi [Arabic], 2008).

For explicitly comparative works on reality TV, see E. Mathjis and J. Jones, eds., *Big Brother International: Formats, Critics and Publics* (London: Wallflower Press, 2004). Two forthcoming volumes take a deliberately global approach, including M. M. Kraidy and K. Sender, eds., *Real Worlds: The Global Politics of Reality Television* (London and New York: Routledge, forthcoming) and L. Baruh and J. H. Park, eds., *Reel Politics: Political Discourse and Reality Television* (Cambridge and New York: Cambridge University Press, forthcoming).

Nestor García-Canclini remains a foremost inspiration on the nexus of modernity, popular culture, politics, and postcolonial predicaments. See his *Hybrid Cultures: Strategies for Entering and Leaving Modernity* (Minneapolis: University of Minnesota Press, 1994), *Consumers and Citizens: Multicultural Conflicts in Globalization* (Minneapolis: University of Minnesota Press, 1998), and *La Globalización Imaginada* (Mexico City: Paidós, 1999).

Bibliography

'Abbas, Faisal (August 6, 2005). Satan's academy. *Asharq al-Awsat* [Arabic].

—— (June 18, 2006). Showtime president: Saudi television viewership rate higher than in Europe or North America. *Asharq al-Awsat* [Arabic].

—— (August 9, 2007). Merger of Rotana and LBC channels: Shares to be offered on U.A.E. stock exchange. *Asharq al-Awsat* [Arabic].

'Abbud, Ghada (February 10, 2005). Teenagers sinking their teeth into new technology. *Arab News.*

About Future TV, http://www.futuretvnetwork.com/Default.aspx?page=aboutus (accessed May 20, 2008).

'Abdullatif, Kamal (1999). *Modernity and History: A Critical Dialogue with Some Questions in Arab Thought* (Casablanca: Afriqia al-Sharq [Arabic]).

'Abdulrahim, Yahya and Jum'a, 'Imad (April 3, 2004). Sadness takes over the Kuwaiti Street. *Al-Watan* [Arabic].

Abou Nasr, Maya (February 4, 2004a). Competition is intense for slots on talent show's 2nd season. *Daily Star.*

—— (February 4, 2004b). Who wants to be a Superstar? 12,000 do. *Daily Star.*

Abukhalil, As'ad (2003). *The Battle for Saudi Arabia: Royalty, Fundamentalism, and Global Power* (New York: Seven Stories Press).

—— (2008). Determinants and characteristics of Saudi role in Lebanon: The post-civil war years, in *Kingdom without Borders: Saudi Arabia's Political, Religious and Media Frontiers,* ed. M. al-Rasheed (New York: Columbia University Press), 79–88.

Abuzeid, Rania (July 6, 2008). Alwaleed expands media empire. *The National.*

Abu-Lughod, Lila. (2005). *Dramas of Nationhood* (Chicago: University of Chicago Press).

Abushaybah, Khaled (April 17, 2005). Saudi youth danced into the morning hours in celebration of "Hisham the bulldozer." *Al-Hayat* [Arabic].

Abuzaid, Muhammad (October 30, 2005). Computer disks ... a new media to jump over taboos. Their stars are Osama Bin Laden, Sadat and video clip [female] artists. *Asharq al-Awsat* [Arabic].

Adelkhah, Fariba (2000). *Being Modern in Iran* (New York: Columbia University Press).

Agnew, Richard (August 21, 2005). The Arabian kings of cash. *Arabian Business.*

Ahmed, Leila (1992). *Women and Gender in Islam: Historical Roots of a Current Debate* (New Haven: Yale University Press).

'Akeel, Maha (January 10, 2005). Camera phones legal but individual restrictions apply. *Arab News*.

'Akoum, Caroline (December 17, 2006). Downtown Beirut ... a theater for "reality TV" whose heroes are demonstrators and politicians and analysts. *Asharq al-Awsat* [Arabic].

—— (August 13, 2007). Has the era of Arab media alliances arrived? *Asharq al-Awsat* [Arabic].

al-A'ali, Muhammad (May 1, 2005). MPs may block reality show. *Gulf Daily News*.

al-Ahmad, Iqbal (September 14, 2003). Superstar's MPs. *Al-Qabas* [Arabic].

al-Alawi, D. (January 12, 2003). Bahrain launches new TV channel. *Gulf Daily News*.

al-'Ariss, Ibrahim (April 9, 2007). Awareness. *Al-Hayat* [Arabic].

al-'Ariss, Ibrahim (July 11, 2007). What if ... ? *Al-Hayat* [Arabic].

al-Atrash, Rasha (March 8, 2005). "Freedom Square": "Zoom In" on Arab viewers. *Assafir* [Arabic].

—— (March 9, 2005). In defense of "Zoom In." *Assafir* [Arabic].

—— (March 12, 2005). The new Future TV: One political battle ... waged with many forms and programs. *Assafir* [Arabic].

—— (July 20, 2005). Media Page Editor, Assafir, personal interview, Adma, Lebanon.

—— (December 1, 2006). Television the Hailer ... and the present inform the absent! *Assafir* [Arabic].

al-Azmeh, Aziz. (1993). *Islams and Modernities* (London: Verso).

al-Baba, Hakam (March 17, 2005). Wishing for a return to the pre-print era: How do Syrian media confront Syrian reality? *Al-Quds al-Arabi* [Arabic].

—— (April 6, 2005). The Camera Rules the World: Star Academy for Arab leaders. *Al-Quds al-Arabi* [Arabic].

al-Barazi, 'Ayed and Muhammad, Ghada (September 11, 2003). A legislative Superstar threatens Information Minister with the platform and al-Tabtaba'i considers Lebanon a "source of silliness and spoiledness." *Al-Rai al-Aam*.

al-Bishr, Badreiah. (April 19, 2005). Star Academy's democracy. *Asharq al-Awsat* [Arabic].

—— (2007). *The "Tash Ma Tash" Battles: A Reading of the Prohibition Mentality in Saudi Society* (Casablanca, Morocco, and Beirut, Lebanon: Arab Cultural Centre [Arabic]).

al-Bizri, Dalal (January 23, 2005). The truthful "reality" which is kept away from television screens. *Al-Hayat* [Arabic].

al-Dabib, Munira A. (March 11, 2005). These programs aim to destroy the social tissue, especially the youth. *Al-Riyadh* [Arabic].

al-Dakhil, Munira M. (February 27, 2005). Destructive Academy is harmful to the family. *Al-Riyadh* [Arabic].

al-Dawyan, Wafa' M. (March 22, 2005). *Star Academy*: A sincere invitation to ikhtilat. *Al-Riyadh* [Arabic].

al-'Enezi, Hamed A. (March 19, 2005). *Star Academy* ... the other terrorism. *Al-Riyadh* [Arabic].

al-Fadl, Nabil (September 22, 2003). Thank you Superstar. *Al-Rai al-Aam* [Arabic].

al-Fatwaki, Samir (August 30, 2005). A technique for manufacturing leaders. *Al-Quds al-Arabi* [Arabic].

al-Ferzli, Elie (March 10, 2005). Televisual quality's contagion. *Assafir* [Arabic].

Algerian television forced to shut down *Star Academy* after widespread criticism in mosques (February 4, 2006). *Al-Quds al-Arabi* [Arabic].

al-Ghaneem, Muhammad (July 11, 2007). The bay'a's second anniversary: Building foundations for a new stage of modernization and progress. *Al-Riyadh* [Arabic].

al-Ghaddhami, 'Abdullah M. (2005). *The Tale of Modernity in the Kingdom of Saudi Arabia* (Beirut and Casablanca: Arab Cultural Center [Arabic]).

al-Hadath (March 7, 2004). The Reality TV Phenomenon, Marwan Matni, Producer; Shada 'Omar, Host. Adma, Lebanon: Lebanese Broadcasting Corporation [Arabic].

al-Hajiri, Quboul (January 9, 2007). King 'Abdullah's era opened spaces for the media. *Elaph* [Arabic].

al-Hamad, Turki (2001). *Arab Culture in the Era of Globalization* (Beirut and London: Al-Saqi [Arabic]).

——— (June 19, 2005). It is in the concept that all the meaning resides. *Al-Bayan* [Arabic].

al-Hekmi, Ibrahim (February 4, 2006). Shahd Barmada: I am participating in an artistic program unrelated to politics. *Al-Quds al-Arabi* [Arabic].

al-Hekmi is Superstar for 2006. (February 7, 2006). *Assafir* [Arabic].

al-Humaydan, Sawsan (May 15, 2005). Crisis hits Saudi homes because of television shows coinciding with final exams. *Asharq al-Awsat* [Arabic].

al-Hussaini, Amira (May 3, 2005). MPs simply won't give up fretting over petty issues. *Gulf Daily News*.

al-Ibrahim, Walid (March 7, 2008). Al-Ruba'i ... names "al-Arabiya" and departed. *Asharq al-Awsat* [Arabic].

al-Jabban, Munir (February 20, 2004). Star Academy channel ... ideas for dialogue. *Asharq al-Awsat* [Arabic].

al-Jacques, Sana' (January 23, 2004). Star Academy on LBC "represents reality" with amateurs but with outstanding professionalism. *Asharq al-Awsat* [Arabic].

——— (August 13, 2004). The equation merges geography and economics in rumor wars: *Superstar 2* between the authenticity of the voice and the majority of votes. *Asharq al-Awsat* [Arabic].

——— (August 12, 2007). Pierre Al-Daher: "Sheikh" ... and "Godfather." *Asharq al-Awsat* [Arabic].

al-Jallad, Majdi (July 9, 2008). The Law to "slaughter" satellite television ... and Facebook! *Al-Masry al-Youm* [Arabic].

al-Jammal, Gaby (March 10, 2005). Phenomena that do not found new Lebanon. *Assafir* [Arabic].

al-Jasem, Waleed J. (April 6, 2004). If I were a clergyman. *Al-Watan* [Arabic].

al-Khammash, Faisal (January 17, 2007). After he announced partial solutions to stock market problems ... Michel Hayek's predictions attract the attention of Saudis. *Al-Hayat* [Arabic].

al-Khairy, Amina (December 8, 2006). National "Reputation." *Al-Hayat* [Arabic].

al-Khoury, Sylvana (March 18, 2005). The original and the copy/image. *Annahar* [Arabic].

al-Khudr, Muhammad (February 4, 2006).... And Syrians are unfazed. *Al-Hayat* [Arabic].

al-Madhoun, Rassem (July 19, 2006). War ... The most widespread and most credible reality TV. *Al-Hayat* [Arabic].

al-Majid, Hamad (June 20, 2005). Islamists and Liberals: They share the blame...! *Asharq al-Awsat* [Arabic].

al-Makaty, Safran S., Douglas A. Boyd, and G. N. Van Tubergen (2000). A Q study of reactions to Direct Broadcast Satellite television programming in Saudi Arabia, in *Civic Discourse and Digital Age Communications in the Middle East*, ed. L. A. Gher and H. Y. Amin (Stamford, CT: Ablex, 2000), 191–206.

al-Maraj, Rasheed Muhammad (January 10, 2008). Vigorous economic growth in Bahrain. Speech by His Excellency Rasheed Muhammad Al Maraj, Governor of the Central Bank of Bahrain, at the Strategic Forum on the Bilateral Trade and Investment Opportunities in Banking and Finance, London.

al-Mashnouq, Nuhad (March 27, 2006). Listen to me, O rida. *Assafir* [Arabic].

al-Matayri, Amal Muhammad (February 28, 2004). Star Academy: An attempt to inculcate Western traditions in the selves of Muslims. *Al-Watan* [Arabic].

al-Matrafi, S. (April 22, 2005). Star Academy winner told to leave Riyadh. *Arab News*.

al-Mesh'el, Muhammed Nasser (April 5, 2004). Star Academy ... An art of moral decadence. *Al-Watan* [Arabic].

al-Mezel, Muhammad (March 2, 2004). Bahrainis split on reality TV show. *Gulf News* [Arabic].

al-Mousawi, Sayyid Diya' (March 19, 2005). Bahraini democracy, pros and cons. *Al-Hayat* [Arabic].

al-Mughni, Haya (Jan.–Mar. 1996). Women's organizations in Kuwait, *Middle East Report 198*: 32–5.

——— (2000). Women's movements and the autonomy of civil society in Kuwait, in *Feminist Approaches to Social Movements, Community and Power*, vol. 1, *Conscious Acts: The Politics of Social Change*, ed. R. L. Teske and M. A. Tétreault (Columbia: University of South Carolina Press), 170–87.

——— (2001). *Women in Kuwait: The Politics of Gender* (London: Al-Saqi.).

al-Mughni, Hala and Tétreault, Mary Ann (2004). Engagement in the public sphere: Women and the press in Kuwait, in *Women and Media in the Middle East: Power through Self-Expression*, ed. N. Sakr, (London: I. B. Tauris. Al-Musawi), 120–37.

al-Munajjid, Muhammad S. (March 19, 2004). Satan Academy [akademiyat al-Shaytan wal-Superstar], http://www.islamway.com/?iw_s=Lesson&iw_a=view&lesson_id=28385 (accessed March 30, 2005).

al-Musawi, Muhsin J. (2006). *Arab Poetry: Trajectories of Modernity and Tradition* (London: Routledge).

al-Na'amy, Saleh (April 23, 2005). *Eye on Palestine ... a look at human life*. *Asharq Al-Awsat* [Arabic].

al-Najmi, Hassan (March 24, 2005). "Are you happy now? Muhammad 'Attiya sings for Diana Carzon." *Al-Riyadh* [Arabic].

al-Nakt Rahme, Zakiyya (March 17, 2005). Audiovisual media cover the opposition in its independence uprising (Independence Intifada) and "spaces" more heated than demonstrations [Investigation]. *Annahar* [Arabic].

al-Osaimi, Najah (April 17, 2005). Saudi wins Star Academy 05 Contest. *Arab News*.

al-Qabah, Ranim (February 8, 2005). Victory goes to the Saudi ... And to the Syrians the thanks of voters. *Al-Hayat* [Arabic].

al-Qahs, Muhhamed Faleh (March 23, 2004). Star Academy made Islamic societies poised to fall and suffering from old age (al-kuhula). *Al-Watan* [Arabic].

al-Qassem, Anwar (February 24, 2005). Will Syrian media get out of the cave? *Al-Quds al-Arabi* [Arabic].

al-Rashed, Abdelrahman (October 12, 2005). The fatwa crisis. *Asharq al-Awsat* [Arabic].

al-Rasheed, Madawi (1998). The Shi'a of Saudi Arabia: A minority in search of cultural authenticity, *British Journal of Middle Eastern Studies* 21 (5): 121–38.

al-Rasheed, M. (2002). *A History of Saudi Arabia* (Cambridge: Cambridge University Press).

——— (2007). *Contesting the Saudi State: Islamic Voices from a New Generation* (Cambridge: Cambridge University Press).

——— (April 12, 2008). The Saudi sect joins Lebanon's seventeen sects. *Al-Quds al-Arabi* [Arabic].

———, ed. (2008). *Kingdom without Borders: Saudi Arabia's Political, Religious and Media Frontiers* (New York: Columbia University Press).

al-Roomi, Samar (2007). Women, blogs and political power in Kuwait, in *New Media in the New Middle East*, ed. P. Seib (New York: Palgrave Macmillan), 139–55.

al-Rshaid, Aisha (August 12, 2004). Who is Super Star of the Arabs in 2004: Yasir 'Arafat or Muammar al-Qaddhafi? *Al-Watan* [Arabic].

———. Journalist, *Al-Watan*, personal interview, Kuwait, November 16, 2006.

al-Ruba'i, Ahmad (March 23, 2005). The Kuwaiti "Battle" over *Star Academy*. *Asharq al-Awsat* [Arabic].

al-Shammari, Nuwayr Sa'd (March 23, 2004). Corruption Academy. *Al-Watan* [Arabic].

al-Shammari, Sa'd (May 18, 2004). Kuwait: Restraints on concerts prohibit dancing. *Asharq al-Awsat* [Arabic].

——— (May 8, 2004). *Star Academy* crisis threatens the future of Kuwait's information minister and its repercussions may lead to a cabinet reshuffle by the end of the month. *Asharq al-Awsat* [Arabic].

——— (October 3, 2004). *Star Academy* increases opportunities to interrogate Kuwait's information minister. *Asharq al-Awsat* [Arabic].

al-Shatti, Salem (February 17, 2004). Muhammed Al-Tabtaba'i to "son Bashar": Go back to your parents and do not be an instrument in the hands of religion's enemy with which they strike at Islam. *Al-Rai al-Aam* [Arabic].

al-Shawwa, Maher (2005). "Star Academy 2": A patriotic "prime" and the exit of Syrian Joey Bassous. *Mulhaq-Annahar* [Arabic].

——— (August 1, 2005). Journalist, *Dalil Annahar*, personal interview, Beirut, Lebanon.

al-Sweel, Farah (July 26, 2008). Turkish soap opera flop takes Arab world by storm. Riyadh: Reuters.

al-Tabtaba'i: Celebrating *Star Academy* sends the wrong message to Kuwaiti youth'. (2004, April 4). *Al-Qabas* [Arabic].

Alterman, Jon (1998) New media, new politics? *Washington Institute for Near East Policy*.

al-Za'ir, Sa'id M. (2008). *Television and Social Change in Developing Countries* (Beirut: Dar Wa Maktabat al-Hilal and Jeddah: Dar al-Shuruq [Arabic]).

al-Zaidi, Mufid (2003). *The al-Jazeera Channel: Breaking Taboos in the Arabic Media Space* (Beirut: Dar-al-Tali'a [Arabic]).

al-Zayn, Hassan (February 17, 2005). "Reality TV" in political spectacle. *Assafir* [Arabic].

Amin, Hussein and Boyd, Douglas A. (1994). The development of direct broadcast satellite television to and within the Middle East, *Journal of South Asian and Middle East Studies* XVIII (2): 37–50.

Analysis: Saudi rulers ease their grip on the media, BBC Monitoring Media Services, May 28, 2004. London: British Broadcasting Corporation.

An Arab idol is crowned (August 30, 2004). *New York Times*, 8.

Anderson, Benedict (1993). *Imagined Communities: Reflections on the Origins and Spread of Nationalism* (London: Verso).

Andrejevic, Mark (2004). *Reality TV: The Work of Being Watched* (Lanham, MD: Rowman and Littlefield).

——— (2006). Reality TV is undemocratic. *Flow*, http://flowtv.org/?p=11 (accessed October 1, 2006).

Anta Wal Hadath and the Ramadan drama crisis (September 20, 2007). *Al-Riyadh* [Arabic].

Appadurai, A. (1996). *Modernity at Large: Cultural Dimensions of Globalization* (Minneapolis: University of Minnesota Press).

Arab "Big Brother" seen as American plot: Reality-TV opponents say U.S. seeking takeover by infiltrating minds (May 6, 2004). *WorldNetDaily.com*.

Arab idol a battle of nations (August 13, 2003). Beirut: Associated Press.

Arab Media in the Information Age (2006). Abu Dhabi: The Emirates Center for Strategic Studies and Research.

Arab network suspends Big Brother show (March 2, 2004). Manama, Bahrain: MSANET and News Agencies.

Arab television channels attack Zoghbi poll and consider it manipulated (January 1, 2006). *Asharq al-Awsat* [Arabic].

Armbrust, Walter, (1996). *Mass Culture and Modernism in Egypt* (New York: Cambridge University Press).

Aslama, Minna and Mervi Pantti, M. (2006). Talking alone: Reality TV, emotions and authenticity, *European Journal of Cultural Studies* 9 (2): 167–84.

'Atef, Muhammad (January 31, 2007). Saudi singer Wa'd: I offered a song to Lebanese television so they asked to delete scenes depicting Hassan Nasrallah and I refused! *Al-Quds al-Arabi* [Arabic].

'Awwad, Mayssa (February 6, 2005). No "reality" outside the academy.

Ayish, Muhammad I. (1997). Arab television goes commercial: A case study of the Middle East Broadcasting Center, *Gazette: The International Journal for Communication Studies* 59: 473–94.

'Ayntrazi, Tariq (December 20, 2005). General Manager, Future TV, personal interview, Dubai, UAE.

Ayoub, Sabah (February 7, 2006). When reality turns against the image. *Assafir* [Arabic].

'Azour, Salim (December 23, 2006). Transcontinental Saudi influence! *Al-Quds al-Arabi* [Arabic].

Baaklini, Abdo (1978). The Kuwaiti legislature as ombudsman: The legislative committee on petitions and complaints, *Legislative Studies Quarterly* 3 (2): 293–307.

Badi, Ibrahim (January 22, 2006). Is it a conspiracy ... or reality? *Al-Hayat* [Arabic].

——— (February 14, 2006). Where is new television technology taking us? ... Viewers are now able to retrieve broadcasts they miss. *Al-Hayat* [Arabic].

——— (December 16, 2006). "Gulf Pages" follows "Live with Us" in Beirut ... Saudis behind the cameras ... anchors or emigrants? *Al-Hayat* [Arabic].

Badr, Anwar (2005). Mehdi Dakhlallah himself was considered to sing beyond the group! Syrian media out of its epoch ... and banning publications continues. *Al-Quds al-Arabi* [Arabic].

Bahrain bids farewell to Star Academy 4 (January 21, 2007). *Al-Hayat* [Arabic].

Bahrain Economic Development Board 2008, http://www.bahrainfs.com (accessed April 28, 2008).

Bahrain MPs seek to grill minister on reality TV show (February 26, 2004). *Gulf News*, http://www.gulf-news.com/ (accessed March 1, 2004).

Bahrain refuses to grant mobile phone jamming licenses to mosques (February 22, 2006). *Al-Quds al-Arabi* [Arabic].

Bahry, Louay (May 1997). The opposition in Bahrain: A Bellwether for the Gulf? *Middle East Policy* 5 (2): 42.

——— (2000). The socioeconomic foundations of the Shiite opposition in Bahrain, *Mediterranean Quarterly* (Summer): 129–43.

Baji, Ali (March 8, 2004). 80% of citizens watch *Star Academy*. *Al-Qabas* [Arabic].

Bakhtin, Mikhail (1981). *The Dialogical Imagination: Four Essays*, ed. M. Holquist and trans. C. Emerson and M. Holquist (Austin: University of Texas Press).

Bannout, Hiyam (March 13, 2005). Life at Future TV after al-Hariri "Frame Without Image." *Al-Ra'i al-Aam.* [Arabic].

Baqer, Muhammad (September 22, 2003). Aisha Al-Rshaid: I say to *al-muta'aslemeen*: You aptly failed!! ... and you are not the National Assembly's people. *Al-Watan* [Arabic].

Baqer, Ya'coub Ahmad (April 2, 2004). Star Academy ... and the Western invasion. *Al-Qabas* [Arabic].

Barnett, Michael (1998). *Dialogues in Arab Politics* (New York: Columbia University Press).

Bassam, Camillia (June 4, 2005). Reality TV ... and realism. *Asharq al-Awsat* [Arabic].

Because of their political activities, Israel considers Nancy and Maria and Haifa to pose a danger. Al-Arabiya.net (September 14, 2005).

Belqziz, 'Abdullah (2007). *The Arabs and Modernity: A Study in the Writings of the Modernists* (Beirut: Center for Arab Unity Studies [Arabic]).

Bennett, W. Lance (2005a). News as reality TV: Election coverage and the democratization of truth, *Critical Studies in Media Communication* 22 (2): 171–7.

——— (2005b). Beyond pseudoevents: Election news as reality TV, *American Behavioral Scientist* 49 (3): 364–78.

——— (2008). Changing citizenship in the digital age, in *Civic Life Online: Learning How Digital Media Can Engage Youth*, ed. L. Bennett (Cambridge, MA: MIT Press), 1–24.

Bennis, Muhammad (2004). *Fractured Modernity* (Casablanca: Toubqal Press [Arabic]).

Big Brother opener sparks controversy (April 2004). *Arabian Business* 59–60: 60.

Bilal, Najeh (April 14, 2004). University students: *Star Academy* is dangerous and silly ... But we are fed up on serious and boring political programs. *Al-Siyassah* [Arabic].

Biltereyst, Daniel (2004). *Big Brother* and its moral guardians: Reappraising the role of intellectuals in the *Big Brother* panic, in *Big Brother International: Formats, Critics and Publics*, ed. E . Mathjis and J . Jones (London: Wallflower Press), 9–15.

Blanford, Nicholas (2006). *Killing Mr. Lebanon: The Assassination of Rafik Hariri and its Impact on the Middle East* (London and New York: I.B. Tauris).

Blanks, Jonah (2001). *Mullahs on the Mainframe* (Chicago: University of Chicago Press).

Bluetooth in Saudi Arabia prospers in lost time (February 10, 2005). *Al-Hayat* [Arabic].

Bolter, Jay David and Grusin, Richard (1999). *Remediation: Understanding New Media* (Cambridge, MA: MIT Press).

Boorstin, Daniel (1961). *The Image – Or What Happened to the American Dream* (London: Weidenfeld and Nicholson).

Borgmann, Albert (1999). *Holding on to Reality: The Nature of Information at the Turn of the Millennium* (Chicago: University of Chicago Press).

Bouhaji, Hana' (February 28, 2004). Islamists demonstrate in Bahrain against al-Ra'is and request its shutdown. *Asharq al-Awsat* [Arabic].

Bou Nassar, Joseph (August 10, 2005). Media Editor, *Annahar*, personal interview, Beirut.

Bourdieu, Pierre (1996). *Sur la télévision* (Paris: Raisons d'Agir Éditions).

Boyd, Douglas A. (1970). Saudi Arabian television, *Journal of Broadcasting* 15 (1): 73–8.

——— (1971). Saudi Arabian television, *Journal of Broadcasting* 15 (1): 73–8.

——— (1980). Saudi Arabian broadcasting: Radio and television in a wealthy Islamic state, *Middle East Review* 12 (4)/13 (1): 20–7.

——— (1991). Lebanese broadcasting: Unofficial electronic media during a prolonged civil war, *Journal of Broadcasting and Electronic Media* 35 (3): 269–87.

——— (1999). *Broadcasting in the Arab world: A survey of the electronic media in the Middle East*, 2nd ed (Ames: Iowa State University Press).

——— (2001) "Saudi Arabia's international media strategy: Influence through multi-national ownership," in *Mass Media, Politics and Society in the Middle East*, ed. K. Hafez (Cresskill, NJ: Hampton Press), 43–60.

Boyd, Douglas A. and Najai, A.M. (1984). Adolescent television viewing in Saudi Arabia, *Journalism Quarterly* 61 (2): 295–301, 351.

Brand, Laurie A. (1994a). Economics and shifting alliances: Jordan's relations with Syria and Iraq, 1975–81, *International Journal of Middle East Studies* 26 (3): 393–413.

——— (1994b). *Jordan's Inter-Arab Relations: The Political Economy of Alliance-Making* (New York: Columbia University Press).

Braude, Joseph (October 5, 2006). Rock the Casbah, *Radar Magazine*, http://www.radar online.com/features/2006/10/the_prince_of_pop.php (accessed November 1, 2007).

Brooks, Peter (1976). *The Melodramatic Imagination: Balzac, Henry James, Melodrama, and the Mode of Excess* (New Haven, CT: Yale University Press).

Brubaker, Rogers (1996). *Nationalism Reframed: Nationhood and the National Question in the New Europe* (Cambridge: Cambridge University Press).

Budangji, Fatin (February 15, 2008). Dialogue or no dialogue? That's the real question. *Arab News*.

Burke, Kenneth (1970). *Language as Symbolic Action* (Berkeley: University of California Press).

Cantellli, Fabrizio and Paye, Olivier (2004). *Star Academy*: un objet pour la science politique? In *Star Academy: Un objet pour les sciences sociales?*, ed. Yves Cartuyvels (Bruxelles, Belgique: Publications des Facultés universitaires Saint-Louis), 65–89.

Cartuyvels, Yves, ed. (2004). *Star Academy: Un objet pour les sciences sociales?* (Bruxelles, Belgique: Publications des Facultés universitaires Saint-Louis).

Censure: La LBCI en appelle au conseil d'état (March 28, 1997). *L'Orient-Le Jour.*

Charland, Maurice (1987). Constitutive rhetoric: The case of the Peuple Québécois, *Quarterly Journal of Speech* 73 (2): 133–50.

Chayban, Badih. (August 25, 2003). LBCI celebrates 18th anniversary with prominent media figures. *Daily Star.*

Choueiri: It's time to raise ad spending (December 3, 2006). *Campaign Middle East.*

Cochrane, Peter (October 2007). Saudi Arabia's media influence, *Arab Media and Society*, http://www.arabmediasociety.com/articles/downloads/20071001153449_AMS3_Paul_Cochrane.pdf (accessed November 1, 2007).

Cole, Juan R. I. (1998). *Modernity at the Millennium: The Genesis of the Baha'i Faith in the Nineteenth-Century Middle East* (New York: Columbia University Press).

Coleman, Stephen (2006). How the other half votes: Big Brother viewers and the 2005 British General Election Campaign, *International Journal of Cultural Studies* 9 (4): 457–79.

——— (2007a). From big brother to Big Brother: Two faces of interactive engagement, in *Young Citizens and New Media: Learning for Democratic Participation*, ed. Peter Dahlgren (New York: Routledge), 21–39.

——— (2007b). How democracies have disengaged from young people, in *Young Citizens in the Digital Age: Political Engagement, Young People and New Media*, ed. Brian Loader (London: Routledge), 166–85.

Communiqué by the Lebanese Broadcasting Corporation (March 24, 1994). *The Beirut Review* 7: 167.

Corner, John (2002). Performing the real: Documentary diversions, *Television and New Media* 3 (3): 255–69.

Couldry, Nick (2002). Playing for celebrity: Big Brother as a ritual event, *Television and New Media* 3 (3): 283–93.

——— (2003). *Media Rituals: A Critical Approach* (London: Routledge).

——— (2004). Liveness, "reality," and the mediated habitus from television to the mobile phone, *The Communication Review* 7: 353–61.

Couldry, Nick and Tim Markham (2007). Celebrity culture and public connection: Bridge or chasm? *International Journal of Cultural Studies* 10 (4): 403–21.

Country profile: Saudi Arabia (July 28, 2006), http://news.bbc.co.uk/1/hi/world/middle_east/country_profiles/791936.stm (accessed December 30, 2006), London: British Broadcasting Corporation.

Crystal, Jill and Abdallah al-Shayeji (1998). The Pro-democratic agenda in Kuwait: Structure and context, in *Political Liberalization and Democratization in the Arab World*, vol. 2, ed. Bahjat Korany, Rex Brynen, and Paul Noble (Boulder, CO: Lynne Rienner), 101–26.

Dabbous-Sensenig, Dima (2006). To veil or not to veil: Gender and religion on Al-Jazeera's Islamic Law and Life, *Westminster Papers in Communication and Culture* 3 (2): 60–85.

Dahlgren, Peter (1995) *Television and the Public Sphere* (London: Sage).

——— (2006). Doing citizenship: The cultural origins of civic agency in the public sphere, *European Journal of Cultural Studies* 9 (3): 267–86.

———— (2009). *Media and Political Engagement: Citizens, Communication and Democracy* (New York: Cambridge University Press).

Dakhlallah: Syria has a promising future and its media in transition from dirigiste to purposeful (November 16, 2004). *Al-Hayat* [Arabic].

Dalla, Fadia (March 10, 2005). Reality TV … an Eastern execution with a Western ethos. *Al-Bayan* [Arabic].

Darrous, Sabine (1998). Franjieh orders big shake-up of LBCI politics. New, non-Christian staff may be added to station's news team. *Daily Star*.

———— (October 2, 2000). Storm swirls around LBCI as Franjieh turns screws to bring station to heel. *Daily Star*.

Davies, Fiona (2004). Al-Rais has fallen silent (Geneva: European Broadcasting Union).

Dayan, Daniel and Elihu Katz (1992). *Media Events: The Live Broadcasting of History* (Cambridge, MA: Harvard University Press).

Deeb, Lara. (2006). *An Enchanted Modern* (Princeton, NJ: Princeton University Press).

Deibert, Ronald J. (1997). *Parchment, Printing, and Hypermedia: Communication in World Order Transformation* (New York: Columbia University Press).

Dekmejian, Richard (2003). The liberal impulse in Saudi Arabia, *The Middle East Journal* 57 (3): 381–99.

Delli Carpini, Michael and Bruce Williams (2001). Let us infotain you, in *Mediated Politics*, ed. L. Bennett and R. Entman (Cambridge and New York: Cambridge University Press), 160–81.

Dick, Marlin (November 28, 1998). LBCI says it will haul public into revolutionary age of digital TV. *Daily Star*.

Diab, Wafa'i (January 2, 2004). The year of *infiraj*, realism and disasters. *Asharq al-Awsat*.

Doumato, Eleanor A. (1992). Gender, monarchy and national identity in Saudi Arabia, *British Journal of Middle Eastern Studies* 19 (1): 31–47.

Eddy, William (1963). King Ibn Sa'ud: Our faith and your iron, *Middle East Journal* 17 (3): 257–63.

Edelman, Murray (1995). *From Art to Politics: How Artistic Creations Shape Political Conceptions* (Chicago: University of Chicago Press).

Eickelman, Dale F. (1998). Inside the Islamic reformation, *Wilson Quarterly* 22 (1): 80–9.

———— (2000). Islam and the language of modernity, *Daedelus* 129 (1): 119–35.

Eisenstadt, S. N. (2000). Multiple modernities, *Daedelus* 129 (1): 6.

Elias, Hanna Elias (1993). *La presse arabe* (Paris: Maisonneuve et Larose).

El-Nawawy Mohammed and Adel Iskandar (2002). *Al-Jazeera: How the Free Arab News Network Scooped the World and Changed the Middle East* (Boulder, CO: Westview).

El-Oifi, Mohamed (December 2006). Voyage au coeur des quotidiens panarabes, *Le Monde Diplomatique*.

Elster, Jon, ed. (1998). *Deliberative Democracy* (New York: Cambridge University Press).

Erlanger, Steven (August 22, 2004). Palestinian carries a tune and the hope of his people. *The New York Times*, 10.

Et maintenant … la censure préventive (March 29, 1997). *L'Orient-Le Jour*.

Fakher, Muhammad (April 20, 2004). University students: Bashar is a national symbol and his victory is a triumph for Kuwait. *Al-Qabas* [Arabic].

Family Battle! (March 6, 2004). *Al-Qabas* [Arabic].

Fandy, Mamoun (1999). *Saudi Arabia and the Politics of Dissent* (New York: Palgrave Macmillan).

Fattah, Hassan (March 8, 2005). Pro-Syria party in Beirut holds a huge protest. *The New York Times*, A1.

Fatwa on *Star Academy* (2004). Standing Committee for Scientific Research and the Issuing of Fatwas. Medina: Saudi Arabia.

Fatwas did not affect the popularity of *Star Academy* (April 5, 2004). *Al-Qabas* [Arabic].

Fawwaz, 'Ali (August 25, 2008). Saudi cinema gambles on the future. *Al-Akhbar* [Arabic].

Felski, Rita (1995). *The Gender of Modernity* (Cambridge, MA: Harvard University Press).

First young woman to win the title ... Shadha Hassoun Triumphs for Iraq in Star Academy 4 (April 2, 2007). *Al-Hayat* [Arabic].

Fiske, John (1996). *Media Matters* (Minneapolis: University of Minnesota Press).

Fordham, Alice (August 15, 2008). Bombs and Botox in Beirut. *Times Online*, http://www.timesonline.co.uk/tol/comment/columnists/guests_contrib (accessed August 15, 2008).

Francis, Tony (July 18, 2007). Media ... in Arabic. *Al-Hayat* [Arabic].

Frierson, Elizabeth B. (2004). Gender, consumption and patriotism: The emergence of an Ottoman public sphere, in *Public Islam and the Common Good*, ed. A. Salvatore and D. F. Eickelman (Leiden, the Netherlands: Brill), 99–125.

Future TV showed them and they went to Al-Manar to clarify: Two youth confirm they are Lebanese (March 12, 2005). *Assafir* [Arabic].

Gabler, Neil (1998). *Life the Movie: How Entertainment Conquered Reality* (New York: Knopf).

Gambill, Gary C. and Ziad K. Abdelnour (2002). Prince Al-Walid bin Talal, Saudi Billionaire, *Middle East Intelligence Bulletin*, 4 (9), http: www.meib.org/articles/0209_med1.htm (accessed November 1, 2007).

Gaonkar, Dilip P. (1999). On alternative modernities, *Public Culture* 11 (1): 1–18.

García-Canclini, Nestor (1994). *Hybrid Cultures: Strategies for Entering and Leaving Modernity* (Minneapolis: University of Minnesota Press).

———— (1998). *Consumers and Citizens: Multicultural Conflicts in Globalization* (Minneapolis: University of Minnesota Press).

Gelvin, James (1999). Modernity and its discontents: On the durability of nationalism in the Arab Middle East, *Nations and Nationalisms* 5 (1): 71–89.

Ghabra, Shafeeq (1997). Kuwait and the dynamics of socio-economic change, *Middle East Journal* 51 (3): 358–72.

Ghosn, Zaynab (March 18, 2005). Free-to-air channels pull the rug from under encrypted channels. *Assafir* [Arabic].

Giddens, Anthony (1990). *The Consequences of Modernity* (Palo Alto: Stanford University Press).

Gillespie, Michael A. (2008). *The Theological Origins of Modernity* (Chicago: University of Chicago Press).

Girard, Laurence (November 6, 2001). MBC, la pionnière des chaînes arabes, quitte Londres, *Le Monde*.

Göle, Nilüfer. (2000). Snapshots of Islamic modernities, *Daedelus* 129 (1): 91–117.

Green Light: A reality show of another kind (June 1, 2005). *Al-Riyadh* [Arabic].

Gruzinski, Serge (1999). *La Pensée Métisse* (Paris: Fayard).

Guaybess, Tourya (2003). De L'État Émetteur a L'Émetteur État dans le Champ. Télévisuel Égyptien, in *Mondialisation et nouveaux médias dans l'espace arabe*, ed. F. Mermier (Paris: Maisonneuve et Larose), 103–23.

Habeas, Abed (August 23, 2004). Palestinian singing finalist tunes into nationalism. *Boston Globe*.

Habermas, Jürgen (1998). *Between Facts and Norms* (Cambridge, MA: MIT Press).

Habib, Osama (December 3, 2003). Alwaleed buys large stake in LBC SAT. *Daily Star*.

Habib, Vicky (November 19, 2004). Dreams TV after the reality TV storm abates … what if television can fulfill your wishes? *Al-Hayat* [Arabic].

——— (January 7, 2005). Politics and the misery of reality are television's two stars. *Al-Hayat* [Arabic].

——— (July 19, 2005). Media Reporter and Critic, *Al-Hayat*, personal interview, Beirut, Lebanon.

——— (August 6, 2007). From "closer to reality" to "so that you know more"… Al-Arabiya changes its motto while insisting that its professional essence does not change. *Al-Hayat* [Arabic].

Haddad, Viviane (March 8, 2005). French language colors conversations and songs in Star Academy. *Asharq al-Awsat* [Arabic].

——— (April 23, 2005). A new wave of Arab reality TV shows poised to be launched. *Asharq al-Awsat* [Arabic].

——— (September 17, 2006). Lebanese satellite channels compete for Saudi media personalities. *Asharq al-Awsat* [Arabic].

Hafez, Kai, ed. (2008). Introduction to *Arab Media: Power and Weakness* (New York: Continuum), 1–16.

Hajj-'Abdi, Ibrahim (April 28, 2005). Diana Jabbour: Why don't we turn the screen into a bridge between citizens and the state? *Al-Hayat* [Arabic].

Hammond, Andrew (August 9, 2007). Saudi media empire tries to counter opposition. Riyadh: Reuters.

——— (October 2007). Saudi Arabia's media empire: Keeping the masses at home, *Arab Media and Society*, http://www.arabmediasociety.com/articles/downloads/20071001152622_AMS3_Andrew_Hammond.pdf.

Hammoud, 'Abdulhalim (2008). *Reality TV: Humans in the Cage of the Image* (Beirut: Dar al-Hadi [Arabic]).

Hamzawy, Amr (2006). The Saudi labyrinth: Evaluating the current political opening. *Carnegie Papers on Democracy and Rule of Law, 68* (Washington, DC: Carnegie Endowment for International Peace).

Hartley, John (2007). "Reality" and the Plebiscite, in *Politicotainment: Television's Take on the Real*, ed. K. Riegert (New York: Peter Lang), 21–58.

Haugbolle, Sune (2006). Spatial transformations in the Lebanese "Independence Intifada," *Arab Studies Quarterly* XIV (2): 60–77.

Haydar, Diya' (February 28, 2005). A "painful event" produces "patriotic night." *Assafir* [Arabic].

——— (March 9, 2005). Al-Manar is mother of the bride and Future TV last wellwisher. *Assafir* [Arabic].

Hayek, Georges (February 25, 2005). Televisual division! *Annahar* [Arabic].

Hazin, Ghassan (April 19, 2005). When reality and reality TV collide. *Al-Hayat* [Arabic].

Hermes, Joke (2005). *Re-reading Popular Culture* (Oxford: Blackwell).

Hermes, Joke and Dahlgren, Peter (2006). Cultural studies and citizenship, *European Journal of Cultural Studies* 9 (3): 259–65.

Hervieu-Léger, D. (2003). Pour une sociologie des "modernités religieuses multiples": une autre approche de la "religion invisible" des sociétés européennes, *Social Compass* 50 (3): 287–95.

Hicks, Neil and al-Najjar, Ghanim (1995). The utility of tradition: Civil society in Kuwait, in *Civil Society in the Middle East*, vol. 1, ed. A. R. Norton (Leiden, the Netherlands: Brill), 186–213.

Higgins, Andrew (May 11, 2005). Royal flush: After high hopes, democracy project in Bahrain falters; Gulf kingdom reverses course as calls for change swell; lessons for the Middle East; a web site rallies opposition. *Wall Street Journal*, A1.

Hill, Annette (2002). Big Brother: The real audience, *Television and New Media* 3 (3): 323–40.

——— (2005). *Reality TV: Audiences and Popular Factual Television* (London: Routledge).

Hill, Annette and Palmer, G. (2002). Editorial: Big Brother, *Television and New Media* 3 (3): 251–4.

Hisham is arrested in Riyadh (April 22, 2005). *Assafir* [Arabic].

Holmes, Su (2004). "But this time you choose!" Approaching the "interactive" audience in reality TV, *International Journal of Cultural Studies* 7 (2): 213–31.

Hourani, Albert (1983). *Arabic Thought in the Liberal Age: 1789–1939* (Cambridge: Cambridge University Press).

How to spend it. (April 24, 2008). *The Economist*.

Huwayli, 'Ali (January 12, 2006). Lebanon's uniqueness in the Arab media system. *Al-Hayat* [Arabic].

Ibrahim, Youssef M. (June 29, 1992). Saudis pursue media acquisitions, gaining influence in the Arab world. *New York Times*, D8.

Ida'at: Dr. Aliya Sh'ayb (October 20, 2004). Turki Al-Dakhil, host. Dubai: Al-Arabiya [Arabic].

In spite of fatwas prohibiting it Arab youth are saying: Yes to Star Academy (April 4, 2004). *Al-Siyassah* [Arabic].

Issa, Hanadi (July 19, 2005). *Laha Magazine*, personal interview, Beirut, Lebanon.

'Itani, Samir (March 18, 2005). "War of slogans" hotter than demonstrations. *Al-Bayan* [Arabic].

Jaber, Hala (August 17, 2003). Army called out as pop idol starts battle in Beirut. *Sunday Times*, 25.

Jackson, John Jr. (2008) *Racial Paranoia: The Unintended Consequences of Political Correctness* (New York: Basic Books).

Jacobs, Sue (2007). *Big Brother*, Africa is watching, *Media, Culture and Society* 29 (6): 851–68.

Jamal, Amani and Mark Tessler (2008). Attitudes in the Arab World, *Journal of Democracy* 19 (1), http://www.arabbarometer.org/reports/democbarometers.pdf (accessed December 1, 2008).

James, Laura (2006). Whose voice? Nasser, the Arabs and "Sawt al-Arab" radio, *Transnational Broadcasting Journal*, 16, http://www.tbsjournal.comh/James.html (accessed November 1, 2008).

Jaza'iri, Muhammad (April 9, 2005). Al-Manama: Capital of youth contradictions. *Asharq al-Awsat* [Arabic].

Jost, François (2007a). *L'empire du Loft* (Paris: La Dispute).

——— (2007b). *Le culte du banal. De Duchamp à la télé-réalité* (Paris: CNRS).

Jost, François, and Muzet, Denis (2008). *Le Téléprésident: Essai sur un pouvoir médiatique* (Paris: L'Aube).

Judge hears arguments in LBCI case (February 27, 2001). *Daily Star*.

Kandiyoti, Deniz (1994). Identity and its discontents: Women and the nation, in *Colonial Discourse and Post-Colonial Theory: A Reader*, ed. P. Williams and L. Christman (New York: Columbia University Press).

Katzman, Kenneth (March 14, 2005). *Bahrain: Key issues for U.S. policy* (Washington, DC: Congressional Research Service).

Kassir, Samir (2004). *Considerations sur le Malheur arabe* (Paris: Actes Sud).

Kawakibi, Salam (1977). Le Rôle de la télévision dans la relecture de l'histoire, *Monde arabe Maghreb Mashrek* (158): 47–55.

Kaya, Ibrahim (2004). Modernity, openness, interpretation: A perspective on multiple modernities, *Social Science Information* 43 (1): 35–47.

Khairy, Amina (April 13, 2005). Zizi exited ... and mobile phone companies won. *Al-Hayat* [Arabic].

——— (May 23, 2006). "Reality" in official eyes. *Al-Hayat* [Arabic].

Khaled, Nour (August 14, 2007). Allo Tash ma tash: Saudi drama soon on mobile phones. *Al-Akhbar* [Arabic].

Khalidiyyah, Juhayna (December 11, 2006). "Reality TV" triumphs in open air studios? *Assafir* [Arabic].

Khalil, Joe F. (2004). Blending in: Arab television and the search for programming ideas. *Transnational broadcasting Journal* 13, http://www.tbsjournal.com/Archives/Fall04/khalil.html (accessed February 15, 2006).

——— (2005). Inside Arab reality television: Development, definitions and demystification, *Transnational broadcasting Journal* 15, http://www.tbsjournal.com/Archives/Fall05/khalil.html (accessed February 15, 2006).

Khan, Riz (2005). *Alwaleed: Businessman, Billionaire, Prince* (London: William Morrow).

Khatib, Lina (2006). *Filming the Modern Middle East: Politics in the Cinemas of Hollywood and the Arab World* (London: I. B. Tauris).

——— (2007). Television and public action in the Beirut spring, in *Arab Media and Political Renewal: Community, Legitimacy and Public Life*, ed. N. Sakr (London: I. B. Tauris), 28–43.

Khiabany, Gholam (2007). Iranian media: The paradox of modernity, *Social Semiotics* 17 (4): 479–501.

Khoury, Rosy (March 12, 2005). Television photographers ... first witnesses to the event. *Al-Hayat* [Arabic].

Kohn, Margaret (2000). Language, power and persuasion: Toward a critique of deliberative democracy, *Constellations* 7 (3): 408–29.

Kolakowski, Leszek (1990). *Modernity on Endless Trial*, trans. Stefan Czerniawski, Wolfgang Freis, and Agnieszka Kolakowska (Chicago: University of Chicago Press).

Kraidy, Marwan M. (1998a). Broadcasting regulation and civil society in postwar Lebanon, *Journal of Broadcasting and Electronic Media* 42 (3): 387–400.

———— (1998b). Satellite broadcasting from Lebanon: Prospects and perils, *Transnational Broadcasting Studies 1*, http://www.tbsjournal.com/Archives/Fall00/Kraidy2. htm (accessed June 15, 1999).

Kraidy, M. M. (1999a). The global, the local, and the hybrid: A native ethnography of glocalization, *Critical Studies in Mass Communication* 16 (4): 458–78.

———— (1999b). State control of television news in 1990s Lebanon, *Journalism and Mass Communication Quarterly* 76 (3): 485–98.

———— (2000a).Transnational satellite television and asymmetrical interdependence in the Arab world: A research note, *Transnational Broadcasting Studies*, 5, http://www.tbsjournal.com/Archives/Fall00/Kraidy.htm (accessed November 1, 2007).

———— (2000b). Television talk and civic discourse in postwar Lebanon, in *Civic Discourses in the Middle East and Digital Age Communications*, ed. L. Gher and H. Amin (Norwood, NJ: Ablex), 1–17.

———— (2002). Arab satellite television between regionalization and globalization, *Global Media Journal* 1 (1), http://lass.calumet.purdue/edu/cca/gmj/new_page_1.htm (accessed January 15, 2003).

———— (2005) *Hybridity, or the Cultural Logic of Globalization* (Philadelphia, PA: Temple University Press).

———— (2006a). Governance and hypermedia in Saudi Arabia, *First Monday* 11 (9), http://firstmonday.org/issues/special11_9/kraidy/index.html (accessed December 30, 2006).

———— (2006b). Popular culture as a political barometer: Lebanese-Syrian relations on *Superstar, Transnational Broadcasting Studies*, June, http://www.tbsjournal.com (accessed November 1, 2007).

———— (2006c). Reality television and politics in the Arab world (preliminary observations), *Transnational Broadcasting Studies* [peer-reviewed paper edition] 2 (1): 7–28, http://www.tbsjournal.com/Kraidy.html (accessed November 1, 2007).

———— (2007a). Idioms of contention: *Star Academy* in Lebanon and Kuwait, in *Pan-Arab Media, Democracy, and the Public Sphere*, ed. N. Sakr (London: I. B. Tauris), 44–55.

————(2007b). Saudi Arabia, Lebanon, and the changing Arab information order, *International Journal of Communication* 1 (1): 139–56, http://ijoc.org/ojs/index.php/ijoc/article/view/18/22 (accessed February 10, 2008).

———— (2008a). Critical transculturalism and Arab satellite television: Theoretical explorations, in *Global Communications: Toward a Transcultural Political Economy*, ed. P. Chakravartty and Y. Zhao (Lanham, MD: Rowman and Littlefield), 189–200.

———— (2008b). The Arab audience: From Activity to Interactivity, in *Arab Media: Power and Weakness*, ed. K. Hafez (New York: Continuum), 77–88.

———— (2008c). *Arab Media and U.S. Policy: A Public Diplomacy Reset*, Policy Brief (Muscatine, IA: The Stanley Foundation), http://stanleyfdn.org/publications/pab/PAB08Kraidy.pdf (accessed December 30, 2008).

———— (2008d). Arab states: Emerging consensus to muzzle media? *Arab Reform Bulletin* 6 (2). Carnegie Endowment for International Peace, Washington, DC, http://www.carnegieendowment.org/publications/index.cfm?fa=view&;id=19968 &prog=zgp&proj=zdrl,zme-kraidy (accessed June 1, 2008).

———— (2009). Reality TV, gender and authenticity in Saudi Arabia, *Journal of Communication*, 59, 345–66.

Kraidy, Marwan M. and Khalil, J. (2007). The Middle East: Transnational Arab television, in *The Media Globe: Trends in International Mass Media*, ed. L. Artz and Y. Kamalipour (Lanham, MD: Rowman and Littlefield), 79–98.

—— (2008). Youth, media, and culture in the Arab world, in *International Handbook of Children, Media and Culture*, ed. Sonia Livingstone and Kristin Drotner (London: Sage), 330–44.

—— (2009, in press). *Arab Television Industries* (London: Palgrave Macmillan/ British Film Institute).

Kulynych, Jessica (1997). Performing politics: Foucault, Habermas and postmodern participation, *Polity* 30 (2): 315–46.

Kuwait bans concerts involving women entertainers (May 25, 2004). *Arab News*.

Kuwaiti fatwa prohibits *Star Academy* concert in Kuwait (May 25, 2004). *Al-Bayan* [Arabic].

Kuwaiti MP demands a ban on *Star Academy* concert in the country (May 2004).

Kuwaiti MPs to question minister over concert (May 9, 2004). *Arab News*.

La Future Television dément les accusations don't elle fait l'objet (August 13, 2003). *L'Orient-Le Jour*.

Lacroix, Stéphane (Spring 2005). Post-Wahhabism in Saudi Arabia? *ISIM Review* 15: 17.

Lacroix, S. (2005). Islamo-liberal politics in Saudi Arabia, in *Saudi Arabia in the Balance: Political Economy, Society, Foreign Affairs*, ed. P. Aarts and G. Nonneman (New York: New York University Press), 35–56.

Lamloum, Olfa (2004). *Al-jazira, miroir rebelle et ambigu du monde arabe* (Paris: La Découverte).

Lang, Gladys Engel, and Lang, Kurt (1984). *Politics and Television Reviewed* (Beverly Hills, CA: Sage).

LBC finally merged with Rotana! (August 9, 2007). *Al-Akhbar* [Arabic].

LBCSAT and Rotana Television channels merge to form media powerhouse (August 9, 2007). Riyadh, Saudi Arabia: Company Press Release.

LBCSAT and Rotana channels merge in one entity (August 9, 2007). *Al-Riyadh* [Arabic].

Le Guay, Damien (2005). *L'empire de la télé-réalité: ou comment accroître le "temps de cerveau humain disponible"* (Paris: Presses de la Renaissance).

Le Pottier, Gaëlle (2003). Le monde de la télévision satellitaire au Moyen-Orient et le rôle des libanais dans son développement, in *Mondialisation et nouveaux médias dans l'espace arabe*, ed. F . Mermier (Paris: Maisonneuve et Larose), 43–72.

Lebanese satellite channel LBC with new and varied programming bouquet (October 23, 2006). *Al-Riyadh* [Arabic].

Lebanon's youth and reality TV-1 (April 22, 2004). *Annahar* [Arabic].

Lebanon's youth and reality TV-2 (April 23, 2004). *Annahar* [Arabic].

Lebling, Robert (April 22, 2005). From Beirut to Jeddah: A desk editor reminisces. *Arab News*.

Lerner, Daniel (1964). *The Passing of Traditional Society: Modernizing the Middle East* (New York: Free Press).

Les chaînes de télévision libanaises sont-elles allées trop loin? (December 22–8, 1997), *Vision* 25.

Letter from the chairman (June 14, 1996), www.lbci.inco.com.lb (accessed July 1, 1996).

Leurre et la manière (December 1997). *L'Orient-Express*, 25, 76.

Lewis, Justin (2004). The meaning of real life, in *Reality TV: Remaking Television Culture*, ed. S. Murray and L. Ouellette (New York: New York University Press), 288–302.

Lichtblau, Klaus (1999). Differentiations of modernity, *Theory, Culture and Society* 16 (3): 1–30.

Liebes, Tamar and Elihu Katz (2007). "No More Peace!": How disaster, terror and war have upstaged media events, *International Journal of Communication* 1 (1), http://ijoc.org/ojs/index.php/ijoc/article/view/44/23 (accessed February 10, 2008).

Longva, Anh Nga (1993). Kuwait women at a crossroads: Privileged development and the constraints of ethnic stratification, *International Journal of Middle East Studies* 25: 443–56.

Loqman, Faruq (1997). *Internationalizing the Arab Press: Hisham and Muhammad 'Ali Hafizh* (Jeddah: Saudi Distribution Company [Arabic]).

Lynch, Marc (2005). *Voices of the New Arab Public: Iraq, Al-Jazeera, and Middle East Politics Today* (New York: Columbia University Press).

Lynch, M. (2008). Political opportunity structures: Effects of Arab media, in *Arab Media: Power and Weakness*, ed. K. Hafez (New York: Continuum), 17–32.

Maalouf, Lynn (January 14, 2004). Western television craze makes assured debut on region's networks. *Daily Star*.

MacFarqhar, Neil (March 5, 2004). A kiss is not just a kiss to an angry Arab TV audience. *The New York Times*.

———— (March 13, 2005). Hezbollah leader's new fray: Lebanese politics. *The New York Times*.

MacKenzie, Tyler (2004). The best hope for democracy in the Arab world: A crooning TV "idol"? *Transnational Broadcasting Studies* (13), http://www.tbsjournal.com/Archives/Fall04/mackenzie.html (accessed October 15, 2005).

Madkour, Mona (March 14, 2005). Plastic surgery give men handsomeness and youth … the alternative is "kharab byout." *Asharq al-Awsat* [Arabic].

Mancini, Paolo and David Swanson (1996). Politics, media, and modern democracy: Introduction, in *Politics, Media and Modern Democracy*, ed. D. Swanson and P. Mancini (Westport, CT: Praeger), 1–28.

Mandel Khan, Gabriele (2001). *L'écriture arabe: alphabet, style et calligraphie* (Paris: Flammarion).

Mandour, Sahar (February 28, 2005). A "Jumblati" moment in "the academy." *Assafir* [Arabic].

Mansour, Muhammad (December 13, 2007). LBC's welcome to Saudi productions: Media charlatanism harmful to both sides! *Al-Quds al-Arabi* [Arabic].

———— (March 7, 2008). Al-Arabiya five years after its launch: A necessity imposed by al-Jazeera and continuity shaped its identity. *Al-Quds al-Arabi* [Arabic].

Marghalani, Khalid, Philip Palmgreen, and Douglas A. Boyd (1998). The utilization of direct broadcasting satellite broadcasting (DBS) in Saudi Arabia, *Journal of Broadcasting and Electronic Media* 42 (3): 297–313.

Martín-Barbero, Jesus (1993). *From the Media to Mediations: Communication, Culture and Hegemony* (London: Sage).

Mathjis, Ernest (2002). Big Brother and critical discourse: The reception of Big Brother in Belgium, *Television and New Media* 3 (3): 311–22.

Mathjis, Ernest and Janet J. Jones, eds. (2004). *Big Brother International: Formats, Critics and Publics* (London: Wallflower Press).

Mazhloum, Hussain Dib (April 11, 2005). A coup against the resistance with the public of Superstar! *Al-Quds al-Arabi* [Arabic].

McAdam, Doug, Sidney Tarrow, and Charles C. Tilly (2001). *Dynamics of Contention* (Cambridge and New York: Cambridge University Press).

McAlister, Melani (2005). *Epic Encounters: Culture, Media, and U.S. Interests in the Middle East since 1945* (Berkeley: University of California Press).

McCarthy, Anna (2007). Reality television: A neoliberal theater of suffering, *Social Text* 25 (4): 17–41.

Mcclenahan, William (April 26, 2004). It's either the Mossad, the CIA, neo-cons, or Osama bin Laden. *The Daily Star*.

Mcleod, Kembrew (1999). Authenticity within hip-hop and other cultures threatened with assimilation, *Journal of Communication* 49 (4): 134–50.

McClintock, Anne (1997). No longer in future heaven: Gender, race and nationalism, in *Dangerous Liaisons: Gender, Nation and Postcolonial Perspectives*, ed. A. McClintock, A. Mufti, and E. Shohat (Minneapolis: University of Minnesota Press), 89–112.

Médias-Le différend a la LBC paraît réglé. *L'Orient-Le Jour* (October 3, 2000).

Mellor, Noha (2008). Bedouinisation or liberalisation of culture? The paradox in the Saudi monopoly of the Arab media, in *Kingdom without Borders: Saudi Arabia's Political, Religious and Media Frontiers*, ed. M. Al-Rasheed (New York: Columbia University Press), 353–74.

Mer'i, Zahra (March 22, 2005). Shenanigans, zajal and lies: Covering demonstrations the Lebanese way. *Al-Quds al-Arabi* [Arabic].

——— (February 4, 2006). Shahd Barmada: I participate in an artistic program unrelated to politics, *Al-Quds al-Arabi* [Arabic].

Mernissi, Fatima (1987). *Beyond the Veil: Male-Female Dynamics in Modern Muslim Society* (Bloomington: Indiana University Press), 353–74.

Meyer, Katherine, Helen Rizzo and Youssef Ali (1998). Islam and the extension of citizenship rights to women in Kuwait, *Journal for the Scientific Study of Religion* 37 (1): 131–44.

Meyer, Thomas (2002). *Media Democracy: How the Media Colonize Politics* (Cambridge: Polity).

Miles, Hugh (2005). *Al-Jazeera: How Arab TV News Challenges America* (New York: Grove Press).

Miller, Toby (1993). *The Well-Tempered Self: Citizenship, Culture and the Postmodern Subject* (Baltimore, MD: Johns Hopkins University Press).

Mimicking Western Programs and Imposing Them on Arabs, Episode 1. (March 3, 2004). Bila Hudud (Ahmad Mansour, Host). Doha, Qatar: al-Jazeera.

Mimicking Western Programs and Imposing Them on Arabs, Episode 2. (March 10, 2004). Bila Hudud (Ahmad Mansour, Host). Doha, Qatar: al-Jazeera.

Minister of Information calls on journalists to hold on to "freedom of expression" and to relinquish "the vocabulary of confrontation" ... Syria towards "controlling" electronic publishing in a new media law (April 15, 2005). *Al-Hayat* [Arabic].

Mishkhas, Abeer (March 9, 2004). Do we give our children what they want? *Arab News*.

——— (January 13, 2005). Tilting at the wrong windmills. *Arab News*.

———— (January 27, 2005). Who's who out there? *Arab News*.

Mitchell, Timothy (2000). *Questions of Modernity* (Minneapolis: University of Minnesota Press).

Moaddel, Mansour (2006). The Saudi public speaks: Religion, gender, and politics, *International Journal of Middle Eastern Studies* 38: 79–108.

Moran, Albert (1998). *Copycat Television: Globalization, Program Formats, and Cultural Identity* (Luton, U.K.: University of Luton Press).

Mouawad, Jad (September 16, 1998). Ad firms cast keen eye on TV ratings. More accurate audience figures sought as $50m revenue carrot is dangled. *Daily Star*.

Moussa, George (February 11, 2004). Superstar 2: Why the insistence on turning the contest into a tribal battle? *Al-Hayat* [Arabic].

———— (February 27, 2005). "Star Academy" also ... takes "a patriotic stand." *Al-Hayat* [Arabic].

———— (April 13, 2005). Will Star Academy triumph over reality TV? *Al-Hayat* [Arabic].

Mroue, Bassem (August 18, 2003). Arab world's version of "American Idol" has nationalistic bent, and vehement fans (Beirut: Associated Press).

Mshawrab, Ibrahim. Media and Variety Editor, *Al-Bayan*, personal interview, Dubai, June 17, 2005.

Muhammad, Afra' (October 31, 2005). The weblog is an oasis of freedom that escapes state censorship ... personal diaries to build bridges between young Arabs. *Al-Hayat* [Arabic].

Muhammad al-Saqr on Kuwait's press, *Middle East Report*, 180 (Jan.–Feb. 1993): 20.

Mufreh, Sa'diyya (March 6, 2004). *Star Academy*: A detailed reading on paper of details of life on the air (1): Star Academy fills the Arab world and preoccupies its people between believing, denying, rejecting and agreeing. *Al-Qabas* [Arabic].

———— (March 7, 2004). *Star Academy*: A detailed reading on paper of details of life on the air (2): The program's critics are its most avid daily followers, in secret. *Al-Qabas* [Arabic].

Muntasir, Huda (April 3, 2004). Bashar won ... and 'Atiya triumphed. *Al-Watan* [Arabic].

Muqalled, Diana (March 5, 2005). Lebanese developments ... confuse the media. *Asharq al-Awsat* [Arabic].

———— (March 12, 2005). The Zoom war! *Asharq al-Awsat* [Arabic].

Murdock, Graham (1993). Communications and the constitution of modernity, *Media, Culture and Society* 15: 521–39.

Murshid, Safinaz Z. (February 29, 2004). Reality TV – The Real Deal. *Arab News*.

Mustafa, Mustafa (April 18, 2009). "Scientists" also like stardom. *Al-Akhbar* [Arabic].

Naji, 'Abdulsattar (April 5, 2004). Kuwait gives a hero's welcome to Star Academy star Al-Shatti. *Asharq al-Awsat* [Arabic].

Nasrallah, Muhammad R. (February 9, 2004). The extremists' generation ... and Star Academy's generation! *Al-Riyadh* [Arabic].

New Saudi law to jail, lash cellphone porn users (April 16, 2005). Riyadh, Saudi Arabia: Reuters.

Nizhameddin, 'Arfan (March 6, 2006). Questions and answers on the Arabs' reality. *Al-Hayat* [Arabic].

On the Screen (July 30, 2008). *Al-Akhbar* [Arabic].

O'Reilly, Marc J. (1999). Oil monarchies without oil: Omani and Bahraini security in a post-oil era, *Middle East Policy* 6: 78–92.

'Ouayss, Rasha (January 2005). Arab media moguls, *Forbes Al-Arabiya* 1 (8) [Arabic].

Ouellette, Laurie and James Hay (2008). *Better Living Through Reality TV: Television and Post-Welfare Citizenship* (New York: Blackwell).

Oussy, Hoshenk (April 9, 2007). The screen and the event … nothing new in mode of treatment. *Al-Hayat* [Arabic].

Palmer, Gareth (2002). Big Brother: An experiment in governance, *Television and New Media* 3 (3): 295–310.

Pan Arab song contest fuels passions in Jordan (August 17, 2003), *Jordan Times*.

Parssinen, Catherine (1980). The changing role of women, in *King Faisal and the Modernization of Saudi Arabia*, ed. W. A. Beling (Boulder, CO: Westview Press), 145–70.

Peters, John D. (1999). *Speaking Into the Air: A History of the Idea of Communication* (University of Chicago Press).

——— (2001). Witnessing, *Media, Culture and Society* 23 (6): 703–23.

Peterson, John E. (2002). Bahrain's first steps towards reform under Amir Hamad, *Asian Affairs* 33 (2): 216–27.

Pettman, Jindy J. (1992). *Women, Nationalism and the State: Towards an International Feminist Perspective*, Occasional Paper 4 in Gender and Development Studies, Asian Institute of Technology, Bangkok.

Pierre Daher and LBCI shares (September 9, 1998). *Daily Star*.

Pierre El Daher: Man of the year (1996). *Arab Ad* 6 (1).

Power, Carla (August 8, 2005). Look who's talking, *Newsweek International*, 50–1.

Prince Al-Waleed Bin Talal: Man of the year (1999). *Arab Ad* 9 (1): 8–17.

Prince Al-Waleed: We will continue our journey in supporting Saudi youth and discovering and nurturing their artistic and athletic talents (April 20, 2005). *Al-Riyadh* [Arabic].

Prince Talal bin 'Abdulaziz: Politics of exclusion pushes us to found a party to participate in public governance (September 7, 2007). *Al-Quds al-Arabi*.

Protests prompt MBC to suspend "Big Brother" reality TV show (March 2, 2004). *Gulf News*.

Qusti, Raid (April 20, 2007). National Dialogue chief says no boundaries in forums. *Arab News*.

Rabahi, Tawfiq (July 17, 2007). Saudi loyalty and dissent … from abroad, and war of attrition in Qassem and Haddad's topics. *Al-Quds al-Arabi* [Arabic].

Rabi'a, 'Ali (November 24, 2006). Bahrain: A model of American-style reform. *Al-Quds al-Arabi* [Arabic].

Radi, Lamia (October 26, 2007). Le Liban, Mecque régionale de la chirurgie esthétique. *L'Orient-Le Jour* (Agence France Press).

Raveendran, K. (January 17, 2004). Are the Lebanese taking over Dubai? *The Daily Star*.

"Reality" programs between rejection, acceptance … and embarrassment (February 27, 2004). *Al-Anbaa'* [Arabic].

Reality TV in Kuwaiti Jaridat al-Founoun (Arts Newspaper) (May 19, 2004). *Asharq al-Awsat* [Arabic].

Renan, Ernest (1996). *Qu'est-ce Qu'une une Nation? What Is a Nation?* Intro. Charles Taylor, trans. W. R. Taylor (Toronto: Tapir Press).

Responding to harsh criticism of his government's policies: Egypt's prime minister contributes for the first time to a blog amidst bloggers' astonishment (August 9, 2008). Alarabiya.net.

Restrictions on concerts in Kuwait (May 18, 2004). *Al-Bayan* [Arabic].

Reuters: Saudi Arabia built a media empire to overshadow criticism of its leaders and its policies (August 10, 2007). *Al-Quds al-Arabi* [Arabic].

Rheault, Magali (December 21, 2007). *Saudi Arabia: Majorities Support Women's Rights* (Washington, DC: Gallup).

Rizq, Ghassan (March 1, 2005). When did screens see such a scene? New [Bikr] television coverage for Arab crowds made by youth in downtown Beirut. *Assafir* [Arabic].

——— (March 9, 2005). The crowd's television imagination takes over politics. *Assafir* [Arabic].

Roux Dominique, et Teyssier, *Les Enjeux de Télé-réalité.* Economica, 2003.

Roy, Olivier (2004). *Globalized Islam: The Search for a New Umma* (New York: Columbia University Press).

——— (2008). *The Politics of Chaos in the Middle East* (New York: Columbia University Press).

Rugh, William A. (1980). Saudi mass media and society in the Faisal era. In *King Faisal and the Modernization of Saudi Arabia,* ed. W. A. Beling (Boulder, CO: Westview Press), 125–44.

——— (2004). *Arab Mass Media: Newspapers, Radio, and Television in Arab Politics* (Westport, CT and London: Praeger).

Russell, James A. (May 15, 2003). Political and economic transition on the Arabian peninsula: Perils and prospects. *Gulf Wire Perspectives.*

Ruwaida 'Attiya: I cherish singing and do not seek fame or money (May 27, 2004). *Al-Bayan* [Arabic].

Ryan, Curtis R. (2006). The odd couple: Ending the Jordanian-Syrian "cold war," *The Middle East Journal* 60 (1): 33–56.

Sabry, Tarik (2005). The day Moroccans gave up couscous for satellites: Global TV, structures of feeling, and mental emigration, *Transnational Broadcasting Studies,* 14, http://www.tbsjournal.com/Archives/Spring05/sabry.html (accessed December 30, 2005).

Sa'ib, Rania (2003). Manufacturing sensationalism: Reality TV stirs admirers and detractors in the Middle East. *Al-Watan* [Arabic].

Sakr, Naomi (November 2001). Reflections on the Manama Spring: Research questions arising from the promise of political liberalization in Bahrain, *British Journal of Middle Eastern Studies* 28 (2): 229–31.

Salameh, Ghassan (1980). Political power and the Saudi state, *MERIP Reports,* no. 91.

Saleh, Hussain (February 27, 2005). A deshdasha, a ghutra and a 'qal and "bakhnaq" in Star Academy's celebration of Kuwait's holidays. *Al-Rai al-Aam.* [Arabic].

Salman, Talal (March 8, 2005). A calm discussion of explosive emotions! *Assafir* [Arabic].

Salvatore, Armando and Eickelman, Dale F., eds., *Public Islam and the Common Good* (Leiden, the Netherlands: Brill).

Saudi clerics consider LBC and Rotana to be sin [Razheela] channels (May 11, 2005). *Al-Quds al-Arabi* [Arabic].

Saudi fatwa against liberals raises fears of their exposure to attacks (July 9, 2007). *Al-Quds al-Arabi* [Arabic].

Saudi Internet Rules (2006), http://www.albab.cohm/media/docs/Saudi.htmmedia/ docs/Saudi.htm (accessed December 30, 2006).

Saudis become refugees cinematically as they celebrate *Kif al-Hal* as the first popular release movie (November 12, 2006). *Al-Riyadh* [Arabic].

Scannell, Paddy (2002). Big Brother as a television event, *Television and New Media* 3 (3): 271–82.

Schleifer, Abdallah (2002). Super news center setting up in London for al-Hayat and LBC: An interview with Jihad Khazen and Salameh Nematt, *Transnational Broadcasting Journal*, 9, http://www.tbsjournal.com/Archives/all02/LBC (accessed September 10, 2005).

Schleusener, Luke (February 2007). From Blog to street: The Bahraini public sphere in transition, *Arab Media and Society*, http://arabmediasociety.sqgd.co.uk/topics/index .php?t_article=45 (accessed March 1, 2007).

Schneidermann, Daniel (2004). *Le cauchemar médiatique* (Paris: Denel/Folio Documents).

Scott, Joan W. (1986). Gender: A useful category of historical analysis, *American Historical Review* 91 (5): 1053–75.

Shobaili, Ali S. (1971). *A historical and analytical study of broadcasting and press in Saudi Arabia*. PhD diss., Ohio State University, Columbus.

Sengupta, Somini (October 24, 2002). Bahrain's women take a step toward political power. *New York Times*, A3.

Senoussi, 'Ayyash (April 14, 2006). Algerian television director to al-Hayat: *Star Academy* violated the contract and threats are our daily bread. *Al-Hayat* [Arabic].

Shadid, Anthony (May 1, 2006). A newsman breaks the mold in Arab world. *New York Times*.

Shaheen, Bashir (2003). A loser look at Alarabiya's new identity, *Tasmim: The Arab Design and Creativity Magazine* [Gitex 2003 issue]: 3–6.

Shapiro, Samantha M. (January 2, 2005). The war inside the Arab newsroom. *New York Times*.

Sheikh Saleh Kamel (1998). Featured interview, *Transnational Broadcasting Journal*, 1 (1) http://www.tbsjournal.com (accessed September 15, 2005).

Shobkoshi, Hussain (May 6, 2006). Academy politics. *Asharq al-Awsat* [Arabic].

Siddiqi, Moin A. (June 2001). Bahrain: Financial hub of the Middle East, *Middle East* 313: 37.

Snapshots (February 15, 2005). *Assafir* [Arabic].

Snobar, Andrawes (May 2008). *Arab Reality TV Shows* (Amman, Jordan: Arab Advisors Group).

"Star Academy 2" returns after forced interruption … and the public still brings back the stars of the first season (February 25, 2005). *Asharq al-Awsat* [Arabic].

Star Academy brings "reality TV fever" to LBCI (December 9, 2003). *Asharq al-Awsat* [Arabic].

Star Academy "weapon of mass destruction" (April 3, 2004). *Middle East Online*, http://www.middle-east-online.com/english/?id=9498=9498&;format.

Stars return to politics … a job or a search for the audience? (August 14, 2005). *Asharq al-Awsat* [Arabic].

Straubhaar, Joseph (2007). *World TV: From Global to Local* (London: Sage).

Street, John (1997). *Politics and Popular Culture* (Philadelphia, PA: Temple University Press).

——— (2004). Celebrity politicians: Popular culture and political representation, *British Journal of Politics and International Relations* 6 (4): 435–52.

Struggle between liberal and religious movements over the media ... Turki al-Faisal in Amman to participate in reform conference (April 10, 2007). *Al-Quds al-Arabi* [Arabic].

Sulayman, Bandar (February 27, 2005). Joey the Syrian exits the academy ... of Lebanon. *Al-Rai al-Aam* [Arabic].

Taha, 'Ali-Muhammad (April 28, 2004). Al-Qaradawi: Reality TV programs occupy the youth of the umma and is an instrument of cultural invation. *Asharq al-Awsat* [Arabic].

Taha, Huweida (August 15, 2007). Media raising questions about her regional role: Egypt in the grip of its president. *Al-Quds al-Arabi* [Arabic].

Taylor, Charles (1999). Two theories of modernity, *Public Culture* 11 (9): 153–74.

Technology "morals" in a Saudi study and a Bahraini law (January 4, 2006). Al-Arabiya. net [Arabic].

Television series ... on the mobile phone screen (October 25, 2005). *Asharq al-Awsat* [Arabic].

Tétreault, Mary Ann (1991). Autonomy, necessity, and the small state: Ruling Kuwait in the twentieth century, *International Organization* 45 (4): 565–91.

——— (2000). Gender, citizenship, and state in the Middle East, in *Citizenship and the State in the Middle East*, ed. N. A. Butenschon, U. Davis, and M. Hassassian (Syracuse, NY: Syracuse University Press), 70–87.

——— (2001). A state of two minds: State cultures, women and politics in Kuwait, *International Journal of Middle East Studies* 33: 203–20.

——— (2003). Advice and dissent in Kuwait, *Middle East Report* 226: 36–9.

Tétreault, Mary Ann and Al-Mughni, Haya (1995). Gender, citizenship, and nationalism in Kuwait, *British Journal of Middle Eastern Studies* 22 (1/2): 64–80.

The programs that made our lives a source of entertainment for others (April 23, 2005). *Asharq al-Awsat* [Arabic].

The endeavours of Gulf countries to meet WTO requirements (2001), *Arab Law Quarterly* 16 (1): 49–51.

The Lebanese artist Melhem Zayn: Beautiful voices are absent from Star Academy (April 23, 2004). *Asharq al-Awsat* [Arabic].

The reality of Reality TV in the Middle East (March 7, 2004), http://www.albawaba.com /news/printArticle.php3?sid=271966&;lang=e (accessed April 1, 2004).

Thompson, John (1995). *The Media and Modernity: A Social Theory of the Media* (Stanford, CA: Stanford University Press).

Toumson, Roger (1998). *Mythologie du métissage* (Paris: Presses Universitaires da France).

Traboulsi, Fawwaz (2008). Saudi expansion: The Lebanese connection, 1924–1952, in *Kingdom without Borders: Saudi Arabia's Political, Religious and Media Frontiers*, ed. M. Al-Rasheed (New York: Columbia University Press), 65–78.

Trofimov, Yaroslav (October 25, 2001). Bahrain's bold rebuff to its Islamic rebels: Democracy and rights. *Wall Street Journal*, A1.

——— (2007). *The siege of Mecca* (New York: Doubleday).

Turkish serials pushes Arab drama to break taboos (August 5, 2008). *Al-Quds al-Arabi* [Arabic].

Turkish serials ... stole people's minds (July 7, 2008). *Al-Riyadh* [Arabic].

Turner, Graeme (2006). The mass production of celebrity: "Celetoids," reality TV and the "demotic turn," *International Journal of Cultural Studies* 9 (2): 153–65.

Understanding Bahrain's third parliamentary elections (November 2006). Durham, U.K.: Center for Iranian Studies.

Unfair practice (September 19, 1993). *Daily Star*.

U.S.-Bahrain accord stirs Persian Gulf trade partners (December 4, 2004). *New York Times*, W1.

Van Zoonen, Liesbet (2004). Imagining the fan democracy, *European Journal of Communication* 19 (1): 39–52.

—— (2005). *Entertaining the Citizen: When Politics and Popular Culture Converge* (Lanham, MD: Rowman and Littlefield).

Vattimo, Gianni (1992). *The Transparent Society* (Baltimore, MD: Johns Hopkins University Press).

Waisbord, Silvio (2004). McTV: Understanding the global popularity of television formats, *Television and New Media* 5 (4): 359–83.

Walid, Tawfiq: Superstar presented distinguished voices and Star Academy did not (April 30, 2004). *Al-Bayan* [Arabic].

Wallin, Michelle (December 24, 2004). U.S.-Bahrain accord stirs Persian Gulf trade partners. *New York Times,* W1.

Watenpaugh, Keith D. (2006). *Being Modern in the Middle East: Revolution, Nationalism, Colonialism, and the Arab Middle Class* (Princeton, NJ: Princeton University Press).

Wazin, 'Abdo (November 30, 2006). The street and the image. *Al-Hayat* [Arabic].

Wedeen, Lisa (1999). *Ambiguities of Domination: Politics, Rhetoric and Symbols in Contemporary Syria* (Chicago: University of Chicago Press).

—— (2008). *Peripheral Visions: Publics, Power, and Performance in Yemen* (Chicago: University of Chicago Press).

We must go past TV meters, says OMG boss (September 24, 2006), *Campaign Middle East*, 6.

Wheeler, Deborah L. (2006). *The Internet in the Middle East: Global Expectations and Local Imaginations in Kuwait* (Albany: State University of New York Press).

Wilson, Scott and Williams, Daniel (April 17, 2005). A new power rises across Mideast. *Washington Post*, A01.

Yamani, Mai (2008). Saudi Arabia's mask, in *Kingdom without Borders: Saudi Arabia's Political, Religious and Media Frontiers*, ed. M. Al-Rasheed (New York: Columbia University Press), 323–34.

Yassin, Said (September 16, 2005). Fifi Abdo confronts corruption and smuggling of antiquities. *Al-Hayat* [Arabic].

Yazbeck, Samar (January 7, 2005). The televisual image and split (infissam) reality. *Al-Hayat* [Arabic].

Zakaria, Hiba (February 27, 2005). Celebrating the holidays: Star Academy in "Kuwaiti Night." *Al-Watan* [Arabic].

Zaraqet, 'Ali (August 10, 2007). Local television wakes up to cinema: Lebanese films on LBC and Saudi films on Future TV. *Assafir* [Arabic].

Zayani, Mohammed and Sofiane Sahraoui (2007). *The Culture of Al-Jazeera: Inside an Arab Media Giant* (Jefferson, NC: McFarland and Company).

Index

Modernity (*cont.*)
  as battle of representations, 8, 18,
    92–4, 103
  and gender, 14, 197
  and hybridity, 13
  as image vs. reality, 40, 45
  and nation-states, 17, 27
  as negotiation with the West, 15,
    40, 56, 71
  as rival versions of reality, 15
  taming of, 192–213
Montesquieu, 140
Moore, George Edward, 22
Multiple modernities, 8, 16–18, 219.
  See also modernity
Muqalled, Diana, 174
Murr TV (MTV), 78, 83–4
Muruwwah, Jamil, 77
Muruwwah, Kamel, 74
muyu'a, 128, 197. *See also* effeminacy

Najjar, Ramsay, 42–3, 85
Nasrallah, Hassan, 35, 177, 194
National Broadcasting Network
  (NBN), 78
National identity
  and *Star Academy*, 105, 135
  and *Superstar*, 163
  and women, 125, 162, 196
Nationalism, 5, 18, 37, 58, 135,
    142, 163, 183, 191, 195–6, 204
  as constitutive rhetoric, 18
  as episodic, 18, 196
  and pan-Arab nationalism, 17,
    124, 151, 156
  as performance, 151
  and self-definition, 195
New TV, 25, 53, 78, 156, 168, 177,
  186
New York Times, 152, 178
Nga Longva, Anh, 125
Nujum al-'Ulum [Stars of Science],
  212

Omnicom Media Group (OMD), 10
Ottoman Empire, 26–7

Patriotism, 35, 133–4, 144, 151,
  161, 171, 196
Paye, Oliver, 38
Peters, John, 115, 164
Pettman, Jan Jindy, 162
Poetry, 209–11
Politics. *See also* entertainment-
  politics as contention, 200
  nexus in Arab world as
    performance, 200
  rhetoric, symbols, and ritual in, 28
  as spectacle, 27
Pop Idol. See Superstar
Prince al-Waleed bin Talal, 82
Prince Khalid Bin Musa'id, 72
Prince Nayef Bin 'Abdulaziz, 75
Public space, 34
  and gender, 97, 107
  and modernity, 4
  and politics, 45

Qassir, Samir, 154, 183, 190
Qatar, 23, 71
Qatar Foundation for Education,
  Science and Community
  Development, 212
Qordahi, George, 79

Rabahi, Tawfiq, 88
Radio Riyadh, 75
Radio Sawa, 194
Reality, 42, 113. *See also* authenticity
  as battle of representations, 45
  definition of, 198, 200
  vs. image, 202, 210
Reality Television
  and consumption, 208
  and democratization, 198–201
  and "demotic turn," 34
  and Endemol, 9, 32, 54, 61

Titles in the Series

C. Edwin Baker, *Media, Markets, and Democracy*

C. Edwin Baker, *Media Concentration and Democracy: Why Ownership Matters*

W. Lance Bennett and Robert M. Entman, eds., *Mediated Politics: Communication in the Future of Democracy*

Bruce Bimber, *Information and American Democracy: Technology in the Evolution of Political Power*

Murray Edelman, *The Politics of Misinformation*

Frank Esser and Barbara Pfetsch, eds., *Comparing Political Communication: Theories, Cases, and Challenges*

Hernan Galperin, *New Television, Old Politics: The Transition to Digital TV in the United States and Britain*

Myra Marx Ferree, William Anthony Gamson, Jürgen Gerhards, and Dieter Rucht, *Shaping Abortion Discourse: Democracy and the Public Sphere in Germany and the United States*

Daniel C. Hallin and Paolo Mancini, *Comparing Media Systems: Three Models of Media and Politics*

Robert B. Horwitz, *Communication and Democratic Reform in South Africa*

Philip N. Howard, *New Media Campaigns and the Managed Citizen*

Richard Gunther and Anthony Mughan, eds., *Democracy and the Media: A Comparative Perspective*

L. Sandy Maisel, Darrell M. West, and Brett M. Clifton, *Evaluating Campaign Quality: Can the Electoral Process Be Improved?*

Pippa Norris, *Digital Divide: Civic Engagement, Information Poverty, and the Internet Worldwide*

Adam F. Simon, *The Winning Message: Candidate Behavior, Campaign Discourse*

Gadi Wolfsfeld, *Media and the Path to Peace*